The Jewish Community of Rome

Supplements
to the
Journal for the
Study of Judaism

Editor

John J. Collins
The Divinity School, Yale University

Associate Editor

Florentino García Martínez
Qumran Institute, University of Groningen

Advisory Board

J. DUHAIME − A. HILHORST − P.W. VAN DER HORST

A. KLOSTERGAARD PETERSEN − M.A. KNIBB − H. NAJMAN

J.T.A.G.M. VAN RUITEN − J. SIEVERS − G. STEMBERGER

E.J.C. TIGCHELAAR − J. TROMP

VOLUME 113

The Jewish Community
of Rome

From the Second Century B.C.
to the Third Century C.E.

by

Silvia Cappelletti

BRILL

LEIDEN · BOSTON

2006

This book is printed on acid-free paper.

Library of Congress Cataloging-in-Publication Data

Cappelletti, Sylvia.
    The Jewish community of Rome : from the second century B.C. to the
third century C.E. / by Sylvia Cappelletti.
        p. cm. — (Supplements to the Journal for the Study of Judaism,
ISSN 1384-2161 ; v. 113)
    Includes bibliographical references (p.) and index.
    ISBN-13: 978-90-04-15157-4
    ISBN-10: 90-04-15157-5 (hardback : alk. paper)
    1. Jews—Italy—Rome—History. 2. Catacombs—Italy—Rome. 3. Jewish
inscriptions—Italy—Rome. 4. Rome (Italy)—Ethnic relations. I. Title. II.
Series.

DS135.I85R6227 2006
937'.6004924—dc22

                                                                2006044021

ISSN 1384-2161
ISBN-10 90 04 15157 5
ISBN-13 978 90 04 15157 4

PRINTED IN THE NETHERLANDS

CONTENTS

ACKNOWLEDGEMENTS

This book is a revised version of a doctoral dissertation presented at the University of Pisa, Italy, in June 2004. The thesis was prepared under the supervision of Daniele Foraboschi, Professor of Roman History, University of Milan, to whom I am immensely grateful for his invaluable guidance and support, and also for his warm friendship. I would like to express my deep gratitude to Lucio Troiani, Professor of Roman History, University of Pavia, who read my work and helped me greatly with insightful comments and important suggestions. I am deeply indebted to Professor John Collins, who accepted this book in the series and read the present version, offering important advice.

I am thankful to all the Professors of my Doctoral program, Umberto Laffi, Professor of Roman History, who chairs the course, Cesare Letta, Professor of Roman History, and Biagio Virgilio, Professor of Greek History, whose lessons I could attend during the three years of my doctorate. I would like to thank deeply Simonetta Segenni, Professor of Roman History, who always encouraged me and discussed with me parts of the book while in progress. I am very grateful to Maria Modena Mayer, Professor of Hebrew Literature, University of Milan, who read an early version of this book and suggested some illuminating comments.

In preparing the thesis for publication I have benefited from improvements suggested by Prof. Joseph Mélèze-Modrzejewski whose studies and brilliant seminars at the École Pratique des Hautes Études, Paris, Sorbonne, helped me greatly. I also profited from the studies of Giulio Firpo, Professor of Roman History, University of Chieti and from the helpful comments of Cinzia Vismara, Professor of Classical Archaeology, University of Cassino, who read a draft of the archaeological section.

Scholars whose academic interests are diverse, Federica Cordano, Professor of Greek History, Piergiuseppe Michelotto, Professor of Roman History, and Adriano Savio, Professor of Numismatics, and all Professors of the Department of Antiquities, University of Milan, offered me starting points or helped me simply by being available for discussion.

I wish to thank Dr. La Barbera, Soprintendenza Archeologica di Roma, who allowed me to study unpublished material and to visit the catacombs of Villa Torlonia.

Finally, a special thanks to Dr. Angelica Amoroso, Department of English, University of Leicester, for proof-reading the manuscript.

Clearly, I alone am responsible for the contents and the possible inaccurancies of this book.

SECTION ONE

INTRODUCTION

THE ORGANIZATION OF THE COMMUNITY

A cursory reading of the Jewish inscriptions of Rome seems to reveal the organization of the community in some detail. Unfortunately, this evidence gives only superficial and scanty pieces of information. We know of the existence of eleven synagogues whose names are mentioned in the inscriptions,[1] but we do not have any information on their juridical status and on the relationship between the Jewish hierarchy and the Roman administration. Two points are actually debated: the eventual equalization of the synagogues with the *collegia sacra* as a result of the policy Caesar supported towards the Jews in the years 49–46 B.C.,[2] and the existence of a central γερουσία, a council with officers and representatives from all the congregations.[3]

I

The equalization of the synagogue with the *collegium* is based upon passages of Suetonius and Flavius Josephus. In the first passage it is said that Caesar, some time after 46 B.C., dissolved all the *collegia* except those of ancient foundation.[4] In reorganizing the *collegia* he meant to control guilds and groups of great political weight in those years. The content of the *lex* depends entirely on this passage. Considering the scarce pieces of information we have on the constitutions of the *collegia* in the Caesarian period, we cannot say which *collegia* Suetonius was referring to with the words *antiquitus constituta*.

---

[1] Synagogue of the Agrippesians (JIWE II, 170, 562, 549, 130?), Augustesion (JIWE II, 96, 189, 194, 542, 547, 169?), Calcaresians (JIWE II, 69, 98, 165, 558, 584), Campesians (JIWE II, 288, 560, 577, 1?), Elea (JIWE II, 406, 576), Hebrews (JIWE II, 2, 33, 578, 579), Secenians (JIWE II, 436), Siburesians (JIWE II, 338, 428, 451, 452, 527, 557), Tripolitans (JIWE II, 166), Vernaclesians (JIWE II, 106, 114, 117, 540?), Volumnesians (JIWE II, 100, 163, 167, 577).
[2] Of this opinion E. Schürer 1973–1986, II.2, pp. 112–113, J.B. Frey 1930, p. 275, H.J. Leon 1995², p. 10, E. Smallwood 1981, pp. 133–134 e A. Rabello 1980, pp. 719–720.
[3] According to J. Juster 1914, I, pp. 444–446; S. Krauss 1922, pp. 137–140; G. La Piana 1927, pp. 360–363; S. Baron 1952, II, p. 199.
[4] Suet., *Vita Iul.*, 42, 3: *Cuncta collegia praeter antiquitus constituta distraxit.*

Between 64 and 55 B.C., the sources registered two *senatus consulta*[5] and a *lex*[6] that, in different ways, hit those *collegia* that supposedly operated against the interest of the State, taking part to the political fights violently. Consequently, the object of Caesar's policy could have been the congregations Clodius created in 58 B.C.[7] with the *lex Clodia* that had survived the severe legislation of 56–55 B.C.:[8] the *collegia* founded before then and known for their public utility went untouched. This is not the only problem that affects this passage. The belonging of the *lex Iulia de collegiis* to the corpus of Caesarian laws is debated. Mommsen, in fact, supposed that it was enacted by Augustus.[9] Apart from this passage, the main evidence for including this lex in the Caesarian corpus is an inscription mentioning the law[10] and a reference to the law in the Suetonian "Life of Augustus".[11] In the years of the civil war following the death of Caesar, many

---

[5] The first was enacted possibly in 64 B.C.: it is doubtful which collegia were involved and what was the nature of this act. Some scholars support the idea of a suspension only of the congregations linked to the ludi Capitalicii, mainly professional collegia and collegia cultorum Larum, while others think that all the collegia were indistinctly suppressed. A general bibliography in H. Royden 1988, pp. 4–5 and B. Marshall 1985, p. 94. The second act (dated to 56 B.C.) concerns those political groups that influenced the votes with violence.

[6] It is the lex Licinia de sodaliciis mentioned in the passage of Cicero (see note 5) and enacted in 55 B.C. J.P. Waltzing 1895–1900, I, p. 112 nr. 2.

[7] Asconius, *Comm. In Pis.*, 7–8, 11–23: *Diximus L. Pisone A. Gabinio coss. P. Clodium tr. pl. quattuor leges perniciosas populo romano tulisse:* [. . .] *tertiam de collegiis restituendis novisque instituendis, quae ait ex servitiorum faece constituta.* Idem, 6, 14–15: *Post VI deinde annos quam sublata erant* (i.e. the s.c. of 64 B.C.), *P. Clodius tr. pl. lege lata restituit collegia.* H.L. Royden 1988, p. 7.

[8] Cic., *In Pis.*, 4, 9: *Conlegia non ea solum quae senatus sustulerunt restituta, sed innumerabilia quaedam nova ex omni faece urbis ac servitia concitata.* The study of the collegia is of the greatest importance to understand the policy of Clodius: Cicero himself remarks that Clodius, in reopening these organizations, could control wide strata of the Roman population, both citizens and freedmen, even those who could not vote. As Fezzi shows (L. Fezzi 2001, pp. 274–278), the contemporaries were divided on this reform and often did not understand its political importance. Walzing 1895–1900, I, p. 97.

[9] Th. Mommsen 1850, III, pp. 114–115, resumed by J.P. Waltzing 1895–1900, I, pp. 114–122. Of the opposite opinion de Robertis 1938, pp. 177–178, resumed by Royden 1988, p. 7.

[10] CIL VI 2193 (= VI 4416): *Dis Manibus. | Collegio Symphonia|corum qui sacris publi|cis praestu sunt quibus | senatus c(oire) c(ollegium) c(onstituere) permisit e | lege Iulia ex autoritate | Aug(usti) ludorum causa.* Royden (Royden 1988, p. 7) quotes this inscription among the sources of the *lex Julia* enacted by Caesar, while Waltzing (J.P. Waltzing 1895–1900, I, p. 114) refers it to Augustus.

[11] Suet., *Aug.*, 32: . . . *plurimae factiones titulo collegi novi ad nullius non facinoris societatem coibant. Igitur . . . collegia praeter antiqua et legitima dissolvit.*

political groups named themselves as *collegia* without the official approval of the Senate: Augustus, in an unknown year,[12] dissolved these groups except the *collegia antiqua et legitima*. The first term echoes the passage in Iul. 42 and apparently recalls the same *collegia* Caesar had preserved, while the second adjective is more precise and refers to the congregations whose statute had been approved by a *lex*, possibly the *lex Iulia de collegiis* of Caesar.[13] In the passage of Suetonius no reference to the synagogues can be found.

The second piece of evidence is a passage of Flavius Josephus in which an officer of unknown identity in the name of Julius Caesar grants the Jews of Parium[14] freedom of worship, of following their customs and of gathering money for the communal meals.[15] He also mentions a διάταγμα in which Caesar had forbidden the foundations of θίασοι in the town, but had allowed the Jews to meet and share communal meals according to the use and the law of their fathers. This is the only passage mentioning an act of Caesar that concerned the freedom of assembly of the Jews: the synagogues are apparently considered equal to the *sacra collegia*.

According to Miriam Pucci,[16] this text is built on the same pattern

---

[12] According to Huelsen (P.W. s.v. *collegium* col. 408) it probably happened in 7 B.C., when he hold the censorship and organized the collegium fabrum tignariorum. Of this opinion also Momigliano (A. Momigliano 1966, pp. 523 sg.)

[13] Royden (H. Royden 1988, p. 8) supposes that Augustus' act was an edict.

[14] Marcus, editor of the Loeb edition, and Moraldi, editor of the UTET Italian edition, accept the reading Παριανῶν suggested by Juster (Juster 1914, I, p. 142 n. 4). The town should be identified with Parium, a site placed on the coasts of the Troas. Conversely, Schürer (E. Schürer 1973–1986, II, p. 116) suggests the reading Παρίων: the place should be identified with the isle of Paros, near Delos, mentioned further on.

[15] Flav. Jos., *Ant.*, XIV, 213–216: "Ἰούλιος Γάιος στρατηγὸς ὕπατος Ῥωμαίων Παριανῶν ἄρχουσι βουλῇ δήμῳ χαίρειν. Ἐνέτυχόν μοι οἱ Ἰουδαῖοι ἐν Δήλῳ καί τινες τῶν παροίκων Ἰουδαίων παρόντων καὶ τῶν ὑμετέρων πρέσβεων, καὶ ἐνεφάνισαν, ὡς ὑμεῖς ψηφίσματι κωλύετε αὐτοὺς τοῖς πατρίοις ἔθεσι καὶ ἱεροῖς χρῆσθαι. Ἐμοὶ τοίνυν οὐκ ἀρέσκει κατὰ τῶν ἡμετέρων φίλων καὶ συμμάχων τοιαῦτα γίνεσθαι ψηφίσματα, καὶ κωλύεσθαι αὐτοὺς ζῆν κατὰ τὰ αὐτῶν ἔθη καὶ χρήματα εἰς σύνδειπνα καὶ τὰ ἱερὰ εἰσφερεῖν, τοῦτο ποιεῖν αὐτῶν μηδ' ἐν Ῥώμῃ κεκωλυμένων. Καὶ γὰρ Γάιος Καῖσαρ ὁ ἡμέτερος στρατηγὸς ὕπατος, ἐν τῷ διατάγματι κωλύων θιάσους συνάγεσθαι κατὰ πόλιν, μόνους τούτους οὐκ ἐκώλυσεν οὔτε χρήματα συνεισφέρειν οὔτε σύνδειπνα ποιεῖν. Ὁμοίως δὲ κἀγὼ τοὺς ἄλλους θιάσους κωλύων, τούτοις μόνοις ἐπιτρέπω κατὰ τὰ πάτρια ἔθη καὶ νόμιμα συνάγεσθαί τε καὶ ἑστιᾶσθαι. Καὶ ὑμᾶς οὖν καλῶς ἔχει, εἴ τι κατὰ τῶν ἡμετέρων φίλων καὶ συμμάχων ψήφισμα ἐποιήσατε, τοῦτο ἀκυρῶσαι διὰ τὴν περὶ ἡμᾶς αὐτῶν ἀρετὴν καὶ εὔνοιαν."

[16] M. Pucci Ben Zeev 1996. The epistles are addressed to Ephesus (XIV 225–227

of the other epistles sent by Roman officers to Asian communities
reported in the Antiquities. Consequently, its authenticity should be
granted, but some details arouse doubts.[17] The name of the officer
that enacted the decree is lost. Julius Caesar is called στρατηγὸς
ὕπατος, a title that was no more in use since the beginning of the
first century B.C.[18] Usually θίασος was not the Greek translation of
collegium: Flavius Josephus himself uses this term only in Ant. 213–215,
probably because it did not belong to his vocabulary, but he had
found it in the source mentioning the διάταγμα. According to Gaius,
sodales sunt qui eiusdem collegii sunt, quam Graeci ἑταιρία vocant;[19] literary
and epigraphic sources attest the use of σύστημα[20] and of κολλήγιον,[21]
a translitteration from the Latin word, while a collegium sacrum is usually called ἱερωσύνη.[22] Mason mentions θιασώτης for sodalis, but remarks
that it is a hapax of Cassius Dio.[23] Such a peculiarity cannot even

---

and 230), Cos (XIV 233), Sardis (XIV 235) and Miletus (XIV 244–246). All of
them show an absolute formal unity: the epistles begin with the name of the sender
at the nominative, followed by the name of the people and of the civic officers
respectively in genitive and dative and the salutation χαιρεῖν. The content of the
epistles is privileges Rome granted to the local communities, the emission of senatus consulta or the outcome of arbitrations concerning the Jews; to summarize, the
management of the Roman power concerning the local communities. Pucci defends
the authenticity of these documents and justifies the inaccurancies with an inaccurate use of not-original sources, probably fragmentary copies of Roman documents
translated into Greek. Feldman (L. Feldman – M. Reinhold 1996, p. 82) shares
this position and regards the quotes of this epistle as authentic.

[17] M. Williams 1998, pp. 216–220. The corruption of the text is stressed also by
E. Smallwood 1981, p. 135 n. 52 and E. Schürer 1973–1986, I, p. 116 nr. 36.
Waltzing (J.P. Waltzing 1895–1900, I, p. 113) supports the link of this passage with
the Caesarian intervention on the collegia, but not with the lex Iulia de collegiis,
which he dates to Augustus.

[18] As Williams shows (M. Williams 1998, p. 220 n. 25), the last epigraphic example of a στρατηγὸς ὕπατος is in AE 1967, nr. 532: Γάϊον Κλώδιον Ἀππίου υἱόν
Π[όλχρον], στραταγὸν ὕπατον Ῥωμαίων, τὸν εὐεργέταν καί πάτρ[ωνα], Κυραναῖοι.
Gaius Claudius Pulcher hold the consulship with M. Paperna in 92 B.C.; the inscription belongs to the immediately following years, when he was governor of the newly
annexed province of Cyrenaica. However, Josephus uses this term also in Ant. XIV
233, in the epistle of C. Fannius to Cos (Γάιος Φάννιος Γαίου υἱὸς στρατηγὸς ὕπατος
Κῴων ἄρχουσι χαίρειν); Juster emended ὕπατος with ἄνθυπος (J. Juster 1914, I,
p. 146). Considering these problems, Marcus does not precisely date the document,
and suggests a period between 161 and 44 B.C.

[19] Dig. 47.22.4.

[20] Cass. Dio., H.R., 75.4.6; Plut., Num. 7 (64); SEG (1923) 1.158.

[21] Cass. Dio., H.R., 38.13.2; IGR 1.1314, 3.215; AE 1944 nr. 22.

[22] Usually with the meaning of sacerdotal collegium. For instance Cass. Dio.,
H.R., 53.1.5; 58.12.5.

[23] Cass. Dio., H.R., 56.46.1; 58.12.5. H. Mason 1974, p. 54 e p. 117.

depend on a pattern of the Jewish literature in Greek language: θίασος in fact, does not occur in the New Testament. In the Septuagint, it is used only in a passage of Jeremiah as a translation of בית מרזח, house of feasting.[24]

In the works of Philo the term often recurs to indicate the idea of company,[25] but also general places of aggregation[26] or undefined groups.[27] It is seldom used as synonymous of αἵρησις, to indicate philosophical groups of religious movements.[28] The only passages where θίασος means "place of gathering" are in the *In Flaccum* where the term is used for congregations whose members run a dissolute life,[29] and in the treatise *De specialibus legibus*, in the Greek sense of feminine association.[30]

From a juridical point of view, the passage on Parium can be hardly referred to the Caesarian law on the *collegia*. With apparent inaccuracy, Josephus calls the *lex Iulia de collegiis* a διάταγμα, a decree.[31] The two acts have a different political weight: Suetonius speaks of a re-organization of those *collegia* that were considered politically dangerous, while Josephus says that all the *sacra collegia* were closed, with the exception of the synagogues. Such an open favor towards the Jews of Parium can be hardly justified on the basis of the support

---

[24] Jeremiah 16.5: כי־כה אמר יהוה אל־תבוא בית מרזח Septuagint: Μὴ εἰσέλθῃς εἰς θίασον αὐτῶν καὶ μὴ πορευθῇς τοῦ κόψασθαι καὶ μὴ πενθήσῃς αὐτούς. In the passage from Hebrew to Greek the harshness of a sentence has been attenuated. E. Hatch – H. Redpath 1975, I, p. 652 and L. Köhler – W. Baumgartner 1967–1996, II (1974), p. 599. Supposing a correspondence betwen θίασος and μεστάθεια, both Hatch & Redpath and X. Jacques (X. Jacques 1972, p. 79) quote also Wisdom 12.5, a passage that has some textual problems: R θοῖναν καὶ αἵματος ἐκ μέσου [B² μύσου] μυσταφείας [B¹ S¹ -ᾳ] [A S² μύστας θιάσου] σου.

[25] As in *De plant.* 58; *De ebriet.* 70; *De migr. Ab.*, 90; *De fuga et inv.*, 10; 126; *De somnis* I, 196; II, 10; II, 139; *De vita Mosis* II, 185.

[26] *De mut. nom.*, 198; *De Abr.*, 20; *De spec. leg.* II, 44; III, 169.

[27] *De post.*, 101; *De fuga et inv.*, 28; *De mut. nom.*, 32; *De somnis* II, 277; *De spec. leg.* II, 193; IV 47; *Leg. ad Gaium*, 97.

[28] *De ebriet.*, 94 (Λευιτῶν ὁ θίασος οὗτος); *De fuga et inv.*, 89 (referred to the Levites); *Quod probus* 2 (τὸν μέν οὖν τῶν Πυθαγορείων ἱερώτατον θίασον); *id.*, 85 (he speaks of the Essenes who lived together in communities πρὸς γὰρ κατὰ θιάσους συνοικεῖν οἰκεῖν).

[29] *In Flaccum*, 136–137 (passim): Θίασοι κατὰ τὴν πόλιν εἰσὶ πολυάνθρωποι, ὧν κατάρχει τῆς κοινωνίας οὐδέν ὑγιές, ... σύνοδοι καὶ κλίναι πασονομάζονται ὑπὸ τῶν ἐγχωρίων. ... εἶτα ὅταν τι βουληθῇ διαπράξασθαι τῶν ἀλυσιτελῶν, ἀφ' ἑνὸς συνθήματος ἀθρόως συνέρχονται καὶ τὸ κελευσθέν λέγουσι καὶ δρῶσι.

[30] *De spec. leg.* I, 323: γυναῖκων θιάσους βδελυκτῶν καὶ ἀκολάστων.

[31] According to Mason (H. Mason 1974, p. 127), διάταγμα is the Greek translation of *edictum*.

the local community could have given to Caesar in the years of the civil war.

We have two different pieces of evidence: on one hand, a *lex* Caesar issued to re-organize the *collegia*, with no references to the Jewish assemblies; on the other hand, a corrupted passage of Josephus in which the synagogues are linked with the act of Caesar, but this *lex* is reduced to a διάταγμα addressed exclusively to the town of Parium (κωλύων θιάσους συνάγεσθαι κατὰ πόλιν).

Strong differences between the *sacra collegia* and the synagogues can be recognized. Although most of the sacra collegia—as the synagogues—had to organize the cults, the synagogues organized the funerals and managed the cemeteries, tasks that in the Roman world were carried out by the collegia funeraticia.[32] The charities too were exceptionally developed. Apart from the common meals and the hospitality for poor people the synagogue, as bet-ha-sefer, was a centre for primary school teaching.[33] Since the second century, the Roman community had a rabbinical academy, a yeshivah, probably founded by Rabbi Matthia ben Heresh who is known to have left Palestine before the outbreak of the revolt of Bar Cochba.[34] The presence of a bet-ha-midrash linked with one of the Roman synagogues is probably attested even in an earlier period. According to the Talmud,[35] during the reign of Domitian, Rabbi Gamaliel and his companions

---

[32] On the organization of the collegia funeraticia see J.P. Waltzing 1895–1900, I, pp. 141–154; on the management of the funerals in some professional collegia see II, 484–533.

[33] See Z. Safrai 1994, pp. 181–204.

[34] BT Sanhedrin 32b "Our Rabbis taught: justice, justice shalt thou follow: this means, follow the scholars to their academies (לישיבה), R. Eliezer to Lydda, R. Johanan b. Zakkai to Beror Hail, R. Joshua to Peki'in, Rabban Gamaliel [II] to Jabneh, R. Akiba to Benai Berak, R. Matthia to Rome (רבי מתיא לרומי), R. Hanania b. Taeradion to Sikni . . ."

[35] In the greater towns of Palestine, the bet-ha-midrash was a room outbuilding the synagogue, while in the smaller centres the teaching was undertaken in the synagogue (Z. Safrai 1994, p. 183). Lectures and teaching of the Bible in Diasporan synagogues are attested in Philo. In De somnis II, 126 and De spec. Leg. I, 314 the teaching is generically linked with the synagogues, but in De Spec. Leg. II, 62 it is said: ἀναπέπταται γοῦν ταῖς ἑβδόμαις μυρία κατὰ πᾶσαν πόλιν διδασκαλεῖα φρονήσεως καὶ σωφροσύνης καὶ ἀνδρείας καὶ δικαιοσύνης καὶ τῶν ἄλλων ἀρετῶν . . . A bet-ha-midrash independent from the synagogue is also mentioned in the Acts. After arguments and difficulties with the synagogue of Ephesus, Paul teaches for two years in the school of Tyrannos: Acts 19,9: ἀποστὰς ἀπ' αὐτῶν ἀφώρισεν τοὺς μαθητὰς καθ' ἡμέραν διαλεγόμενος ἐν τῇ σχολῇ Τυράννου. L. Troiani 2002, p. 48.

visited Rome and held rabbinical discussions in synagogue contexts.[36]

According to the Jewish inscriptions, the structures of the synagogues and that of the collegia are not dissimilar. The synagogues are apparently built on the same pyramidal structure of the collegia, themselves shaped on the pattern of the civic administration:[37] the synagogue is ruled by an assembly composed by the most influent members and chaired by an officer. In the collegia, this office was held by magistri or quinquennales,[38] who had to control the application of the statute and had to chair the societal assembly or, in the case of greater associations, a narrow assembly called γερουσία. In the same way, a γερουσιάρχης is attested thirteen times in the Jewish inscriptions:[39] if the γερουσία is to be considered the inner assembly of the synagogue,[40] this officer possibly managed all the duties not related to the cult (of sacerdotal competence), such as the properties of the synagogues, the schools, the gathering of money for the Temple or, after 70 c.e., for the payment of the Jewish tax.[41]

Another point of contact between the two communities is the management of the properties. Two inscriptions mention the φροντιστής.[42] In an inscription found at Syde, Pamphylia,[43] the φροντιστής is the person in charge of the repairs of the synagogue, an office that he shares with the ἀρχισυνάγωγος,[44] often mentioned as yard

---

[36] On the presence of R. Gamaliel, Eleazar b. Azariah, Joshuah ben Hananiah and Akiba in Rome see part II, chapter 5. They appear to have taught in Rome also in BT Abodah Zarah, 54b: "The Elders in Rome were asked . . ." (שאלו את הזקנים ברומי).

[37] Dig. 3, 4, 1: *proprium est ad exemplum reipublicae habere res communes.*

[38] F. de Robertis 1938, pp. 72–73; G. Alföldy 1987, p. 187.

[39] JIWE II, 86, 96, 113, 130, 162, 189, 238, 321, 351, 354, 487, 554, 555. In Italy, this office is attested also in Venosa (JIWE I, 76, 87) as γερουσιάρχον, Castel Porziano (JIWE I, 18) and Pozzuoli (JIWE I, 23).

[40] This point will be debated later on.

[41] Phil. De spec. Leg. I, 143.

[42] JIWE II, 164 and 540.

[43] IJO, II 219 (CIJ n. 781): ['Ἰσά]κις φροντιστὴς τῆς ἁγιωτάτ | [ης] πρώτης συναγωγῆς ἔστην εὑτ | [υχῶς] καὶ ἀνεπλήρωσα τὴν μαρμάρωσιν ἀπὸ | τοῦ ἄμβωνος ἕως τοῦ σίμμα, καὶ ἔσμηξα | [τὰ]ς δύο ἐπταμύξους καὶ τὰ δύο κιονοκέ | φαλα, ἰνδ(ικτιῶνος) ιέ μη(νὸς) δ'.

[44] The ἀρχισυνάγωγος is mentioned six times in the inscriptions of Rome, but this office could be hardly considered as a typical aspect of the Roman community because it is attested both in other centres of the Diaspora (Venosa, Akmonia and Aegina) and in Palestine (mainly at Jerusalem and Caesarea). What his duties were is a debated point. E. Schürer (Schürer 1973–1986, II, pp. 425–453), Juster (Juster 1914, I, pp. 450–453), and, with few differences, Frey (Frey Intr. to the CIJ, pp. XCVII–XCIX) and Leon (Leon 1995², pp. 171–172) regard the ἀρχισυνάγωγος as the chief of the synagogues (CTh XIV,8,4) who could take part in

foreman.[45] Probably, this office was shaped on the pattern of the curator who managed the budget of the professional collegia.[46] Moreover, if we consider the ἄρχων πάσης τιμῆς as the treasurer of the synagogue,[47] his office could be similar to that of the arcarius or of the quaestor whose duty was the management of the arca communis.[48]

The pattern of the collegia is even more evident in the pater synagogae[49] and in the mater synagogae[50] which echo the pater and mater collegii. This office is attested almost exclusively in Rome. As in the collegia, the pater was the most prestigious office within the association: the Roman authorities considered the pater synagogae one of the authorities of the synagogues, together with the priest and the ἀρχισυνάγωγοι.[51] Unlike the patronus, the pater was not appointed with a ceremony, was an honorary office and could be granted to

---

the restoration of the synagogue (as at Aegina and Akmonia) and organize the worship (Acts 13.15). According to Brooten (Brooten 1982, pp. 23–24) the ἀρχισυνάγωγος could have corresponded to the rosh-ha-knesset mentioned in the Mishnah, who was responsible for the worship. In the Gospels, the ἀρχισυνάγωγος appears in the tale of the resurrection of Jairus's daughter, reported in Mark (Mark 5.22; 5.35; 5.36; 5.38) and Luke (Luke 8.49) and in the debate following a recovery on shabbath (Luke 13.14). In both cases, the ἀρχισυνάγωγος runs a synagogue and takes part in the doctrinal debates. This office is referred to in the same terms in the Acts: two ἀρχισυνάγωγοι are mentioned in Corinth (Acts 18.17), one of whom Paul converted to Christianity (Acts 18.8). Much more interesting is a passage where, in describing the community of Antiochia, it is said: μετὰ δὲ τὴν ἀνάγνωσιν τοῦ νόμου καὶ τῶν προφητῶν ἀπέστειλαν οἱ ἀρχισυνάγωγοι πρὸς αὐτοὺς λέγοντες· ἄνδρες ἀδελφοί, εἴ τίς ἐστιν ἐν ὑμῖν λόγος παρακλήσεως πρὸς τὸν λαόν, λέγετε (Acts 13.15). It appears to be a collegial office responsible for the organization of the worship. Recently, Rajak and Noy (T. Rajak – D. Noy 1993, pp. 75–93) suggested to deprive the title of any real power and consider it as a kind of patronage: most of the ἀρχισυνάγωγοι are mentioned in the inscriptions for donatives or for the restoration of the synagogues. They agree with the idea that the ἀρχισυνάγωγοι were bound to only one synagogue. On this subject see also L. Levine 1998, pp. 195–213.

[45] IJO I, Ach58 (CIJ n. 722) from Aegina dated to 300–350 A.D., IJO II, 168 (CIJ n. 766) from Akmoneia in Phrygia and IJO II, Syr5 (CIJ n. 991) from Sepphoris, dated to 4th–5th century A.D.

[46] J.P. Waltzing 1895–1900, I, pp. 406–413.

[47] J.B. Frey, Intr. to CIJ, pp. LXXXXIX–XCI.

[48] J.P. Waltzing 1895–1900, I, pp. 413–415.

[49] JIWE II, 209, 288, 540, 544, 560, 576, 578, 579, 584.

[50] JIWE II, 251, 542, 577.

[51] CTh. XVI,8,4 (1 Dic. 331): Imp. Constantinus hiereis et archisynagogis et patris synagogarum et ceteris qui in eodem loco deserviunt. Hiereos et archisynagogos et patres synagogarum et ceteros qui in synagogis deserviunt ab omni corporali munere liberos esse praecipimus. dat. kal. dec. Constant(ino)p(oli) Basso et Ablavio coss.

people of low social level.[52] The office was probably granted for life to people whose generosity and morality was self-evident.[53]

According to the sources, it cannot be proved that the synagogues were eventually assimilated to the collegia. Apart from some resemblances between the structures of the two kinds of associations and some charities that both of them had, there is no evidence to show a juridical intervention that transformed the synagogues into sacra collegia. Notwithstanding the textual problems, the decree Flavius Josephus mentions has to do more with the benevolence Caesar shows towards the Jews than with the reorganization of the collegia: few lines above, it is remarked that the Jews of Rome too could live according to the Law and could gather money for the communal meals and for the rites. The passages of Suetonius and of Flavius Josephus refer to different aspects of the Caesarian policy towards the associative phenomenon: on the one hand, Caesar possibly reorganized those collegia that had become dangerous centres of power during the civil wars; on the other hand, he could have granted the Jews the right of living accordingly to their Law. Freedom of worship is always mentioned as an acquired right: the legal existence of synagogues probably depended on this point more than on their equalization with the sacra collegia.[54]

II

The presence of a γερουσία, a central assembly able to coordinate the synagogues and to create a net between the community and the Romans, is a debated question.

Evidence of the existence of a γερουσία could be deduced from two offices seldom mentioned in the inscriptions, the γερουσιάρχης[55]

---

[52] J.P. Waltzing 1895–1900, I, pp. 446–449.
[53] Eight πατὴρ συναγωγῆς (JIWE II, 209, 288, 540, 544, 560, 576, 578, 584), a πατήρ (JIWE II, 579) and a *pater* (JIWE II, 210) are attested in Rome. Apparently, this title could be held at any age.
[54] Of this opinion E. Smallwood 1981, p. 135.
[55] JIWE II, 86, 96, 113, 130, 162, 189, 238, 321, 351, 354, 487, 554, 555. This office is attested in Venosa (JIWE I, 76, 87) as γερουσιάρχον, Castel Porziano (JIWE I, 18) and Puteoli (JIWE I, 23).

and the ἀρχιγερουσιάρχης.[56] As we have already seen, the γερουσιάρχης is considered the chief of the γερουσία; his duties and characteristics consequently depend on what we mean by γερουσία. If it was the central assembly,[57] the γερουσιάρχης was actually the head of the community. This opinion is not unanimously shared. Those who support the opposite position base their opinion on some positive evidence.[58] This office is not mentioned in the legal Roman sources that, with some inaccurancies, quote the pater synagogae and the ἀρχισυνάγωγος. In five of the thirteen inscriptions attesting the γερουσιάρχης the term is followed by the name of a synagogue, an element that leads us to see a link with the assemblies of the synagogues. This latter point, though, is quite doubtful. The name of the synagogue could have been added to note the house of prayer he belonged to or a caring attitude he showed towards this synagogue while he was holding the office.

The ἀρχιγερουσιάρχης, not mentioned in the Roman legal sources, is attested only once, in an inscription found in Villa Torlonia and published in 1976. Assuming that the prefix αρχ- has the same hierarchic meaning it has in ἀρχισυνάγωγος,[59] the ἀρχιγερουσιάρχης was literally the head of the γερουσιάρχης. This is not an easy interpretation. If we consider the γερουσιάρχης as the chairman of the central assembly, the existence of an ἀρχιγερουσιάρχης is meaningless. Conversely in reconciling all the pieces of the puzzle, we could suppose, with Margaret Williams,[60] that the γερουσιάρχης was the chairman of the synagogal assembly, while the ἀρχιγερουσιάρχης led the central assembly. This opinion is not completely satisfactory. The evidence we have is too sparse, the inscriptions cannot be dated with

---

[56] JIWE II, 521: Ἐνθάδε κῖτε Ἀναστάσιους ἀρχιγερουσιάρχης υἱὸς Ἀν[ασ]τασίου OIT[.] Noy dates the inscription to the third/fourth century. Fasola at first published it after his excavations in Villa Torlonia in 1976 (U.M. Fasola 1976, pp. 36–37).

[57] As assumed by G. la Piana 1927, p. 549; J. Juster 1914, I, p. 128.

[58] E. Schürer 1973–1986, II.1, p. 98; J.B. Frey, Intr. to CIJ, LXXXV; H.J. Leon 1995², pp. 180–183; L.H. Kant 1987, p. 695; H. Solin 1983, p. 696 nr. 239; D. Noy, notes to JIWE II, 118.

[59] According to H. Solin 1983, p. 696 nr. 239 and M. Williams 1998, p. 226. Accordind to Noy (D. Noy 1999, p. 608) the prefix αρχ- stressed the age rather than the power of this person, while according to Horsley (G.H. Horsley 1982, p. 64) the office was a synymous of γερουσιάρχης. Fasola does not take any sides, and resumes the two opposite positions.

[60] M. Williams 1998, p. 226.

certainty and do not help demonstrate the existence of a central γερουσία. The importance and the meaning itself of these offices depend
almost entirely on the way we interpret the γερουσία.

Among the Roman inscriptions, the ἄρχων is the most frequently
attested office and is frequently followed by appellatives or suffixes
that probably modified its competences.

Two typologies of archons, attested only in Rome and in few
inscriptions, could be related to the existence of a central γερουσία,
the ἄρχων πάσης τιμῆς[61] and the ἐξάρχων.[62]

The interpretation of the ἄρχων πάσης τιμῆς depends on the meaning of the term τιμή. According to the most widely accepted explanation, τιμή could mean "honor", as it frequently appears in the
New Testament.[63] This meaning was not extraneous to Hellenized
Judaism and is frequently used in the Septuagint as the honor due
to God[64] and, with a more ethical shade, the honor due to the person who helps the neighbour[65] or who acts with wisdom,[66] modesty[67]
and respect.[68] Honor could assume a non theoretical value and could

---

[61] This office is attested only three times (JIWE II, 121, 164, 259) in inscriptions found in Vigna Randanini and Monteverde. A fourth further inscription found
in Vigna Randanini shows the title translittered into Latin (JIWE II, 265). Leon
(Leon 1995², pp. 176–177) and Williams (M. Williams 1998, p. 225) consider the
archon alti ordinis as a Latin translation of the ἄρχων πάσης τιμῆς. This office is attested
only in one inscription whose Jewishness has been rejected by Manzella (S. Manzella
1989, pp. 103–112) and Noy (notes to JIWE II, nr. 618): *L. Maecio L. Constantio et |
Maeciae L. Lucianidi et | L. Maecio Victorino et | L. Maeciae Sabbatidi filis | et Iul.
Alexandriae coniugi | fecit b. m. L. Maecius L. | archon s alti ordinis.* Linder (A. Linder
1987, p. 139 nr. 11) connects both the titles with the *maiores Iudaeorum* mentioned
in CIust 1:9:3 (415 C.E.) and CTh 16:8:23 (416 C.E.) and to the ראשׁים נדלים and
to the זקנים of the Jewish sources.

[62] JIWE II,2: ἐνθάδε κεῖτε | Γελάσις ἐξάρχων | τῶν Ἑβρέων· ἐν εἰ|ρήνη ἡ κοίμησις
| αὐτοῦ; JIWE II,4: C(aius) Furfani|us Iulianus | exarchon | qui vixit | annis XXVIII.

[63] This is the fundamental meaning of the term: for instance Romans 12, 10:
. . . τῇ τιμῇ ἀλλήλους προηγούμενοι; 1 Timothy 6, 1: Ὅσοι εἰσὶν ὑπὸ ζυγὸν δοῦλοι,
τοὺς ἰδίους δεσπότας πάσης τιμῆς ἀξίους ἡγείσθωσαν; Hebrews 2, 9: . . . βλέπομεν
Ἰησοῦν διὰ τὸ πάθημα τοῦ θανάτου δόξῃ καὶ τιμῇ ἐστεφανωμένον.

[64] For instance Psalms 28:1: ἐνέγκατε τῷ κυρίῳ δόξαν καὶ τιμήν.

[65] Often with this meaning in the Sapiential books. For instance: Proverbs 22:9a:
Νίκην καὶ τιμὴν περιποιεῖται ὁ δῶρα δούς, τὴν μέντοι ψυχὴν ἀφαιρεῖται τῶν κεκτημένων.

[66] Wisdom 8:10: ἕξω δι᾽ αὐτὴν δόξαν ἐν ὄχλοις καὶ τιμὴν παρὰ πρεσβυτέροις ὁ νέος.

[67] For instance in Sirach 10:28: Τέκνον, ἐν πραΰτητι δόξασον τὴν ψυχήν σου καὶ
δὸς αὐτῇ τιμὴν κατὰ τὴν ἀξίαν αὐτῆς.

[68] For instance the honor due to parents (Exodus 20:12: Τίμα τὸν πατέρα σου καὶ
τὴν μητέρα) or to the husband (Esther 1:20: . . . . καὶ οὕτως πᾶσαί αἱ γυναῖκες
περιθήσουσιν τιμὴν τοῖς ἀνδράσιν ἑαυτῶν ἀπὸ πτωχοῦ ἕως πλουσίου).

become the sign of greater dignity. Consequently, τιμή could be associated with royalty and the power God gives to some individuals.[69] Consequently, it has been supposed that the formula "πάσης τιμῆς" could mean "with all the honors" and suggest an archonship with greater powers. The existence of distinct archonships is evident after the finding of JIWE II, 164.[70] In this inscription the two offices are clearly distinguished in a way that, according to Noy,[71] could suggest the existence of a cursus honorum, of two steps required to acquire the position of φροντιστής. Conversely, the inaccuracy that characterizes the Jewish inscriptions of Rome leads me to believe that the list was compiled in a random order. Surely, the ἄρχων πάσης τιμῆς had a position of some prestige within the community. But which community are we talking about? Considering that the ἄρχων πάσης τιμῆς was never linked with a synagogue, it has been assumed that he was a member of the central γερουσία: his greater power, his distinction from the more common archonship was stressed with the addition of "πάσης τιμῆς". Unfortunately, this attractive theory is not based on any positive evidence. Most of the Jewish inscriptions attest titles that seem to be honorary. Τιμή could be traced back to its most common meaning and denote, instead of a greater power, a superior status the community granted to worthy people.[72]

The interpretation of Frey is completely different. In his opinion, τιμή could mean "material goods": the ἄρχων πάσης τιμῆς managed the financial affairs of the community and was the person in charge of the gathering of the fiscus Iudaicus. Examples from the Hebrew Bible are rare and point to the payment of professional services,[73] to the price of an item[74] or to the estimation for a vow.[75] The term

---

[69] Frequently with this meaning in the Book of Daniel. For instance in Daniel 2:37: . . . καὶ σοὶ ὁ κύριος τοῦ οὐρανοῦ τὴν ἀρχὴν καὶ τὴν βασιλείαν καὶ τὴν ἰσχὺν καὶ τὴν τιμὴν καὶ τὴν δόξαν ἔδωκεν. It is attested also in other books as in 2 Maccabees 4:15: Καὶ τὰς μὲν πατρῴους τιμὰς ἐν οὐδενὶ τιθέμενοι, τὰς δὲ Ἑλληνικὰς δόξας καλλίστας ἡγούμενοι.

[70] JIWE II, 164: οἶκος αἰώνιος. | ἐνθάδε κεῖτε Εὔ|ψυχος δὶς ἄρχ(ων), ἄρχ(ων) π|άσης τειμῆς καὶ φροντισ|τής· ἐν εἰρήνη κοίμησ||ις αὐτοῦ. ἐτῶν νε'.

[71] D. Noy 1999, p. 609.

[72] It is apparently the same phenomenon attested for the ἄρχων διὰ βίου; the two archonship can be compared also for the old age the persons who hold the offices had.

[73] For instance: Sirach 38:1: Τίμα ἰατρὸν πρὸς τὰς χρείας αὐτοῦ τιμαῖς αὐτοῦ καὶ γὰρ αὐτὸν ἔκτισεν κύριος.

[74] For instance: Numbers 20:19: ἐὰν δὲ τοῦ ὕδατός σου πίωμεν ἐγώ τε καὶ τὰ κτήνη, δώσω τιμήν σοι.

[75] For instance: Leviticus 27:2–3: Ὃς ἂν εὔξηται εὐχὴν ὥστε τιμὴ τῆς ψυχῆς αὐτοῦ τῷ κυρίῳ, ἔσται ἡ τιμὴ τοῦ ἄρσενος.

is connected with a tax only in a passage where it is said that Demetrius exempted the Jews from the payment of the salt tax.[76] Flavius Josephus uses τιμή both with the meaning of price[77] and of honor.[78] In the New Testament τιμή has the same meanings attested in the Septuagint, but the term occurs much more frequently.[79] The opinion of Frey can be hardly supported by the evidence we have in the Jewish literary sphere.

The second officer to be considered is the ἐξάρχων: while the ἄρχων was the member of the synagogal assembly, the ἐξάρχων was the member of the central γερουσία. Juster assumed that ἐξάρχων had the same etymology of ἔξαρχος, a term that in the literature of the first century was used to mean an emerging personality, a military leader.[80] However, the morphologic difference is not a minor issue. Moreover, an office with this name is not attested in Diaspora or in Eretz-Israel. A more plausible explanation could be suggested.[81] In Late Antiquity the prefix εξ- was sometimes used to note an office the person had held and subsequently left.[82] That cannot suit the Jewish inscriptions: since these titles are found in funerary inscriptions, all, apart from the lifelong ones, referred to offices the dead had held in the past, not in the year when he died. Moreover, this theory can hardly justify the fact that both titles were mentioned in the same inscription, apart from supposing that the office of ἐξάρχων could be held only by a person who once had been an ἄρχων. But this is pure speculation. As a matter of fact, we have no evidence to interpret the meaning and the importance of this title.

---

[76] 1 Maccabees 10:29: Καὶ νῦν ἀπολύω ὑμᾶς καὶ ἀφίημι πάντας τοὺς Ἰουδαίους ἀπὸ τῶν φόρων καὶ τῆς τιμῆς τοῦ ἁλὸς καὶ ἀπὸ τῶν στεφάνων. The exemption is mentioned also in Flav. Jos., *Ant.* XIII,49 (E. Schürer, 1973–1986, I, pp. 178–179).

[77] For instance: *B.J.* II, 285: Οἱ γὰρ ἐν Καισαρείᾳ Ἰουδαῖοι . . . πολλάκις μὲν κτήσασθαι τὸν τόπον ἐσπούδασαν τιμὴν πολλαπλασίονα τῆς ἀξίας διδόντες. or *B.J.* II, 592: Συνωνούμενος δὲ τοῦ Τυρίου νομίσματος, ὃ τέσσαρας Ἀττικὰς δύναται, τέσσαρας ἀμφορεῖς, τῆς αὐτῆς ἐπίπρασκεν τιμῆς ἡμιαμφόριον.

[78] For instance: *B.J.* II, 208: [Κλαύδιον] ἀρκεῖσθαι γὰρ τῇ τιμῇ τῆς προσηγορίας; oppure *B.J.* I, 461: ". . . οὐ γὰρ βασιλείαν, ἀλλὰ τιμὴν βασιλείας τοῖς υἱοῖς παραδίδωμι.

[79] With the meaning of price of goods τιμή occurs, for instance, in Matthew 27:9 (. . . καὶ ἔλαβον τὰ τριάκοντα ἀργύρια, τὴν τιμὴν τοῦ τετιμημένου ὃν ἐτιμήσαντο ἀπὸ υἱῶν Ἰσραήλ), Acts 4:34 (τὰς τιμὰς τῶν πιπρασκομένων), Acts 4:1–2 (Ἀνὴρ δέ τις Ἀνανίας ὀνόματι . . . ἐπώλησεν κτῆμα καὶ ἐνοσφίσατο ἀπὸ τῆς τιμῆς), Acts 7:16 (ἐτέθησαν ἐν τῷ μνήματι ᾧ ὠνήσατο Ἀβραὰμ τιμῆς ἀργυρίου).

[80] For instance Arrianus, *Tactica*, 10,1 and Elianus, *Tactica*, 9,2. J. Juster 1914, II, p. 214. His theory is resumed by M. Williams 1994, p. 140.

[81] G. La Piana 1927, p. 316, H.J. Leon 1995², pp. 189–190.

[82] Isidorus, *Origines*, 9,3,9: *Exconsules autem dicti, quod iam a consulatu exierint, sive discesserint peracto vicis suae anno*; idem, *op. cit.*, 15, 13, 13: *Exconsul quod a consulatu discesserit.* Symmacus, *Epistola*, 7,126: *Rufini, expraefecti Urbi . . .*

Almost no mention of the organization of the Jewish community is made in the literary sources. Some scholars see a reference to the γερουσία in a well-known passage of Acts which narrates the arrival of Paul at Rome, probably around 60 c.e., and his meeting with important members of the Roman community.[83] Who these Jews were, which offices they held is unknown. This passage simply attests the presence of a hierarchy among the Jews of Rome, for which some Jews enjoyed a greater power, could speak in the name of the whole community, were in touch with the religious authorities of Eretz-Israel and could open a debate on a new sect.[84]

Some aspects of the social and economic life of the community could have required the coordination of a central assembly, as the management of the allotments used as cemeteries. Only the catacomb of Vigna Cimarra,[85] a small cemetery that was partly explored at the beginning of the nineteenth century, has returned inscriptions with the name of only one synagogue: all the other catacombs returned inscriptions mentioning more than one congregation, seven in the case of Monteverde.[86] Possibly, the management (or the property?) of the cemetery was shared by different congregations and the burial place depended on the proximity to the residence of the deceased. An assembly whose members were chosen among all the synagogues could have run these burial areas. But on this point we do not have any certainty. We actually do not know by what right the Jews could enjoy these lands and who was responsible for the Jewish cemeteries under the Roman authorities.

The synagogues could have needed coordination in the election of the members of the courts of justice whose presence is attested in the Imperial period in many centres of the Diaspora. During the first century, the State did not intervene on this point: this question

---

[83] Acts 28:17: Ἐγένετο δὲ μετὰ ἡμέρας τρεῖς συγκαλέσασθαι αὐτὸν τοὺς ὄντας τῶν Ἰουδαίων πρώτους. G. La Piana 1927, pp. 350 sg.

[84] Acts 28:21–22: Οἱ δὲ πρὸς αὐτὸν εἶπαν· ἡμεῖς οὔτε γράμματα περὶ σοῦ ἐδεξάμεθα ἀπὸ τῆς Ἰουδαίας οὔτε παραγενόμενός τις τῶν ἀδελφῶν ἀπήγγειλεν ἢ ἐλάλησέν τι περὶ σοῦ πονηρόν. Ἀξιοῦμεν δὲ παρὰ σοῦ ἀκοῦσαι ἃ φρονεῖς, περὶ μὲν γὰρ τῆς αἱρέσεως ταύτης γνωστὸν ἡμῖν ἐστιν ὅτι πανταχοῦ ἀντιλέγεται.

[85] JIWE II, 406: the synagogue of Elea.

[86] The synagogue of the Agrippesians (JIWE II 170, 130), of the Augustesion (JIWE II, 169, 189, 194, 542), of the Calcaresians (JIWE II, 69, 98, 165, 1), of the Hebrews (JIWE II, 33, 2), of the Tripolitans (JIWE II, 166, 113), of the Vernaclesians (JIWE II, 114, 117, 72) and of the Volumnesians (JIWE II, 577).

possibly fell within the positive attitude the Romans had towards the Jews since Caesar. In some statutes of Diasporan communities the Jewish courts are granted quite a large degree of autonomy in matters concerning the civil law:[87] they could judge cases regarding Jewish habits and the Jewish Law,[88] but they also had the authority to draw up a will or a contract.[89] The chairman usually was a distinguished figure: at Sidon, because of the proximity with the Judaea, the court was chaired by the ἐθνάρχης Hyrcanus II, while at Alexandria this position was held by the ἐθνάρχης of the community who, according to Strabo, had the same powers of a head of state.[90] We do not have any information on communities smaller than Alexandria or farther from Eretz-Israel.

The Roman legislation of Late Antiquity often deals with the Jewish courts of justice. However, our knowledge of their organization is not better. In fact any law specifies the place of meeting of the courts, the number of judges and the legal procedures. The laws

---

[87] At Alexandria, Strab. in Flav. Jos., *Ant.* XIV, 117: Ἐν γοῦν Αἰγύπτῳ κατοικία τῶν Ἰουδαίων ἐστὶν ἀποδεδειγμένη χωρίς, καὶ τῆς τῶν Ἀλεξανδρέων πόλεως ἀφώρισται μέγα μέρος τῷ ἔθνει τούτῳ. Καθίσταται δὲ καὶ ἐθνάρχης αὐτῶν, ὃς διοικεῖ τε τὸ ἔθνος καὶ διαιτᾷ κρίσεις καὶ συμβολαίων ἐπιμελεῖται καὶ προσταγμάτων, ὡς ἂν πολιτείας ἄρχων αὐτοτελοῦς. At Sidon, Flav. Jos., *Ant.* XIV, 194–195: . . . διὰ ταύτας τὰς αἰτίας Ὑρκανὸν Ἀλεξάνδρου καὶ τὰ τέκνα αὐτοῦ ἐθνάρχας Ἰουδαίων εἶναι . . . ἂν δὲ μεταξὺ γενηταί τις ζήτησις περὶ τῆς Ἰουδαίων ἀγωγῆς, ἀρέσκει μοι κρίσιν γίγνεσθαι παρ' αὐτοῖς. At Sardis, Flav. Jos., *Ant.* XIV, 235: Ἰουδαῖοι πολῖται ἡμέτεροι προσελθόντες μοι ἐπέδειξαν αὐτοὺς σύνοδον ἔχειν ἰδίαν κατὰ τοὺς πατρίους νόμους ἀπ' ἀρχῆς καὶ τόπον ἴδιον, ἐν ᾧ τά τε πράγματα καὶ τὰς πρὸς ἀλλήλους ἀντιλογίας κρίνουσι. and *Ant.* XIV, 260: . . . καὶ νῦν εἰσελθόντες ἐπὶ τὴν βουλὴν καὶ τὸν δῆμον παρεκάλεσαν, ἀποκαθισταμένων αὐτοῖς τῶν νόμων καὶ τῆς ἐλευθερίας ὑπὸ τῆς συγκλήτου καὶ τοῦ δήμου τοῦ Ῥωμαίων, ἵνα [. . .] διαδικάζωνται πρὸς αὐτούς, δοθῇ τε καὶ τόπος αὐτοῖς εἰς ὅν συλλεγόμενοι μετὰ κυναικῶν καὶ τέκνων ἐπιτελοῦσι τὰς πατρίους εὐχὰς καὶ θυσίας τῷ θεῷ.

[88] As at Sidon.

[89] As at Alexandria.

[90] The ἐθνάρχης is mentioned also by Philo (*In Flaccum*, 74) but is called γενάρχης. Philo himself says (*Quis rer. div. her.*, 279): ἐθνάρχης γὰρ καὶ γενάρχης ὡς ἀληθῶς ἐστιν οὗτος. His duties are not defined, but he is described as the head of the community. On behalf of the Jewish courts in Egypt their competences are described by Talmudic sources (Toseftà Pe'ah 4:6 and Toseftà Ketubbot 3:1). We do not know whether their iurisdictio was extended only to Alexandria or to the whole of Egypt. It is doubtful when this office was created; the literary sources which refer to the Ptolemaic period, including the Letter of Aristeas, do not mention this title. A papyrus of the 13 B.C. (CPJ II nr. 143 l. 7) mentions a Jewish notary's office clearly connected with the court of justice: ἀδελφὸς Θεόδωρο(ς) καθ' ἥν ἔθετο διαθήκ(ην) διὰ τοῦ τῶν Ἰουδαίων ἀρχείου. We will discuss later on the substitution of the ἐθνάρχης with the γερουσία. P.M. Fraser 1972, I pp. 55–57; M. Stern 1974–1980, nr. 105 pp. 277–282.

are not limited to a specific community, but are generically addressed to the Jews living within the boundaries of the Empire.[91] From the Roman point of view, the core of the problem was the codification of their sphere of competence. With a law Arcadius II enacted in 398 c.e., the iurisdictio of these courts was heavily limited.[92] The Jewish authorities kept only the capacity of judging on questions of *superstitio*; they could also decide by arbitration in civil suits if both parties agreed to be judged by a Jewish court. Consequently the suits between Jews and non-Jews could still take place, but the non-Jewish party had to agree previously to be judged by a Jewish court. In 415 c.e. Theodosius II intervened again on this point and forbade the Jewish courts to judge the Christians: the governor of the province became responsible for the lawsuits between Jews and Christians.[93] Notwithstanding these two laws, the Jewish courts were still in activity. The last known intervention on this question is a law enacted by Arcadius and kept in the Justinian codex that followed the abolition of the patriarchate by few months.[94] In the absence of a central religious authority, the suits concerning the *superstitio* are also moved to regular courts: the Jewish courts could only decide by arbitration in civil suits between two Jewish parties. With regard to the composition of the courts and of the position the judges had within the Jewish communities, the legal sources are the most vague. They are called with periphrasis *qui legi ipsi praesident*[95] or *maiores religionis*

---

[91] *CTh* 2:1:10 addressed to *Iudaei Romano et communi iure viventes*.

[92] *CTh* 2:1:10 (= Bre. II, 1, 10) (3 Febr. 398): Impp. Arcadius et Honorius AA. Ad Eutychianum praefectum praetorio. *Iudaei Romano et communi iure viventes in his causis, quae non tam ad superstitionem eorum quam ad forum et leges ac iura pertinent, adeant sollemni more iudicia omnesque Romanis legibus inferant et excipiant actiones: postremo sub legibus nostris sint. Sane si qui per compromissum ad similitudinem arbitrorum apud Iudaeos vel patriarchas ex consensus partium in civili dumtaxat negotio putaverint litigandum, sortiri eorum iudicium iure publico non vetentur: eorum etiam sententias provinciarum iudices exequatuntur, tamquam ex sententia cognitoris arbitri fuerint adtributi.* dat. III Non. Feb. Constantinopoli Honorio A. IIII et Eutychiano V.C. Coss.

[93] *CTh* 16:8:2 (29 Nov. 330).

[94] *CJust* 1:9:8: Impp. Gratianus Valentinianus et Theodosius AAA. Eutychiano pp. *Iudaei Romano communi iure viventes in his causis quae tam ad superstitionem eorum quam ad forum et leges ac iura pertinent, adeant sollemni more iudicia omnesque Romanis legibus conferant et excipiant actiones. Si qui vero ex communi pactione ad similitudinem arbitrorum apud Iudaeos in civili dumtaxat negotio putaverint litigandum, sortiri eorum iudicium more publico non vetentur. Eorum etiam sententias iudices exsequantur, tamquam ex sententia cognitoris arbitri fuerint attributi.* D III Non. Febr. Constantinopoli Honorio A IIII et Eutychiano conss. [a. 398].

[95] In *CTh* 16:8:2: . . . *Qui devotione tota synagogis Iudaeorum patriarchis vel presbyteris se dederunt et in memorata secta degentes legi ipsi praesident* . . .

suae,[96] but it is remarked that they are subjected to the authority of the patriarch and of the Elders of the Sanhedrin,[97] according to the pyramidal structure that connected the Diaspora with Eretz-Israel.

If we look at Eretz-Israel the picture becomes more complex: in the towns the justice could be delegated to a wise man, a member of the Sanhedrin. From the Amoraic period, the *bet din* where he judged, studied and taught was placed in the synagogue.[98] In this case, the synagogue was actually a *bet din*, a house of justice, and the members of the synagogue as the *hazzan* became the judges. In the literary sources, the Roman synagogue is not only a house of prayer, but also a centre of studies. Although it is not clearly attested, they could have assumed the function of *bet din* from the synagogues of the homeland.[99] Clearly, in this case coordination between synagogues to elect the judges was not necessary.

No definitive evidence has been found to demonstrate the existence of a central γερουσία. One of the most common arguments to support this theory has been the comparison with other great communities of the Diaspora. In fact, the γερουσία is attested in Cyrene[100] and in Alexandria. The Egyptian community could be apparently compared to the Roman centre: the two communities are the most populous ones of the whole Diaspora and the best documented too, even if the Egyptian evidence is of better quality. The Alexandrian Diaspora is of more ancient origin. During Hellenism, the Jews were integrated in the civic body and part of the community was organized in a πολίτευμα. Their conditions changed abruptly with the Roman conquest.[101] The Romans could recognize full citizenship

---

[96] In the *interpretatio* of *CTh* 2:1:10: *Iudaei omnes, qui Romanos esse noscuntur, hoc solum apud religionis suae maiores agant . . .*

[97] *CTh* 16:8:2.

[98] The synagogue as *bet din* is attested both in the New Testament and in the Talmud, although with some important differences. Z. Safrai 1994, pp. 187–190.

[99] On this point any evidence can be found in the Roman inscriptions in Hebrew.

[100] According to a decree enacted in 24 C.E. (CIG III, 5361) to do credit to M. Settius, the officer in charge of the δημόσια πράγματα for the province of Crete and Cyrene. The commmunity of Cyrene had a πολίτευμα whose members were clearly parted from the πολῖται (ll. 16–18) of the town, but were granted some privileges as the possibility of following their customs. In fact, the meetings are arranged according to the Jewish feasts, sukkot (ll. 1–2) and New Moon (l. 24). The inscription mentions nine ἄρχοντες. Their number probably changed in time. The ἄρχοντες probably ran the πολίτευμα. L. Boffo 1994, pp. 204–216.

[101] J. Mélèze-Modrzejewski 1991, pp. 131–133.

only of those who had previously enjoyed civic rights: this category included the Greeks who had the citizenship of the πόλεις of Alexandria, Naukratis and, since 130 c.e., Alcinoopolis, but excluded the Greeks living in the χώρα who obtained only a reduction in the payment of the λαογραφία, the tax the Egyptians had to pay between 14 and 64 years. Even though the Jews were Hellenophones and held the same social positions as the Greeks, they had seldom gained Alexandrian citizenship:[102] they were prevented from obtaining the Roman citizenship. Moreover, not having Greek origin, they could not enjoy tax reductions either. The Romans recognized the Jewish πολίτευμα of Alexandria and granted to its members privileges in religious matters, such as the exemption from answering a summons in the day of shabbat, the possibility of receiving a pecuniary indemnity instead of a measurement of oil during the public distributions, the right of prosecuting for sacrilege the theft of holy books and of replacing the stick with the whip in corporal punishments. Even though the πολίτευμα had a religious and ethnic value, it never took the shape of an independent civic body within the Greek πόλις.[103] With few alterations, the Romans kept its structure. According to Philo,[104] after the death of the γενάρχης in 11 c.e., Augustus sus-

---

[102] A sample of the social declassing the Alexandrian Jews underwent after the Roman conquest is attested in a papyrus of the 5/4 B.C. (CPJ II, 151), written by Ἑλένος, who was the son of an Alexandrian citizen but who could not enjoy the Alexandrian citizenship for unknown reasons (because illegitimate son, because son of a non-citizen mother or because his father gained the citizenship after his birth). He asks to the prefect of Egypt G. Turranius to be exempted from the λαογραφία for having reached the age limits. As Tcherikover remarks (CPJ II, pp. 30–32), the Alexandrian citizenship could be passed to the sons only if both parents were citizens; such a situation was rare among the Jews. Most part of them probably lived the same difficulties Ἑλένος had. The scribe emends the definition of Ἑλένος as Ἀλεξανδρεύς in Ἰουδαῖος τῶν ἀπὸ Ἀλεξανδρε(ίας). According to Delia (D. Delia 1991, p. 26), the correction did not depend on an unfortunate attempt to assume citizenship illegally or on his passage to the status of citizen, but on the necessity to specify his exact status: even if he was born in Alexandria, he was not a citizen but a member of the Jewish community.

[103] As Modrzejewski remarks (J. Mélèze-Modrzejewski 1999, p. 142). Troiani (L. Troiani 1994, pp. 11–22) shows that for the Jews the idea of πολιτεία meant the belonging to the people of Israel and to the Mosaic Law and did not entail any bound with a land (so M. Goodman 1992, p. 61).

[104] In Flaccum, 74: Τῆς γὰρ ἡμετέρας γερουσίας ἣν ὁ σωτὴρ καὶ εὐεργέτης Σεβαστὸς ἐπιμελησομένην τῶν Ἰουδαικῶν εἵλετο μετὰ τὴν τοῦ γενάρχου τελευτὴν διὰ τῶν πρὸς Μάγιον Μάξιμον ἐντολῶν μέλλοντα πάλιν [ἀπ'] Ἀλεξανδρείας καὶ τῆς χώρας ἐπιτροπεύειν . . .

pended this office and placed a γερουσία at the head of the community.[105] However, this evidence is inconsistent with a passage of Flavius Josephus who attests that Augustus "had not forbidden the appointment of the *ethnaches*".[106] Members of the γερουσία are attested under Caligula,[107] while the *ethnarches* is no more mentioned after 10/11 C.E. Consequently Tcherikover assumed that Augustus eventually forbade the appointment of new *ethnarches*,[108] an act that Claudius confirmed few years later. Flavius Josephus (or his source) could have modified the text of the act because it was supposed to be in contrast with the positive policy Augustus had towards the Jews. Stern tried to reconcile the two pieces of evidence and supposed that the ethnarcate was not abolished but subordinated to the γερουσία, whose power Augustus significantly strengthened.[109] The number of people composing the assembly is uncertain; according to the Mishnaic tradition the γερουσία had 71 members,[110] a number corresponding to the 71 benches found during the excavations in the great synagogue of Alexandria. According to the literary sources, the members of the γερουσία held the title of ἄρχων. As we have already seen, the archonship was also the most common title attested in the Jewish inscriptions of Rome. However, this cannot be used as definitive evidence of the existence of a central γερουσία in Rome: as a matter of fact,

---

[105] The existence of a γερουσία in Hellenistic period is a debated question and depends on the interpretation of the §310 of the Letter of Aristeas: καθὼς δὲ ἀνεγνώσθη τὰ τεύχη, στάντες οἱ ἱερεῖς καὶ τῶν ἑρμηνέων οἱ πρεσβύτεροι καὶ τῶν ἀπὸ τοῦ πολιτεύματος οἵ τε ἡγούμενοι τοῦ πλήθους. Fuchs (L. Fuchs 1924, p. 89) connects πρεσβύτεροι both with τῶν ἑρμηνέων and with τῶν ἀπὸ τοῦ πολιτεύματος and infers the existence of a γερουσία at the head of the πολίτευμα in Hellenistic period. Conversely, Tcherikover (Intr. to CPJ I, p. 9) connects οἱ πρεσβύτεροι only with τῶν ἑρμηνέων and rejects such a dating. Both Fraser (P.M. Fraser 1972, II, p. 139 nr. 145) and Stern (M. Stern 1974–1980, I, p. 280) share this opinion.

[106] *Ant.* XIX, 283: τελευτήσαντος τοῦ τῶν Ἰουδαίων ἐθνάρχου τὸν Σεβαστὸν μὴ κεκωλυκέναι ἐθνάρχας γίγνεσθαι βουλόμενον ὑποτετάχθαι ἑκάστους ἐμμένοντας τοῖς ἰδίοις ἔθεσιν καὶ μὴ παραβαίνειν ἀναγκαζομένους τὴν πάτροις θρησκείαν.

[107] *In Flaccum*, 74: ὀκτὼ καὶ τριάκοντα συλλαβὼν τοὺς εὑρεθέντας ἐν ταῖς οἰκίαις εὐθὺς μὲν δῆσαι κελεύει and *In Flaccum*, 76: ἐδηλώθη γὰρ αὐτῷ μεταπεμψαμένῳ πρότερον τοὺς ἡμετέρους ἄρχοντας ὅσα τῷ δοκεῖν ἐπὶ καταλλαγαῖς ταῖς πρὸς τὴν ἄλλην πόλιν.

[108] Tcherikover, *Intr.* to CPJ, vol. I pp. 9–10. To eliminate this contradiction, Reinach (T. Reinach 1924, p. 124 nr. 5) supposes that the text was corrupted and emends ἐθνάρχας with ἀρχόντας.

[109] M. Stern 1974–1980, I, nr. 105 p. 280.

[110] Midrash Sukkoth 5:1. According to the Jewish tradition, the Sanhedrin of Jerusalem had this same number of members (for instance TB Sanhedrin 1:5 and Toseftà Sanhedrin 3:4).

this title is attested in other communities of the Diaspora, where a γερουσία is not supposed to exist.

Some scholars have considered the possibility that the Roman γερουσία was modelled not on the pattern of assemblies attested in other communities of the Diaspora, but on assemblies existing in Eretz-Israel. Such a theory is supported by the observation that most of the Roman community is likely to have come from Palestine, because of free immigration or forced deportation of war prisoners, as we will see. Consequently the organization both of the synagogues and of the γερουσία could have been influenced by patterns of the homeland, first of all the Sanhedrin of Jerusalem.[111] The sources paint different pictures of the functions and of the organization this assembly had. According to Flavius Josephus[112] and to the Gospels,[113] the Sanhedrin was the supreme political and legal body of the country; it consisted of priests, scribes and elders and chaired by the high priests.[114] Conversely, the Talmudic sources describe the Sanhedrin as the supreme legislative assembly on religious matters,[115] and affirm that it consisted of sages and that it was chaired by the *nasi* and the *av bet din*.[116]

Notwithstanding the differences between the συνέδριον and the Sanhedrin, Schürer tried to reconcile the different traditions on the

---

[111] G. La Piana 1927, pp. 362–363.

[112] According to Josephus, the political and legal activities of the Sanhedrin reached the peak during the fights between Hyrcanus II and Herod (Ant. XIV, 168–170 and Ant. XV, 176) and in the suit against the sons of Herod (Ant. XVI, 356 and BJ I, 537).

[113] For example Mark 15:1: Καὶ εὐθὺς πρωὶ συμβούλιον ποιήσαντες οἱ ἀρχιερεῖς μετὰ τῶν πρεσβυτέρων καὶ γραμματέων καὶ ὅλον τὸ συνέδριον; Luke 22:66: Καὶ ὡς ἐγένετο ἡμέρα, συνήχθη τὸ πρεσβυτέριον τοῦ λαοῦ, ἀρχιερεῖς τε καὶ γραμματεῖς, καὶ ἀπήγαγον αὐτὸν εἰς τὸ συνέδριον . . . Acts 4:5–15: Ἐγένετο δὲ ἐπὶ τὴν αὔριον συναχθῆναι αὐτῶν τοὺς ἄρχοντας καὶ τοὺς πρεσβυτέρους καὶ τοὺς γραμματεῖς ἐν Ἱερουσαλήμ, καὶ Ἄννας ὁ ἀρχιερεὺς καὶ Καιάφας καὶ Ἰωάννης καὶ Ἀλέξανδρος καὶ ὅσοι ἦσαν ἐκ γένους ἀρχιερατικοῦ . . . κελεύσαντες δὲ αὐτοὺς ἔξω τοῦ συνεδρίου ἀπελθεῖν . . . Acts 5:21: Παραγενόμενος δὲ ὁ ἀρχιερεὺς καὶ οἱ σὺν αὐτῷ συνεκάλεσαν τὸ συνέδριον καὶ πᾶσαν τὴν γερουσίαν τῶν υἱῶν Ἰσραὴλ . . .

[114] As in Acts 23:6: Γνοὺς δὲ ὁ Παῦλος ὅτι τὸ ἓν μέρος ἐστίν Σαδδοκαίων τὸ δὲ ἕτερον Φαρισαίων ἔκραζεν ἐν τῷ συνεδρίῳ . . .

[115] As in TB Sanhedrin 11:2 and in Toseftà Sanhedrin 7. A list of the duties in TB Sanhedrin 1:5 and in Toseftà Sanhedrin 3:4.

[116] The two groups of sources are debated by E. Schürer 1973–1986, II, pp. 210–218. He thinks that these two offices adopted the tasks described in the Talmud only in the late Mishnaic period.

basis of passages from the Mishnaic treatise Sanhedrin according to which the Sanhedrin was granted wide powers in administrative, legal and political matters.[117] The Sanhedrin is likely to have been in activity between the first century B.C. and the first century C.E. and is supposed to have ceased to exist with the destruction of the Temple.[118] Subsequently, a prestigious assembly working as *bet din* and *yeshivah* was created in Yabneh. The emergence of this assembly is recognised by the late Imperial legislation that speaks of this assembly in terms of the supreme Jewish court and of the supreme authority on the Jews living within the boundaries of the Empire. According to this source, it consisted of *presbyteri* and was chaired by the *patriarcha*.[119] Since the authority recognized that the Sanhedrin before and after the fall of Jerusalem was strong, its organization could have been easily taken as a pattern for other Jewish assemblies. Yet, it was likely to have begun its activity only in the first century B.C., in quite a late period.[120] In the previous time, the organization of the Roman γερουσία may have depended on other patterns. The literary sources of the Hellenistic and Hasmonean period mention a γερουσία composed by Elders and authoritative members of the Jewish people.[121] This assembly was part of the Jewish great

---

[117] In particular Mishnah Sanhedrin 1:5. For the debate on this question see E. Schürer 1973–1986, II, pp. 207–208.

[118] The Mishnah recalls this event: Mishnah Sota 9:11: "Since the Sanhedrin ceased (מסבטלה סנהדרין) all singing ceased at the wedding feasts".

[119] *CTh* 16:8:2: *Qui devotione tota synagogis Iudaeorum patriarchis vel presbyteris se dederunt et in memorata secta degentes legi ipsi praesident.* . . .

[120] The first literary attestation is in Flav. Jos., *Ant.* XIV, 91: Πέντε δὲ συνέδρια καταστήσας εἰς ἴσας μοίρας διένειμε τὸ ἔθνος, καὶ ἐπολιτεύοντο οἱ μέν ἐν Ἱεροσολύμοις οἱ δέ ἐν Γαδάροις οἱ δὲ ἐν Ἀμαθοῦντι, τέταρτοι δ᾽ ἦσαν οἱ ἐν Ἱεριχοῦντι, καὶ τὸ πέμπτον ἐν Σαπφώροις τῆς Γαλιλαίας. The same words appear in *B.J.* I, 170, but here Josephus uses the term σύνοδοι instead of συνέδρια.

[121] Πρεσβύτεροι τοῦ λαοῦ are attested in the period of Judah Maccabaeus (2 Maccabees 1:10; 4:44; 11:27 and 1 Maccabees 7:33). A γερουσία is openly mentioned with Jonathan (1 Maccabees 12:6: γερουσία τοῦ ἔθνους; 11:23: τῶν πρεσβυτέρων Ἰσραήλ; 12:35: τοὺς πρεσβυτέρους τοῦ λαοῦ) and with Simon (1 Maccabees 13:36; 1 Maccabees 14:20; 1 Maccabees 14:28). Its existence is attested also in the book of Judith (on which see note 131) that mentions a γερουσία τῶν πρεσβυτέρων: it represented all the people of Israel and met at Jerusalem (Judith 4:8; 11:14; 15:8). According to Flavius Josephus, the γερουσία was already in activity at the times of Antiochus the Great: *Ant.* XII, 138: . . . παραγενομένους δ᾽ εἰς τὴν πόλιν λαμπρῶς ἐκδεξαμένων καὶ μετὰ τῆς γερουσίας ἀπαντησάντων . . .

assembly, a larger assembly composed of priests, representatives of the people, elders, and notables that gathered rarely to take only the most important decisions on the fate of the Jews.[122] Although it was also the high court both for civil and for religious suits[123]—a peculiarity that the Sanhedrin would subsequently inherit—it was mainly the permanent representative body of the Jews. Such was the assessment of the Syrian kings, who exempted its members and the officers of the Temple from the payment of a group of taxes,[124] while Sparta[125] and Egypt[126] agreed to receive missives from the high priest and from the γερουσία of the Jews.

---

[122] For instance in 1 Maccabees 14:28: Ὀκτωκαιδεκάτῃ Ελουλ ἔτους δευτέρου καὶ ἑβδομηκοστοῦ καὶ ἑκατοσοῦ . . . ἐπὶ συναγωγῆς μεγάλης ἱερέων καὶ λαοῦ καὶ ἀρχόντων ἔθνους καὶ τῶν πρεσβυτέρων τῆς χώρας ἐγνώρισεν ἡμῖν . . . The remembrance of a Great Assembly keeper of the Torah as received through generations, is attested in BT Abot 1a (and Mishnah Abot 1): משה קבל תורה מסיני ומסרה ליהושע ויהושע לזקנים וזקנים לנביאים ונביאים מסרוה לאנשי כנסת הגדולה ("Moses received the Torah at Sinai and transmitted it to Joshua, Joshua to the Elders, and the Elders to the Prophets, and the Prophets to the men of the Great Synagogue").

The spiritual heir of Joshua left to the Elders is mentioned in Judges 2:7: ויעבדו העם את־יהוה כל ימי יהושע וכל ימי הזקנים אשר האריכו ימים אחדי יהושע אשר ראו את כל־מעשה יהוה הגדול אשר עשה לישראל ("The troops had served Yahweh throughout Joshua's days and the days of the elders who outlived Joshua, who had witnessed the whole of Jahweh's great work, which he did on behalf of Israel").

[123] As in the notes of Flavius Josephus to Deuteronomy 17:8–11, Ant IV, 218: ἂν δ' οἱ δικασταὶ μὴ νοῶσι περὶ τῶν ἐπ' αὐτοῖς παρατεταγμένων ἀποφήνασθαι, συμβαίνει δὲ πολλὰ τοιαῦτα τοῖς ἀνθρώποις, ἀκέριον ἀναπεμπέτωσαν τὴν δίκην εἰς τὴν ἱερὰν πόλιν, καὶ συνελθόντες ὅ τε ἀρχιερεὺς καὶ προφήτης καὶ ἡ γερουσία τὸ δοκοῦν ἀποφαινέσθωσαν.

[124] In the letter of thanks Antiochus IV sent to the Jews and to their γερουσία for the help they had given him in the war against Ptolemy IV: Flav. Jos., Ant. XII, 144: . . . ἀπολυέσθω δ' ἡ γερουσία καὶ οἱ ἱερεῖς καὶ οἱ γραμματεῖς τοῦ ἱεροῦ καὶ οἱ ἱεροψάλται ὧν ὑπέρ τῆς κεφαλῆς τελοῦσι καὶ τοῦ στεφανιτικοῦ φόρου καὶ περὶ τῶν ἀλῶν.

[125] Flav. Jos., Ant. XIII, 166: . . . ἀρχιερεὺς Ἰωνάθης τοῦ ἔθνους τῶν Ἰουδαίων καὶ ἡ γερουσία καὶ τὸ κοινὸν τῶν ἱερέων Λακεδαιμονίων ἐφόροις καὶ γερουσίᾳ καὶ δήμῳ τοῖς ἀδελφοῖς χαίρειν. 1 Maccabees 12:6: Ιωναθαν ἀρχιερεὺς καὶ ἡ γερουσία τοῦ ἔθνους καὶ οἱ ἱερεῖς καὶ ὁ λοιπὸς δῆμος τῶν Ἰουδαίων Σπαρτιάταις τοῖς ἀδελφοῖς χαίρειν. The answer in 1 Maccabees 14:20: Σίμωνι ἱερεῖ μεγάλῳ καὶ τοῖς πρεσβυτέροις καὶ τοῖς ἱερεῦσι καὶ τῷ λοιπῷ δήμῳ τῶν Ἰουδαίων. As Schürer remarks (E. Schürer 1973–1986, II, p. 203 nr. 8), there is an apparent correspondence between ἡ γερουσία τοῦ ἔθνους and τοῖς πρεσβυτέροις; all the evidence distinguishes among the High Priest, the γερουσία, the ἱερεῖς e the people (here δῆμος, elsewhere λαός).

[126] 2 Maccabees 1:10: Οἱ ἐν Ἱεροσολύμοις καὶ οἱ ἐν τῇ Ἰουδαίᾳ καὶ ἡ γερουσία καὶ Ιουδας Ἀριστοβούλῳ διδασκάλῳ Πτολεμαίου τοῦ βασιλέως . . .

The importance an assembly assumed in the history of a nation does not necessarily entail that its organization was adopted in other dependent areas. Beside the influence the Sanhedrin and the preceding assembly had on the Jews, no evidence supports the theory that their organizational patterns were actually used in Rome.

On surveying the patterns that could have influenced the creation of the Roman γερουσία, smaller assemblies usually were not taken into account. Flavius Josephus speaks of a council of seven who administrated small towns in Galilee.[127] Although these local assemblies are likely to have acted mainly as legal courts, Josephus calls their members ἄρχοντες, a term that denotes a political power and is often used as the translation of the Hebrew *rashim*, leaders.[128] Josephus again confirms this: in an more generic passage he affirms that in the Galilean towns a group of seven men, chosen among the most influential families, administered justice.[129] Probably, this was a widespread use of Judaic origin, a use that the first Christian community of Jerusalem also took up.[130] This is not the only literary evidence we have of this office. In the Book of Judith, the *archon* is described as having political and administrative power.[131] The ἄρχοντες,

---

[127] Flav. Jos., *B.J.*, II, 570: . . . . τῶν μὲν γηραιῶν ἑβδομήκοντα τοὺς σωφρονεστάτους ἐπιλέξας ἐκ τοῦ ἔθνους κατέστησαν ἄρχοντας ὅλης τῆς Γαλιλαίας, ἑπτὰ δ' ἐν ἑκάστῃ πόλει δικαστὰς [. . .] ἐφ' ἑαυτὸν ἀναπέμπειν ἐκέλευσεν καὶ τοὺς ἑβδομήκοντα.

[128] G. Alon 1980, p. 177; S. Freyne 1980, p. 198; S. Safrai – M. Stern 1974, pp. 414–415; A. Sherwin-White 1963, p. 133; H. Cotton 1999, p. 88.

[129] Flav. Jos., Ant. IV, 287: εἰ δὲ μηδέν ἐπίβουλον δρῶν ὁ πιστευθεὶς ἀπολέσειεν, ἀφικόμενος ἐπὶ τοὺς ἑπτὰ κριτὰς ὀμνύτω τὸν θεόν, ὅτι μηδὲν παρὰ τὴν αὐτοῦ βούλησιν ἀπόλοιτο καὶ κακίαν, οὐδὲ χρησαμένου τινὶ μέρει αὐτῆς, καὶ οὕτως ἀνεπαιτίατος ἀπίτω.

[130] Acts 6:3–6: ἐπισκέψασθε δέ, ἀδελφοί, ἄνδρας ἐξ ὑμῶν μαρτυρουμένους ἑπτά, πλήρεις πνεύματος καὶ σοφίας, οὓς καταστήσομεν ἐπὶ τῆς χρείας ταύτης, ἡμεῖς δὲ τῇ προσευχῇ καὶ τῇ διακονίᾳ τοῦ λόγου προσκαρτερήσομεν. Καὶ ἤρεσεν ὁ λόγος ἐνώπιον παντὸς τοῦ πλήθους καὶ ἐξελέξαντο Στέφανον, ἄνδρα πλήρης πίστεως καὶ πνεύματος ἁγίου, καὶ Φίλιππον καὶ Πρόχορον καὶ Νικάνορα καὶ Τίμωνα καὶ Παρμενᾶν καὶ Νικόλαον προσήλυτον Ἀντιοχέα, οὓς ἔστησαν ἐνώπιον τῶν ἀποστόλων, καὶ προσευξάμενοι ἐπέθηκαν αὐτοῖς τὰς χεῖρας.

[131] Judith 6:14–16 (passim): . . . καὶ κατέστησαν αὐτὸν ἐπὶ τοὺς ἄρχοντας τῆς πόλεως αὐτῶν, οἱ ἦσαν ἐν ταῖς ἡμέραις ἐκείναις, Ὀζίας ὁ τοῦ Μιχα ἐκ τῆς φυλῆς Συμεων καὶ Χαβρις ὁ τοῦ Γοθονιηλ καὶ Χαρχις υἱὸς Μελχιηλ. Καὶ συνεκάλεσαν πάντας τοὺς πρεσβυτέρους τῆς πόλεως . . .; 8:9–10: καὶ ἤκουσεν τὰ ῥήματα τοῦ λαοῦ τὰ πονηρὰ ἐπὶ τὸν ἄρχοντα . . . καὶ ἀποστείλασα τὴν ἄβραν αὐτῆς τὴν ἐφεστῶσαν πᾶσιν τοῖς ὑπάρχουσιν αὐτῆς, ἐκάλεσεν Χαβριν καὶ Χαρμιν τοὺς πρεσβυτέρους τῆς πόλεως αὐτῆς; 10:6: . . . εὕροσαν ἐφεστῶτα ἐπ' αὐτῇ Ὀζίαν καὶ τοὺς πρεσβυτέρους τῆς πόλεως; 13:12: . . . ἐσπούδασαν τοῦ καταβῆναι ἐπὶ τὴν πύλην τῆς πόλεως αὐτῶν καὶ συνεκάλεσαν τοὺς πρεσβυτέρους τῆς πόλεως. The Book of Judith is not included in the canon of the Hebrew Bible. "Quasi fictional narrative", according to Schürer's definition (E. Schürer 1973–1986, III.1, pp. 216–222), it was composed for didactic and parenethic purposes

three in number, cooperate with the πρεσβύτεροι, whose number is not specified, neither it is said what is the relationship between these two offices.[132] Alon argued that the πρεσβύτεροι (zeqenim)—supposedly some of the most influential citizens of the town—formed a legislative assembly; among these, three ἄρχοντες (rashim) were elected in turn and held the executive power.[133] Such an organization could not survive the Roman conquest. He consequently thought about a different distribution of tasks. The rashim could have run the administration of the town and managed the relationship with the Roman authorities, while the zeqenim could have dealt with the religious life of the community. Later sources confirm the existence of this situation. The Talmud can distinguish between the zeqenim and the rashim; the latter had administrative duties in the towns.[134] Again, among the papyri produced during the revolt of Bar Cochba there are letters sent to or received by officers—two in number—who administered the centres in question.[135] This evidence—belonging to different periods and different contexts—suggests that the administrators came from wealthy and influential families. An organizational pattern that requires cooperation between the ἄρχοντες and the πρεσβύτεροι is attested in Diaspora. An interesting text comes from the community of Elche. The inscription (JIWE I, 181) is dated to the fourth century and was placed as partial border of a mosaic that covered the floor of a building whose purposes are not yet clear but that was certainly used by the local community:

ΧΗΟΧΟΝΤΩΝ ΚΕ ΠΡΕΒΥΤϹΡΩΝ

Noy integrates as follows:

---

in Maccabaic period—possibly after Alexander Jannaeus—by a Syrian author. The Hebrew original version went lost, but its existence is confirmed by Origines (*Ad Africanum* 113), while Jerome (Opp. Ed. Vall X,21) mentions an Aramaic version. The text is known through Greek, Latin, Syriac and Ethiopic versions.

[132] The council of the Elders is attested also in the OT, often in connection with the notables of the place. With administrative duties, like in the book of Judith, in Judges 8:14: "At his request, he listed for him the commanders and elders of Succoth, seventy-seven men." 1 Kings 21:8: "So she wrote letters in Ahab's name and sealed (them) with his seal; she sent the letters to the elders and the nobles of his town, who lived with Naboth"; Ruth 4:11: "The all the people who were in the gate and the elders said"; With legal duties in Deuteronomy 19:12.

[133] G. Alon 1980, p. 177.

[134] MShek. 5:2; TB Baba Bathra 8b.

[135] P. Benoit 1961 nr. 42 p. 156; Y. Yadin 1967 nr. 12 p. 59.

⟨εὐ⟩χὴ (?) ⟨ἀρ⟩χόντων κὲ πρε⟨σ⟩βυτ⟨έ⟩ρων

The reading of the last two words is unanimous, although two inaccuracies should be admitted, the omission of the Σ and the wrong writing of the E. The way we should reconstruct the first part of the line is much more debated. Reinach, the first editor, assumes that O was a mistake for AP and can read ⟨προσ⟩ευχὴ ⟨ἀρ⟩χόντων; he deduces that the building was a synagogue. Frey, followed by Lifshitz, suggests that the O was written in place of a C and that AP were both omitted: the final reading was ⟨ἐξ εὐ⟩χῆ⟨ς⟩ (?) ⟨ἀρ⟩χόντων, "according to the vow of the archons . . .". The inscription was placed to show that the mosaic was a voting offering of the ἄρχοντες and the πρεσβύτεροι. Noy accepts the general interpretation of the text but admits only the wrong lettering of the O and reads εὐχή at the nominative. Notwithstanding these uncertainties, at Elche the πρεσβύτεροι and the ἄρχοντες were collegial offices and represented the whole community, according to the pattern attested in Galilee.

Unfortunately, no text of this kind was ever found in Italy. However, if we consider the final functions that the Jewish inscriptions found in this territory had, this peculiarity could no longer sound strange. Almost all the epigraphic evidence, not only the Roman corpus, comes from a funerary context, where the praise of the deceased was more important than the description of the community he belonged to. More pieces of information could be retrieved from commemorative inscriptions a community or a private placed in public buildings, as in the case of the inscription of Castel Porziano,[136] but this category is rarely attested in Italy[137] and is completely absent in Rome.

---

[136] JIWE I, 18: [*synagoga* (?)] *Iudeorum* | [*in col(onia) Ost(iensi) commor*]*antium qui com-para* | [*verunt ex conlat*(?)]*ione locum C(aio) Iulio Iusto* | [*gerusiarche ad m*]*unimentum struen-dum* | [*donavit, rogantib*(?)]*us Livio Dionysio patre et* | | [. . . . .]*no gerusiarche et Antonio* | [. . . . . *dia] biu anno ipsorum, consent(iente) ge*[*r* | *us(ia). C(aius) Iulius Iu*]*stus gerusiarches fecit sib*[*i*] | [*et coniugi] suae lib(ertis) lib(ertabusque) posterisque eorum.* | [*in fro*]*nte p(edes) XVIII, in agro p(edes) XVII.*

[137] JIWE I, 15: Ostia (253–260 C.E. or few years later): *M(arco) Aurel*[*io .*] *f(ilio) Ter(entina) Py*[*ladi*] | A[. .]SCI[. . .] *Scythop*[*oli*] | *p*[*an*]*tomim*[*o sui] tempor*[*is*] | *primo in c*[. . . . .]*to et probato* | *a*[*b imp(eratoribus) Valeriano*] | | [*e*]*t Gal*[*lien*]*o* [- -] | *ex provincia* [*Iuda*]*e*[*a . . . . . . post*] | *mortem patr*[*is s*]*ui Iud*[*ae; item de*]*cu* | *rioni civitat*[*iu*]*m Ascalo*[*nitan*]*orum et* | *Damascen*[*or*]*um. Huic s*[*ecu*]*ndus* | | *ordo Augus*[*ta*]*lium non solum* | *propter memo*[*ri*]*am patr*[*i*]*s eius, sed* | *et propter plenam* [*ipsius pe*]*ritiam postul*[*antibus*] | *omnibus pariter civibus* [- -] [--].

Conversely, if we look at the two offices alone, the results are quite different. The ἄρχων, well attested in all the Diaspora, is mentioned 41 times at Rome and, according to this evidence, is likely to have been an easy office.

The data regarding the adjective πρεσβύτερος are opposite: it is seldom attested in Italy and is usually mentioned in inscriptions dated to a later period than the Roman corpus. The term follows the name of the deceased only in one inscription of the fifth century found at Sofiana (Gela)[138] and in a contemporary text of Venosa (JIWE I, 75), a bilingual written in Hebrew characters. Actually it is a matter of isolated cases. It is hard to establish whether the adjective meant an office or the age of the deceased, as it occurs with νήπιος,[139] παρθένος[140] and νεώτερος.[141] The use of the term πρεσβίτερες ascribed to three women of Venosa in inscriptions of the fifth century seems more pertinent to our aims: one of these appears to have died at 38 years, still rather young.[142] Although it is hard to show, the women of the Jewish community of Venosa could have had a role in the religious activities of the synagogue, as happened in the same period in the Church of Southern Italy: in 494 Pope Gelasius sent an epistle to the bishops of Lucania, Bruzzio and Sicily in which he condemned the presence of women who officiated at mass and administered the Sacraments.[143]

JIWE I, 17: Porto (IV C.E.): [- - -] σὺν [. . . . . .κ]αὶ Θεοδώ | [ρου (?) κα]ὶ Ἑλλὴλ φρον | τιστῶν.

[138] JIWE I, 157: Ἀττί | νις βρε⟨σ⟩β | ύτερο | ς. Two inscriptions of the fourth/fifth century with the term πρεσβύτερος (JIWE I, 148; I, 149) were found at Catania, but their Jewishness is doubtful.

[139] JIWE II, 288, 337; simile JIWE II, 214: [- -]e infan | [ti- - dul]cissime | [- -] us et Vi | [- -]s amato | [- - parent?]es fecerunt.

[140] JIWE II, 30, 357, 525, 552.

[141] JIWE II, 557: ἐντάδε κεῖται | Νεικόδημος | ὁ ἄρχων | Σιβουρησίων καὶ | πᾶσι φειλητὸς | | αἰτῶν λ᾿ ἡμερ(ῶν) μβ᾿ | θάρι Ἀβλάβι νεώτερε οὐ | δεὶς ἀθάνατος.

[142] JIWE I, 59: τάφος | Βερωνικέ | νις πρεσβιτε | ρες ετ φιλια | Ἰωσέτις. JIWE I, 62: τάφως | Μαννίνες πρεσ | βιτέρες τιγάτερ Λον | γίνι πατέρις, ἰνγόνιν | Φαυστίνι πατέρις | | ἐτῶν λη᾿. JIWE I, 71: τάφος Φα | υστίνες πρεσ | βιτέρες. שלום

Noy remarks the peculiarity of the expression "πρεσβιτέ | ρες ετ φιλια", as the presence of the patronymic should make the indication of seniora to distinguish this woman from an homonym iuniora unnecessary. The argument is strong, but without knowing how old the woman was when she died, we can not definitively exclude the possibility that she was simply an old woman.

[143] In particular Ep. 14,26: Nihilominus impatienter audivimus, tantum divinarum rerum subisse despectum, ut feminae sacris altaribus ministrare firmentur . . . A Christian inscription of the half of the fifth century mentions a presbitera. (CIL X, 8079: B(onae) m(emoriae)

With regard to Rome, it is hard to say whether the office of πρεσβύτερος is attested: it all depends on the reconstruction of two inscriptions where this title seems to be mentioned.

The first inscription (JIWE II, 176) is extremely fragmentary:

[- -]ΗΤΡΟ
[- -]ωρος
[- -]υτερος
[- -]ιτε

Frey makes large integrations and reads on ll. 1–2 Μητρόδωρος[144] while on l. 3 πρεσβύτερος: this latter integration is accepted by Leon and Schürer.[145] L. 4 could possibly be integrated with [ἐνθάδε κ]ῖτε or [ὧδε κ]ῖτε, corresponding to the usual formula ἐνθάδε κεῖται, "here lies".[146] Considering the wide lacuna in the text, Noy does not accept any integration. With regard to line 3, he stresses that before the υ, one could see faint traces of a letter that Frey reads as a B but that he thought it could also be a P, an O or a Θ.

Difficulties of different nature concern the second inscription (JIWE II, 24):

ἐνθ⟨ά⟩δε
κῖται Σά
ρα ΟΥΡΑ π
ρεσβύτ⟨η⟩ς

The term ΟΥΡΑ is considered a wrong transcription of the Latin names Ursa[147] or Vera.[148] However, this is unlikely because double names in which the Hebrew name precedes the Latin or Greek one are never attested among the Jewish inscriptions of Rome. Another crux is the reconstruction of the η on line 4. The version here quoted is that of Noy: he assumes that the ν was a wrong lettering, a mistake

---

s(acrum). *Leta presbitera | vixit annos XL, menses VIII, dies VIIII | quei bene fecit maritus. | Processit in pace pridie | idus Maias.* On the presence of female priests see: G. Otranto 1982, pp. 341–360.

[144] The name Μητρόδωρος is not attested among the Jewish inscriptions of Rome.

[145] H.J. Leon 1995², p. 181, p. 321; E. Schürer (Schürer 1973–1986, II.1, p. 98) accepts the reconstruction of Frey.

[146] The first formula is the most common among the Roman Jewish corpus: see the index at p. 544 of JIWE II. The second formula is attested in Rome in JIWE II, 237, 238, 239, 459?, 463.

[147] Attested as Οὖρσος (JIWE II, 253).

[148] The name is not attested, but we have the variant Βηριάνη (JIWE II, 481, 453).

the lapicide did in composing the text. Neither Frey nor Leon suggests any alternative integration and transcribe πρεσβυτνς. Πρεσβύτ⟨η⟩ς should be a masculine form, but it is preferred to πρεσβὺτ⟨ι⟩ς for the resemblance between the shape of ν and η, that could have facilitated the mistake. If we accept Noy's reconstruction, then we need to bear in mind that this is actually the only Italian inscription bearing the adjective in question. The choice of πρεσβύτ⟨η⟩ς instead of πρεσβύτερα could not depend on the fact that the deceased was a woman: although of different periods, the three women of Venosa that we have already mentioned are called πρεσβίτερες, while at Rabat in Cyprus a person named Eulogia has the appellative of πρεσβύτερα. The literary evidence we have on the office always mentions the term with the suffix -υτερος/α: actually, the Roman evidence is likely to suggest the age of the deceased, not an office she hold within the community.

Given this situation, we do not have any evidence of the presence in Rome of a role that, as described in the literature, was recurring and prestigious enough to be mentioned in funerary inscriptions. We have to conclude prudentially that this title was not used in Rome and that the Galilean pattern of the council of the zeqenim was not followed in this community.

After surveying all the evidence we have on the γερουσία, the (natural) conclusion is that no general council was ever attested in Rome. Despite the fact that a kind of cooperation is likely to have existed in a large community such as that of Rome, as occurred in other centres of the Diaspora, we have only scanty and faint traces of this reality, whose interpretation ultimately depends on an a priori assumption of the existence of the central assembly itself.

SECTION TWO

THE HISTORICAL DEVELOPMENT

ORIGINS

The Jewish presence in Rome is apparently attested in a controversial passage of Valerius Maximus, which mentions the expulsion
from Rome both of the Jews and of the Chaldaeans in 139 B.C.[1]
This passage has severe textual problems, as it is inserted within a
large lacuna that runs between I, 1, 21 e I, 5,1, filled by two late
epitomizers.

As Lane shows, we have at least three traditions of manuscripts;
each one of these basically quotes different versions.[2]

The most widespread tradition is reported only in a Vatican codex
of the ninth century (Vat. Lat. 4929) published by Angelo Mai in
1831.[3] Kempf used this codex in publishing Valerius Maximus in
1853, as the following editors did also.[4] The epitome is due to Julius
Paris who possibly lived in the fifth century.[5]

> *Cn. Cornelius Hispalus praetor peregrinus, M. Pompilio Laenate L. Calpurnio
> cos., edicto Chaldeos circa decimum diem abire ex urbe atque Italia iussit, leuibus
> et ineptis ingeniis fallaci siderum interpretatione quaestuosam mendaciis suis cali-
> ginem inicientes. Idem Iudaeos, qui Sabazi Iouis cultu Romanos inficere mores
> conati erant, repetere domos suas coegit.*

Apart from few details that we will see later on, Julius Paris mentions a ban of expulsion addressed by the praetor peregrinus *Cn.
Cornelius Hispalus* to the Chaldaeans and the Jews, for trying to introduce the cult of Juppiter Sabazius in Rome.

We have two other versions of this passage. Before Mai's discovery, we knew of a different version of Paris, transcribed by the codex

---

[1] *Facta ac dicta memorabilia* I, 3,2.
[2] E. Lane 1979, pp. 35–38.
[3] According to J. Briscoe, editor of the Teubner edition (Stuttgart 1998, intr.
p. I), with whom Shakleton Bailey, editor of Loeb edition, agrees (Cambridge Mass.:
Harvard University Press 2000, intr. p. 5). Faranda, editor of the Italian UTET
edition (Torino: Unione tipografico-editrice torinese 1971, p. 25), dates the codex
to the tenth century, as Lane does.
[4] In Teubner edition, in Loeb edition and in two Italian editions, the already
mentioned UTET edition and Giardini edition (Pisa 1986, vol. III). Les Belles
Lettres (editor R. Combès, Paris 1995), lets the lacuna.
[5] The Vat. 4929 and Nepotionus are quoted from the Teubner edition, while
the codex Bernensis 366 from Lemaire edition of 1822.

Bernensis 366 (ninth century) and the Codex Berolinensis 46 (four-teenth century), depending on the foregoing codex. This version was used in all the printed editions published from the sixteenth cen-tury—as Aldus' edition of 1502—to the beginning of the nineteenth century, as the editions of Kappius (1782) and Lemaire (1822).

> *C. Cornelius Hispallus, praetor peregrinus, M. Popilio Laenate, Cn. Calpurnio coss., edicto Chaldaeos intra decimum diem abire ex urbe atque Italia iussit: levibus et ineptis ingeniis, fallaci siderum interpretatione, quaestuosam mendaciis suis cali-ginem enicientes. Idem, qui Sabazii Iovis cultu simulato mores Romanos inficere conati sunt, domos suas repetere coegit.*

In this second version the Jews are not mentioned.

The third tradition is preserved in another Vatican codex (Vat. 1321). Mai published this manuscript in 1831 and dated it to the fourteenth century. Kempf and all the following editors published this version alongside the one presented in Vat. Lat. 4929, in two parallel columns.[6] The lacuna in I,3,2 is filled with the epitome of Januarius Nepotianus, an epitomizer of the sixth century whose text often diverges from that of Paris in introducing details that proba-bly do not depend on Valerius Maximus.

> *Caldeos igitur Cornelius Hippalus urbe expulit et intra decem dies Italia abire ius-sit, ne peregrinam scientiam uenditarent. Iudeos quoque, qui Romanis tradere sacra sua conati erant, idem Hippalus urbe exterminauit, arasque priuatas e publicis locis abiecit.*

Nepotianus mentions the ban of the Chaldaeans and of the Jews but leaves out the believers of Juppiter Sabazius.

The versions of the two epitomizers are inconsistent on the infor-mation concerning the fate of the Jews. In regard to Paris' manu-script, the work of philology has not been able to definitively remove all the doubts about this tradition. J. Briscoe, Teubner editor of Valerius Maximus, could reconstruct the moment when the Bernensis codex came into contact with the Vat. Lat. 4929. According to Schultz's research, Briscoe supposed that the author of the second codex was Henricus Auxerrensis, pupil of Servus Lupus, a scholar of Carolingian age who died in 862. Lupus emended Valerius twice. In his first work, between 859 and 862, he apparently did not know

---

[6] Including the above mentioned editions.

Paris: he did not use him in the *Excerpta Valeriana* that he was composing nearly in that same period either.

In his last year of life, Lupus works again on the Exempla, this time using Paris: in 862 he had possibly read Paris' epitome.

In Billanovich's opinion,[7] Henricus could have drawn up the Vat. Lat. 4929 before Lupus' death: in this context, Lupus could have introduced Paris' epitome, while compiling his second version of the Exempla, the version ultimately preserved in Cod. Bernensis 366. As Briscoe shows, the two traditions are often completely different.[8] This is evident in the passage we are studying. It is possible that Lupus used a source of the Vatican manuscript, which Henricus probably drew only after his master's death.

To summarize, around 860 in a narrow circle of scholars two different versions of Paris circulated independently, the first fixed in the work of Lupus (cod. Bern. 366), the second drawn upon by Henricus (cod. Vat. Lat. 4929), who also gathered pieces of information from a new unknown source.

Lane criticized Billanovith's reconstruction, but did not yet know the opinion of Briscoe, which was published twenty years later. He supposes that the lost passage of Valerius Maximus regarding year 139 reported the issuing of three bans of expulsions, respectively against the Chaldaeans (this ban is unquestionable because mentioned by all the manuscripts), against the believers of Juppiter Sabazius and against the Jews.[9] Julius Paris probably reported only the ban against Chaldaeans and Jews, while omitting the expulsion of the believers of Sabazius. The editor of codex Vat. Lat. 4929 could have gathered the two traditions,[10] placing a *Iudaeos* before the relative clause (*qui Sabazi Iouis cultu Romanos inficere mores conati erant*), a confusion that was probably induced by the peculiar structure of the sentence and by the assonance between Juppiter Sabazius and Yahwè Sabaoth.

---

[7] E. Billanovich 1956, pp. 319–353.

[8] According to Faranda (intr. pp. 32–33), Vat. Lat. 4929 keeps the general structure of the original text, but changes some titles and omits or corrects some *exempla*. Moreover, in the introduction, Paris mentions 10 books, while the original *Exempla* should have been in 9.

[9] Lane's opinion is rejected in footnotes both by Briscoe and by Solin (H. Solin 1983, p. 606 n. 25), but is accepted by Goodman (M. Goodman 1994, pp. 82–83).

[10] Or a lost manuscript from which Vat. Lat. 4929 depends.

This passage has been greatly debated in the past:[11] it was used as evidence of syncretism between Judaism and the cult of Sabazius or as an abortive attempt to translate Judaism into a language that could be understood by non-Jews. Otherwise, if we reject the versions commonly published, we have two irreconcilable accounts of the same event, the ban of the Chaldaeans: the first adds a supplementary expulsion of the believers of Juppiter Sabazius, while the second reports the news regarding the Jews. The only source mentioning the Jewish ban is consequently Nepotianus, who is often considered less authoritative than Paris.[12] As we will see, Nepotianus

---

[11] E. Johnson (E. Johnson 1984, pp. 1538–1613) stresses the two possible readings of this passage: it can be considered as evidence of religious syncretism of a Jewish group, or as a wrong transcription due to the epitomizers. The first theory is backed up by those scholars who suppose the existence of Jewish heterodox groups, open to a Jewish interpretation of pagan cults. Even if the cult of Sabazius, a Phrygian god, is attested in Athens in the fifth century (Aristophanes, *Wasps* 8–10; *Birds*, 876; *Lysistrata*, 388; *Horae* frag. 566 ed. Edmonds), it was widespread only during the Imperial period. The first pieces of evidence we have in Rome are of the first century C.E., but the cult reaches the peak of diffusion in the third century (P.W. s.v. *Sabatius*). Often confused with Dionysus, Sabazius is identified with Zeus only (and not always as a decree from Sardis shows, L. Robert 1975, pp. 306–330) in Asia Minor. The most ancient inscription mentioning the cult of Zeus-Sabazius dates back to the 134–135 B.C. and has been found in Pergamus. According to Cumont, the ban of 139 B.C. was addressed to a community of Phrygian or Thracian Jews converted to Juppiter-Sabazius. On the contrary, Schürer stresses the chronological proximity to the first Jewish embassy and supposes that the embassadors themselves urged the ban of this heterodox group: the letter sent by Λεύκιος ὕπατος alludes to Jewish refugees who should be returned to Simon. In Marcel Simon's more moderate opinion (M. Simon 1976, pp. 52–65), the formula was created by Jews who wanted to make Judaism understandable to pagans, an opinion already expressed, with few differences, by Bickermann in 1937 (Bickerman 1937, p. 134, nr. 3).

The version of Vat. 4929 is not questioned by those scholars who equate this formula with Yahwè Sabaoth (κύριος Σαβαώθ in the Septuagint) or with Yahwè Shabbath either, as suggested by Leon (H.J. Leon 1995[2], p. 2) and Solin (H. Solin 1983, p. 606 n. 25). Schürer rejects this latter interpretation (E. Schürer 1973–1986, III.1, p. 74). When and why this transcription was made is questionable. *T* could be a corruption of the name of God due to the source of Valerius Maximus, to Julius Paris or to medieval copists (according to Lane's theory, with which P. Schäfer agrees, 1999, p. 71). But this formula could also be an interesting piece of evidence of the attempt of the State to identify a condemned cult with a well-known god (as Johnson sharply suggests, E. Johnson 1894, p. 1603). As Stern stresses, Nepotianus is silent on Juppiter Sabazius, but mentions the Jewish attempt to introduce *sacra sua* in Rome (M. Stern 1974–1980 I, n. 147a).

[12] As by Shakleton Bailey (Loeb ed., intr. p. 5); Faranda (intr. p. 34) stresses that Nepotianus quotes only the first 21 chapters of the work, corresponding to Val. Max. I–III 2,7.

reports anachronistic details, while the Vatican codex preserves precious elements perfectly pertaining to a fresh, not yet rooted, community.

The expulsion of the Chaldaeans is unquestionable. We have pieces of information on the dating and on the reason why the ban was enacted both by Nepotianus and by Julius Paris. Nepotianus presents a brief, precise account; Paris mentions the consuls,[13] Hispalus' title[14] and an exhaustive description of the count of indictment; unlike Nepotianus, his words have a moralistic tone.

Conversely, the section regarding the Jews has greater problems. The Jews were expelled in 139 B.C., the same year of the ban against Chaldaeans. Alessandrì uses this dating to confute the issue of the ban itself.[15] Around the middle of the second century, after a first contact due to the action of Q. Mummius and T. Manlius during the negotiations pending between Judas Maccabaeus and the Syrian king in 164,[16] the relationships between Judaea and Rome become more frequent. According to a tradition mentioned in I Macc. and in Flavius Josephus—tradition that Alessandrì accepts but that part of the scholarship considers at least questionable[17]—we know that

---

[13] The *praenomen* of Calpurnio Piso is Cneus, not Lucius as Paris refers; they both were praetor in 142 B.C. T. Broughton 1951, vol. I, p. 481.

[14] C. Cornelius Scipio Hispalus is mentioned in CIL I², 15, but with the cognomen Hispanus.

[15] S. Alessandrì 1968, pp. 187–198.

[16] 2 Macc., 14: 16–21; Polybius, 31,1.

[17] Some authoritative positions emerge within the huge bibliography concerning the problem of the treaties between Judaea and Rome. At the end of nineteenth century, a group of scholars led by Mendellsohn aroused doubts on the authenticity of the treaty as quoted in I Macc. (I. Mendelsohn, *Senatus consulta Romanorum quae sunt in Josephi Antiquitatibus*, Acta societatis philologiae Lipsiensis 5 (1875), pp. 91–100), but we have to wait until the early twentieth century for Willrich to reject the treaty as a whole (H. Willrich, *Urkundenfälschung in der hellenistisch-jüdischen Literatur*, 1924, pp. 44–50). He affirms that Judaea and Rome entered official relationships under John Hyrcanus I, according to a debated statement of Flavius Josephus (*Ant.* XIV, 206). Yet, the treaty of 161 B.C. should not be considered a forgery, but, according to another passage of Flavius Josephus (*Ant.* XII, 419), it should be dated to the period when Judah was a high priest, i.e. during the kingdom of Aristobulus I, called Judah. Niese (B. Niese 1900, pp. 268sg.) rejects the authenticity of the treaties quoted in I Macc., but accepts the possibility of official relationships between the two countries, as attested by Justin XXXVI and Diod. XL,2. The guidelines given to these studies by Willrich are rejected by Täubler (E. Täubler 1913, pp. 239–254) who can recognize within the words of I Macc. the structure of a *senatus*

Jewish embassies went to Rome. The first embassy, probably dated
to 161, should have allowed the stipulation of an alliance between
Rome and the Maccabean government (ruled, in that period, by
Judas): a copy of the treaty was probably engraved on bronze and
kept in the Capitol.[18] In 143/2 the Senate invited Simon, who had
succeeded his brother Jonathan, to renew the alliance: a second
embassy reached Rome, formed the alliance and exchanged gifts
with the Roman authorities.[19] At this time, the Senate drew up a
letter suggesting that the king of Syria and Egypt recognize the independence and the integrity of the Jewish State. As a matter of fact,
Rome considers Judaea under its protection, but only apparently on
equal terms: Syria and Egypt, who had long fought for the control
of the area, had to answer to Rome for their policy towards the
Jews. Momigliano dated the letter to 139, because he identified the
Leukios upatos, who signed the letter in the name of Rome, with praetor Lucius Valerius, who was in charge that year.[20] A few years later,
in 134 B.C., John Hyrcanus sent a third embassy requiring the help
of Rome in the long lasting war against Demetrius, king of Syria.[21]
The Roman intervention was immediate: the alliance with Judaea
was renewed and Demetrius was ordered to give up some strongholds.

In this period the relationships between Rome and Judaea were
excellent, even though Rome showed signs of interest in the Middle-
East: as a matter of fact, through the pacts with Judaea, Rome was

---

consultum; the original text was probably modified and corrupted when it was translated before being introduced in I Macc., a detail that could itself prove the antiquity of the passage. As already suggested by Niese, Flavius Josephus quotes a letter
addressed to Cos by Γαίος Φάννιος Γαίου υἱὸς στρατηγὸς ὕπατος asking protection
for the Jewish embassadors who carried back διατάγματα of the Senate: the consul
should be C. Fannius Strabo, appointed in 161 B.C. Momigliano (A. Momigliano
1930, pp. 159–162) agrees with Täubler and confutes the reference to *Ant.* XIV,
206, the most important element supporting a late dating of the treaties. The position of Täubler is shared by Schürer (E. Schürer 1973–1986, II.1, p. 172). Sordi, in
both her works (M. Sordi 1952, pp. 509–519; M. Sordi 1972, pp. 96–104), considers the authenticity of the treaties as proved, and studies them only in their political importance. More recently, Bar Kochva (B. Bar Kochva 1989, pp. 530–533),
in studying the relationships between Rome, Judaea and Syria in 164, accepts the
Maccabaean tradition even if he changes its dating slightly. On the problem see
also E. Gruen 1984 II, pp. 745–751.

[18] I Macc. 8:17–32; Flav. Jos., *Ant.* XII, 414–419.
[19] I Macc. 12:1–4; Flav. Jos., *Ant.* XIII, 163–165 and 169–170.
[20] A. Momigliano 1930, pp. 152–153.
[21] Flav. Jos., *Ant.* XIII, 259–266.

legitimated to intervene in the complex political situation of the area. Consequently, the positive picture Alessandrì drew of the relations between Judaea and Rome should be moderated: although both parts received benefits, with these alliances the position Rome had in Eastern Mediterranean was actually strengthened.

It is hard to evaluate how these embassies could have influenced the policy of the State towards the Jewish presence in Rome. According to the general picture he offers of the relations between the two governments, Alessandrì rejects the possibility of an expulsion: such an act could have caused the breakdown of the alliance. In my opinion, the two events cannot be related. Rome could have banned an unwelcome group even in presence of an embassy whose members belonged to the same group. Rome seems to maintain a steady policy towards the Jews, dealing separately with Eretz-Israel and with each community of the Diaspora, whose behaviour often made this policy easier. The Western Diaspora apparently does not react to the dramatic fall of Jerusalem in 70 C.E. and to the revolt of Bar Kochba; consequently, the Empire does not carry out any reprisal towards these peripheral areas. The Roman community is not an exception: notwithstanding the attempts to link the bans delivered under Tiberius and Claudius with the events in Judaea, these acts were possibly the consequences of local problems. Apparently this is also the situation in 139: the praetor peregrinus intervened to expel two (or three) groups of strangers whose cults and activities were considered dangerous for the *mores Romani*. Even in the words of the epitomizers, the ban is not referred to the Jews as a whole, but to that group of Jews who were in Rome in 139.

By what right a group of Jews was in Rome in this year is not clear. Nevertheless the officer who enacted the ban was the *praetor peregrinus*, who had the *provincia* of *iurisdictio* on suits between *peregrini* or between *cives* and *peregrini*.[22] The Jews—and the Chaldaeans—were consequently *peregrini*, did not enjoy civic rights and could be banned without a trial. The information we have does not help us understand whether it was a deep-rooted community or a group of Jews passing through. The second possibility is more reliable. In this period,

---

[22] According to annalistic sources, this office was introduced in the last year of the first Punic war. Its province is not subjected to the *ius civile* but to *ius gentium*. G. Scherillo – A. Dell'Oro 1987, pp. 219–220.

Rome had not yet supremacy in the Eastern Mediterranean, while the Jewish Diaspora was attested in Asia and Northern Africa. The attraction Rome had for the Jews during the second century B.C. cannot be compared to that of the Imperial period. In my opinion, the Jewish presence was sporadic. A confirmation of this hypothesis can be grasped from the words of Julius as they appear in Vat. 4929. While Nepotianus, in referring to the ban, says *Iudaeos . . . Hispalus urbe exterminavit*, Paris chooses the expression *Iudaeos . . . repertere domos suas coegit*. If the ban consisted in "going back home", we have to conclude that the permanent address of the expelled Jews was not Rome.

According to Bickermann,[23] this sentence should be read almost literally: the praetor banned the Jews and ordered them to return to their usual addresses, under the control of the Roman authorities. But Judaea at that time was not a Roman territory: these Jews should have originally come from Southern Italy, an area Rome conquered decades before. This is an interesting interpretation. Nevertheless, the sources speak of the ban, but not of the intervention of an army to take the Jews back to their original country. On this point, the subsequent expulsions are more ambiguous: Tacitus says that in 19 C.E. the Jews were expelled from Rome, while Suetonius and the Acts speak of a ban regarding Italy, supposing wide-ranging controls. Clearly, if we accept Lane's reading of the passage, this interpretation should be rejected: in fact, the sentence is to be referred not to the Jews but to the Chaldaeans.

From this debated detail a positive conclusion can be drawn: the original Jewish community, probably transitory, was composed of *peregrini*. The picture of Philo,[24] who in the Augustan age speaks of a community composed of freedmen who came to Rome as war prisoners, cannot be related to these years and is different from the community that Valerius Maximus himself could see. Many communities founded in the Eastern Diaspora had a military origin, due to deportations or to compulsory colonizations promoted by the Hellenistic kingdoms of Syria and Egypt.[25] Guignebert links the pres-

---

[23] E. Bickerman 158, p. 147.
[24] Phil., *Legatio ad Gaium*, 159–161.
[25] In regard to Egypt, during the third century plots of land were assigned to Jewish soldiers in Arsinoitis, according to a custom already attested in Elephantine in the time of Psammaticus I, while Ptolemy I sent Jewish settlers to Cyrenaica

ence of a Jewish community in Rome with the arrival of prisoners captured and taken to the city after the end of the Syrian war: the Syrian army could have included Jews after Judaea had been conquered by Antiochus III in 199 B.C.[26] Nevertheless, as *servi*, the Jews should have become *liberti* in a few years and were not subjected to the *iurisdictio* of a praetor pregrinus. More likely, after the first alliance between Rome and Judaea, groups of Jewish traders created a market in Southern Italy and lived temporarily in Rome, for political and economic purposes.[27] A development similar to that of a Greek *emporion* has sometimes been recognised in the Jewish Diaspora:[28] the communities of Dora and Ascalon expanded their trades in the first century B.C. with the help of the Hasmoneans, and a similar origin is supposed for the community of Dikaiarcheia, attested in contemporary sources.[29] In this case, the Jews had the status of *peregrini*, as a consequence of the alliance between Rome and Judaea.[30]

Other details are not clear. As Alessandrì remarked, the praetor could not have ordered the destruction of the altars simply because the Jews could not built altars in public places. This act was felt as a natural consequence of condemning a cult: in 186 B.C. consuls ordered the destruction of *arae* and *signa* dedicated to Bacchus,[31] while

---

with defensive purpose. This policy was shared by Syria. Seleucus I moved settlers to Antiochia and Seleucus II sent 2,000 families of the Babylonian Diaspora to Lydia and Phrygia to reinforce these rebellious areas. E. Bickerman 1991, pp. 68–73; pp. 125–128; pp. 133–135.

[26] C. Guignebert 1950, p. 235.

[27] As Philo says, the core of the community was on the Western banks of Tiber, in *Transtiberim regio*, an area naturally devoted to fluvial trades and linked to the Mediterranean routes through the harbor of Ostia.

[28] E. Smallwood 1981, p. 181.

[29] Flav. Jos., Ant. XVII, 138; B.J., II, 104. This area has returned some of the most ancient pieces of evidence of Jewish epigraphy of the peninsula, sealed by the eruption of 79 C.E. Three graffiti have been found in Pompeii: JIWE I, 38: *Sodom[a] | Gomora*; JIWE I, 39: *POINIUM | CHEREM* (probably, a transliteration from Greek and from Hebrew); JIWE I, 40: TPY|ΛES | Ἰουδαικός (scratched on four amphorae). A fourth inscription comes from Herculaneum: JIWE I, 41: *David*. In Naples there is a long inscription of doubtful origin, but which dates back to 70/95 C.E. according to its content: JIWE I, 26 (CIJ I 556): *[Cl]audia Aster | [H]ierosolymitana | [ca]ptiva. Curam egit | [Ti(berius)] Claudius Aug(usti) libertus | [Pro(?)]culus. Rogo vos fac(ite) | | [prae]ter licim ne quis | [mi]hi titulum deiciat cu|[ra]m agatis. vixit annis | XXV.* Finally, Puteoli has yielded JIWE I, 23: *Ti. Claudius Phi|lippus dia viu et | gerusiarches mace-riam duxit.*

[30] A. Rabello 1996, p. 142.

[31] Livy, 39,18,7: *Datum deinde consulibus negotium est, ut omnia Bacchanalia Romae primum, deinde per totam Italiam diruerent, extra quam si qua vetusta ara aut signum consecratum esset.*

in 19 C.E. Tiberius ordered the destruction of the vestments and the holy vessels belonging to the temple of Isis, whose cult had been forbidden that year.[32] This passage could hardly be referred to the synagogues, because no sacrificial altar could be built inside. It was strictly forbidden to reproduce the holy vessels or elements of the Temple, particularly the altar:[33] a Jew could offer sacrifices only in Jerusalem,[34] while the synagogue, whose existence is debated for such an early period, quickly takes the shape of a house of study (bet-ha-midrash) and a house of prayer (προσευχή).[35] This section of the text, omitted by the two versions of Paris, was possibly introduced by Nepotianus.[36]

According to both epitomizers, the ban was issued as a consequence of Jewish proselytism, an activity the Jews engaged in to convert the Romans to their faith and corrupt their *mores*.[37] The charge of pros-elytism occurs frequently in the bans that regarded the Roman com-munity during the first century, and are considered truthworthy by those scholars who see in proselytism a trait not of Talmudic Judaism only. As Martin Goodman among others shows,[38] proselytism could have hardly developed during the late-Republic and in the early Imperial period. Moreover, the Roman community was newly founded and could not have reached the organization required for such wide-spread propaganda. A group of scholars agrees that the problem for Roman authorities was not proselytism itself, but a new, unwelcome

---

[32] Suet., *Tib.*, 36.

[33] BT Menahot 28b; 'Abodah Zarah 43a; Rosh Hashanah 21 a,b: "A man can not make a house after the design of the Temple, or a porch after the design of the Temple porch, or a courtyard after the design of the Temple court, or a table after the design of the table [in the Temple], or a candlestick after the design of the candlestick [in the Temple]. He may, however, make one with five, six or eight [branches], but with seven he may not make one, even though it be of other metal."

[34] Moreover, while the Temple was operating, the construction of a sacrificial altar was felt as a sign of religious split, as it happened on Mount Gerazim, when the Samaritans constructed a rival temple to Jerusalem.

[35] An in-depth study of the origin and structure of the synagogues and of the evidence found in Eretz-Israel and Diaspora in D. Urman – P. Flesher 1994.

[36] Bickerman (E. Bickerman 1958, pp. 137–151), with whom Goodman agrees (M. Goodman 1994, pp. 82–83), suggests that the *arae* were private altars built for groups of Romans interested in Judaism and subsequently destroyed.

[37] Vat. 4929 uses the term *inficere*, that occurs also in Tacitus in reference to proselytes (Tac., Ann. II, 85.4: . . . *quattuor milia libertini generis ea religione infecta*)

[38] M. Goodman 1994.

religious presence in Rome. Even so, opinions on this passage differ.[39] According to Goodman[40] and Solin,[41] the ban was the institutional reaction to the spreading of oriental cults in Rome, cults considered extraneous and dangerous to the *mores*: the Jews should have made the same mistake that the believers of Bacchus did when they tried to practise their cult publicly, without authorization. According to others[42]—I think more prudently—the point lies in the reaction of the Roman population to a new cult. As happens in subsequent periods, the peculiar lifestyle of the Jews makes their presence evident in the social fabric of a city, strengthening the idea that their cult could attract people and could be dangerous for the traditional *mores*.

With few differences, the charge of corrupting the *mores* is addressed both to the Chaldaeans and to the Jews: the ones are accused of influencing weak minds with their *scientia*, and the others of introducing their cult in Rome looking for new followers. Considering the low quality of the text, we could suppose that, in an unknown stage of the transmission of the news, the memory of the charge against the Jews was lost: Valerius Maximus, or one of his sources, could have filled in the gap addressing to the Jews the charges which were originally addressed only to the Chaldaeans.

These details were probably added by the epitomizers or by a late common source: in the late Antiquity or in the high Middle-Ages evidence of Jewish propaganda increases, and proselytism is recognised as a peculiarity of Talmudic Judaism.[43] Paris and Nepotianus—who worked in the fifth and sixth centuries—or one of their sources, could have received the passage without the charge addressed to the Jews and could have introduced the charge that was most frequently brought against the Jews of their age, proselytism.

Groups of Jews probably frequented Southern Italy from the middle of the second century, as a result of the treaties between Rome and

---

[39] This problem apparently does not trouble Schürer (E. Schürer 1973–1986 III.1, p. 75) and Leon (H. Leon 1995², p. 4) who do not discuss the tradition as passed on by both epitomizers. Even with great doubts on the dating, Feldman (L.H. Feldman 1993, p. 301) supports the idea of a missionary activity in Rome, but suggests that the aim was to spread only few observances. So Bickerman (E. Bickerman 1958, pp. 137–151).

[40] M. Goodman 1994, pp. 82–83.

[41] H. Solin 1983, p. 606.

[42] P. Schäfer 1999, p. 154.

[43] M. Goodman 1994, pp. 109–152.

Judaea. In 139 B.C. some Jews were expelled from Rome where they probably lived: the *peregrinitas* could not protect them from a ban. We cannot say why this ban was issued, since proselytism is a doubtful phenomenon in such an early age.

II

Some decades passed by with no further news on the Roman community. In October 59 B.C. action was brought against L. Valerius Flaccus, propraetor of Asia, with the charge *de repetundis*.[44] One of the injured parties[45] was the Jewish communities of Asia who accused the governor of having confiscated the gold they used to send to the Temple each year. Cicero undertook his defence[46] and conveys the idea of a populous, even influential community.[47] When and why the Roman Jews could have begun to take part in political life is unknown. Havas links this passage with Catiline's conspiracy, the transfer of the aurum coronarium to Jerusalem and the prohibition of exporting gold voted by Senate during the consulship of Cicero.[48] According to Havas, the Catilinarii should have tried to form an alliance with the Sadduceans in Palestine, who violently opposed Roman supremacy in the area, in the attempt to finance a revolt in Judaea with the gold of the Temple and to find new funds in the

---

[44] Subject of the Pro Flacco.

[45] Flaccus is accused of corruption. The charge, supported by D. Lelius Balbus with the assistance of C. Appuleius Decianus and L. Herrenius Balbus as *subscriptores*, is brought by groups with a different range of interests. The whole province accuses him of having imposed an extraordinary taxation to arm a navy and fight the piracy in the Aegean Sea (§27–33); Akmonia (§34–38), Dorylaion (§39–41), Temnos (§42–51) and Tralles (§52–59) complain about the illegal confiscation of public founds, partially gathered (as in Tralles) to organize games in honor of Flaccus' father. The Jews of Asia denounce the confiscation of the gold sent to Jerusalem but seized by the governor himself (§66–69); some citizens claim to have undergone abuses of power (§70–93).

[46] Cicero can quickly reject the charge brought by the Jews: the confiscation is the legitimate consequence of an edict that Flaccus issued and that followed the policy Cicero promoted during his consulship. The gold was eventually kept in the provincial treasury. Apart from this, it was an act of fair severity *huic autem barbarae superstitioni resistere.*

[47] Cic., *Pro Flacco*, 66: *Ob hoc crimen hic locus abs te, Laeli, atque illa turba quaesita est; scis quanta sit manus, quanta concordia, quantum valeat in contionibus.* And later in §67: *Huic autem barbarae superstitioni resistere severitatis, multitudinem Iudaeorum flagrantem non numquam in contionibus pro re publica contemnere gravitatis summae fuit.*

[48] L. Havas 1983, pp. 233–248.

properties the Jews had in Italy. This plot could have prompted a revolt in Italy, in the Middle-East and, possibly, in all the Romanised Diaspora. She lists as evidence the references Cicero makes in the *Pro Flacco*,[49] and the already mentioned act that he prompted when the fight against Catiline was at its acme. According to a passage from the speech *In Vatinium*, Cicero sent Vatinius to Puteoli to block the remittance of gold to Judaea that the local community was organizing.[50] The Jews were also involved in the suppression of the collegia in 64 B.C. (attested by Asconius);[51] their assemblies of prayer were forbidden and the synagogues closed. As Miriam Pucci has recently shown,[52] this complex theory unfortunately finds few confirmations in the sources. If the existence of anti-Roman feelings in some Jewish groups after Pompey had profaned the Temple is attested, the link between these groups and the Catilinarii and the involvement of Italian Jews in the plot are questionable. Even Cicero's statement on the supposed influence that the Jews had on the public assemblies seems extreme: no other Latin source mentions the presence of Jews in the Roman assemblies. Even if it is possible that in the 60s the Roman Jews were part of the *plebs urbana* often involved in the political struggles of the late Republic, an active participation of the community in riots or revolts is never recorded.[53] The same lack of evidence regards also the *aurum coronarium*. No act concerning the liability of transporting gold to Palestine has been preserved: it is possible that this trafic was never regulated, and that it was included in the right accorded to the Jews τοῖς πατρίοις ἔθεσι καὶ ἱεροῖς χρῆσθαι.[54] According to Cicero, Flaccus suspended a custom protected by the law and justified himself saying he delivered this act to block an illegal remittance of gold and to resist a barbarous religion, *barbarae superstitioni resistere*: even if he had the possibility of doing it, Cicero does not link the Jews with Catiline. In such a case, I think we have a significant evidence *ex silentio*.

---

[49] As Schäfer shows (P. Schäfer 1999, pp. 255–259).

[50] Cic., *In Vatinium*, 12: *missusne sis a me consule Puteolos, ut inde aurum exportari et argentum prohiberes.*

[51] Asconius, *Comm. In Pis.*, 6, 9–15.

[52] M. Pucci Ben Zeev 2001, pp. 9–24.

[53] As in the way Roman Jews mourned Caesar's death: Suet., *Iul.*, 85.4.

[54] As we have already seen, διατάγματα granted this right to communities of *provincia Asiae*, quoted by Flavius Josephus in the XIV book of the *Antiquities*.

With regard to the *In Vatinium*, the passage Havas mentions shows only a temporary block of the exporting of gold and silver, but is silent on the Jews, whose involvement cannot be proved. Even the existence of a Jewish community in Puteoli in this period is doubtful. We can suppose that the Jews already frequented Italian harbours during the first century B.C.: otherwise, the first evidence—both epigraphic and literary—regarding the Jewish presence can be dated no earlier than the first century C.E..

The equalization of synagogues with collegia has already been discussed. Moreover, this act could have regarded only professional, not religious collegia, that were not involved in the suppression of the ludi Campitalicii.

The speech reports some precious details. During the trial, the Jewish community of Rome was numerous and was part of the plebs urbana. The demographic increase was probably recent and due to Pompey's campaign in the East. In the autumn 63 B.C., after a siege which lasted three months,[55] Pompey succeeded in forcing a passage

---

[55] The chronology of the fall of Jerusalem is dabated. It is certainly possible that Temple area was seized in the autumn of 63, because of the number of events that occured between the beginning of the siege (*Ant.* XIV, 38) in spring 63 and the final seizure, but the exact day is unknown. Strabo (*Geog.*, 16.2.40: κατελάβετο δ', ὥς φασι, τηρήσας τὴν τῆς νηστείας ἡμέραν, ἡνίκα ἀπείχοντο οἱ Ἰουδαῖοι πάντος ἔργου) and Cassius Dio (*H.R.*, XXXVII 16,2: νῦν δὲ τὰς τοῦ Κρόνου δὴ ὠνομασμένας διαλείποντες, καὶ οὐδὲν τὸ παράπαν ἐν αὐταῖς δρῶντες, παρέδωκαν τοῖς Ῥωμαίοις καιρὸν ἐν τῷ διακένῳ τούτῳ τὸ τεῖχος διασεῖσαι) link up this event with the shabbath: the Romans exploited the sabbatic rest to attack the northern wall. Flavius Josephus' evidence is complex: while in *B.J.* I, 146 he dates the violation to a generic shabbath, in *Ant.* XIV, 66 (καὶ γὰρ ἁλούσης τῆς πόλεως περὶ τρίτον μῆνα τῇ τῆς νηστείας ἡμέρᾳ κατὰ τὴν ἐνάτην καὶ ἑβδομηκοστὴν καὶ ἑκατοστὴν ὀλυμπιάδα ὑπατευόντων Γαίου Ἀντωνίου καὶ Μάρκου Τυλλίου Κικέρωνος...) he says that it was the Yom Kippur of 63. The date could justify the attitude of the priests who do not stop offering sacrifice while the Romans were attacking. This date is usually rejected (an exception J. Goldstein 1989, vol. II, p. 349). As Schürer shows (E. Schürer I, p. 239 n. 23), Flavius Josephus in the passage of the Antiquities probably misunderstood his non-Jewish sources, Strabo, Posidonius, Nicolaus of Damascus and Livy, historians that he openly mentions as sources for the war of Pompey (*Ant.* XIV, 68: .... πάντες οἱ τὰς κατὰ Πομπήιον πράξεις ἀναγράψαντες, ἐν οἷς καὶ Στράβων καὶ Νικόλαος καὶ πρὸς αὐτοῖς Τίτος Λίβιος ὁ τῆς Ῥωμαικῆς ἱστορίας συγγραφεύς). According to studies (R. Goldenberg 1979, pp. 414–447; P. Schäfer 1999, pp. 117–131) on this question, in the Graeco-Roman world the idea that shabbath was a day of penance was widespread. Aly (W. Aly 1957, pp. 165–170) supposes that non-Jewish people could mistake shabbath for Yom Kippur, on the basis of Leviticus

through the northern wall, entered the Temple and slaughtered the partisans of Aristobulus who were defending the area.[56] When on 28 September 62, Pompey celebrated the triumph in Rome,[57] a massive number of Jews was brought into the Capital as war prisoners, while Aristobulus II and his family were compelled to precede the chariot of the winner,[58] as would happen in 71 C.E. to Simon bar Giora.

To summarize: in 59 B.C. there is the first unquestionable reference to a Jewish community living permanently in Rome. In this period, the community was probably already composed of freedmen, even if the number of slaves should have been high, considering the chronological proximity to Pompey's war. This trend is maintained in the following years: the political instability that affects Judaea compels Rome to intervene frequently. In 57, a year after the reduction of Syria to consular province, Aulus Gabinius had to suppress an insurrection led by Aristobulus and Alexander: according to Flavius Josephus, 3,000 Jews were killed and as many Jews were captured.[59] A few years later, in 51, the governor of Syria C. Cassius Longinus

---

16,31 in which this festivity is called "shabbath of the shabbaths". This theory cannot be shared because it assumes an in-depth knowledge of the Bible that is in contrast with a superficial observation of the Jewish costumes: Yom Kippur is an annual festivity. Flavius Josephus, as Jew, would never have called shabbath the great day of penance, the Yom Kippur. In Feldman's opinion (L. Feldman 1984, p. 55), the passage of the Antiquities could describe not only Yom Kippur but also 9 Ab (July/August), a fateful day of penance in which tragedies as the destruction of the Second Temple had happened, according to the tradition. Smallwood (E. Smallwood 1981, pp. 565–567) remarks that the soldiers of Hyrcanus would not have attacked the Temple in the holy festivity of Yom Kippur.

[56] Apart from Flavius Josephus (*Ant.* XIV, 58–73; B.J. I, 141–151), the siege is described by Cassius Dio (*H. R.*, XXXVII, 16, 1–4), Strabon (*Geog.* XVI, 2,40–41), Appian (*Hist. Rom.* XII, 106; XVI, 50), Livy (*Epit.*, 102) and Tacitus (*Hist.* V,9).

[57] Flavius Josephus omits the triumph. A rather long description can be found in Plutarchus (*Pompeius*, 45,1–4) who does not mention how many prisoners were brought into Rome, and in Appian (*Hist. Rom.*, XII, 116–117). Plinius' account is brief but reports both the date and the official announcement of the triumph (*N.H.*, VII, 26, 98: *Triumphi quem duxit a.d. III Kal. Oct. M. Pisone M. Messala coss. Praefatio haec fuit . . .*), while Cassius Dio simply mentions the event (*H.R.*, XXXVII, 21, 1–4).

[58] *Ant.* XIV, 79; *B.J.*, I, 157–158; Appian (*Hist. Rom.* XII, 117) wrongly thinks that Aristobolus was killed at the end of the triumph. He died in 49 B.C.

[59] *Ant.* XIV, 85: καὶ ἀναχωρεῖ μὲν ἐγγὺς Ἱεροσολύμων Ἀλέξανδρος, συμπεσόντων δὲ ἀλλήλοις ἐκεῖ καὶ μάχης γενομένης κτείνουσι μὲν οἱ Ῥωμαῖοι τῶν πολεμίων περὶ τρισχιλίους, ζωγροῦσι δὲ οὐκ ἐλάττους. B.J. I, 163: . . . καὶ κατὰ τὴν μάχην ἑξακισχιλίους ἀποβαλών, ὧν τρισχίλιοι μὲν ἔπεσον τρισχίλιοι δὲ ἐζωγρήθησαν, φεύγει σὺν τοῖς καταλειφθεῖσιν εἰς Ἀλεξάνδρειον.

had to suppress another revolt which has broken out when the Parthians had breached the Syrian boundaries and had arrived in Antioch. According to Flavius Josephus, in the seizure of Tarichaea 30,000 Jews were captured.[60] These figures are to be considered indicative of a massive number of prisoners; nevertheless, it is possible that during the second half of first century B.C. groups of Jews were brought into Rome and, after being manumitted, remained in town and enlarged the local community. It is in this period that the Roman community possibly took the shape Philo described: a populous community made of freedmen who were once war prisoners.

Finally, one last detail often neglected by scholarship has to be pointed out:[61] according to Cicero, the *aurum coronarium* was gathered not only in Rome but in the whole of Italy.[62] We could suppose that groups of Jewish slaves were sold or bought in other towns of the peninsula, where they stayed after the manumission. This forced movement intercepted by literary sources has to be added to free activities of traders that, notwithstanding the bad relationships between Judaea and Rome, probably continued to frequent the Italian markets. Well before the archaeological and epigraphic evidence, groups of Jews were present in Rome and, probably, in the whole of Italy, Jews that, as commonly happened in Diaspora, did not want to forget their identity.

---

[60] *Ant.* XIV, 120: Ταριχαίας μὲν οὖν προσπεσὼν εὐθέως αἱρεῖ, καὶ περὶ τρισμυρίους ἀνθρώπους ἀνδραποδίζει; B.J. I, 180: . . . καὶ Ταριχαίας μὲν ἑλὼν εἰς τρεῖς μυριάδες Ἰουδαίων ἀνδραποδίζεται.

[61] Schürer stresses this problem in a footnote (E. Schürer 1973–1986, I, p. 241 n. 29).

[62] Cic., *Pro Flacco*, 67: *Cum aurum Iudaeorum nomine quotannis ex Italia et ex omnibus nostris provinciis Hierosylimam exportari soleret, Flaccus sanxit edicto ne ex Asia exportari liceret.*

TIBERIUS

I

In 19 c.e. the Jews were expelled from Rome. The main sources attesting the ban are Flavius Josephus, Tacitus and Suetonius; Seneca and a passage of Cassius Dio known through indirect tradition support the information with scanty and questionable details.

The account of the events Tacitus[1] and Suetonius[2] give is similar. The act is issued to hit both the Egyptian cult of Isis and Judaism: the aim is to limit the activities of *externae caerimoniae*, cults that were seen as extraneous to Roman tradition. Young Jews have to undergo a special call-up and are sent to Sardinia, an area with an unhealthy climate. All the other Jews are banned.

The close resemblances between the accounts suggest the use of a common source,[3] possibly the *senatus consultum* itself or an intermediate work that quotes the act, a theory supported by the presence of two expressions that recur, with few changes, in both authors. The first—*ea superstitione*—is equivocal: in fact the cult *ea* refers to is unveiled only by the context. In the beginning of the passage, Tacitus mentions an *actio de sacris Aegyptiis et Iudaicis pellendis*,[4] but refers *superstitio* only to the Jews, whose youngsters were sent to Sardinia, as Flavius Josephus and Suetonius show. Conversely, Suetonius links *ea* with the cult of Isis, which is easy to recognize in the details of the

---

[1] Tac., *Ann.* II, 85:4: *Actum et de sacris Aegyptiis Iudaicisque pellendis, factumque patrum consultum, ut quattuor milia libertini generis ea superstitione infecta, quis idonea aetas, in insulam Sardiniam veherentur, coercendis illic latrociniis et, si ob gravitatem caeli interissent, vile damnum; ceteri cederent Italia, nisi certam ante diem profanos ritus exuissent.*

[2] Suet., *Tib.*, 36: *Externas caerimonias, Aegyptios Iudaicosque ritus compescuit, coactis qui superstitione ea tenebantur religiosas vestes cum instrumento omni comburere. Iudaeorum iuventutem per speciem sacramenti in provincias gravioris caeli distribuit, reliquos gentis eiusdem vel similia sectantes urbe summovit, sub poena perpetuae servitutis nisi obtemperassent.*

[3] According to Stern (M. Stern 1974–80, II, p. 113). According to Williams (M. Williams 1989, p. 766), Suetonius and Tacitus personally saw the *senatus consultum*: the differences depend on narrative choices.

[4] According to Goodyear (F.R. Goodyear 1981, p. 441), without the evidence of Suetonius and Flavius Josephus, the passage could indifferently refer to both cults. Syme (R. Syme 1958, II, p. 468) stresses the absence of details on the punishment of the Isis' believers, which sounds paradoxical in an annalistic work.

religiosas vestes and the *instrumenta*.[5] The second expression—*ob gravitatem caeli* in Tacitus and *gravioris caeli* in Suetonius—clarifies the reference to Sardinia in Suetonius's passage which does not mention this detail openly.

There are many similarities but also a few differences. While Suetonius mentions an act of Tiberius in an undefined year of his government, Tacitus states that it was a *senatus consultum* and dates it indirectly, through the annalistic course of his work. Moreover, he adds details on the punishment inflicted on the Jews: 4,000 young Jews were sent to Sardinia to fight the brigandage, and not, in general, to the provinces with a bad climate.

Conversely, Suetonius can complete the account of Tacitus with important details. According to him, the ban was addressed only to the Jewish community of Rome, not to all Jews living in Italy. Moreover, he can remember the punishment of the believers of Isis, which Tacitus omitted.[6] The ban itself differs on some important points. Tacitus involves the whole community (*ceteri*) and marks the possibility of avoiding the ban with an abjuration, while Suetonius includes in the expulsion Jews by birth (*eiusdem gentis*) and proselytes (*similia sectantes*) and reports the risk of perpetual slavery for those who refuse to leave Rome.

These passages are inserted in quite a similar context. Tacitus links the passage with the acts Tiberius issued to reaffirm a traditional morality. The foregoing chapter (§85) reports a senatorial decree forbidding prostitution to those women who had a close relative of equestrian rank: the debate arose after acts of prostitution made by Vestilia, a matrona whose vicissitudes Tacitus briefly summarizes.

---

[5] Stern (M. Stern 1974–80, II, p. 112) and Jackson (J. Jackson, Tacitus, *The Annals* (ed. J. Jackson), Loeb Classical Library, Cambridge Mass.: Harvard University Press; London: W. Heinemann 1962) translate *coactis qui superstitione ea tenebantur* as "compelling all who were addicted to such superstitions": the ambiguity is resolved by making *ea* refer to both cults. Smallwood (E. Smallwood 1981, p. 204 n. 10) and Goodyear (F. Goodyear 1981, p. 441 n. 2)—and most of the reviewers—link *vestes* and *instrumenta* with the Egyptian cult and stress the proximity to the text of Suetonius: they translate *ea* with "the former superstition". The problem is not resolved. Tacitus is aware (*Hist.* V, 5, 10–11) that in the Temple, during Hannukah and Sukkoth, there were players of flutes and tympana, who could not be confused with the dionysiac cult *sed quia sacerdotes eorum tibia tympanisque concinebant, hedera vinciebantur vitisque aurea templo reperta, Liberorum patrem coli, domitorem Orientis, quidam arbitrati sunt, nequaquam congruentibus institutis.*

[6] According to Goodyear and Smallwood.

Chapter 87, which follows the account of our events, relates the large dowry Tiberius gives to a Vestal who had served Rome all her life and the appointment of a new Vestal chosen among girls of ancient nobility. Tacitus's contempt for foreign cults emerges from the words he chooses to describe the events—a point on which the scholarship unanimously agrees—but also from the context in which the event is inserted, after a senatorial act that reaffirms an Augustan morality and before the intervention of the Emperor that praises one of the most ancient religious institutions of Rome.

In regard to Suetonius, chapters 30–33 report acts that Tiberius issued in order to reaffirm the priority of the senate, the independence of the magistracy and of the courts to prevent the judges from being corrupted. In chapters 34–35 Tiberius reaffirms the importance of more severe habits, reduces the number of games and the salary of the actors, and exiles those *matronae* that renounced their rank and registered themselves as prostitutes to the list of the edils to avoid a charge of adultery.

Josephus's account is rather different.[7] In the attempt to justify two contemporary expulsions, he builds a semi-fictional story with, as protagonists, two *matronae* both deceived by cheats belonging to the two communities. Tiberius responds to these outrages with two distinct acts. The similarities between these sections emerge clearly in the structure of the story and in important details: the protagonists are women of high rank (ἀξίωμα) and their husbands (both named

---

[7] *Ant.* XVIII, 65: Καὶ ὑπὸ τοὺς αὐτοὺς χρόνους ἕτερόν τι δεινὸν ἐθορύβει τοὺς Ἰουδαίους καὶ περὶ τὸ ἱερὸν τῆς Ἴσιδος τὸ ἐν Ῥώμῃ πράξεις αἰσχυνῶν οὐκ ἀπηλλαγμέναι συντυγχάνουσιν. καὶ πρότερον τοῦ τῶν Ἰσιακῶν τολμήματος μνήμην ποιησάμενος οὕτω μεταβιβῶ τὸν λόγον ἐπὶ τὰ ἐν τοῖς Ἰουδαίοις γεγονότα...

Ant. XVIII, 81–84: Ἦν ἀνὴρ Ἰουδαῖος, φυγὰς μὲν τῆς αὐτοῦ κατηγορίᾳ τε παραβάσεων νόμων τινῶν καὶ δέει τιμωρίας τῆς ἐπὶ αὐτοῖς, πονηρὸς δὲ εἰς τὰ πάντα. Καὶ δὴ τότε ἐν τῇ Ῥώμῃ διαιτώμενος προσεποιεῖτο μὲν ἐξηγεῖσθαι σοφίαν νόμων τῶν Μωυσέως, προσποιησάμενος δὲ τρεῖς ἄνδρες εἰς τὰ πάντα ὁμοιοτρόπους τούτοις ἐπιφοιτήσασαν Φουλβίαν τῶν ἐν ἀξιώματι γυναικῶν καὶ νομίμοις προσεληλυθυῖαν τοῖς Ἰουδαϊκοῖς πείθουσι πορφύραν καὶ χρυσὸν εἰς τὸ ἐν Ἱεροσολύμοις ἱερὸν διαπέμψασθαι, καὶ λαβόντες ἐπὶ χρείας τοῖς ἰδίοις ἀναλώμασιν αὐτὰ ποιοῦνται, ἐφ᾽ ὅπερ καὶ τὸ πρῶτον ἡ αἴτησις ἐπράσσετο. Καὶ ὁ Τιβέριος, ἀποσημαίνει γὰρ πρὸς αὐτὸν φίλος ὢν Σατορνῖνος τῆς Φουλβίας ἀνὴρ ἐπισκήψει τῆς γυναικός, κελεύει πᾶν τὸ Ἰουδαϊκὸν τῆς Ῥώμης ἀπελθεῖν. οἱ δὲ ὕπατοι τετρακισχιλίους ἀνθρώπους ἐξ αὐτῶν στρατολογήσαντες ἔπεμψαν εἰς Σαρδὼ τὴν νῆσον, πλείστους δὲ ἐκόλασαν μὴ θέλοντας στρατεύεσθαι διὰ φυλακὴν τῶν πατρίων νόμων. Καὶ οἱ μὲν δὴ διὰ κακίαν τεσσάρων ἀνδρῶν ἠλαύνοντο τῆς πόλεως.

Σατορνῖνος) sue successfully against the two communities with the positive help of Tiberius. The first scholar who studied this problem was Rogers, who suggests a complex, doubtful theory.[8] In his opinion, there was only one woman, whose *nomen* was reported in the first episode, and the *cognomen* in the second one;[9] she became a Jew, but was finally attracted to the cult of Isis, because of a kind of religious syncretism. In two distinct moments she was deceived by believers of both cults, a fact that caused two scandals and two independent acts of expulsion. Rogers could not support this reconstruction with positive evidence. The most interesting detail consists in the identification of Σατορνῖνος with *G. Sentius Saturninus*, consul in 4 c.e. and promoter of the *lex Aelia Sentia*. The link the family had with Syria, where both his father Gaius and his brother Gnaeus were *legati Augusti pro praetore*,[10] could have helped the creation of clientel as bonds with the Jewish community of Rome.

In my opinion, a single episode was probably split into two very similar stories, which Josephus created with the aim of justifying the *senatus consultum* and redeeming the communities (especially the Jewish one) from any responsibility: he stresses the attitude of the Jews, many of whom "refused to serve for fear of breaking the Jewish law" and blames the wickedness of the four men who caused the banishment of the whole community. The style in which the two episodes are told is very similar too. The first part, when the tricks against the matronae take the scene, has a semi-fictional tone that recalls Hellenistic romances,[11] while in the second section, with the official reactions of the Emperor, the facts are reported with a dry, severe style. This change and the resemblances between §§83–84 of the 18th book of the Antiquities and the accounts of Tacitus and Suetonius suggest the use of a Roman common source.[12] As the other histori-

---

[8] R.S. Rogers 1932, pp. 254–255.

[9] Only one woman is attested with this name, a Baebia Fulvia Claudia Paulina Gratia Maxilla (CIL VI 1361).

[10] His father *Gaius* was in Syria in the last decade before Christ, while his brother *Gnaeus* was *comes* of Germanicus during his mission in the East and succeeded to Piso as *legatus Augusti* in Syria. The presence of Gnaeus in the East in 19 C.E. contrasts with the quickness of his intervention against the Roman Jewry: his brother Gaius could be recognised as the husbund of Fulvia.

[11] S. Heyob 1975, pp. 115–119. Heyob also stresses the apologetic attempt to distinguish Judaism from other oriental cults.

[12] According to Norden (E. Norden 1966, p. 246), in §§83–84 Josephus used a Roman annalistic source different from the one used for the account on Judaea

ans, Josephus reports that the whole community was banned except 4,000 young Jews who were sent to Sardinia after a special call-up: those who refused to leave Rome (in respect of the Law, he adds) were punished. He does not mention the *senatus consultum*, but probably knows it: the consuls were in fact the material executors of this act.

II

According to Tacitus's evidence, the ban was issued during the consulship of *M. Stilanus* and *L. Norbanus*.[13] The passages of Suetonius and Flavius Josephus, which do not present any element useful for dating, are dated on the basis of Tacitus.[14] Nonetheless, some observations have to be made on Josephus' account and on the context this passage is inserted in, that could lead one to suppose a completely different dating. The Parthian excursus, which culminated with Germanicus' expedition and his untimely death in 19 C.E., is concluded in chapter 54. The account on the Middle-East lasts up to chapter 89, with the facts that occur in Judaea and Samaria under the government of Pontius Pilatus. Josephus dedicates most of this section to reporting Jewish revolts, usually caused by Roman actions felt as provocations (the exposition of pictures of the Emperor in Jerusalem and the use of part of the gold belonging to the Temple to build an aqueduct, besides the bloody repression of a Samaritan revolt). In this context both the vicissitudes of Jesus, not already reported (§§63–64), and the expulsion of the Jews from Rome (§§65–84) are mentioned. While the first insertion is in accordance with the chronology and with the facts Josephus was reporting, the same cannot be said for the second one. In Norden's opinion, this section of the 18th book has a composite structure.[15] From chapter 53 to chapter 89 we have a dry, annalistic style, with the story divided into

---

and Samaria, and recognises it in Cluvius Rufus, whose work he supposes to have been used for all the events in Rome up to Neronian age. Hadas Lebel (M. Hadas-Lebel 1994, pp. 99–106) agrees with a suggestion of Feldman and supposes the use of an oral source for books 18–20: Josephus probably gathered stories and evidence of Imperial slaves and freedmen near to Tiberius, Caligula and Agrippas II, whose identities she can suggest.

[13] Tac., Ann. II, 59.
[14] As Stern suggests (M. Stern 1974–1980, II, pp. 70–71).
[15] E. Norden 1966, pp. 245–261.

στάσεις and θόρυβοι, a style able to give unity to the whole section. These terms occur almost at every paragraph and recall an articulation based on war's episodes that is typical of the Roman annalistic historiography, as is shown, for example, in the first ten books of Livy.[16] Consequently, he supposes that, in relating the events that occurred in Judaea/Samaria, Josephus used an annalistic source near to the governor of Syria, instead of an oral Jewish source. Nonetheless, the story is interrupted twice. Chapters 63–64 are one of the most debated parts of the Antiquities: the so called *Testimonium Flavianum*, where the tale of Christ is summarized and it is said ὁ χριστὸς οὗτος ἦν, is considered an interpolation of a Christian author for preaching purposes, written before the *Symbolum Nicaeanum* and modeled on the I Epistle to the Corinthians.[17] Chapters 65–84 outline a θόρυβος, a term that occurs also in the first sentence ἕτερόν τι δεινὸν ἐθορύβει τοὺς Ἰουδαίους; nonetheless, it is different both for the subject (the expulsion of the Jews and the Egyptians) and for the semi-fictional style which contrasts with the tone of this part of the 18th book and with the account of the punishment given to the two groups. Why Josephus decided to tell this episode here is questionable.

According to Smallwood, it was a conscious choice due to a superficial knowledge of the facts.[18] In her opinion, Josephus knew the issuing of the ban but could date it only vaguely, during the reign of Tiberius. Consequently, he decided to place it in a troubled period in the relationship between Judaea and Rome, during the government of Pontius Pilatus, whose misrule and bloody repressions he recalls. This policy apparently was not limited to Judaea: Philo remarks that, during his last year of power, Sejanus cooled the relationship between the Jewish Diaspora and the Roman community: in 31 c.e. Tiberius had to reaffirm the Roman policy of friendship towards the Jews.[19] Linking all these events, Smallwood can

---

[16] Many passages by Livy are marked with the terms *tumultus, turbae* and *motus*. The expression ἕτερόν τι δεινὸν ἐθορύβει τοὺς Ἰουδαίους reminds us of the Livian sentence *sequitur aliud in urbe nefas*, which occurs, for example, in II, 44 (E. Norden 1966, p. 248).

[17] I Corinthians 15:3–5: Παρέδωκα γὰρ ὑμῖν ἐν πρώτοις, ὃ καὶ παρέλαβον, ὅτι Χριστὸς ἀπέθανεν ὑπὲρ τῶν ἁμαρτιῶν ἡμῶν κατὰ τὰς γραφὰς καὶ ὅτι ἐτάφη καὶ ὅτι ἐγήγερται τῇ ἡμέρᾳ τῇ τρίτῃ κατὰ τὰς γραφὰς καὶ ὅτι ὤφθη Κηφᾷ εἶτα τοῖς δώδεκα.

[18] E. Smallwood 1956, pp. 314–329 and M. Stern 1974–80 II, pp. 70–71.

[19] Phil., *Leg. ad Gaium*, 159–161: Τοιγαροῦν οἱ πανταχοῦ πάντες, εἰ καὶ φύσει διέκειντο πρὸς Ἰουδαίους οὐκ εὐμενῶς, εὐλαβῶς εἶχον ἐπὶ καθαιρέσει τινὸς τῶν

highlight two distinct events which occurred during the reign of
Tiberius:[20] an expulsion that Tacitus dates in 19 c.e. and a cooling
of the relationship between Romans and Jews in the years around
the death of Sejanus. Flavius Josephus, who was vaguely aware of
both the facts, could have linked the events and placed the ban
around 30 c.e.[21] This clever reconstruction can eliminate what should
be considered a chronological inaccuracy, but has great limits nonetheless. Josephus (or his source) shows an extensive knowledge of the
act and of its content, in accordance with what both Tacitus and
Suetonius say: can we easily suppose that he was aware of the details
of the expulsion but was completely unaware of its dating?

In the 18th book Josephus apparently does not follow a strict
chronological order in relating the facts.[22] The news of the replacement of Valerius Gratus as procurator of Judaea and Samaria in 26
c.e. (§35) is followed by the long Parthian excursus (§§39–52) which
closes with the death of Antiochus king of Commagenes (§53), the
intervention of Germanicus in the East and his death. With chapter 54 we are in 19 c.e.. Josephus then resumes the thread of the
events interrupted in §35 and talks about the decade when Pilatus
ruled over Judaea until his final replacement with Vitellius after the

---

Ἰουδαικῶν νομίμων προσάψασθαι· καὶ ἐπὶ Τιβερίου μέντοι τὸν αὐτὸν τρόπον, καίτοι
τῶν ἐν Ἰταλίᾳ παρακινηθέντων, ἡνίκα Σηιανὸς ἐσκευώρει τὴν ἐπίθεσιν. 160 ἔγνω γάρ,
εὐθέως ἔγνω μετὰ τὴν ἐκείνου τελευτήν, ὅτι τὰ κατηγορηθέντα τῶν ᾠκηκότων τὴν Ῥώμην
Ἰουδαίων ψευδεῖς ἦσαν διαβολαί, πλάσματα Σηιανοῦ τὸ ἔθνος ἀναρπάσαι θέλοντος,
ὅπερ ἢ μόνον ἢ μάλιστα ᾔδει βουλαῖς ἀνοσίοις καὶ πράξεσιν ἀντιβησόμενον ὑπὲρ τοῦ
παρασπονδηθῆναι κινδυνεύσαντος αὐτοκράτορος. 161 καὶ τοῖς πανταχόσε χειροτο-
νουμένοις ὑπάρχοις ἐπέσκηψε παρηγορῆσαι μὲν τοὺς κατὰ πόλεις τῶν ἀπὸ τοῦ ἔθνους,
ὡς οὐκ εἰς πάντας προβάσης τῆς ἐπεξελεύσεως, ἀλλὰ ἐπὶ μόνους τοὺς αἰτίους—ὀλίγοι
δὲ ἦσαν—, κινῆσαι δὲ μηδὲν τῶν ἐξ ἔθους, ἀλλὰ καὶ παρακαταθήκην ἔχειν τούς τε
ἄνδρας ὡς εἰρηνικοὺς τὰς φύσεις καὶ τὰ νόμιμα ὡς ἀλείφοντα πρὸς εὐστάθειαν.
This passage is summarised in Eusebius, HE II, 5, 6–7: πρῶτον δὴ οὖν κατὰ
Τιβέριον ἐπὶ μὲν τῆς Ῥωμαίων πόλεως ἱστορεῖ Σηιανόν, τῶν τότε παρὰ βασιλεῖ πολλὰ
δυνάμενον, ἄρδην τὸ πᾶν ἔθνος ἀπολέσθαι σπουδὴν εἰσαγηοχέναι, ἐπὶ δὲ τῆς Ἰουδαίας
Πιλᾶτον, κατὰ ὃν τὰ περὶ τὸν σωτῆρα τετόλμητο, περὶ τὸ ἐν Ἱεροσολύμοις ἔτι τότε
συνεστὸς ἱερὸν ἐπιχειρήσαντά τι παρὰ τὸ Ἰουδαίοις ἐξόν, τὰ μέγιστα αὐτοὺς ἀναταρά-
ξαι. Philo speaks first of the problems that affected the Jews in Italy and then of
Sejanus' policy towards the Roman community. Conversely, Eusebius affirms that
Sejanus attacked all the Jews living in the Empire almost in the same period when
Pilatus was attacking the Temple and some Jewish previleges.
[20] The expression ὑπὸ τοὺς αὐτοὺς χρόνους should be a general reference to the
times of Tiberius.
[21] E. Smallwood 1956, pp. 322–329.
[22] A. Galimberti 2001, pp. 99–100.

repression of the Samaritan revolt: "And so Pilate, after having spent ten years in Judaea, hurried to Rome in obedience to the orders of Vitellius, since he could not refuse. But before he reached Rome, Tiberius had already passed away." We are in March 37 c.e. Consequently, we cannot be sure which events Josephus was referring to in saying ὑπὸ τοὺς αὐτοὺς χρόνους, incipit of the digression on the Roman community. The account on Pilatus is not logically linked with the Parthian excursus, with the death of Germanicus and with the *senatus consultum* against the Roman Jews: instead, it is linked with the replacement of Valerius Gratus, narrated several chapters before, and seems to be an independent unit that uses a different annalistic source well-informed on the events that occurred in the Middle-East. The chronological reference in §65 should not be attributed to the government of Pilatus, but to the death of Germanicus. This theory is easier than that of Smallwood and can justify why Josephus, who knew the content of the ban, actually ignored its dating. Unfortunately, it cannot explain why he decided to insert this event eleven chapters after the logical point, causing evident confusion in the chronology.

The events that occurred in Rome are unquestionably linked with the years that preceded Pilatus. According to Norden, the organization of the material on the basis of four θόρουβοι helps give unity to the whole section.[23] He argues that this structure could have a chronological aim too: heterogenous material gathered from different sources is organized and shaped into a rigid annalistic scheme. He could support his reconstruction with a positive evidence: if we eliminate §§63–64, an interpolation, the end of §62 (καὶ οὕτω παύεται ἡ στάσις) is perfectly linked with the beginning of §65 (ἕτερόν τι δεινὸν ἐθορύβει τοὺς Ἰουδαίους).

Norden's analysis is easier than that of Smallwood, but leads to the same conclusions: Josephus ignores the dating of the ban and places it during the years of Pilatus probably because of a political interpretation of the events.

It could be useful to remember that, after the replacement of Pilatus, Josephus goes on with the events of 36–37 c.e., the return of Pilatus to Rome and the arrival of Vitellius in Jerusalem.[24] In

---

[23] E. Norden 1966, pp. 248–249.
[24] Josephus anticipates the death of Tiberius at this point.

Easter 36[25] (§§90–95) Vitellius replaces the high priest Caiaphas with Jonathan and, by order of Tiberius, declares war on Artabanus III (§§96–105), quickly obtaining a treaty of peace and the delivery of prisoners. He has just begun the war against Aretas IV king of Nabataea when he receives the news of the death of Tiberius. He makes the army swear loyalty to Gaius, interrupts the expedition and withdraws the troops to Antiochia: it is March 37 c.e. The thread of the events that happened in 19 c.e. is never resumed and is of secondary importance in the economy of the 18th book.

III

Very little is known about the act and the reason why it was issued. The sources do not help on this question, particularly on the identification of the groups the ban was referring to. According to Tacitus, *quattuor milia libertini generis ea superstitione infecta* were brought to Sardinia to fight brigandage. *Ceteri* had to leave Italy if they did not reject their faith within a prearranged date. Suetonius clarifies Tacitus' statement and affirms that only young Jews were sent to provinces with unhealthy climate *per speciem sacramenti*, while all the other Jews and *similia sectantes* were expelled. Finally, Flavius Josephus says that the community was banned except 4,000 young Jews who were sent to Sardinia; those who decided not to answer the call-up because of the Jewish Law risked heavy punishments.

As we can see, the evidence varies. According to Tacitus, the ban should have concerned only converted pagans: 4,000 of these, probably on military age, were brought by force into Sardinia, while "all the others" had to leave Italy. Neither category pertains to Jews by birth. We cannot tell how many Jews lived in Rome, but their number certainly increased after the fall of Jerusalem. We will discuss this problem later on. Apart from the discussion of Jewish attitudes towards proselytism in such an early period, massive conversions require an established, well-organised community, for which we have no clear evidence.[26] Partial conversions of people attracted by the

---

[25] On the problem regarding the visits—possibly two—of Vitellius to Jerusalem and the moment when Pilatus was replaced see A. Galimberti 2001, pp. 88–91.

[26] The only evidence we have of the Julio-Claudian age is the already mentioned passage by Philo.

Jewish style of life were actually more frequent: in case of danger or open persecution (as during the government of Domitian), this category of "Judaizers" abandoned their new habits so that they would not be confused with those who had truly become Jews. We have a firsthand evidence of this behaviour in Tiberian age in a passage by Seneca who remembers that during his youth, under the pressure of his father, he decided to interrupt his vegetarian diet to avoid being confused with a Jew.[27] What Tacitus apparently affirms is that the ban aimed to eradicate proselytism from Rome by moving all the new members of the community away from Italy. Such a serious decision was consequently determined by a phenomenon that increased so much in that period that it generated no less than 4,000 conversions only in Rome. These figures are too high.[28] We could suppose that Tacitus was inaccurate and meant to include both the Jews and the proselytes in the expression *ea supersitione affecta*: the community as a whole, and not only its new members, should have been included in the 4,000 Jews who were sent to Sardinia. But this interpretation is supported by no evidence and does not exclude that a mass of proselytes was eventually expelled.

Flavius Josephus' evidence is entirely different. He does not mention the proselytes: the ban concerned only the Jews, many of whom refused to answer the special call-up and appealed to the exemption which was probably granted by the Imperial authority. Their Jewish identity cannot be discussed. In my opinion the silence of Josephus on the proselytes is more apparent than real. The sources describe the proselyte as a member of the community, a person who shared with the Jews by birth all the precepts of Judaism, included the circumcision for the men and the ritual bath for the women.[29] The males who were over the age of twenty had to send half a shekel to the Temple each year, as all other Jews. They formed a distinct group within the synagogue: the scrolls of Qumran mention the pros-

---

[27] Sen., *Ep. Mor.* CVIII, 22: *In primum Tiberii Caesaris principatum iuventae tempus inciderat. Aliogena tum sacra movebantur, sed inter argumenta superstitionis ponebatur quorundam animalium abstinentia. Patre itaque meo rogante, qui non columniam timebat, sed philosophiam oderat, ad pristinam consuetudinem redii. Nec difficiliter mihi, ut inciperem melius cenare, persuasit.*

[28] But this is the opinion of Radin (M. Radin 1915, pp. 306–307) and Abel (E. Abel 1968, p. 385).

[29] Not all rabbinic sources agree on this point: according to Rabbi Joshua and Rabbi Yehudah ben Ila'i (JT Bikkurim 1.4.64a; BT Yebamoth 46a) the immersion was enough.

elytes as fourth, after the Priests, the Levites and the Israelites.[30] A similar piece of evidence comes from a different context and belongs to a different period: the well-known inscription of Aphrodisias, dated to the third century, in the list of the δεκανία τῶν μαθετῶν mentions three proselytes after sixteen Jews and before two "Judaizers".[31] In Rome, the proselytes are attested in seven inscriptions, two of which pertained to women that had changed their original names to Jewish ones.[32] The scarcity of the findings is possibly due to the low number of full-conversions, an act that required a complete change of life, but also to the decision of the parents of the deceased to avoid mentioning the non-Jewish origin of their relative. Most probably Josephus included the proselytes in the number of the Jews expelled from Rome. Unlike the account of Tacitus, the proselytes are not the main object of the ban.

The accounts of Suetonius and Flavius Josephus have important details in common: both of them distinguish between the Jewish youngsters, who were driven away from Rome with a call-up, and the rest of the community which was expelled together with those who shared the same faith, namely the proselytes. Like Josephus, Suetonius does not attach any importance to the proselytes: the ban regards all the community, even if on different levels.

We could deduce who the ban was attached to on the basis of the distinction between a first group who had to answer the call-up and a second group that was abruptly expelled. This could depend on criteria other than sex and age. According to Tacitus, the Jews sent to Sardinia were *libertini generis*, an expression that described the

---

[30] CD 14:4.

[31] J. Reynolds – R. Tannenbaum 1987, pp. 5–6: face a l. 13 (Σάμουλ ἀρχιδέ[κανος] προσ[ήλυτος]), l. 22 (Εἰωσῆφ Εὐσεβίου προσ[ήλυτος]), l. 27 (Ἰωσῆς προσ[ήλυτος]).

[32] JIWE II, 62, 218, 224, 392?, 489, 491, 577. JIWE II, 577: *Beturia Pau|lla {f} domi | heterne quos|tituta que bi|xit an(nos) LXXXVI meses VI | | proselyta ann(os) XVI | nominae Sara, mater | synagogarum Campi | et Bolumni | {b} en irenae ay cymisis | 10 | autis* JIWE II, 62: *Felicitas pro|selita ann(orum) VI NVENN || Peregrina | quae vixit | ann(os) XLVII. Patr|onus venemerenti.* The restoration of line 2 is debated. Frey suggests an integration with the female name Noemi. Müller reads Felicitas as a Jewish name and Nunna (attested also in CIL VI 2431) as her first name, an African name. Leon (H.J. Leon 1995², p. 332) and Noy suppose, prudentially, that it was the wrong writing for *nomine*: *Felitas nomine Peregrina* as *Beturia Paulla nomine Sara.* The three proselytes of Aphrodisia have Jewish names.

status of the freedman in society.[33] Consequently, we should suppose that there were 4,000 slaves just set free and still in military age.[34] This number is too high.[35]

Nonetheless, we cannot tell how many Jewish freedmen lived in Rome even in a later, better attested period. The inscriptions exalt the faith of the dead, or his position within the community, but usually omit his status and position in the Roman society.

Philo, who was in Rome in the years of Gaius, describes a community integrated in the social fabric of the Capital, present in many areas but particularly concentrated in *Trastiberim*.[36] This community basically consisted of *liberti*, who reached Italy as war prisoners and were subsequently freed by their masters. The most important campaign in Judaea before the first revolt is that of Pompey who brought back to Rome a number of slaves so high that, according to Reinach, it caused the true beginning of the community.[37] Even when the war was over, violent revolts could not be stemmed in Judaea: Gabinius and Cassius captured several prisoners[38] and so did Sosius when he had to put down the revolt of Pitolaos in 37 B.C.[39] According to

---

[33] Gai, *Inst.* 1,11: *Libertini, qui ex iusta servitute manumissi sunt.* S. Treggiari 1969, pp. 52–53; contra Mommsen (*Droit public roman* [n-4], VI,2, pp. 4–5) who refers the terms to the freedmen and their sons on the basis of Suet., *Claudius*, 24.1.

[34] M. Williams 1989, p. 770.

[35] The passage is inaccurate: M. Stern 1974–80, II, p. 72; E. Smallwood 1981, pp. 207–208, P. Schäfer 1999, p. 156; F. Goodyear 1981, p. 442; M. Pucci Ben Zeev 2001, p. 11.

[36] Phil., *Leg. ad Gaium*, 155: τὴν πέραν τοῦ Τιβέρεως ποταμοῦ μεγάλην τῆς Ῥώμης ἀποτομὴν [ἣν] οὐκ ἠγνόει κατεχομένην καὶ οἰκουμένην πρὸς Ἰουδαίων. Ῥωμαῖοι δὲ ἦσαν οἱ πλείους ἀπελευθερωθέντες · αἰχμάλωτοι γὰρ ἀχθέντες εἰς Ἰταλίαν ὑπὸ τῶν κτησαμένων ἠλευθερώθησαν, οὐδὲν τῶν πατρίων παραχαράξαι βιασθέντες.

[37] T. Reinach 1893, p. 46 based on *Ant.* XIV, 79, where Josephus briefly describes the triumph of Pompey. This thesis ignores the ban of 139 B.C., but marks the scarcity of evidence that we have for the period before 19 A.D. This migration, as the one that probably happened in 70 C.E., can not be quantified.

[38] *Ant.* XIV, 119–120: Κράσσος δὲ πάντα διοικήσας ὃν αὐτὸς ἐβούλετο τρόπον, ἐξώρμησεν ἐπὶ τὴν Παρθυαίαν· καὶ αὐτὸς μὲν οὖν σὺν ἅπαντι διεφθάνη τῷ στρατῷ, ὡς καὶ ἐν ἄλλοις δεδήλωται, Κάσσιος δὲ εἰς Συρίαν φυγὼν καὶ περιποιησάμενος αὐτὴν Πάρθοις ἐμποδὼν ἦν ἐκτρέχουσιν ἐπὶ αὐτὴν διὰ τὴν κατὰ Κράσσου νίκην. Αὖθις δὲ εἰς Τύρον ἀφικόμενος ἀνέβη καὶ εἰς τὴν Ἰουδαίαν. Ταριχαίας μὲν οὖν προσπεσὼν εὐθέως αἱρεῖ, καὶ περὶ τρισμυρίους ἀνθρώπους ἀνδραποδίζει, Πειθόλαόν τε τὴν Ἀριστοβούλου στάσιν διαδεγμένον κτείνει.

[39] *Ant.* XIV, 487–489: Τοῦτο τὸ πάθος συνέβη τῇ Ἱεροσολυμιτῶν πόλει ὑπατεύοντος ἐν Ῥώμῃ Μάρκου Ἀγρίππα καὶ ὀγδοηκοστῆς καὶ πέμπτης ὀλυμπιάδος, τῷ τρίτῳ μηνί, τῇ ἑορτῇ τῆς νηστείας, ὥσπερ ἐκ περιτροπῆς τῆς γενομένης ἐπὶ Πομπηίου τοῖς Ἰουδαίοις συμφορᾶς· καὶ γὰρ ὑπὸ ἐκείνου τῇ αὐτῇ ἑάλωσαν ἡμέρα, μετὰ ἔτη εἴκοσι ἑπτά. Σόσσιος δὲ χρυσοῦν ἀναθέμενος τῷ θεῷ στέφανον ἀνέζευξεν ἀπὸ Ἱεροσολύμων, Ἀντίγονον ἄγων δεσμώτην Ἀντωνίῳ.

Philo—and to Tacitus—the Jewish community of Rome was mostly
made up of freedmen who once were war prisoners. Miriam Pucci
supposes that the sons or nephews of the freedmen should also be
numbered among these *liberti*: the peculiarity of Jewish life could
have fostered quick manumissions.[40] Beside testamentary manumissions, the Romans allowed informal manumissions that nevertheless
did not grant full citizenship to the freedman.[41] Those who were
freed through this procedure remained slaves formally, and were
bound to their *patronus* both in economic and in private life.[42] Nevertheless, the *lex Iunia* granted Roman citizenship to the *latini Iuniani*
and their wives if the couple had a son of more than one year of
age. (Gai. *Inst.* I,29). Consequently, only part of the Jewish freedmen who lived in Rome was not protected by citizenship and could
be expelled: all the others, who received full citizenship, could be
compelled to answer a call-up (Suetonius in fact uses the traditional
formula, *per speciem sacramenti*) but could not be easily banned. Probably
the Roman Jews were not involved in military service, as Josephus
shows when he says that most of them refused to set off because of
the Jewish Law. We do not know whether this community (as that
of Ephesus)[43] was exempted from the military service. Josephus does
not denounce the end of a privilege (of which there are no traces),[44]
but attests the hostility the Jews had towards military life, during
which important precepts such as the alimentary rules and the sab-
batical rest could not be respected.

Another important piece of information on the status of the group
expelled comes again from Suetonius who states that those who
refused to leave Rome had to undergo the *poena perpetuae servitutis*.
This is a most ambiguous expression. We only know one *lex* forbidding the possibility of manumitting entirely: the *lex Aelia Sentia*,

---

[40] M. Pucci Ben Zeev 2001, p. 11.

[41] The slave who was freed by a *civis Romanus* gained citizenship, but enjoyed
less rights: he was excluded from all religious and public positions, from the equestrian rank and from the Senate, had limited voting rights and had to serve his
patronus. The status of his sons was better, but in the Republican period they were
excluded from public positions, both of senatorial and of equestrian rank. The
nephews were perfectly integrated. F. Schultz 1995, p. 106; T. Mommsen 1969,
vol. III, pp. 420 sg.

[42] Frag. Dosith. 5: *manebant servi*; Gai., *Inst.*, III, 56: *ex iure Quiritium servos fuisse*.
On *lex Iunia* see F. Schultz 1995, p. 191 e G. Fabre 1981, pp. 55–59.

[43] *Ant.* XIV, 262–264; on this passage see T. Rajak 1984, pp. 116–118.

[44] *Contra* A. Galiberti 2001, p. 105.

promoted in 4 C.E. by the consuls *Sp. Aelius Cato* and *C. Sentius* as
part of the Augustan policy on manumissiones.[45] This *lex* integrated
the *lex Fufia Caninia* issued in 2 B.C. concerning the testamentary
manumissiones,[46] while the *lex Aelia Sentia* provided restrictions on
non-testamentary manumissiones. By and large, the *manumissio in
fraudem creditorum* is forbidden[47] and age limits are provided both for
the *manumissor*[48] and for the *manumissus*:[49] a *consilium* had to ratify acts
that did not respect these limits.[50] The *lex Aelia Sentia* was thought
to limit the access of freedmen to full citizenship: the manumission
was not forbidden, but the freedmen joined the status of *peregrinus
dediticius* on the condition that they lived 100 milia from Rome: *ut
eiusdem condicionis liberi fiant, cuius condicionis sunt peregrini dediticii (Inst.
I,13).*[51] Those who remained in town risked becoming slaves again

---

[45] Suet., *Aug.*, 40, 3: *Magni praeterea existimans sincerum atque ab omni collusione peregrini ac servilis sanguinis incorruptum servare populum, et civitates Romanas parcissime dedit et
manumittendi modum terminavit.*

[46] *Inst.* 1,7: *Lege Fufia Caninia certus modus constitutus erat in servis testamento manumit-
tendis.* The law allowed the manumission only of part of the *familia*, in decreasing
percentage with the number of slaves a *patronus* had. F. Schultz 1995, p. 191.

[47] *Inst.* 1,6,1: *Non tamen cuicumque volenti manumittere licet. Nam is qui in fraudem creditorum
manumittit nihil agit, quia lex Aelia Sentia impedit libertatem.*

[48] Who could not be less than 20 years old. *Inst.* 1,6,4: *Eadem lege Aelia Sentia
domino minori annis vigenti non aliter manumittere permittitur, quam si vindicta apud consilium
iusta causa manumissionis adprobata fuerint manumissi.* Continued with the list of the *iustae
manumissiones.*

[49] The minimum age was thirty. Gai. *Inst.*, 1, 18.

[50] Gai. *Inst.*, I,20. In Rome the *consilium* was made of 10 members, 20 in the
provinces. In Domitian age, its prerogatives are undertaken by the *collegium decurio-
num*, R. Leonard 1925, coll. 2321–2322.

[51] The juridical value of this expression is debated. It is mentioned in the *constitutio antoniniana*, where this category is excluded from citizenship. Schultz (F. Schultz
1995, p. 104, p. 107 nr. 69) compares their status to that of the *peregrini* belonging
to the State: they have autonomy (not juridically granted), can follow their laws but
cannot take part in the comitia, are prevented from reaching the senatorial and
equestrian ranks and, in the Republican period, cannot enter the legions. They cannot obtain Roman citizenship. The *peregrini dediticii* should actually be the *dediticii
Aeliani.* This opinion is shared by Scherillo – Dell'Oro (G. Scherillo – A. Dell'Oro
1987, p. 388) who points out that the *lex Aelia Sentia* was repealed only in Justinian
period: even after the issue of the *constitutio Antoniniana* the *dediticii Aeliani* still existed.
Momigliano (A. Momigliano 1967, p. 3), and Stroux (J. Stroux 1933, pp. 286–287)
accept the definition of *peregrinus dediticius* given by Gaius (1,14) in a passage that
Schultz considered interpolated: *vocantur autem peregrini dediticii hi qui quondam adversus
populum Romanum armis susceptis pugnaverunt, deinde victi se dederunt.* The *deditus* whose
status could not be reduced to the categories provided by the law becomes *dediticius.* This could explain why the *peregrini dediticii lege Aelia Sentia* had no civil rights
and could not enjoy Roman citizenship: according to Gaius (1,26) *dediciorum numero
sunt nec ulla lege aut senatus consulto aut constitutione principali aditus illis ad civitatem Romanam*

with no possibilities of being freed.[52] Apparently this law does not regard the Jewish community and was never applied to *peregrini* who ignored a ban. We can suppose that it was enforced on those Jews *dediticii Aeliani* who had not left Rome after being freed, but their number was certainly small. What Suetonius says (if it is a well-grounded information), shows the presence of a small number of newly freed slaves in 19 C.E.: it cannot refer to the community as a whole at all.

Not all the Jews arrived in Rome as war prisoners: some groups could have come to the Capital from the motherland, or from other centres of the Diaspora, of their own free will. The inscriptions, which give a picture of two centuries later, show a sporadic presence of Jews who were not born in Rome. Apart from Οὐρσάκιος (JIWE II, 238), who was born in Aquileia, and Ἀμάχιος, who was born in Catania (JIWE II, 515), all the other texts that mention the place of birth report towns of the Eastern Mediterranean and of Africa. Four of the deceased came from the Syro-Palestinian area, from Caesarea[53] (JIWE II, 459 and JIWE II, 112), Sepphoris (JIWE II, 60) and Tiberias (JIWE II, 561), while the fifth was born in Arca Libani[54] (JIWE II, 568). A man was born in Laodicea[55] (JIWE II, 183), while a woman is said to be Achaean (JIWE II, 503). A Μάξι-μος Θαβρακενός certainly came from Numidia (JIWE II, 508), while the identification of Tripolis mentioned in an inscription found in Monteverde (JIWE II, 113) is more doubtful.[56] Thanks to the important contribution of the inscriptions of Villa Torlonia, the overall picture of the Jewish immigration to Rome changed completely from

---

datur. According to Mommsen (T. Mommsen 1969, vol. III p. 716), Schulten (P.-W., vol. IV, e s.v. *dediticii*) and Bickerman (E. Bickerman 1926, p. 17), the *dediticius* in Gaius I, 14 should be referred to all the people who do not belong to a *civitas* whose autonomy Rome recognised and did not have a Roman or Latin citizenship.

[52] Gai, *Inst.*, I, 27.

[53] In consideration of JIWE II, 112 (Κεσαρεὺς τῆς Παλεστίνης) the Caesarea above mentioned is identified with Caesarea in Palaestina. Vismara (C. Vismara 1987, pp. 119–121) identifies it with Caesarea in Mauritania. Noy (in commenting upon the text) recalls a town in Asia Minor.

[54] The inscription is lost, but was transcribed in the 19th century.

[55] Identified with Laodicea ad Lycum in Phrygia (E. Smallwood 1981, p. 126) or Laodicea ad Mare in Syria (H. Leon 1995², p. 239).

[56] According to Noy, Τρίπολις without any further indication should indicate the Syrian town. A Τρίπολις is attested also in Asia Minor and in Lybia.

the times of the research done by Leon and Smallwood. Even if the
provenance from the Middle-East is still well attested, we have traces
of a south-north immigration that was excluded before the publication of the report on Villa Torlonia's catacombs. Nevertheless, as
Leon remarked,[57] we have no traces of an immigration from the rich
communities of Egypt and Cyrenaica.[58] However, the evidence is too
small and too late to allow definitive conclusions.

The status of the Jews of non-Roman origin is uncertain and
differentiated. Those Jews who were citizens in Judaea after the death
of king Archelaos and before 70 C.E. were considered *peregrini*, as all
the other provincials:[59] they were not protected in case of ban. In
Judaea there were also Jews who were *cives Romani*, whose status had
probably been gained thanks to a *manumissio* made by a *cives*, and
Jews who were *servi*.[60] Many Jews could have also come from communities of the Diaspora whose right depended on accords between
the authorities of their places of residence and Rome.[61]

According to this analysis, the social composition of the community
is in contrast with the simplified picture depicted by the sources.
Both the expulsion and the call-up regarded a limited number of Jews:
even Flavius Josephus does not mention the suspension of Jewish
rights. The ban hits Jews *peregrini* (so to speak, inhabitants of Judaea
who lived in Rome at the time) and, probably, slaves freed with
informal *manumissiones* but who were not yet citizens (the most
numerous category). The overall number was not high. The compulsory call-up involved more people, because it regarded the freedmen and their families, with limits due to sex and age. Tacitus and
Suetonius do not remark the exceptionality of the act (that possibly

---

[57] H. J. Leon 1995[2], pp. 238–240.
[58] As a matter of fact, it is not strange. The inscriptions date to the third century and, after the revolt under Trajan, the Jewish presence in Egypt and Cyrenaica
was dramatically reduced.
[59] From 63 B.C. to 6 C.E. and during the reign of Agrippa I (41–44 C.E.) Judaea
was a vassal state, formally independent but actually controlled by Rome. From
6 C.E. to 66 C.E., when the Jewish war broke off, Judaea was annexed to the
province of Syria and ruled first by a *praefectus*, then by an Imperial *procurator* resident
in Caesarea Maritima. A.M. Rabello 1980, p. 725; A. Momigliano 1967, p. 5.
[60] A.M. Rabello 1980, p. 725.
[61] As Rajak shows (T. Rajak 1984), there was not a Roman charter of the Jewish
rights, as Juster supposed. Their rights depended on their places of residence. On
the value the term πολιτεία had for the Jews see L. Troiani 1994, pp. 11–22.

was legal), but the harshness of the destination, an area whose weather could cause casualties.

The act was certainly traumatic for the community but did not have severe consequences: after less than thirty years, under the reign of Claudius, the community was still flourishing, apparently not wounded by the ban of 19.

IV

In regard to the reason that induced the government to issue a ban of expulsion, the sources again suggest different interpretations.

The explanation Josephus offers of the ban is considered untrustworthy, both for the semi-fictional style in which the tale is told—as Williams shows[62]—and for the extraordinary disproportion between the fault of a few Jews and a punishment that involved the whole community. The tale is not mentioned elsewhere. In any case, Fulvia is a woman of high social standing: the violent reaction of the Senate (and of the Emperor too) could be due to the spreading of the Jewish faith not only among the plebs but also among the high ranks. This detail could be echoed in the passages of Suetonius and Tacitus. None of them can explain the *senatus consultum*, but some signals suggest what their position was. Tacitus almost explicitly blames the Romans who converted to Judaism: these are the only ones responsible for the ban. This is not Suetonius's opinion: the proselytes are mentioned only at the end of the passage and with no emphasis. While Tacitus forgets the Egyptians, Suetonius also mentions their punishment: the Roman State had to intervene against both communities, not only against the Jews. As we have already seen, the two historians place the event within a series of reforms the Senate provided to control the customs and the efficiency of the Imperial bureaucracy. However, the question is observed from two different points of view. Tacitus does not stress this link, and exaggerates the criticisms against the Jews, reporting only their punishment and using harsh language. Suetonius reads the act against the Egyptians and the Jews as part of a general policy of control of foreign cults: *Externas caerimonias, Aegyptios Iudaicosque ritus compescuit*...

---

[62] M. Williams 1989, pp. 775–777.

In spite of the differences, what emerges from both authors is an attack of the State not against the Jewish (and the Isiac) cult itself, but against its spreading in Roman society. Most probably, the conflicts between Roman Jewry and Roman State under Tiberius and Claudius are caused by proselytism. However, it is debated whether these acts were the answer to an open activity of proselytism promoted by the community, or to the (unwilled) presence of proselytes in high society. The difference between the two positions depends on the way the behaviour of the community is judged. In my opinion, the presence of proselytes is not enough to require a missionary activity openly promoted by the community: the peculiarity of Jewish life, exceptional in antiquity, could be enough to attract pagans.

In the first place, the most significant support comes from a controversial piece of evidence by Cassius Dio.[63] The passage is quoted, out of context, by John of Antioch, a Christian historian of the seventh century. The reference to the events of 19 c.e.—which Smallwood suggested but which is also supported by Stern and Abel[64]—is at least questionable. According to Boissevain, the facts can refer to the period between 17 and 20 c.e.: the reason for dating them to 19 c.e. depends on the similarity with what Tacitus and Suetonius say.[65] Even if John had quoted the passage in its integrity, the differences with the other authors are unquestionable: the *senatus consultum* and the punishment of the believers of Isis are not mentioned, while an active proselytism developed by the Jews "who arrived in large number in Rome" is seen as responsible. In the period between the war of Pompey and the fall of Jerusalem the sources do not talk about mass arrival from Judaea. Apparently, the movement during the first and second centuries c.e. is due to the transportation of war prisoners to the market of the Capital and of Italy. Most probably, after the war of Bar-Kochba, when the Jews were forbidden to live in *Aelia Capitolina*, the flow of Jews from the motherland increased. According to Schäfer, who resumes a thesis already expressed by

---

[63] Cass. Dio, *Hist. Rom.* LVII, 18,5a: Τῶν τε Ἰουδαίων πολλῶν ἐς τὴν Ῥώμην συνελθόντων καὶ συχνοὺς τῶν ἐπιχωρίων ἐς τὰ σφέτερα ἔθη μεθιστάντων, τοὺς πλείονας ἐξήλασεν.

[64] E. Smallwood 1956, pp. 318–322; M. Stern 1974–80, II, p. 70; E. Abel 1968, pp. 383–386.

[65] Cass. Dio, *Historiarum romanarum quae supersunt* (ed. U.P. Boissevain), Berlin: Weidmann 1955 (1st ed. 1895–1931).

Goodman and Williams,[66] proselytism could not have been an activity of the community in such an early date: probably Cassius Dio attributed to the first century a situation which actually existed in the third century.[67]

Williams is probably right in suspecting that the event as narrated by John is not that of 19 C.E. The passage has too many inaccuracies to be used as the only evidence of the presence of a missionary activity promoted by Roman Jewry within the pagan society of the Capital.

However, it is almost unquestionable that large strata of the Roman society were actually attracted by Judaism. The Jewish community, its peculiar style of life, the consciousness of its identity, could easily make an impression in a pagan society. As the episode on Fulvia shows, it was not odd that a *matrona* sent money to the Temple. The State, in this period as in others, is negatively impressed by partial as well as by full conversions. As we will see, Domitian in the nineties attacks these groups of partially converted Romans, of "Judaizers". Seneca echoes this attitude: in a passage quoted by Augustine, he is worried about the spreading of Judaism in Roman society and remarks with disappointment that the Jews, unlike most people, knew the reasons of their cults and did not celebrate meaningless rites.[68]

The *senatus consultum* was probably issued for the presence of *externae caerimoniae* among the plebs urbana and among Romans of high social standing, not for a missionary activity supported by the local community. In this period, the Jewish style of life seems to be sufficiently attractive in itself.

---

[66] M. Goodman 1992, p. 70; M. Williams 1989, pp. 767–768.

[67] P. Schäfer 1999, pp. 157–158.

[68] *De superstitione*, in Aug., *De Civitate Dei*, VI, 11: *De illis sane Iudaeis cum loqueretur, ait: "Cum interim usque ea sceleratissimae gentis consuetudo convaluit ut per omnes iam terras recepita sit; victi victoribus leges dederunt." Mirabatur haec dicens et quid divinitus ageretur ignorans subiecit plane sententiam qua significaret quid de illorum sacramentorum ratione sentiret. Ait enim: "Illi tament causas ritus sui noverunt; maior pars populi facit quod cur faciat ignorat."*

CLAUDIUS

A new intervention against the Jewish community of Rome occurred during the reign of Claudius. In an unknown year the Senate enacted a ban of expulsion together with (or before) a ban forbidding the gatherings: the holy service is eventually forbidden. The literary evidence, Acts, Suetonius and Cassius Dio, contradict each other. Apart from the worsening of the relationships between Jews and Roman authorities, tension was mounting within the community itself because of the preaching of the first Christians.

I

The expulsion is mentioned in a passage of Acts: Paul arrives in Corinth from Athens and meets Aquila and Priscilla, a Jewish couple who has converted to Christianity, and who has escaped from Rome because of the ban.[1] The two do not stop a long time in Corinth: later on they are with Paul in Ephesus,[2] a fact confirmed by a passage in the first epistle to the Corinthians probably written during the Ephesian stay.[3] After a while, the couple is again in Rome; we could suppose that the Emperor had eventually dropped his repressive policy. Paul, in the final greeting of the Epistle to the Romans, includes among the first names those of Aquila and Priscilla, who had probably become two close friends of his, and had possibly attained a position of priority in the community.[4] They are mentioned

---

[1] Acts, 18:1–3: Μετὰ ταῦτα χωρισθεὶς ἐκ τῶν Ἀθηνῶν ἦλθεν εἰς Κόρινθον. Καὶ εὑρών τινα Ἰουδαῖον ὀνόματι Ἀκύλαν, Ποντικὸν τῷ γένει προσφάτως ἐληλυθότα ἀπὸ τῆς Ἰταλίας καὶ Πρίσκιλλαν γυναῖκα αὐτοῦ, διὰ τὸ διατεταχέναι Κλαύδιον χωρίζεσθαι πάντας τοὺς Ἰουδαίους ἀπὸ τῆς Ῥώμης, προσῆλθεν αὐτοῖς καὶ διὰ τὸ ὁμότεχνον εἶναι ἔμενεν παρὰ αὐτοῖς, καὶ ἠργάζετο· ἦσαν γὰρ σκηνοποιοὶ τῇ τέχνῃ.

[2] Acts 18, 18–19: Ὁ δὲ Παῦλος ἔτι προσμείνας ἡμέρας ἱκανὰς τοῖς ἀδελφοῖς ἀποταξάμενος ἐξέπλει εἰς τὴν Συρίαν, καὶ σὺν αὐτῷ Πρίσκιλλα καὶ Ἀκύλας, κειράμενος ἐν Κεγχρεαῖς τὴν κεφαλήν, εἶχεν γὰρ εὐχήν. Κατήντησαν δὲ εἰς Ἔφεσον κἀκείνους κατέλιπεν αὐτοῦ, αὐτὸς δὲ εἰσελθὼν εἰς τὴν συναγωγὴν διελέξατο τοῖς Ἰουδαίοις.

[3] I Cor. 16:19: Ἀσπάζονται ὑμᾶς ἐν κυρίῳ πολλὰ Ἀκύλας καὶ Πρίσκα σὺν τῇ κατ᾽ οἶκον αὐτῶν ἐκκλησίᾳ. A. Robertson – A. Plumber 1967, p. XXVII.

[4] Rom. 16:3–5: Ἀσπάσασθε Πρίσκαν καὶ Ἀκύλαν τοὺς συνεργούς μου ἐν Χριστῷ Ἰησοῦ, οἵτινες ὑπὲρ τῆς ψυχῆς μου τὸν ἑαυτῶν τράχηλον ὑπέθηκαν, οἷς οὐκ ἐγὼ μόνος

also in the second Epistle to Timothy, whose date and authenticity as a Pauline epistle is questionable.[5]

The idea is that of a ban that regarded all Jews living in Rome. Some inaccuracies have been noticed. The term πάντες suggests that the ban involved the community as a whole, not only a few members or a particular group. This information, however, is in contrast with the statement of Cassius Dio, who affirms that at the time of Claudius the Jews were too numerous to be banned from the Capital. Such a ban would pose the same problems discussed in connection with the intervention of Tiberius: in this period the community was probably composed of freedmen and citizens who could hardly be expelled *sine causa*. The passage does not state precisely why the ban was enacted, a secondary detail in a non historical piece of literature. The involvement of Aquila and Priscilla apparently shows the presence of Jewish Christians among the Jews expelled from Rome. This is a debated question: the passage fails to say whether Aquila and Priscilla were still Christian when they left Rome or if they were converted when they reached Corinth and met Paul. In the first case, the Christian community was involved in the ban of Claudius. In my opinion, the passage does not allow us to take any sides on this point. The silence of Acts on the involvement of the Christians could derive from the fact that the ban officially concerned only the Jews. Why should we stress a contrast between Romans and Christians in a period when the Christian community in Rome was relatively small?

The author of Acts, in presenting Ἀκύλας, calls him Ἰουδαῖος. This detail has been used to show the non-involvement of the Christians in the event.[6] In this case, Ἰουδαῖος does not indicate a geographical origin: the man was born in Pontus, not in Judaea. In the Jewish inscriptions of Rome Ἰουδαῖος is interpreted as a way to note that a dead person belonged to the Jewish community regardless of his place of birth.[7] Such an indication had a religious value:

εὐχαριστῶ ἀλλὰ καὶ πᾶσαι αἱ ἐκκλησίαι τῶν ἐθνῶν, καὶ τὴν κατ᾽ οἶκον αὐτῶν ἐκκλησίαν.

[5] II Tim., 4:19: Ἄσπασαι Πρίσκαν καὶ Ἀκύλαν καὶ τὸν Ὀνησιφόρου οἶκον. On the problems concerning the authenticity and the dating of this epistle see R. Brown 2001, pp. 859–893, L. Johnson 2001, pp. 319–330.

[6] Among others M. Sordi 1995, p. 263.

[7] On this problem see M. Williams 1997, pp. 249–262.

the deceased stands out for his fidelity to the Law. In Acts it is applied to Christians converted from Judaism: apart from Aquila, we know Timothy, the son of a Jewish woman,[8] and Apollos, a Jew of Alexandria who became a Christian.[9] In Acts, Paul twice states that he is a Jew by birth and in Gal. 2:15 he says: ἡμεῖς φύσει Ἰουδαῖοι καὶ οὐκ ἐξ ἐθνῶν ἁμαρτωλοί.[10] The term Ἰουδαῖος is also used to design those Christians who behave as Jews with regard to the precepts of the Law. Peter reminds Cornelius that a Jew was forbidden to have contacts with strangers,[11] while in the community of Iconius there was a Jewish group that could be easily distinguished from the unconverted Jews.[12] This idea is present in Paul's Epistles too: in Gal. 2:12–13 Paul remarks (with negative accents) that in Antioch the Jewish Christians led a separate life from the pagan Christians.[13] The term occurs in Pauline thought and is the core of the Epistle to the Romans, where Ἰουδαῖος is debated not only in the comparison between the Christian message and the Law, but also in the section concerning the difficult fusion between Christians of pagan and of Jewish origins.[14]

The passage of Acts cannot be easily dated. We know that Aquila and Priscilla had a house and had set up a trading activity when Paul reached Corinth: the Apostle lived and worked with them for a while. According to Acts, Paul was charged because he had led the people to worship God in a way opposite to the Law.[15] The

---

[8] Acts 16:1: καὶ ἰδοὺ μαθητής τις ἦν ἐκεῖ ὀνόματι Τιμόθεος, υἱὸς γυναικὸς Ἰουδαίας πιστῆς, πατρὸς δὲ Ἕλληνος.

[9] Acts 18:24: Ἰουδαῖος δέ τις Ἀπολλῶς ὀνόματι, Ἀλεξανδρεὺς τῷ γένει, ἀνὴρ λόγιος, κατήντησεν εἰς Ἔφεσον, δυνατὸς ὢν ἐν ταῖς γραφαῖς.

[10] Acts 21:39: Εἶπεν δὲ ὁ Παῦλος· ἐγὼ ἄνθρωπος μέν εἰμι Ἰουδαῖος, Ταρσεὺς τῆς Κιλικίας, οὐκ ἀσήμου πόλεως πολίτης; Acts 22:3: Ἐγώ εἰμι ἀνὴρ Ἰουδαῖος, γεγεννημένος ἐν Ταρσῷ τῆς Κιλικίας, ἀνατεθραμμένος δὲ ἐν τῇ πόλει ταύτῃ.

[11] Acts 10:28: ὑμεῖς ἐπίστασθε ὡς ἀθέμιτόν ἐστιν ἀνδρὶ Ἰουδαίῳ κολλᾶσθαι ἢ προσέρχεσθαι ἀλλοφύλῳ.

[12] Acts 14:1–2: Ἐγένετο δὲ ἐν Ἰκονίῳ κατὰ τὸ αὐτὸ εἰσελθεῖν αὐτοὺς εἰς τὴν συναγωγὴν τῶν Ἰουδαίων καὶ λαλῆσαι οὕτως ὥστε πιστεῦσαι Ἰουδαίων τε καὶ Ἑλλήνων πολὺ πλῆθος. Οἱ δὲ ἀπειθήσαντες Ἰουδαῖοι ἐπήγειραν καὶ ἐκάκωσαν τὰς ψυχὰς τῶν ἐθνῶν κατὰ τῶν ἀδελφῶν.

[13] Gal. 2:12–13: πρὸ τοῦ γὰρ ἐλθεῖν τινας ἀπὸ Ἰακώβου μετὰ τῶν ἐθνῶν συνήσθιεν· ὅτε δὲ ἦλθον, ὑπέστελλεν καὶ ἀφώριζεν ἑαυτὸν φοβούμενος τοὺς ἐκ περιτομῆς. καὶ συνυπεκρίθησαν αὐτῷ καὶ οἱ λοιποὶ Ἰουδαῖοι, ὥστε καὶ Βαρναβᾶς συναπήχθη αὐτῶν τῇ ὑποκρίσει.

[14] Notes to Rom. 1,16–11,36 by C. Cranfield 1986–87 and W. Gotbrod 1968, vol. IV coll. 1167–1172.

[15] Acts 18:12–14: Γαλλίωνος δὲ ἀνθυπάτου ὄντος τῆς Ἀχαΐας κατεπέστησαν

chairman of the trial was the governor *L. Iunius Gallio*, whose pro-
consulate can be dated, according to an inscription, between spring
51 and spring 52 c.e.[16] We do not know when Paul arrived in
Corinth. In 18,11 it is said that Paul ἐκάθισεν δὲ ἐνιαυτὸν καὶ μῆνας
ἓξ διδάσκων ἐν αὐτοῖς τὸν λόγον τοῦ θεοῦ: according to some scholars,
this interval corresponded to his entire stay.[17] In this time, a long
period of quiet (18:1–11) was followed by disagreements and clashes
with the local community (18:12–18). After the trial, Paul did not
leave the town immediately, but remained ἡμέρας ἱκανάς: although
we suppose that Paul postponed his departure for one or two months,
he should have arrived in Corinth in the winter of 50/51 c.e. not
long before the appointment of new governor. Conversely, according to Boffo, who resumes a position already expressed by Gabba,
18:11 does not indicate the passage from a period of peace to a
period of opposition with the local community:[18] even the first section mentions the clash with some Jews who were attending Paul's
preaching in the synagogue (18:6). The detail of the eighteen months
Paul spent in Corinth makes sense only as a way of suggesting a

---

ὁμοθυμαδὸν οἱ Ἰουδαῖοι τῷ Παύλῳ καὶ ἤγαγον αὐτὸν ἐπὶ τὸ βῆμα λέγοντες ὅτι παρὰ
τὸν νόμον ἀναπείθει οὗτος τοὺς ἀνθρώπους σέβεσθαι τὸν θεόν.

[16] SEG III (1927) nr. 389 (Ditt., Syll. 801): Τιβέρ[ιος Κλαύδιος Καῖσ]αρ Σ[εβαστ]ὸς
Γ[ερμανικός, δημαρχικῆς ἐξου]|σίας [τὸ ΙΒ, αὐτοκράτωρ τ]ὸ κϛ', π[ατὴρ π]ατρί[δος—
ca. 14—χαίρειν]. | Πάλ[αι μὲν τ]ῆι π[όλει τῃ] τῶν Δελφῶ[ν ἦν ο]ὐ μό[νον εὔνους |
ἀλλ' ἐπιμελὴς τῆς τυ]|χῆς, ἀεὶ δ' ἐτήρη[σα τὴ]ν θρησκεί[αν τ]οῦ Ἀπό[λλωνος | τοῦ
Πυθίου· ἐπεὶ δὲ] | νῦν λέγεται καὶ [πολ]ειτῶν ἔρη[μο]ς εἶναι, ὥ[ς μοι ἄρτι | ἀπήγγειλε
Λ. Ἰού]|νιος Γαλλίων ὁ φ[ίλος] μου κα[ὶ ἀνθύ]πατος, [--- τοὺς Δελφοὺς] | ἔτι ἕξειν
τὸν πρ[ότερον κόσμον ἐντελ]ῆ, ἐ[ντέλλομαι---ἐξ ἄλ]|λων πόλεων καλ[εῖν εὖ γεγονότας
εἰς Δελφοὺς ὡς νέους | κατοίκους καὶ] | αὐτοῖς ἐπιτρέ[πειν ἐκγόνοις τε τὰ] πρεσ[βεῖα
πάντα ἔχειν τὰ τῶν Δελ]|φῶν ὡς πολε[ίταις ἐπ' ἴσῃ καὶ ὁμοίᾳ· ε]ἰ μέν γάρ τι[νες--- ὡς
πολεῖ]|ται μετῳκίσ[αντο εἰς τούτους τοὺ]ς τόπους, κρ[---] | [το]ύτους [---]ν πάντως
ε[---] | [---]σθη· οἵτινε[ς δὲ---] | [---]ι καὶ τὸ συναύ[ξειν---] | [---ὥσπε]ρ ἐπὶ τῶν
ἀνα[---] |ἀνα[---φ]ημι. [Τ]οῖς μέντ[οι---] | εἰς τῶν [---]ειασε ἐντέλλομαι ἵν[α---] |
κατὰ προ[σῆκον πάντων] τῶν ἐν αὐτῷ γεγραμ[μένων μηδὲν] | ἐριστὸ[ν ᾖι]. This inscrip-
tion was found in Delphi in 1905. The date of the proconsulship of *L. Iunius Gallio
Annaeanus* is supported by Claudius' titulature: l.2 mentions his 26th imperial accla-
mation, during his 12th tribunicia potestas, between 25th January and 1st August
52 C.E. Claudius answers a previous epistle sent by the governor, who was still in
office when Claudius was writing the answer: consequently, the proconsulship of
Gallio should be dated to a period between spring 51 and the beginning of
summer 52. The month the governors reached the provinces to which they had
been appointed is debated. L. Boffo 1994, pp. 321–333. On the meeting between
L. Gallio and Paul see L. Troiani 2002, pp. 47–54.

[17] Among others J. Wiseman 1979, pp. 503–505.

[18] L. Boffo 1994, p. 254.

chronological sequence. Consequently, Paul arrived in winter 50/51 C.E., a year and a half before the appointment of Gallio, and was likely to have remained in Corinth no less than thirty months.[19] Then, Aquila and Priscilla reached Corinth in the winter of 49 or 50 C.E. When Paul joined the couple, they had arrived not long before (προσ-φάτως), an extremely vague adverb. Although what the passage says does not allow a definitive reconstruction, the overall picture seems to suggest that the ban was enacted in 49 C.E. rather than in 41 C.E.

II

Suetonius agrees with the author of Acts and attests a decree of expulsion against the Jewish community of Rome.[20] The text has many problems.

The event is not dated and is inserted within a non-datable context. However, Orosius quotes Suetonius' passage and places it in 49 C.E., on the basis of a passage by Flavius Josephus, now lost.[21] Orosius' quotation is roughly correct, but an important detail is changed: he writes *impulsore Chresto* as *impulsore Christo*, implying the involvement of the Christians in the turmoil that provoked the ban. This *variatio* probably was not due to Orosius, but to an intermediate source in which Orosius found the passage by Suetonius. Harnack in this source acknowledged the Chronicle of Jerome, a work Orosius usually looked up.[22] Although we suppose an intermediate passage between Suetonius and Orosius, the authority of Orosius in dating the event is not undermined, as Harnack thought. According to Orosius, a passage by Flavius Josephus supported 49 C.E.: the lack of a source does not mean that the person who quotes it makes a mistake, but that he offers a piece of information that cannot be verified in any way. To summarize, a late source, depending on an

---

[19] L. Barrett 1994–1998, vol. II p. LVI e pp. 870–871.

[20] Suet., *Claud.*, 25,4: *Iudaeos impulsore Chresto adsidue tumultantis Roma expulit.*

[21] Orosius, *Adversus Paganos* VII, 6,15: *Anno eiusdem (sc. Claudii) nono expulsos per Claudium urbe Iudaeos Iosephus refert. Sed me magis Suetonius movet, qui ait hoc modo: Claudius Iudaeos impulsore Christo adsidue tumultuantes Roma expulit; quod, utrum contra Christum tumultuantes Iudaeos coherceri et conprimi iusserit, an etiam Christianos simul velut cognatae religionis homines voluerit expelli, nequaquam discernitur.*

[22] A. von Harnack, *Chronologische Berechnung des "Tags von Damaskus"*, SPrAW 1912, p. 673 quoted by H. Bottermann 1996, p. 55.

unknown passage, dates the ban to a year that may correspond to what Acts say.

As in Acts, Suetonius's passage attests a crisis in the relationship between the community and Rome: all the Jews who lived in the town are expelled. The author of Acts uses the term πάντες and Suetonius similarly suggests a ban against all Roman Jews. He does not mention the Christians explicitly, but affirms that in Rome there was an agitator called Chrestus. The involvement of the Christians in this event depends entirely on the way Chrestus is interpreted. The presence of a Christian community in Rome dates back to early 54 c.e., when Paul wrote the Epistle to the Romans.[23] In the period that preceded the arrival of Paul (spring 63)[24] groups of Christians probably frequented the Capital. Their organization is not clear.[25] According to the Epistle to the Romans, the community was exemplary in the faith (Rom. 16:19: ἡ γὰρ ὑμῖν ὑπακοὴ εἰς πάντας ἀφίκετο) and was largely composed of pagans converted to Christianity, rather than of Jewish Christians (Rom. 16:5–15). Contacts between the Jewish and the Christian communities cannot be excluded. In the last chapter of Acts, Paul arrives in Rome and is welcomed by "the first of the Jews" who, worried about the presence of the Apostle, ask information on the new sect known to be cause of conflicts among the Jews of the Diaspora.[26] In Marta Sordi's opinion, this passage shows that the Christians did not clash with the Jewish com-

---

[23] This is the traditional dating of the Epistle to the Romans. H. Bottermann 1996, p. 62.

[24] According to Marta Sordi; the arrival of Paul is traditionally dated to 60 C.E. It all depends on the date of the governorship of Felix, mentioned in Acts 24:27: Διετίας δὲ πληρωθείσης ἔλαβεν διάδοχον ὁ Φῆλιξ Πόρκιον Φῆστον, θέλων τε χάριτα καταθέσθαι τοῖς Ἰουδαίοις ὁ Φῆλιξ κατέλιπε τὸν Παῦλον δεδεμένον. On the problem see M. Sordi 1960, p. 401 and G. Rinaldi 1991, p. 452.

[25] According to M. Sordi (M. Sordi 1995, p. 262), pieces of information can be found in the epistle to the Philippesians, which she supposed to have been written during the imprisonment of 61–63. This letter describes a local community, mild in preaching (1:12–14) and mainly composed of pagans converted to Christianity. However, the letter should be dated back to the two-year period when he was imprisoned in Caesarea (58–60) or to an unknown imprisonment during the Ephesian stay.

[26] Acts 28:17–22 passim: Ἐγένετο δὲ μετὰ ἡμέρας τρεῖς συγκαλέσασθαι αὐτὸν τοὺς ὄντας τῶν Ἰουδαίων πρώτους· . . . οἱ δὲ πρὸς αὐτὸν εἶπαν· ἡμεῖς οὔτε γράμματα περὶ σοῦ ἐδεξάμεθα ἀπὸ τῆς Ἰουδαίας οὔτε παραγενόμενός τις τῶν ἀδελφῶν ἀπήγγειλεν ἢ ἐλάλησέν τι περὶ σοῦ πονηρόν. Ἀξιοῦμεν δὲ παρὰ σοῦ ἀκοῦσαι ἃ φρονεῖς, περὶ μὲν γὰρ τῆς αἱρέσεως ταύτης γνωστὸν ἡμῖν ἐστιν ὅτι πανταχοῦ ἀντιλέγεται.

munity before the arrival of Paul and, consequently, were not involved in the ban of 49 C.E.: according to what Paul himself says, the community did not stand out for its missionary ardour and avoided the conflict with Jews, preferring to preach to pagans. She supposes that Ἰουδαῖος had a "confessional", not an ethnic value: when Aquila left Rome, he was still of Jewish faith, he was not yet a Christian.[27] In my opinion, what the passage says is more radical. The Jews knew Paul by reputation and knew that he preached a new message; however, they did not know the content, and the danger, of this αἵρησις. Apparently, before Paul, the Christian message was yet not preached within the Jewish community of Rome. But the Epistle to the Romans attests that the Christians formed an organised community well before his arrival. In contrast with what probably happened, the author of Acts stresses the unlikely ignorance of the Jews to strengthen the function of "founder" that Paul played. Probably, little importance can be attached to the statments of this passage.[28]

Let us go back to Suetonius's passage. The name Chrestus is well attested among the freedmen:[29] if we sustain the view that the events of 49 C.E. were limited to the Jewish environment, then we should suppose that an unknown Jew triggered disturbances (*adsidue tumultantes*) among the Jews of Rome, who were eventually expelled. The passage means: "Since the Jews constantly made disturbances at the instigation of Chrestus, he expelled them from Rome." The adverb *adsidue* corresponds to what we know of the community in the early Imperial period. Under Tiberius part of the community was expelled, while in 41, according to Cassius Dio, Claudius already enacted a decree that forbade the Jews to meet.

We do not know the root of this discontent: the Jews, the Romans and other ethnic groups lived together in peace; Rome did not see social crises like that of Alexandria in 38–41 C.E. It was supposed that there was a link between the events that occurred in Rome and the situation in Eretz-Israel, where violent revolts broke out in the

---

[27] M. Sordi 1995, pp. 264–269.

[28] M. Simon 1981, pp. 40–45.

[29] H. Bottermann 1996, p. 59. Among the pagan inscriptions in Latin language *Chrestianus* occurs as a *cognomen*. For instance, CIL VI, 24944: *D M | M(ontanus) T(yche) Drusi (servi) pa(rent)es | Primicinio qui vixit | ann(os) XXXXII dies VII | Faustus Antoniae Drusi (servi) ius emit | Iucundi Chrestiani oll(a?)*; CIL VI 1056. 2 l. 3: *Agid(ius) Chresti(anus)*.

period between the death of Herod and the fall of Jerusalem.[30] One of these crises occurred in 49. In 41–44 Judaea was ruled by Agrippa I, who had lived in Rome since his youth and had made bonds of friendship with Caligula and Claudius. At his untimely death Judaea was joined to the province of Syria. Probably there was bitter disillusionment among those who had believed in a rebirth of Palestine. Suetonius's passage could attest the presence of Jews in Rome, who preached the freedom of Judaea from the Roman yoke: the violence of this nationalism could depend on the activity of the Zealots.[31] Anti-Roman sentiment was probably widespread among the Christians of Jewish birth, because in the thirteenth chapter of the Epistle to the Romans Paul warns his brothers not to yield to anti-Roman feelings.

However, according to the sources, the Jews of Rome never took any sides on Palestine. It has been repeatedly remarked that there is a gap between what happened in Judaea and the reaction in Diaspora: the Diasporan communities do not eventually intervene during the Jewish war and the revolt of Bar-Kochba, while the participation of Judaea in the revolt under Trajan is questionable. It could hardly be understood why a community would have risked its own existence because Judaea was made a province, but was actually indifferent to the destruction of the Temple.

Chrestus is not mentioned anywhere else; in Slingerland's opinion, he was probably a well-known figure, or Suetonius would have stressed the obscurity of his origins, putting a *quondam* before his name.[32] But this seems to be a too subtle argumentum ex silentio.

We could suppose that Chrestus was an incorrect spelling of Christus, the Greek translation of the Hebrew Messiah. The Jews were not led by a man called Chrestus, but by someone whose name is unknown who acted as a Messiah and preached a revolt against the Romans.[33] In the same period, Judaea was often shaken by revolts in which social aspects were mixed with millennial expectations, fomented by such men as the "false prophets" of Flavius Josephus. Consequently, we should argue that the Messianic message arrived

---

[30] M. Borg 1972/73, p. 205.
[31] S. Benko 1980, p. 105. Contra H.D. Slingerland 1997, p. 230.
[32] H.D. Slingerland 1997, pp. 179–219.
[33] E. Köstermann 1967, p. 456.

in Rome carried from the motherland by prisoners or immigrants: though possible, this hypothesis cannot be verified.

Other theories have been suggested. The ban was thought to have been the answer to violent proselytism promoted by important members of the Jewish community, one of whom was the Chrestus mentioned by Suetonius. But a fracture between a part of the community open to proselytism and a part who opposed any missionary activities is not attested in this period.

Instead, if the facts occurred in 49 are related to those of 41 described by Cassius Dio,[34] it could be argued that Claudius enacted two decrees. In a first instance, he targeted Jewish proselytism through the closure of their meeting places, the synagogues. This decree, enacted in 41, triggered disturbances that had the same consequence seen at the time of Tiberius: the community, or most probably some violent elements of it, was expelled. However, this theory touches one of the most debated points of Roman Judaism, the presence of a missionary activity promoted by the Jews in the first centuries of the common era. But its existence in such an early period is at least questionable.

Most probably, the events of 49 are related to the first contacts between the rising Christian community and the Jewish community. The transcription of the name of Christ as *Chrestus* is not necessarily a mistake, and the change Orosius (or his source) made to the original passage by Suetonius should not be considered a misinterpretation. The literature of the third and fourth centuries attests that the two terms were interchangeable, a problem studied in depth by the Apologists who warned people about this dangerous alteration of the holy name of Christ.[35] Bottermann reviews all the stages:[36] probably the pagans, or the non-Jewish Christians, could not understand the meaning of Χριστός and interpreted it not as the translation of the Hebrew Messiah, but as the surname of Ἰησοῦς. Such

---

[34] According to important scholars who suppose that proselytism was already a widespread practice in first century C.E.: E. Smallwood 1981, p. 205 and H. Solin 1983, p. 687.

[35] Tert., *Ap.* 3,5: *Nunc igitur, si nominis odium est, quis nominum reatus? Quae accusatio vocabulorum, nisi si aut barbarum sonat aliqua vox nominis, aut infaustum aut maledicum aut impudicum? Christianos, vero, quantum interpretatio est, de unctione deducitur. Sed et cum perperam Chrestianus pronuntiatur a vobis (nam nec nominis certa est notitia penes vos), de suavitate vel benignitate compositum est. Oditur itaque in hominibus innocuis etiam nomen innocuum.*

[36] H. Bottermann 1996, p. 89.

a name, however, was not in use and was modified into the more common Χρηστός. This process was certainly a reformulation of meaning due to misunderstanding and ignorance, but it was also an interesting phonetic phenomenon: in the spoken language the rather incomprehensible Χριστός was almost exactly alike the adjective χρηστός and the name *Chrestus*. The sounds "e" or "η" was often written as "i" or "ι" in the Greek and in the Latin languages of the first centuries of the common era: the iotacism of the vowel η and of the diphthong ει is attested in the Jewish[37] and in the Christian inscriptions of Rome, among which we have examples of the term *christianus* written as *chrestianus*.[38] It was not a local phenomenon: the iotacism is standard in the Christian inscriptions written in Greek language found in Asia Minor, in particular in the Phrygian area.[39] Most of this group of inscriptions dates back to the third century, evidence of the persistence of this phenomenon in later period. In regard to the *nomen Christianum*, the editor of the codex Sinaiticus, dated to the sixth century, uses χρηστιανός in the three passages of the New Testament where this term occurs.[40]

This does not mean that Suetonius thought that Jesus preached in Rome and caused clashes with the local Jewish community. Suetonius shows a good knowledge of Christianity when he recalls the Neronian persecution; on this occasion he uses the version in "i" of the nomen Christianum.[41] Tacitus, who was a contemporary of Suetonius, calls the Christians *Chrestiani* but can outline briefly and correctly the life of Jesus of Nazareth and the development of the new faith, which he distinguishes from Judaism.[42]

We cannot ascribe this mistake to the source of Suetonius either, who, although aware of the content of the Christian faith, could have inexplicably decided not to correct his source. In the middle

---

[37] According to Leon, it was almost a rule of writing (H.J. Leon 1995², p. 123).
[38] For instance CIL VI 24944; VI 1056. see note 29.
[39] E.P. Gibson 1978. SEG 28 (1978), nr. 1078.
[40] Acts 11:26; 26:28; I Petr. 4:16.
[41] Suet., *Nero*, 16,2.
[42] Tac. *Ann.* 15,44: *Ergo abolendo rumori Nero subdidit reos et quaesitissimis poenis affecit, quos per flagitia invisos vulgus Chrestianos appellabat. Auctor nominis eius Christus Tiberio imperitante per procuratorem Pontium Pilatum supplicio adfectus erat; repressaque in praesens exitiabilis superstitio rursum erumpebat, non modo per Iudaeam, originem eius mali, sed per urbem etiam, quo cuncta undique atrocia aut pudenda confluunt celebranturque.*

of the first century, the Roman authorities probably had a vague knowledge of the life of Christ and could circumscribe it to Palestine. But, most probably, they knew the importance of resurrection in the new faith, and could distinguish Christianity from Judaism: the procurator Phestus, in referring to Herod Agrippas II the charges the Jews brought against Paul, says that he "had some disputes with him about religion, and about a certain Jesus, who was dead, but whom Paul asserted to be alive" (Acts 25:19).

An inscription was thought to show the picture the Romans had of the death of Christ in a moment near to the events.[43] This inscription forbids the exhumation of bodies, their removal and damage to the grave stones. It was acquired by the Frohner collection (and then by the Cabinet des Médailles of the Biblioteque Nationale of Paris) in 1898 from the antiquities market, not from the place of excavation: the tradition according to which it was found in Nazareth is considered doubtful by the editors. Palaeography suggests that it dated back to the first century; the identification of the Καῖσαρ who enacted the decree is debated too, but there is a general agreement on recognising him as a member of the Julio-Claudian family.[44] According to some scholars, the text is the Imperial answer to the

---

[43] SEG VIII (1937) nr. 13: (vac.2) Διάταγμα Καίσαρος. | Ἀρέσκει μοι τάφους τύνβους | τέ, οἵτινες εἰς θρησκείαν προγόνων | ἐποίησαν ἢ τέκνων ἢ οἰκείων, || τούτους μένειν ἀμετακεινήτους· | τὸν αἰῶνα· ἐὰν δέ τις ἐπιδίξῃ τι | νὰ ἢ καταλελύκοτα ἢ ἄλλῳ τινὶ | τρόπῳ τοὺς κεκηδευμένους | ἐξερριφφότα ἢ εἰς ἑτέρους | τόπους δόλῳ πονηρῷ με | τατεθεικότα ἐπ᾽ ἀδικίᾳ τῇ τῶν | κεκηδευμένων ἢ κατόχους ἢ λί | θους μετατεθεικότα, κατὰ τοῦ | τοιούτου κριτήριον ἐγὼ κελεύω || γενέσθαι καθάπερ περὶ θεῶν | ε[ἰ]ς τὰς τῶν ἀνθρώπων θρησ{κ} | κ[εί]ας· πολὺ γὰρ μᾶλλον δεήσει | τοὺς κεκηδευμένους τειμᾶν. | καθόλου μηδενὶ ἐξέστω μετα | | κεινῆσαι· εἰ δὲ μή, τοῦτον ἐγὼ κε | φαλῆς κατάκριτον ὀνόματι | τυμβωρυχίας θέλω γενέσθαι. The history of the studies on this inscription is found in L. Boffo 1994, pp. 321–322.

[44] Cumont, who was the first editor of the stone, thinks of Augustus (F. Cumont 1930, pp. 241–266). According to the Christian interpretation of the stone, the καῖσαρ was Tiberius who, immediately after the death of Jesus, took measures against the stealing of bodies, after Pilatus had informed him of the rumours about the resurrection and the disappearance of Jesus' body. The inscription was not from Nazareth but from Judaea, the area Pilatus controlled. On the contrary, those who support the provenience from Nazareth, date the inscription to Claudius who annexed Galilee in 44 (E. Smallwood 1981, p. 213; H.J. Leon 1995², p. 24 e M. Guarducci 1941–42, pp. 85–98). According to Marta Sordi (M. Sordi 1957, pp. 91ss.), the καῖσαρ was Nero, and the διάταγμα was part of his anti-Christian persecution. De Visscher (F. De Visscher 1963, pp. 164–165) dates the inscription to the time of Herod who was accused of having violated the graves of David and Solomon, while Brown (quoted by da L. Boffo 1994, p. 325) supposes that it was produced after the revolt of Bar Kochba.

rumour the Jews spread, according to which the disciples of Jesus had profaned his grave and had hidden the body in a secret place to support a false resurrection.[45] If the stone comes from Galilee, the διάταγμα could be referred to Claudius, because Galilee was annexed to the province of Judaea after the death of Agrippa I in 44 C.E.[46] Consequently, we have evidence of the persistence of anti-Christians rumours years after the crucifixion, but we also have proof of the good level of knowledge the Romans had on the main point that divided the Jews and the Christians. Cadbury suggests a link between the διάταγμα and the events in Rome: Claudius, after several clashes between the two communities, could have enacted a decree forbidding Christianism both in Rome and in its original areas.[47]

The Christian interpretation of this stone is not based on positive evidence. No elements of the text can be easily ascribed to a Christian environment, and its finding in Nazareth is questionable. The inscription is more "Jewish" than "Christian". The Roman funerary laws do not provide capital punishment for those who violate a grave, but only the payment of a fine: Carcopino supposed that this inscription was the Imperial answer to a letter the governor of Judaea sent, asking help for an extraordinary event, such as the riots that broke out in Jerusalem in 8 A.D., during which the Samaritans scattered the bones of the dead on the Temple area.[48] According to other scholars, this inscription shows the adaptation of Roman law to the local custom, well attested in provincial contexts: the Jewish habit of the double sepulture (largely attested both in Jerusalem and in the later necropolis of Beth She'arim) is not forbidden, but the

---

[45] See the foregoing note: M. Sordi, E. Smallwood, H. Leon, M. Guarducci, G. De Sanctis (G. De Sanctis 1929–1931, pp. 13–17).

[46] With Agrippa's untimely death in 44 C.E. most of these territories entered into the Roman province of Judaea. After the death of Claudius, Agrippa II, who had received from the Emperor the kingdom of Chalkis in 52 C.E., obtains Tiberias, Tarichaeae, Julias and 14 villages around these towns, and probably some territories in Southern Peraea, cut off from the rest of his reign. After the fall of Jerusalem he regained the territories he had lost during the Jewish war. His reign was incorporated in the province of Syria at his death, whose date is debated. S. Freyne 1980, pp. 68–91.

[47] H. J. Cadbury 1955, p. 117.

[48] Fl. Jos., *Ant.* XVIII, 29–30. J. Carcopino 1931, pp. 77–92.

Romans prevented its uncontrolled spreading and remarked the importance of the ritual rules on the transportation of the bones.[49]

The point that divided the Jews and the Christians was the preaching of the life, death and resurrection of Christ, a name that the Roman police certainly heard from both the parties. We may suppose that "impulsore Chresto" referred to the issue that divided the orthodox Jews and the Christian Jews, so to speak, the interpretation of Jesus' mission. As we have already seen, in that period Chrestus could stand for Christus, both in a Jewish and in a Christian context. Consequently, we could argue that in Rome there were harsh disturbances between the Jews and the Christians, as happened in Corinth and Ephesus during the stay of Paul. But in Rome the relations between Romans and Jews, still on bad terms, degenerated, and after an enquiry that Suetonius echoes, it was decided that part of the Jewish community who lived in town had to move away. In the 40s, the Romans could hardly distinguish Christianity from Judaism: it is possible that among these Jews there were also some Christians.

III

The information given by Acts and by Suetonius could refer to the same event: the same cannot be said of the passage by Cassius Dio.[50] According to this evidence, Claudius was prevented from expelling the whole community, which was too numerous to be banned, and decided to forbid them to gather. The passage cannot be easily dated. According to Suetonius and Acts, the ban should date back to 49, while, according to Cassius Dio, the ban was issued at the beginning of the reign of Claudius, and was one of the acts Claudius issued in his first year of government, i.e. 41 C.E.

The historian does not attach great importance to the event: as in Suetonius, the ban is one of Claudius's interventions to control

---

[49] Among others Luzzatto (G.I. Luzzatto 1942, p. 232) and Boffo (L. Boffo 1994, pp. 330–332).
[50] Cass. Dio, *Hist. Rom.*, LX,6,6: Τούς τε Ἰουδαίους πλεονάσαντας αὖθις, ὥστε χαλεπῶς ἂν ἄνευ ταραχῆς ὑπὸ τοῦ ὄχλου σφῶν τῆς πόλεως εἰρχθῆναι, οὐκ ἐξήλασε μέν, τῷ δὲ δὴ πατρίῳ βίῳ χρωμένους ἐκέλευσε μὴ συναθροίζεσθαι.

the associations and their meeting places. After having told the news about the Jews, Dio reminds us that Claudius τάς τε ἑταιρείας ἐπαναχθείσας ὑπὸ τοῦ Γαΐου διέλυσε, and closed the *tabernae* to curb episodes of drunkenness and disorder. As in the past, the places where people could meet were negatively seen by government, probably because they were considered a dangerous point of gathering of political dissent. The synagogues are superficially compared to collegia. The aim of Claudius was not to stop the activities of the collegia but to prevent people from gathering. The closure of the synagogues actually meant that the Jews were forbidden to celebrate their rites. The act was harsh, but, according to Cassius Dio, was not addressed solely to the Jews.

The act was issued with a double purpose: on the one hand, Claudius wanted to control the mass living in Rome (not only the Jews),[51] on the other hand, he meant to prevent the meeting of political groups, even in unconventional places such as the *tabernae*. In the words of Cassius Dio, Claudius did not have an anti-Jewish policy: although he made the life of the Roman community difficult, he stressed that the Jews could continue using the ancestral way of life (τῷ δὲ δὴ πατρίῳ βίῳ χρωμένους). The problem of the government was the number of Jews who lived in Rome. But apart from the possible return of members expelled under Tiberius, we are not informed of mass-arrival of Jews in the middle of the first century. Rome was a multiethnic city, where groups coming from all the provinces lived together in harmony and (usually) did not clash with the administration of the town. Cassius Dio does not mention the reason of the friction between the authorities and the Roman Jewry; but if the act aimed at breaking up the community, the problem was probably of public order. Proselytism has been suggested again. This activity had to be organised and probably emerged in a city context. To prevent proselytism, Claudius should have acted against those who organised this activity and against their meeting places: forbidding the cult was a side effect. This situation may correspond to what Cassius Dio says. Unfortunately, as we have already said, proselytism could hardly be dated back to the first century.

---

[51] Meaningful is the use of ὄχλος and of πλῆθος to stress the presence of high number of people.

As for Suetonius' passage, it has been thought that riots burst out within the community because of the preaching of Christians: according to Acts, the place dedicated to teaching was usually the synagogue. The authorities could have intervened in the violent reaction of the Jews with the closure of the synagogues, the place where the disorders had broken out. However, Dio should have stressed the presence of divisions within the community and not the high number of Jews in Rome, which from this point of view is a secondary problem. Moreover, the presence of Christians in Rome in the early 40s is questionable: in this period the organization of the Church was still growing up in the Middle-East.

The event that occurred in Rome could be linked to the well-known judgement of the Jews as "common plague for the whole world" that closed Claudius' epistle to the Alexadrians.[52] As Mélèze-Modrzejewski shows, the Emperor cannot be accused of anti-Judaism.[53] The epistle, that the *praefectus Aegypti L. Aemilius Rectus* published on 10 November 41, in the section regarding the Jews, is the conclusive act of a trial begun on the eve of the Calends of May (the *Acta* use the Egyptian date of 5 Pachon), in which a Graeco-Alexandrinian

---

[52] *CPJ*, sez. VIII, n° 153: 73 Τῆς δὲ πρὸς Ἰουδαίους ταραχῆς καὶ στάσεως, μᾶλλον δ᾽ εἰ χρὴ τὸ ἀληθὲς 74 εἰπεῖν τοῦ πολέμου, πότεροι μὲν αἴτιοι κατέστησαν, καίπερ 75 ἐξ ἀντικαταστάσεως πολλὰ τῶν ἡμετέρων πρεσβέων, 76 φιλοτειμηθέντων καὶ μάλιστα Διονυσίου τοῦ Θέων[ο]ς ὅμως 77 οὐκ ἐβουλήθην ἀκριβῶς ἐξελένξαι, ταμιευόμενος ἐμαυτῶι 78 κατὰ τῶν πάλειν ἀρξαμένων ὀργὴν ἀμεταμέλητον· 79 ἁπλῶς δὲ προσαγορεύωι ὅτι ἂν μὴ καταπαύσηται τὴν ὀλέ—80 θριον ὀργὴν ταύτην κατ᾽ ἀλλήλων αὐθάδιον ἐγβιασθήσομαι 81 δῖξαι ὗόν ἐστιν ἡγεμὼν φιλάνθρωπος εἰς ὀργὴν δικαίαν μεταβεβλη— 82 μένος. Διόπερ ἔτι καὶ νῦν διαμαρτύρομε εἵνα Ἀλεξανδρεῖς μὲν 83 πραέως καὶ φιλανθρόπως προσφέροντε Ἰουδαίο<ι>ς τοῖς 84 τὴν αὐτὴν πόλειν ἐκ πολλῶν χρόνων οἰκοῦσει (*col.* 5) 85 καὶ μηδὲν τῶν πρὸς θρησκείαν αὐτοῖς νενομισμένων 86 τοῦ θεοῦ λοιμένωνται ἀλλὰ ἐῶσιν αὐτοὺς τοῖς ἔθεσιν 87 χρῆσθαι ὗς καὶ ἐπὶ τοῦ θεοῦ Σεβαστοῦ, ἅπερ καὶ ἐγὼι 88 διακούσας ἀμφοτέρων ἐβεβαίωσα· καὶ Ἰουδέοις δὲ 89 ἄντικρυς κελεύωι μηδὲν τῶν πρὸς πλήωι ὧν πρότερον 90 ἔσχον περιεργάζεσθαι μηδὲ ὥσπερ ἐν δυσεὶ πόλεσειν κα—91 τοικοῦντας δύο πρεσβείας ἐκπέμπειν τοῦ λοιποῦ, 92 ὦ μὴ πρότερόν ποτε ἐπράκθη, μηδὲ ἐπισπαίειν 93 γυμνασιαρχικοῖς ἢ κοσμητικοῖς ἀγῶσει, 94 καρπουμένους μὲν τὰ οἰκῖα ἀπολα<ύ>οντας δὲ 95 ἐν ἀλλοτρίᾳ πόλει περιουσίας ἀπθόνων ἀγαθῶν, 96 μηδὲ ἐπάγεσθαι ἢ προσείεσθαι ἀπὸ Συρίας ἢ Αἰγύπ<τ>ου 97 καταπλέοντας Ἰουδαίους, ἐξ οὗ μείζονας ὑπονοίας 98 ἀνανκασθήσομε λαμβάνειν. εἰ δὲ μή, πάντα 99 τρόπον αὐτοὺς ἐπεξελεύσομαι καθάπερ κοινήν 100 τεινα τῆς οἰκουμένης νόσον ἐξεγείροντας. Ἐὰν 101 τούτων ἀποστάντες ἀμφότεροι μετὰ πραότητος 102 καὶ φιλανθροπείας τῆς πρὸς ἀλλήλους ζῆν ἐθελήσητε, 103 καὶ ἐγὼι πρόνοιαν τῆς πόλεως ποήσομαι τὴν ἀνατάτωι 104 καθάπερ ἐκ προγόνων οἰκίας ὑμῖν ὑπαρχούσης. The first editor was Bell (H.I. Bell 1924). The text is integrally published also in *Select Papyri*, II n° 212, Loeb Classical Library 1934 and in M.P. Charlesworth 1939, pp. 3–5.

[53] J. Mélèze – Mordzejewski 1991, pp. 141–150.

delegation composed of the gymnasiarch Isidorus and the chanchellor Lampo accused Agrippa I, a close friend both of Caligula and of Claudius, who appointed him king of Judaea in 41.[54] The trial can be reconstructed thanks to the *Acta Isidori*, transcribed in three papyri written between the end of the second and the beginning of the third century.[55] Agrippa is charged with menacing the pax Romana with a policy of separatism and independence that is considered typical of the Jews. Isidorus, who was aware of the bonds of friendship between Claudius and Agrippa, complains about the negligence of the government in repressing the Jews and insinuates the complicity of the Emperor in the alleged conspiracy against the Jews, with the aim of forcing Claudius to condemn his friend, so that he would not seem impartial. The plan is unsuccessful: Isidorus is charged with crimen calumniae, connected with the crimen maiestatis: Isidorus had actually accused the Emperor of managing the State badly. The two prosecutors are sentenced to death and undergo the damnatio memoriae: in the prologue to the Epistle, their names are not mentioned within the Alexandrian delegation that reached Rome to pay tribute to the new Emperor in April 41. According to the Acta, on this occasion Claudius's policy was certainly not anti-Jewish. He was aware that the trial was the result of tensions between two ethnic groups, a tension so strong that it is described as a πόλεμος. At the end of the epistle, he ordered the Greeks to respect Jewish rights; but the Jews had to renounce the request for new privileges—such as taking part in the games—and were prevented from sending separate embassies and from encouraging free immigration from Eretz-

---

[54] Musurillo (H. Musurillo 1979, pp. 123–124), in summerazing the comments of the editors, remarks that the dating of the papyri depends on the identification of Agrippa. If it was Agrippa I (as suggested by T. Reinach 1924, pp. 113–144) the trial occurred in 41, when the king was in Rome for the death of Caligula and the appointment of Claudius. On the contrary, if it was Agrippa II (as suggested U. Wilken 1909, pp. 783–839), the trial occurred in 52–53, the period that he spent in Rome. Musurillo supports the second hypothesis and unties the trial of Isidorus from the epistle to the Alexandrinians.

[55] Two fragments (BGU 511 e P. Cairo Inv. 10448) of unknown provenance, but belonging to the same scroll, make up the first papyrus. Musurillo (H. Musurillo 1979, p. 117) dates them to the late second century. Bell (Archiv X (1932), pp. 5–16) dates the second papyrus (P. Lond. Inv. 2785) to the beginning of the third century. The recto of the third papyrus is dated to the end of the second or the beginning of the third century, while the verso is dated to a previous period (H. Musurillo 1979, p. 118).

Israel and Syria. Conversely, they would be condemned because "fomenters of the common plague of the ancient world". This sentence, used in the past to show the anti-Jewish attitude of Claudius, is a reference to the trial of Isidorus, whose name is not mentioned because condemned to the damnatio memoriae, or, to say it better, it is almost a quotation of the charge Isidorus moved against the Agrippa and, by extension, against the Jews. In my opinion, there is no relation between the trial and the events we are studying, except for the place where both of them occurred: Rome. It could be argued that the Jews, worried about the dangerous consequences the trial could have had, caused disorders to which Claudius answered with the act forbidding assemblies.[56] But no evidence supports this hypothesis.

According to Marta Sordi, the migratory phenomenon mentioned in the Epistle should have involved not only Egypt, but also Rome, causing two distinct interventions, the one mentioned by Cassius Dio, the other exposed in the Epistle.[57] However, the two cities had a different social fabric. According to Philo, the Jews lived in two of the five areas that formed Alexandria:[58] their presence was evident. Since the Hellenistic period, the proximity to Judaea and the richness of the Egyptian communities favoured the immigration.[59] Possibly in the second half of second century B.C., the community was organised into a πολίτευμα, and could live according to their πατρίοις νόμοις.[60] Claudius realistically suggested that this community should

---

[56] As happened during the trial against Flaccus in 59 B.C. However, the action against Agrippa was brought into the Imperial palace, without that popular participation that Cicero censured.

[57] M. Sordi 1995, pp. 265–269.

[58] Phil., *In Flaccum*, 55: πέντε μοῖραι τῆς πόλεώς εἰσιν, ἐπώνυμοι τῶν πρώτων στοιχείων τῆς ἐγγραμμάτου φωνῆς· τούτων δύο Ἰουδαικαὶ λέγονται διὰ τὸ πλείστους Ἰουδαίους ἐν ταύταις κατοικεῖν· οἰκοῦσι δὲ καὶ ἐν ταῖς ἄλλαις οὐκ ὀλίγοι σποράδες. In the Diadoches period the Jews lived near the harbour; the permanent occupation of the other two areas was the result of the demographical increase. Flav. Jos., *B.J.* II, 488: διέμενεν δ' αὐτοῖς ἡ τιμὴ καὶ παρὰ τῶν διαδόχων, οἳ καὶ τόπον ἴδιον αὐτοῖς ἀφώρισαν, ὅπως καθαρωτέραν ἔχοιεν τὴν δίαιταν, ἧττον ἐπιμισγομένων τῶν ἀλλοφύλων. Flav. Jos., *C. Ap.* II, 33: ἐλθόντες ἀπὸ Συρίας ᾤκησαν πρὸς ἀλίμενον θάλατταν γειτνιάσαντες ταῖς τῶν κυμάτων ἐκβολαῖς. Flav. Jos., *C. Ap.* II, 36: οὐκ οἶδα δὲ τί ποτ' ἂν ἔλεγεν Ἀπίων, εἰ πρὸς τῇ νεκροπόλει κατῴκουν καὶ μὴ πρὸς τοῖς βασιλικοῖς ἦσαν ἱδρυμένοι.

[59] On the Jews in Egypt see J. Mélèze-Modrzejewski 1991, J. Mélèze-Modrzejewski 2003 a, J. Barclay 1996, pp. 50–79, the preface of W. Horbury – D. Noy, *Jewish Inscriptions of Greco-Roman Egypt*, Cambridge: Cambridge University Press 1992.

[60] Neither Flavius Josephus nor Philo mention the presence of a Jewish πολίτευμα

not be increased with arrivals from Eretz-Israel to avoid tensions
with the Greeks, who felt their existence menaced by the growing
number of Jews who lived in town. On the contrary, the social structure of Rome was not shaped in two contrasting ethnic groups, but
was characterized by people coming from all over the *oikumene* and
living together, usually in peace.[61] Among these, the Jews were not
prevalent.[62] According to Philo, in this period, the community increased
because of the arrival of war prisoners that remained in town after
being freed.[63] The increase was limited and controlled by the authorities: it could not cause distress to the government.

The increase Cassio Dio mentions is hardly a complaint for their
overwhelming number, it possibly means that the Jews were too
numerous to be expelled.

IV

There are important differences in the accounts of the events happened in Rome under Claudius. On the one hand, Cassius Dio mentions a decree forbidding the assemblies and dates it to 41; on the
other hand, Suetonius, Orosius and Acts speak of a ban of expul-

---

at Alexandria in Hellenistic times. The pubblication of P.Pol.Jud.—a corpus of
papyri from Herackleopolis dated to 144/3–133/2—re-opened the debate on this
organization, its origins and legal status. On this problem see: S. Honigman 2002,
S. Honigman 2003, *Intr. to* P.Pol.Jud., pp. 4–9; on the status questionis before the
publication of P.Pol.Jud. see G. Luederitz 1989.

[61] D. Noy 2000.

[62] The number of Jews who lived in Rome cannot be easily estimated. According
to Flavius Josephus (*B.J.* II, 80; *Ant.* XVII, 300), in 4 B.C. 8,000 Jews attended the
arrival of a Judean delegation asking the deposition of Archelaos, Herod's son.
Tacitus (*Ann.* II, 85,4) affirms that 4,000 Jews *libertini generis* were sent to Sardinia,
as we have already seen. On this basis, it has been suggested that 20,000/60,000
Jews lived in Rome. The range depends on the death-rate the authors suppose.
Vogelstein – Rieger (H. Vogelstein – P. Rieger 1986, I, p. 38), Solin (H. Solin
1983, pp. 698–701) and Mazzoleni (D. Mazzoleni 1976, p. 289) support a maximum of 40,000 Jews, while Juster (J. Juster 1914, I, p. 9), Leon (H.J. Leon 1995²,
p. 135), Smallwood (E. Smallwood 1981, p. 169) and Grayzel (S. Grayzel 1947,
p. 140) prefer a number of 50,000 Jews. According to these scholars, the Jewish
population was between two per cent and eight per cent of the overall population
of Rome (estimated as one million of inhabitants in the first century).

[63] Phil., *Leg. ad Gaium*, 155: τὴν πέραν τοῦ Τιβέρεως ποταμοῦ μεγάλην τῆς Ῥώμης
ἀποτομὴν [ἣν] οὐκ ἠγνόει κατεχομένην καὶ οἰκουμένην πρὸς Ἰουδαίων. Ῥωμαῖοι δὲ
ἦσαν οἱ πλείους ἀπελευθερωθέντες· αἰχμάλωτοι γὰρ ἀχθέντες εἰς Ἰταλίαν ὑπὸ τῶν
κτησαμένων ἠλευθερώθησαν, οὐδὲν τῶν πατρίων παραχαράξαι βιασθέντες.

sion and place it in 49. In contrast with the other historians, Cassius claims that in 41 the community was too numerous to be expelled: we do not know what could have changed in the following eight years to make this hypothesis reliable.

To reconcile all the evidence,[64] some scholars have tried to place the two events in the same year. Stern stresses that Tacitus in the 12th book of the Annales does not report the ban of the year 49, a meaningful silence from one of the few authors mentioning the expulsion of the 19 c.e. A large lacuna covers the VII–X books and the first chapters of the XI book, where the history of Rome from 37 to 47 c.e. is recorded. Consequently, it cannot be excluded that Tacitus mentioned the ban precisely in that place. However, this argument can be rejected: Tacitus may have deliberately failed to report the ban if it involved a low number of people,[65] as he probably did. Then, Stern supposes that the only act Claudius enacted was to forbid the assemblies: he had thought to expel the Jews but had rejected the proposal after considering their number. In the meantime, the rumour of the ban had spread among the community, triggering voluntary departures, as the experience of Aquila and Priscilla shows.[66]

According to Schürer, in the first instance, Claudius decided to expel the Jews, as Tiberius had previously done, but changed his mind and forbade the assemblies for fear of disorders. This too was a heavy punishment for the Jews, many of whom decided to leave Rome. Some remained in Latium (as the scholium to Juvenal attests), some went farther (as the passage of Acts shows). The event cannot be placed in 41, as Cassius Dio suggests, because in that year Claudius probably reaffirmed the privileges of the Jews.[67] No details support the traditional dating of the passage to 41: the act forbidding assemblies is mentioned as one of Claudius' positive interventions during

---

[64] A further evidence in the *Scolia ad Iuvenalem*, edited in the fifth century: *Dignus Aricinus qui mendicaret ad axes: Qui ad portam Aricinam sive ad clivum mendicaret inter Iudaeos, qui ad Ariciam transierant ex urbe missi.* The passage attests the presence in Aricia of Jews coming from Rome. It can be dated both to the reign of Tiberius (A. Momigliano 1934, p. 30, p. 96) and of Claudius (E. Schürer 1973–1986, III, p. 63 e J. Juster 1914, I, p. 180 nr. 9).

[65] Differently from the ban of 19, that involved also the believers of Isis.

[66] M. Stern 1974–1980 II, p. 116.

[67] Flav. Jos., *Ant.* XIV, 287–292.

his reign, it is not inserted within a chronological sequence. On the contrary, Suetonius, Acts and Orosius clearly attest an intervention in 49. Tacitus's silence may not be a problem: while a ban was an important, exceptional act, a decree forbidding assemblies was relatively frequent in Rome, and was possibly not worth mentioning.[68] Schürer is ambiguous in dealing with Orosius: he considers his statement untrustworthy but uses him for the dating of the event. Apart from this, both Stern and Schürer interpret the flight of Aquila and Priscilla as a voluntary departure, while according to Acts they were compelled to leave Rome.

In my opinion it is not necessary to read too much into the passages to harmonize their meaning: the sources are not in contradiction because they report two distinct events that happened at the distance of eight years. On the one hand, there is a decree forbidding assemblies enacted in 41 and involving all the Jews living in Rome; on the other hand, there is a ban of expulsion provided in 49 against some dangerous members of the community. They were two different interventions whose causes were probably different too.

This hypothesis is apparently inconsistent with the statement that the community was too numerous to be expelled. This is actually a valuable piece of information. According to Philo, the community was numerous and lived in the Transtiberim, but was also attested in other areas.[69] Most of the Jews were war prisoners who had been freed after some years: consequently, we may suppose that they were liberti or citizens. After twenty years of good relationships, in 41 something happens between the community and the authorities: according to Cassius Dio, Claudius wants to punish the whole community and thinks about an expulsion. As the previous ban of 19 had shown, the Jewish group could not be entirely expelled not because they were too numerous (as Cassius supposes), but because they were protected by their status. In 41 Claudius' attention had turned to the whole community not to a few of its members.

The Jews could not be banned, but their activities were controlled and paralysed. In 41 both the ἑταιρίαι and the synagogues were blocked. We do not know why the Emperor intervened, but his aim

---

[68] E. Schürer 1973–1986, III, pp. 77–79.
[69] Phil., *Leg. ad Gaium*, 155.

was to dismember the links within the community. Most probably it was a problem of public order.

In 49 the situation changed. The beginning of the Christian preaching and the reaction of the Jews caused tension with the authorities. On this occurrence, the ban of expulsion could be provided not against the whole community but against a few dangerous members after a regular trial. According to Acts, Aquila and Priscilla were compelled to leave Rome because of the ban Claudius had enacted.

VESPASIAN

With the fall of Jerusalem and the destruction of the Temple, the religious, political and moral core of Judaism disappeared. We do not know how the Jewish community of Rome reacted both to the war and to the defeat: the sources do not attest aid sent to Eretz-Israel or disturbances in Rome. According to Flavius Josephus, the community was apparently indifferent to the grand triumph that Vespasian and Titus celebrated in the spring of 71. The ancient historians do not stress this astonishing position: they were interested in what happened in Judaea, while events that occurred in Diaspora were reported only if they had consequences on the motherland. In the Bellum Iudaicum, Josephus mentions revolts only in the final phases of the war, when the fate of Judaea had been decided. According to the debated chronology of the 7th book, the Egyptian revolt broke out after (or more probably during) the siege of Masada, so to speak, after the destruction of Jerusalem and the fall of the fortresses of Herodeion, Machairous and Iardan.[1] The community of Cyrene revolted even later.[2] Tacitus speaks of the war in the well-known passages of the 5th book of the Historiae. His account, interrupted by the so called archaeologia Iudaica in which he describes the habits, the origin and the history of the Jews, is again suspended with the beginning of the siege of Jerusalem and the organization of the Roman camp. It is April 70. In chapter V, 13 he resumes the account of the war against the Bataves, interrupted in IV, 79. From chapter V, 26 onwards, the text was lost: we do not know how he described the fall of Jerusalem and the end of the war. Flavius Josephus and Tacitus do not speak of political repercussions in the relationship between the Romans and the Jews of Diaspora. Apparently the Romans preserved the rights of the Diasporan communities, probably because they kept a neutral position during the war. According to Josephus, immediately after the end of the war, Antioch tried to expel the Jewish community or to suppress their

---

[1] *BJ* VII, 407.
[2] *BJ* VII, 437.

rights, which had been granted since the Seleucids.[3] Titus, who was
in Syria at the time,[4] goes to Antioch, grants audience to the two
factions, and confirms the Jewish rights.[5] In those years the Jewish
world was probably divided into two parties, one opposing Rome—
the position that caused the war—, the other trying to reach a compromise with Rome, a position that prevailed in Diaspora.

One of the most important consequences of the war was the dispersion of thousands of war prisoners all over the Empire.

I

As Jonathan Price remarks,[6] the estimates of groups or of popula-
tions mentioned not only in Flavius Josephus but in all ancient literature is usually untrustworthy. Clerical errors in the handwritten
tradition, the absence of scientific criteria, sometimes the bad faith
of the author himself, often cause mistaken estimates. To evaluate
the demographic impact of the fall of Jerusalem on the Jewish society both of Eretz-Israel and of the Diaspora, we would need to know
how many people lived in the city during the siege and how many
prisoners Rome captured. Flavius Josephus felt the importance of
this problem and justified the high number of dead and prisoners
recalling that the siege had begun during Passover of 70, when
Jerusalem overflowed with pilgrims coming from all over Judaea:[7]
"The whole nation had been shut up by fate as in a prison, and
the city when war encompassed it was packed with inhabitants".[8]

---

[3] *BJ* VII, 41–111.

[4] *BJ* VII, 39–40. Titus was in Berytus and celebrated games (with Jewish prisoners) for his father's birthday (17th November). In VII, 41 it is said: γένεσθαι δὲ
συνέβη περὶ τὸν καιρὸν τοῦτον . . . the temporal connection is unclear also because
the account of the difficulties the Antiochian community had is interrupted in VII,
42. In VII, 96 Flavius Josephus remarks that Titus, after a long stay in Berytus
(χρόνον μὲν τινα διέτριβεν ἐν Βηρυτῷ), embarked on the trip to Zeugma on the
Euphrates where Vologesis wanted to pay tribute to him (according to VII, 105).
During this trip, probably late in the winter, he visited some Syrian towns, celebrated grand games (using Jewish prisoners again) and stopped in Antioch to set-
tle the question (VII 105: οὐδὲ ὑπέμεινεν ἐν Ἀντιοχείᾳ Τίτος).

[5] *BJ* VII, 111: οὐ μὴν οὐδὲ τοῦτο Τίτος ἐπένευσεν αὐτοῖς, ἀλλ᾽ ἐάσας πάντα κατὰ
χώραν τοῖς ἐπ᾽ Ἀντιοχείας Ἰουδαίοις ὡς πρότερον εἶχον εἰς Αἴγυπτον ἀπηλλάττετο.

[6] J. Price 1992, p. 205.

[7] *BJ* VI, 421: ἀπὸ γὰρ τῆς χώρας ὅλης ἐπὶ τὴν τῶν ἀζύμων ἑορτὴν συνεληλυθότες
ἐξαπίνης τῷ πολέμῳ περιεσχέθησαν . . .

[8] *BJ* VI, 428: εἰς εἱρκτὴν ὑπὸ τῆς εἱμαρμένης πᾶν συνεκλείσθη τὸ ἔθνος, καὶ ναστὴν
ὁ πόλεμος τὴν πόλιν ἀνδρῶν ἐκυκλώσατο.

He remarks that the figure of 2,700,000 Jews that he proposes were present in Jerusalem on that occasion is confirmed by an official enquiry the governor of Syria Cestius made in 63 and sent to Nero to show him the importance of the city.[9] The calculus is based on the number of sacrifices offered in the Temple during Pesach: the priests counted 255,600 sacrifices. Considering an average of ten table-companions per sacrifice, the people in charge calculated about 2,700,000 Jews who were present at that time in Jerusalem. The calculus is rounded up because of the occasional presence of more than ten table-companions. The figure recalls the 3,000,000 inhabitants mentioned in BJ II, 280,[10] but it is unanimously rejected by scholarship. However, no agreement has been reached as to how many people lived in the city in peacetime. Jeremias, on the basis of the extension and the demographic density of the city suggests a figure of 25,000/30,000 inhabitants in peacetime, which increased (on traditional data) to 100,000 during the festivals.[11] On the same basis, Michel and Baurnfield calculate 70,000/80,000 Jews living in the city,[12] 100,000/150,000 according to Avi-Yonah.[13] Armstrong agrees with this last estimate and, with Sanders,[14] assumes that in the Herodian period an average of 300,000/500,000 pilgrims visited the Temple each year.[15] Garner, on the basis of excavation data, supposes that in 4 B.C., the year when Herod died, 40,000 Jews lived in Jerusalem.[16] As Price stresses, this kind of study based on archaeological data presents an additional problem: Jerusalem was not

---

[9] *BJ* VI, 422–427. C. Cestius Gallo, consul in 42 C.E., was appointed governor of Syria in 63 but was actually subordinated to Corbulo who had taken charge of the operations against the Parthians (Tac. *Ann.* XV 25:3: *Syriaeque exsecutio C. Cestio, copiae militares Corbuloni permissae; et quinta decuma legio ducente Mario Celso e Pannonia adiecta est.*). When the war was over, Cestius resumed the military offices of a *legatus Augusti pro pretore.*

[10] *BJ* II, 280: μέχρι μὲν οὖν ἐν Συρίᾳ Κέστιος Γάλλος ἦν διέπων τὴν ἐπαρχίαν, οὐδὲ πρεσβεύσασθαί τις πρὸς αὐτὸν ἐτόλμησαν κατὰ τοῦ Φλώρου· παραγενόμενον δὲ εἰς Ἱεροσόλυμα τῆς τῶν ἀζύμων ἑορτῆς ἐνεστώσης περιστὰς ὁ δῆμος, οὐκ ἐλάττους τριακοσίων μυριάδων, ἱκέτευον ἐλεῆσαι τὰς τοῦ ἔθνους συμφορὰς καὶ τὸν λυμεῶνα τῆς χώρας Φλῶρον ἐκεκράγεσαν.

[11] J. Jeremias 1969, pp. 77–84.

[12] O. Michel – O. Baurnfield, Flavius Josephus, *De Bello Judaico*, Bad Homburg-Munich 1959–1969, II.2, 207–208.

[13] M. Avi-Yonah 1968, pp. 98–125.

[14] E.P. Sanders 1992, p. 128.

[15] K. Armstrong 1996, p. 126; p. 133.

[16] G. Garner 1986, pp. 39–48.

homogeneously inhabited, and the best known area—the upper city—had a low demographic density.[17]

With the advance of the Roman armies, waves of refugees reached Jerusalem and joined the inhabitants and the pilgrims. At the beginning of 67 Samaria (BJ III, 307–309; III, 414; IV, 130), Galilee and the Golan hills (BJ IV, 83–120) had already been conquered and the ways to the north-western coasts of Judaea had been obstructed. In the first months of 68, Vespasian occupied the Peraea and the Decapolis (BJ IV, 416), blocking all communications with the Transjordan area and the Jordan Valley where he camped the tenth legion (BJ IV, 449–450, 486). Cerealius, moving from south-west, conquered the western hills of Idumaea and Judaea (BJ IV, 443) and camped the fifth legion in Adida.

Since the end of 68—before the death of Nero—Jerusalem could control only a narrow line of hills in the north, while in the east and in the south it had access to the desert around the Dead Sea, to the fortress of Masada that defended the fertile area around Engaddai (BJ IV, 400), and to the central part of Idumaea, through which there was still a free way to the Negev and to Arabia. The plan of Vespasian was successful. Jerusalem controlled only deserted areas, which in the long run caused heavy problems in provisioning. Masses of people escaping from the war flocked into the city, the only free, defensible area of Judaea that could still be reached.[18] According to Flavius Josephus, 2,000 inhabitants of Tiberias fled to Jerusalem,[19] as did all the inhabitants of some Peraean villages,[20] and an indefinite number of people from a village on Mount Tabor[21]

---

[17] J. Price 1992, p. 209.

[18] *BJ* IV, 89: οὐ γὰρ ὀλίγον αὐτῷ πόνον ἑώρα περὶ τοῖς Ἱεροσολύμοις λειπόμενον, ἅτε δὴ βασιλείου μὲν οὔσης τῆς πόλεως καὶ προανεχούσης ὅλου τοῦ ἔθνους, συρρεόντων δὲ εἰς αὐτὴν τῶν ἐκ τοῦ πολέμου διαδιδρασκόντων. Tac. *Hist.* 5.12.4: *Atque per avaritiam Claudianorum temporum empto iure muniendi struxere muros in pace tamquam ad bellum, magna conluvie et ceterarum urbium clade aucti; nam perniciosissimus quisque illuc perfugerat eoque seditiosius agebant.*

[19] *Vita* 354: τί δ᾽; οὐχὶ καὶ κατὰ τὴν τῶν Ἱεροσολυμιτῶν πολιορκίαν δισχίλιοι Τιβεριέων ἐξητάσθησαν, οἱ μὲν πεπτωκότες οἱ δὲ ληφθέντες αἰχμάλωτοι;

[20] *BJ* VI, 201: γυνή τις τῶν ὑπὲρ τὸν Ἰορδάνην κατοικούντων, Μαρία τοὔνομα . . . διὰ γένος καὶ πλοῦτον ἐπίσημος, μετὰ τοῦ λοιποῦ πλήθους εἰς τὰ Ἱεροσόλυμα καταφυγοῦσα συνεπολιορκεῖτο.

[21] *BJ* IV, 61: καὶ οἱ μὲν τὸ Ἰταβύριον καταλιπόντες ἐπὶ Ἱεροσολύμων ἔφευγον, οἱ δ᾽ ἐπιχώριοι πίστεις λαβόντες, ἐπιλελοίπει δ᾽ αὐτοὺς ὕδωρ, τό τε ὄρος καὶ σφᾶς αὐτοὺς Πλακίδῳ παρέδοσαν. Mount Tabor is in Southern Galilee.

and from Gamala[22] before the fall of these centres. Probably these are only the most representative cases: smaller groups could have left their houses and reached Jerusalem without being recorded. The more it became evident that the last action for freedom was to be fought around the Temple, the more frequent was the arrival of people who wanted to take part in the defence of the city and reached Jerusalem together with their families, as occurred with the refugees from Gischala (BJ IV, 106–107). Among these there were many allies of revolutionary leaders, as Jesus the Galilean, who reached Jerusalem in 67, and John of Gischala who took with him volunteers from Tyre and Galilee and called an Idumean army (Flavius Josephus speaks of 20,000 men)[23] during the agitated overthrow of Ananos' government in winter 67–68. Not all the soldiers came from Eretz-Israel: Cassius Dio mentions the presence of Babylonian Jews,[24] Josephus that of τὰ πέριξ ἔθνα συννοσοῦντα (BJ III,3). We can agree with Price, who supposes that the volunteers coming from non-combatant areas certainly had deep ideals, but also considerable goods, so that they could earn their living for a long period away from home.[25]

In estimating how many people underwent the siege another element should be taken into consideration: the defections. The number of people that tried to quit the city increased enormously in the months before the fall: subterranean passages dug by deserters were found out and walled up.[26]

According to Flavius Josephus, during the war 97,000 Jews were captured, while 1,100,000 died in the siege.[27] It is not clear on what

---

[22] *BJ* IV, 62: τῶν δ' ἐπὶ τῆς Γαμάλας οἱ παραβολώτεροι μὲν φευγόντες διελάνθανον, οἱ δ' ἀσθενεῖς διεφθείροντο λιμῷ. Gamala is in Decapolis.

[23] *BJ* IV, 235: συνταχθέντες δ' εἰς δύο μυριάδας παραγίνονται πρὸς τὰ Ἱεροσόλυμα, χρώμενοι τέσσαρσιν ἡγεμόσιν . . .

[24] C. Di., *Hist. Rom.*, 65.4.3: καὶ οἱ Ἰουδαῖοι πολλοὶ μὲν αὐτόθεν πολλοὶ δὲ καὶ παρὰ τῶν ὁμοήθων, οὐχ ὅτι ἐκ τῆς τῶν Ῥωμαίων ἀρχῆς ἀλλὰ καὶ ἐκ τῶν πέραν Εὐφράτου . . .

[25] J. Price 1992, pp. 83–84.

[26] J. Price 1992, p. 95: it is a narrow passage in the outer wall. According to Price (pp. 95–101; pp. 135–142), there were two waves of flight, the first after the overthrowing of Ananos in the winter of 67/68, the second after the fall of the second defensive wall on 12nd Artemisios 70. During the siege smaller groups tried to escape, but their flight was violently prosecuted by the men of John of Giscala and Simon bar Giora.

[27] *BJ* VI, 420: τῶν μὲν οὖν αἰχμαλώτων πάντων, ὅσα καθ' ὅλον ἐλήφθη τὸν πόλεμον, ἀριθμὸς ἐννέα μυριάδες καὶ ἑπτακισχίλιοι συνήχθη, τῶν δὲ ἀπολομένων κατὰ πᾶσαν τὴν πολιορκίαν μυριάδες ἑκατὸν καὶ δέκα.

basis he calculated these figures. Although most of the prisoners were possibly taken during the siege, the sources mention groups of Jews captured elsewhere. On 5 Desios 68[28] Vespasian moved from Caesarea to Jerusalem through north-western Judaea, a hilly area, and took the toparchiae of Gophna and Acrabetta and the villages of Bethela and Ephraim (that he garrisoned); on his way he carried out massacres and took a large number of prisoners.[29] The attitude of Cerealius was even more violent. He moved northwards, he easily occupied some villages of Idumea superior[30] and besieged Hebron: according to Josephus prisoners were not taken and the towns were set on fire.[31] This figure cannot be compared to other estimates made in antiquity and seems unlikely, or, at least, difficult to evaluate.

After the final fall of Jerusalem, Titus asked Fronto to decide what to do with the prisoners:[32]

> Fronto put to death all the seditioners and brigands, information being given by them against each other; he selected the tallest and most handsome of the youth and reserved them for the triumph; of the rest, those over seventeen years of age he sent in chains to the works in Egypt, while multitudes were presented by Titus to the varius provinces, to be destroyed in the theatres by swords or by wild beasts; those under seventeen were sold.

Not all the prisoners taken in the siege, whatever their number was, were sold as slaves. Two groups were formed, according to age and

---

[28] *BJ* IV, 550–552. The Macedonian month of Desios roughly corresponds to June. Using a joint narrative technique, Josephus resumes the manoevres of Vespasian, which account had been interrupted in IV, 502 when the news of the death of Nero (9th June 68) reached the future emperor, and he decided to interrupt the campaign against Jerusalem and sent Titus to Rome to support Galba. When Galba died (15th January 69) Titus returned to Judaea. After the account of the civil wars among Jewish parties in the winter of 66 and 67 (*BJ* IV, 503–544), Josephus summarizes the war between Galba, Otho and Vitellius (*BJ* IV, 545–549) and concludes with the suicide of Otho on 16th April 69 and the imperial appointment of Vitellius.

[29] *BJ* IV, 551: φθόρα δ' ἦν πολλῶν καταλαμβανομένων καί συχνούς ἠχμαλωτίζετο.

[30] *BJ* IV 552–553: Josephus mentions the villages of Κάφεθρα e di Καφαραβίς.

[31] *BJ* IV, 554.

[32] *BJ* VI, 417–418: ὁ δὲ [Φρόντων] τούς μὲν στασιώδεις καὶ λῃστρικοὺς πάντας ὑπ' ἀλλήλων ἐνδεικνυμένους ἀπέκτεινε, τῶν δὲ νέων τοὺς ὑψηλοτάτους καὶ καλοὺς ἐπιλέξας ἐτήρει τῷ θριάμβῳ. Τοῦ δὲ λοιποῦ πλήθους τοὺς ὑπὲρ ἑπτακαίδεκα ἔτη δήσας ἔπεμψεν εἰς τὰ κατ' Αἴγυπτον ἔργα, πλείστους δ' εἰς τὰς ἐπαρχίας διεδωρήσατο Τίτος φθαρησομένους ἐν τοῖς θεάτροις σιδήρῳ καὶ θηρίοις· οἱ δ' ἐντὸς ἑπτακαίδεκα ἐτῶν ἐπράθησαν. Transl. by H.St.J. Thackeray, Cambridge, Mass.: Harvard University Press; London: W. Heinemann, 1928.

to physique. Only the men are mentioned in this passage: what happened to the women is unknown.[33] It is hard to follow the groups of prisoners: Josephus never specifies when and in what number the Jews were sold as slaves in the provinces of the Empire. We know that Titus, during his long stay in the Middle-East from autumn 70 to spring 71, frequently held games in which Jewish prisoners were compelled to fight: at least during the journey in Syria, an indefinable number of prisoners were kept for this purpose. Grand games were held at Caesarea[34] and at Berytus[35] to celebrate the birthday of Domitian (24th October) and Vespasian (17th November). Around the end of 70, Titus moved from Berytus towards Syria and held games in all the towns along his way.[36] This statement suggests that such a show was probably put up not only on official occasions such as the two Imperial birthdays. With great political acumen, Titus decided not to organise games in Antioch, where he was called to expel the Jewish community or to suspend their rights. A rejoicing crowd welcomed him and pressed for harshness against the Jews, but Titus defended and re-affirmed the rights the Jews had enjoyed since the Seleucids.[37] We have already discussed this point. During the long journey towards Egypt the prisoners are not mentioned; after visiting Jerusalem again, Titus reached Alexandria, where he decided that Simon and John—together with 700 young Jews tall and of good looking—had to be sent to Rome for the triumph.[38] This passage is inconsistent with VI, 417–418: Fronto should have chosen the prisoners for the triumph already in Jerusalem, parting them from groups destined to the mines and to the games. A group of prisoners were sent directly to Egypt: should we suppose that Titus chose the 700 prisoners from among these? Josephus cannot help us reconstruct their movements.

---

[33] In chapter VI, 414 Josephus reports that Titus, in front of πολὺ πλῆθος τῶν περιόντων ordered to kill only those who put up resistance, and τὸ λοιπὸν πλῆθος ζωγρεῖν. Nevertheless, the soldiers killed the old and the weak too (VI, 415).

[34] *BJ* VII, 37–38.

[35] *BJ* VII, 39.

[36] *BJ* VII, 96.

[37] In both his stays in Antioch, before and after the journey to Zeugma. *BJ* VII, 100–111.

[38] *BJ* VII, 118: τῶν αἰχμαλώτων δὲ τοὺς μὲν ἡγεμόνας Σίμωνα καὶ Ἰωάννην, τὸν δ᾽ ἄλλον ἀριθμὸν ἑπτακοσίους ἄνδρας ἐπιλέξας μεγέθει τε καὶ κάλλει σωμάτων ὑπερβάλλοντας, προσέταξεν εἰς τὴν Ἰταλίαν αὐτίκα μάλα κομίζεσθαι, βουλόμενος αὐτοὺς ἐν τῷ θριάμβῳ παραγαγεῖν.

Let us return to the fall of Jerusalem. Josephus informs the reader on the number of prisoners who died of hardship, hunger or in the arena in the period immediately following their capture. While Fronto was deciding their fate, around 11,000 Jews starved to death—for lack of grain, for cruelty of the guardians or because they themselves refused food that was considered impure.[39] In the following chapter we are informed that around 97,000 men died in the war.[40] What was the relation between these two figures? The source of this information is clearly unknown, consequently we cannot evaluate whether this figure also included those who died immediately after the fall of Jerusalem. The number of prisoners who survived the siege was going to dwindle because of the games. According to Josephus, in Caesarea 2,500 Jews died,[41] while an undefined but high number of prisoners (πλῆθος) died in Berytus[42] and in the Syrian towns.[43]

Some conclusions can be drawn. The figures Josephus attests are highly untrustworthy, while the description of the fate of the prisoners presents dark points and obvious contradictions. This was not a priority for Josephus who was much more interested in describing the policy Titus promoted in the months that elapsed from the fall of Jerusalem and his embarkation in Alexandria. It can also explain his precision in reporting Titus' movements, of which he gives a plausible chronology,[44] and the long excursus on the community of Antioch that preludes his entrance in the town.

Josephus gives us some interesting pieces of information. At the end of the siege the number of prisoners was high but not comparable to the amount of dead people, whose number increased during the winter. Josephus is imprecise in reporting these figures, but he uses the term πλῆθος almost regularly. After hours of massacre

---

[39] *BJ* VI, 419: ἐφθάρησαν δὲ αὐτῶν, ἐν αἷς διέκρινεν ὁ Φρόντων ἡμέραις, ὑπ' ἐνδείας χίλιοι πρὸς τοῖς μυρίοις, οἱ μὲν ὑπὸ μίσους τῶν φυλάκων μὴ μεταλαμβάνοντες τροφῆς, οἱ δ' οὐ προσιέμενοι διδομένην· πρὸς δὲ τὸ πλῆθος ἦν ἔνδεια καὶ σίτου.

[40] *BJ* VI, 420.

[41] *BJ* VII, 38: ὁ γὰρ ἀριθμὸς τῶν ἔν τε ταῖς πρὸς τὰ θηρία μάχαις ἔν τε ταῖς ἀλληλοκτονίαις ἀναιρουμένων καὶ τῶν καταπιμπραμένων πεντακοσίους ἐπὶ τοῖς δισχιλίοις ὑπερέβαλε.

[42] *BJ* VII, 40: τὸ δὲ τῶν αἰχμαλώτων πλῆθος τὸν αὐτὸν τρόπον ὡς πρόσθεν ἀπώλλυτο.

[43] *BJ* VII, 96: . . . καὶ δι' ὧν ἤει πόλεων τῆς Συρίας ἐν πάσαις θεωρίας τε συντελῶν πολυτελεῖς καὶ τῶν Ἰουδαίων τοὺς αἰχμαλώτους εἰς ἐπίδειξιν τῆς ἑαυτῶν ἀπωλείας ἀποχρώμενος . . .

[44] The scholarship widely accepts the sequence of the events and of Titus' movement between the fall of Jerusalem and his departure from Egypt.

the survivors were a πλῆθος,[45] so that Titus was compelled to order to kill only those who put up resistance and to take prisoners τὸ λοιπὸν πλῆθος; after days of hesitation, Fronto keeps a group of prisoners for the triumph, and manages all the others (τοῦ λοιποῦ πλήθους) differently;[46] in the meantime, because of the mass of prisoners the Romans had captured, grain begins to be lacking and people starve to death;[47] in the games at Berytus a mass of prisoners (τὸ δὲ τῶν αἰχμαλώτων πλῆθος) died.[48] As emerges in the whole account of the siege, Jerusalem was overcrowded, notwithstanding the famine, the dead in action and the massacres that occurred when the town fell, and the prisoners were so numerous that Josephus uses a term that can be translated as "multitude of people, crowd, mass". No quantitative meaning can be attached to this term.

Another point concerns the origin of the fighters. Not all of them came from Jerusalem: groups arrived not only from other areas of Eretz-Israel urged by the Roman menace or convinced to fight for the defence of the Temple, but also from Babylonian Diaspora. The Jews who were caught during the siege came from different economic and cultural backgrounds, but in Flavius Josephus's account they are marked by a traditional piety, in which the Temple has a primary importance, a piety probably different from the one that existed in Egypt or in the periphery of the Diaspora.

In regard to Rome, we know that around a thousand young, good-looking prisoners take part in the triumph, but we do not know their fate after the celebrations. Most of the historians that studied the Roman community suppose that in the seventies the Jewish population of Rome increased remarkably as a consequence of a mass-arrival of slaves from Judaea.[49] There is no evidence of such a movement. It is possible that other groups of prisoners were sold in the market of the Capital, but we cannot quantify this. The Jewish epigraphic and archaeological sources of Rome, of two centuries later, do not record the event.

---

[45] *BJ* VI, 414: . . . πολὺ δ᾽ ἔτι πλῆθος τῶν περιόντων ἀνεφαίνετο, κελεύει Καῖσαρ μόνους μὲν τοὺς ἐνόπλους καὶ χεῖρας ἀντίσχοντας κτείνειν, τὸ δὲ λοιπὸν πλῆθος ζωγρεῖν.
[46] *BJ* VI, 418.
[47] *BJ* VI, 419.
[48] *BJ* VI, 40.
[49] Among others H. Leon 1995², p. 31; E. Smallwood 1981, p. 519.

The only evidence we have of the presence of Jewish slaves in Italy is an inscription of unknown provenance kept in the Museo Archeologico Nazionale of Naples since 1852, when Mommsen could see it and study it.[50] Frey, probably on the basis of the close similarities with JIWE I, 23,[51] supposes that the inscription came from Marano.[52] No evidence can support this hypothesis and it is actually rejected.[53] It is the funerary inscription of Claudia Aster, who died at 25 (years old), *Hierosolymitana captiva*. Notwithstanding Solin's doubts,[54] the Jewish identity of the woman is confirmed. The name Aster corresponded to the Hebrew אסתר and was probably her sole name before being freed. The relation with Ti. Claudius Proculus, mentioned in the inscription, is not clear. Considering that the name of the woman is Claudia, it is possible that Ti. Claudius Proculus was first her master, than her patronus. In Noy's opinion, he was probably her husband as well.[55] Aster in fact died at 25: according to the lex Aelia Sentia, it was difficult for freed slaves of such an age, while a marriage could simplify the procedure. However, such an important bond could not be omitted in a long text. The woman, taken prisoner with the fall of Jerusalem, was probably sold as a slave, was bought and freed by Ti. Claudius Proculus, and died young in an unknown place. If Aster was captured when she was still a baby, the inscription can be dated to no later than 95 c.e.

II

The second consequence of the fall of Jerusalem was the creation of the Jewish tax. Though Flavius Josephus and Cassius Dio agree

---

[50] JIWE I, 26 (CIJ I 556): [*Cl*]*audia Aster* | [*H*]*ierosolymitana* | [*ca*]*ptiva. curam egit* | [*Ti*(*berius*)] *Claudius Aug*(*usti*) *libertus* | [*Pro*(?)]*culus. rogo vos fac*(*ite*) | | [*prae*]*ter licim ne quis* | [*mi*]*hi titulum deiciat cu* | [*ra*]*m agatis. Vixit annis* | *XXV.* T. Mommsen 1852, p. 370 nr. 6467.

[51] JIWE I nr. 23: *Ti*(*berius*) *Claudius* | *Philippus* | *dia viu et* | *gerusiarches* | *maceriam duxit.* According to onomastics, the inscription can be dated to Claudius or Nero. The only element in common beween the two inscriptions are *praenomen* and *nomen.*

[52] In editing CII I, 556.

[53] See Noy commentary on the inscription.

[54] H. Solin 1983, pp. 658–649, 729.

[55] In the commentary on the text. A slave under thirty years old could be freed only with the positive judgement of a *consilium* (whose composition the law regulates) that was convened also if the *manumissor* was less than twenty years old. (F. Schultz 1995, p. 191).

on the main questions, their evidence differs in important details. According to Josephus,[56] in an undefined moment after the fall of the siege, Vespasian farmed out all Jewish territory and "on all Jews, wheresoever resident, he imposed a poll-tax of two drachmae, to be paid annually into the Capitol as formerly contribuited by them to the Temple in Jerusalem." The tax is clearly linked to the war, but is collected not only in the lands that actually rebelled to Rome, but also among all the Jews living in the Empire. It expressly replaces the annual offering of half a shekel that all Jewish males over twenty years old had to pay to the Temple as a sign of their belonging to the Jewish nation.[57] Apart from the earmarking of the income and the increase in the number of taxable people, apparently there was not any fracture with the past. Josephus specifies the year when the tax is introduced. Vespasian would have provided this act "περὶ δὲ τὸν αὐτὸν καιρόν", with reference to a foregoing dating. After the

---

[56] *BJ* VII, 216–218: **216** Περὶ δὲ τὸν αὐτὸν καιρὸν ἐπέστειλε Καῖσαρ Βάσσῳ καὶ Λαβερίῳ Μαξίμῳ, οὗτος δ' ἦν ἐπίτροπος, κελεύων πᾶσαν γῆν ἀποδόσθαι τῶν Ἰουδαίων. **217** Οὐ γὰρ κατῴκισεν ἐκεῖ πόλιν ἰδίαν αὐτῷ τὴν χώραν φυλάττων, ὀκτακοσίοις δὲ μόνοις ἀπὸ τῆς στρατιᾶς διαφειμένοις χωρίον ἔδωκεν εἰς κατοίκησιν, ὃ καλεῖται μὲν Ἀμμαοῦς, ἀπέχει δὲ τῶν Ἱεροσολύμων σταδίους τριάκοντα. **218** φόρον δὲ τοῖς ὁπου-δηποτοῦν οὖσιν Ἰουδαίοις ἐπέβαλεν, δύο δραχμὰς ἕκαστον κελεύσας ἀνὰ πᾶν ἔτος εἰς τὸ Καπετώλιον φέρειν, ὥσπερ πρότερον εἰς τὸν ἐν Ἱεροσολύμοις νεὼν συντέλουν. Καὶ τὰ μὲν Ἰουδαίων τότε τοιαύτην εἶχε κατάστασιν.

[57] Ex. 30:15: זֶה יִתְּנוּ כָּל־הָעֹבֵר עַל־הַפְּקֻדִים מַחֲצִית הַשֶּׁקֶל בְּשֶׁקֶל הַקֹּדֶשׁ עֶשְׂרִים גֵּרָה הַשֶּׁקֶל מַחֲצִית הַשֶּׁקֶל תְּרוּמָה לַיהֹוָה: כֹּל הָעֹבֵר עַל־הַפְּקֻדִים מִבֶּן עֶשְׂרִים שָׁנָה וָמָעְלָה יִתֵּן תְּרוּמַת יְהֹוָה: הֶעָשִׁיר לֹא־יַרְבֶּה וְהַדַּל לֹא יַמְעִיט מִמַּחֲצִית הַשֶּׁקֶל לָתֵת אֶת־תְּרוּמַת יְהֹוָה לְכַפֵּר עַל־נַפְשֹׁתֵיכֶם

"This is what everyone shall give who is numbered in the census; half a shekel by sanctuary weight—twenty gerahs to the shekel—half a shekel as an offering to the Lord. Every one who is numbered in the census, from twenty years old and upward, shall give the offering of the Lord. The rich shall not give more, and the poor shall not give less than the half shekel, when giving the Lord's offering as atonement for yourselves"; Philo, *De Spec. Leg.*, 1:76–78: **76** Προσόδους δ' ἔχει τὸ ἱερὸν οὐ μόνον ἀποτομὰς γῆς ἀλλὰ καὶ πολὺ μείζους ἑτέρας, αἳ μηδενὶ χρόνῳ φθαρήσεται· ἐφ' ὅσον γὰρ τὸ ἀνθρώπων γένος διαμενεῖ—διαμενεῖ εἰς ἀεί—καὶ αἱ πρόσοδοι τοῦ ἱεροῦ φυλαχθήσονται συνδιαιωνίζουσαι παντὶ τῷ κόσμῳ. **77** Προστέτακται γὰρ ἕκαστον ἀνὰ πᾶν ἔτος ἀπαρχὰς εἰσφέρειν ἀπὸ εἰκοσαετίας ἀρξάμενον. Αἱ δ' εἰσφοραὶ "λύτρα" προσονομάζονται· διὸ καὶ προθυμότατα ποιοῦνται τὰς ἀπαρχάς, φαιδροὶ καὶ γεγηθότες, ὡς ἅμα τῇ καταθέσει μέλλοντες ἢ δουλείας ἀπαλλαγὴν ἢ νόσων ἄκεσιν εὑρίσκεσθαι καὶ βεβαιοτάτην ἐλευθερίαν ὁμοῦ καὶ σωτηρίαν εἰς ἅπαν καρποῦσθαι. **78** Πολυανθρωποτάτου δ' ἔθνους ὡς εἰκὸς καὶ τὰς ἀπαρχὰς ἀφθονωτάτας εἶναι συμβέβηκε· σχεδὸν γοῦν ἀνὰ πᾶσαν πόλιν ταμεῖα τῶν ἱερῶν χρημάτων ἐστίν, εἰς ἃ παραγινομένοις ἔθος ἀπάρχεσθαι. καὶ χρόνοις ὡρισμένοις ἱεροπομποὶ τῶν χρημάτων ἀριστίνδην ἐπικριθέντες, ἐξ ἑκάστης οἱ δοκιμώτατοι, χειροτονοῦνται, σώους τὰς ἐλπίδας ἑκάστων παραπέμποντες· ἐν γὰρ ταῖς νομίμοις ἀπαρχαῖς αἱ τῶν εὐσεβούντων ἐλπίδες εἰσίν.

long account on the twofold triumph in Rome, Josephus resumes
the events that happened in Judaea and reports the dramatic seizure
of the fortress of Machairous (BJ VII, 163–208) and the actions
around the forest of Iardan (BJ VII, 210–215), where those who had
escaped the massacres in Jerusalem had taken refuge. After these
bloody clashes, where, according to Josephus, 5,000 died,[58] the area
could be reorganized (BJ VII, 216–218). With paragraph 219 the
subject changes: the scene moves to Commagene, which the governor
of Syria *Cesennius Peto* occupied "ἤδη δ' ἔτος τέταρτον Οὐεσπασιανοῦ
διέποντος". From this point on, Josephus logically should have recorded
what happened in the fourth year of Vespasian's government, which
ran from 1st July 72 to 1st July 73. At the end of the long excursus on Commagene (BJ VII, 252), without other chronological references, we learn that L. Flavius Silva arrived in Judaea, replaced
Lucilius Bassus, who died when he was still in office,[59] and began
the siege of Masada. Then, during the third year of Vespasian,
Judaea was pacified with the exception of the fortress of Masada:
after these clashes, Vespasian could organize the province and establish the new tax.

It is hard to find evidence that supports this chronology. We do
not know when the triumph was celebrated, even though Josephus
attests that months passed by before Titus could return to Rome.
According to Chambolu, his arrival should be placed in June 71.[60]
Josephus does not report any events before the ceremony, which
could have occurred at the end of the second year of Vespasian as
well, or at the beginning of the third (i.e. in the summer of 71).
Apart from Josephus' short references, the career of the magistrates
mentioned in this occurrence cannot be easily reconstructed. Bassus
is identified with Sex. Lucilius Bassus; *praefectus alae* under Galba,
praefectus utriusque classis under Vespasian, in 71 is appointed *legatus
Augusti* in Judaea, and relieves the military command of Cerealius.[61]
The account of the death and the replacement of Bassus follows the
facts that happened in Commagene, which Josephus dates to the
fourth year of Vespasian: consequently, it has been supposed that

---

[58] Calculating the 1,700 of Machaerus and the 3,000 of Iardan.
[59] *BJ* VII, 252: ἐπὶ δὲ τῆς Ἰουδαίας Βάσσου τελευτήσαντος Φλάυιος Σίλβας
διαδέχεται τὴν ἡγεμονίαν . . .
[60] A. Chambolu 1885, pp. 507–517.
[61] PIR L 379, pp. 99–100.

the governor died in late 72 or in early 73. According to this theory, the fall of Masada was to be dated to the spring 73.[62] The study Eck conducted on the inscription of Urbs Salvia radically changed the reconstruction of the events that occurred in Judaea after 70.[63] The appointment to governor of Judaea—an office of praetorian rank—follows his *adlectio inter praetorios* and *inter patricios*, made (at least the first)[64] during the censorship of Vespasian and Titus. They became censors only in March–April 73.[65] Thus, his departure towards Judaea should have been subsequent to this date. The siege of Masada lasted for months and ended in spring:[66] Eck places the definitive seizure of the fortress on 15 Nisan 74. This reconstruction is inconsistent with Josephus' account, whose sole dating before the fall of Masada is the reference to the fourth year of Vespasian in BJ VII, 219. After this event (μετὰ ταῦτα BJ VII, 409), riots broke out in Egypt, fomented by a group of Sicarii coming from Judaea; the *praefectus Aegypti Ti. Iulius Lupus* suppressed the revolt and received the order to destroy the temple of Leontopolis.[67] The *praefectura* of Lupus is mentioned in

---

[62] *BJ* VII, 401: καὶ τὸ πάθος ἐπράχθη πεντεκαιδεκάτῃ Ξανθικοῦ μηνός. Before Eck, the seizure of Masada was traditionally dated to the spring of 73, as in Schürer (in the revised edition of 1973 the event is dated to 74) Hoelscher (G. Hoelscher 1930, col. 2056), Smallwood (E. Smallwood 1981, p. 381; pp. 366–367) and Wallace (S. Wallace 1938, p. 175 in discussing the date of introduction of the Jewish tax). Niese (B. Niese 1893, p. 211 sg.) and Reicke (B. Reicke 1965, p. 193, p. 216) suggest 72.

[63] AE 1969–1970, nr. 183a: a. on the upper frame. *Ex eis honor[ibus data Urbi]salviensium plebei loca DCL.*

b. [*L. Flavius—f., V]el(ina), Silva Nonius Bassus, co(n)s(ul),* | *pont(ifex), [legat(us) Aug(usti) pro pr(aetore) pr]ovinc(iae) Iudaeae, adlectus inter patricios* | *[a divo Vespasiano et] divo Tito censoribus, ab isdem adlectus inter pr(aetorios), legat(us) leg(ionis) XXI Rap(acis),* | *[trib(unus) pleb(is), quaest(or), trib(unus) mil(itum)] leg(ionis) IIII Scithicae, IIIvir Kapitalis, quinq(uennalis) II, patron(us) col(oniae), suo et* | *[Ann.—ca. 20—]ttae matris item* | *[—ca. 15—]millae uxo[r]is nomine, pecuni[a sua solo suo],* | *[amphitheatrum faciundu]m curavit et [pa]rib(us) [qua]drag(inta) [ord(inariis) dedic(avit)]* W. Eck, *Die Eroberung von Masada und eine neue Inschrift des L. Flavius Silva Nonius Bassus,* ZNW 60–61 (1969–1970), 282–289; id. AE 1969–1970, nr. 183).

[64] It is questionable whether both *adlectiones* occurred during the censorship of Titus and Vespasian: on bibliography see L. Boffo 1994, pp. 305–306.

[65] Dessau, ILS nr. 8903.

[66] Eck corrects the correspondence between Ξανθικός and May according to the Tyrian calendar and compares it with the Hebrew month of Nisan (March/April). The seizure of Masada should be dated to Pesach (14th Nisan) 74. J. Roth rejects this idea and, in consideration of the overwhelming military supremacy of the Romans, figures that the siege lasted no more than seven weeks (J. Roth 1995, pp. 87–110).

[67] *BJ* VII, 407–436; an excursus on the history of the temple of Onias interrupts the account (*BJ* VII, 423–432).

documents dated to the fifth (Egyptian) year of Vespasian and is interrupted by his sudden death, traditionally placed in August 73.[68] According to Josephus' account, the events that occurred between the campaign in Commagene and the Egyptian revolt should be included in the fourth year of Vespasian.[69] What Eck notices is the elasticity Josephus showed in reporting the events: the date of the fourth year referred only to the campaigns in Commagene and Armenia, while the death of Bassus, the appointment of Silva and the seizure of Masada should be placed in the fifth year of Vespasian, from 1st July 73 to 1st July 74 according to epigraphic data. Consequently, the revolt in Egypt was roughly contemporary to the fall of Masada.[70]

Liberius Maximus, who was in charge of the finances in Judaea, is identified with *L. Liberius Maximus*, mentioned in the *Acta Arvalium* (CIL VI, 2059 = ILS 5049) and in a military diploma of 83 C.E. (CIL XVI, 29), in which it is attested that he reached the *praefectura Aegypti*.

To conclude, according to Flavius Josephus the new tax was introduced in the third year of Vespasian, about a year after the celebration of the triumph, and is the last administrative act the Emperor did at the end of the war.

According to Cassius Dio, the new tax is an annual tribute of two denarii set aside for the temple of Juppiter Capitolinus:[71] considering

---

[68] Eck AE 1969–1970, p. 100.

[69] On bibliography that agrees with Eck see again L. Boffo 1994, pp. 302–308.

[70] The dating of Lupus' praetorship was partially established with the discovery of two Egyptian papyri (P. Oxy. XLVI nr. 3279 and P. Mich. XIV, nr. 676): Lupus closed the temple of Leontopolis in the autumn of 74 (H. Schwier 1989, p. 52). Jones (C. Jones 1997, pp. 249–253), connecting all the evidence on this period, supposes that two revolts broke out in Alexandria, but the first was crushed by the praetor L. Peducaeus Colonus between the end of 69 and the beginning of 73, the second, much more violent, broke out in 73/74 with the presence of Palestinian refugees and was crushed by Iulius Lupus. His praetorship is attested in February/March 73 but could have lasted up to the summer of 74, after Masada. Lupus ordered the destruction of the temple of Leontopolis, but the building was definitively levelled by Valerius (?) Paulinus. Cotton discusses the dating of Lupus' government and concludes that he was still in Egypt in 74 (H. Cotton 1989, pp. 157–162).

[71] C. Di., *Hist. Rom.* LXVI, 7, 2: Οὕτω μὲν τὰ Ἱεροσόλυμα ἐν αὐτῇ τῇ τοῦ Κρόνου ἡμέρᾳ, ἣν μάλιστα ἔτι καὶ νῦν Ἰουδαῖοι σέβουσιν, ἐξώλετο. Καὶ ἀπ' ἐκείνου δίδραχμον ἐτάχθη τοὺς τὰ πάτρια αὐτῶν ἔθη περιστέλλοντας τῷ Καπιτωλίῳ Διὶ κατ' ἔτος ἀποφέρειν.

that the Egyptian drachma was exchanged at par with the *denarius*, the two pieces of evidence are not contradictory. However, while Flavius Josephus describes the fiscus Iudaicus as an "ethnic" tax, which all the Jews living within the Empire had to pay, Cassius Dio remarks that only the orthodox Jews were subject to the new taxation, those that "continued to observe their ancestral customs". From his point of view, this was the most important point, not the universality of the tax, nor its bond with the ancient half-shekel offering. We will see a similar religious interpretation of the tax in the evidence that concerns the harsh fiscal policy Domitian promoted against the Jews about fifteen years later. Cassius Dio places the introduction of the tax immediately after the seizure of Jerusalem, months before the reorganization of Judaea: the tax is apparently a political consequence of the fall of the city. It was the second year of Vespasian: Dio's evidence contrasts with that of Josephus. Notwithstanding these differences, they have an important detail in common: both historians stress the continuity between the half-shekel offering and the new tax.

The Jewish tax is attested also in non-literary sources.

A group of 259 ὄστρακα found during the excavation at Apollinopolis Magna (Tell Edfu) in 1937–39 registers the receipts of payment of different taxes, the λαογραφία, the φόρος προβάτων and the τιμὴ οἴνου among others, paid by the Jews who lived in the "fourth area", named as in Alexandria δ᾽ ἄμφοδος. Most of the ὄστρακα date to Vespasian, Titus, Domitian and Trajan; some evidence goes back to Nero, Galba, Otho and Vitellius (CPJ II, 230–36), while 29 documents belong to the period between 151 and 165 c.e. (CPJ II, 375–403). Sixty-nine documents attest the payment of the Jewish tax (CPJ II, 160–229), issued between the fourth year of Vespasian (71–72 c.e.) and the nineteenth of Trajan (116 c.e.), according to the Egyptian calendar. The tax is mentioned also in a late papyrus of Karanis (CPJ II, 460) and in a long papyrus found in Arsinoe (CPJ II, 421). This latter papyrus, divided into three fragments, consists of a report of the ἀμφοδάρχης, the officer in charge of the collection of taxes in Arsinoe, and is dated to the fifth year of Vespasian (72–73).

The name of the tax depends on the dating of the documents. As Tcherikover shows,[72] until the eighth year of Domitian (88–89)

---

[72] CPJ II, pp. 112–113.

the tax is named τιμὴ δηναρίων δύο Ἰουδαίων, which he translates with "the price of two denarii of the Jews", while from the twelfth year of Domitian (92–93) the tax is called Ἰουδαικὸν τέλεσμα, "tax of the Jews". We do not know exactly when this change occurred, because the receipts issued from the eighth to the twelfth years were lost. Some documents suggest that the two names were in use in the same time. In an ὄστρακον of 14th November 80 (CPJ II, 181), the tax bears the official name of τιμὴ δηναρίων δύο Ἰουδαίων, but the collector is called πράκτωρ Ἰουδαικοῦ τελέσματος:[73] before the reform of Domitian the name Ἰουδαικὸν τέλεσμα had already appeared. It also appears in a receipt dated to 18th May 85 (CPJ II, 183) and in the papyrus of Arsinoe, as Ἰουδαικὸν τέλεσμα. The evidence of an ὄστρακον issued in May 108 is more questionable. This receipt registers that Μελχίων Πεσούριος had paid a generic τιμή of four drachmae: two months later, the same person pays the Jewish tax (called correctly Ἰουδαικὸν τέλεσμα) whose value was again four drachmae.[74] Then, it has been supposed that the first receipt shortened the old name of the Jewish tax. However, in Edfu other taxes were called τιμή, as the tax on the wine (τιμὴ οἴνου) and the tax on the grain (τιμὴ πυροῦ): it could have been one of these.

Notwithstanding this important change, the value of the tax and the people who had to pay it, remained the same. What probably changed was its final earmarking. The currency in circulation in Egypt was the drachma: τιμὴ δηναρίων δύο Ἰουδαίων was not the Egyptian name of the tax but probably the Greek translation of *duo denarii Iudaeorum*. As Flavius Josephus and Cassius Dio show, in an unknown moment subsequent to the fall of Jerusalem, Vespasian imposed the payment of two denarii to the temple of Juppiter Capitolinus in Rome on all the Jews living in the Empire. Considering that the Attic drachma was exchanged at par with the denarius, it has been supposed that τιμὴ δηναρίων δύο Ἰουδαίων was the official name of the δίδραχμον attested in the literary sources.[75] The value of the tax was probably the link Josephus stresses with the half-shekel

---

[73] CPJ II, p. 112: Tcherikover affirms that πράκτωρ τιμῆς δηναρίων δύο Ἰουδαίων did not sound right to a Greek, because τιμή meant the "price" of the tax not the tax itself.

[74] A part of the whole amount. CPJ II, 214.

[75] CPJ II, 112–113; S. Wallace 1938, p. 171.

offering. Nehemiah had fixed this offering at half a shekel, and had destined the income to the Temple.[76] This was not the only mean of supporting the Temple: according to biblical evidence,[77] the Temple received frequent donations from those who ruled over Judaea[78] or from private citizens.[79] Moreover, it was possible to give testamentary legacies, in form of cash or of plots of land: the sale proceeds of these properties were kept in the treasury.[80] The Temple also worked as a deposit not only for widows and orphans, categories that the Jewish society usually protected (2 Macc. 3:10), but also for wealthy families (2 Macc. 3:11) and so it was considered, in the words of Josephus, "the general repository of Jewish wealth" (BJ VI, 282). Before the fall of Jerusalem the payment of the half a shekel was still in use[81] and was paid in Eretz-Israel and in the Diaspora with two silver attic drachmae, although well-off people offered golden drachmae sometimes (Toseftà Shekalim 2:4). Talmudic evidence recalls the way the offering was collected. On the first day of Adar (February/March), the high court of Jerusalem (bet-din ha-gadol) sent messengers all over Judaea announcing that the collection was open and that it had to be concluded by the first day of Nisan (March/April);[82]

---

[76] In Neh. 10:33–34 the amount is a third of shekel: "Moreover we obligated ourselves to contribute one third shekel yearly for the service of the house of our God—for the layer bread, for the continual meal offering, for the continual burnt offering, the Sabbaths, the new moons, festivals, and consecrated [gift] offerings and the sin offerings to atone for Israel, and for all the work of the house of our God."

[77] In the Second Temple period large donations of kings are often mentioned. For instance, Darius diverted the income of a satrapy to the Temple to finish the building and to fund the sacrifices (Ezra 7:20–23). Antiochus III gave 20,000 shekalim for the sacrifices and plentiful timber, including the cedar of Lebanon, to restore the Temple (Ant. XII, 140–141), while Demetrius allocated to the Temple the income of the tribute Akko had to pay, plus 15,000 shekalim from his personal treasure (1 Macc. 10:39–45).

[78] In the First Temple period the bond with the monarchy was close. The king was the guarantee of the management of the Temple and of the treasury, and paid for the sacrifices with his personal funds (II Chron. 31:3; Ezek. 45:17). Schürer (E. Schürer 1973–1986 II, p. 271) affirms that the half shekel tax was introduced with the return from the Babylonian exile.

[79] On this problem too we have plenty of evidence. Among others, Alexander, the brother of Philo of Alexandria, made a cover for the gates of the Temple with gold and silver (B.J. V, 53), while Nicator of Alexandria gave a bronze gate worked by Corinthian artisans (BT Yoma 3:10).

[80] Toseftà Shekalim 2:15; Mish. Ar. 8.

[81] Mt. 17:24–25: ἐλθόντων δὲ αὐτῶν εἰς Καφαρναοὺμ προσῆλθον οἱ τὰ δίδραχμα λαμβάνοντες τῷ Πέτρῳ καὶ εἶπαν· ὁ διδάσκαλος ὑμῶν οὐ τελεῖ [τὰ] δίδραχμα; λέγει· ναί.; Ant. XVIII, 312–3.

[82] JT Shekalim 1:1, 45d.

probably these embassies also reached the most important communities of the Diaspora.[83] Since 15th Adar benches of money-dealers appeared everywhere in Eretz-Israel to speed up the operations of exchange that began in the Temple courts on 25th Adar.[84] These offerings were usually destined for the purchase of victims for sacrifices and of incense.[85] The δίδραχμον was exchanged with the Phoenician silver shekel whose average weight was of 14,2 gr;[86] this money was minted in Tyre from 126 B.C. and 56 C.E.[87] An half shekel was exchanged with two attic drachmae. Since 56 C.E., and in particular during the Jewish war, the flow of shekalim from Tyre was blocked and the Jewish authorities decided to mint in autonomy silver shekalim as sacred money to be devoted to the maintainance of the Temple. The money was minted in pieces of one silver shekel, half a silver shekel and a quarter of silver shekel. To conclude, as Wallace shows,[88] Vespasian in introducing the new tax means to recall the ancient offering, but changes its significance, imposing the payment to all Jews (regardless of their age and their sex) and allocating this income to a pagan temple.

The peculiar name the tax had in Egypt may depend on the fact that it was paid with the local currency: the denarii were in use in Egypt and were probably regarded as "goods to buy at the market", as Tcherikover said.[89] Even if the authorities called the tax in a different way, it is possible that at a more informal level it was called "the tax of the Jews", Ἰουδαϊκὸν τέλεσμα, a fact that could explain why this terminology appears in the receipts before the intervention of Domitian. With this Emperor, the bureaucracy adopted Ἰουδαϊκὸν τέλεσμα, the popular name, clearly by order of the central government. The old name of the tax had a symbolic and evoca-

---

[83] In Ant. XVIII, 312–313 the account of the tax-raising in the Babylonian Diaspora: ἔστιν δὲ καὶ Νίσιβις πόλις κατὰ τὸν αὐτὸν τοῦ ποταμοῦ περίρρουν, ὅθεν Ἰουδαῖοι τῇ φύσει τῶν χωρίων πεπιστευκότες τό τε δίδραχμον, ὃ τῷ θεῷ καταβάλλειν ἑκάστοις πάτριον, ταύτῃ κατετίθεντο καὶ ὁπόσα δὲ ἄλλα ἀναθήματα, ἐχρῶντό τε ὥσπερ ταμιείῳ ταῖσδε ταῖς πόλεσιν. ἐντεῦθεν δὲ ἐπὶ Ἱεροσυλύμων ἀναπέμπετο ᾗ καιρός, πολλαί τε ἀνθρώπων μυριάδες τὴν κομιδὴν τῶν χρημάτων παρελάμβανον δεδιότες τὰς Παρθυαίων ἁρπαγὰς ὑποτελούσης ἐκείνοις τῆς Βαβυλωνίας.
[84] JT Shekalim 1:3.
[85] JT Shekalim 4:1.
[86] JT Shekalim 1:7; Toseftà Ketubot 13:3; E. Schürer 1973–1986 II, p. 272.
[87] See E.J. s.v. *Shekel*, coll. 1347–1348.
[88] S. Wallace 1938, pp. 170–171.
[89] CPJ II, 113.

tive value due to its bond with the half-shekel, which was lost in the new definition. Probably, when the restoration of the temple of Juppiter Capitolinus ended, Domitian decided to allocate this income to other necessities.[90] The meaning Vespasian gave to the *fiscus Iudaicus* changed: the tax was no longer the tribute that a defeated nation had to pay to the civic temple of the winner, but a generic tax paid by a large ethnic group living in the Empire.

The amount of the tax was not changed in time. Flavius Josephus and Cassius Dio mention two Attic drachmae, while in Egypt the tax was of eight drachmae and two obols, plus an extra drachma for the ἀπαρχαί. Considering that an Egyptian tetradrachma was worth a denarius, the amount of the tax was the same as in all other provinces. According to Wallace, the two obols consisted of a sur-tax of 6¼%, whose value is questionable, but which is often attested in Egypt.[91] As for other taxes, this amount could be paid in two rates,·the first of 4%, the second of 2½%. Wallace remarks that an obol corresponded roughly to 4% of a tetradrachma and supposes that this amount had to cover the rate of exchange of the Egyptian currency into the Roman currency.[92] The term τιμή used in the first formulation of the tax could be explained as the price of two denarii bought in the local currency: the total amount was 8 drachmae and 2 obols. This could explain the name the tax had in the first period it was collected. Unless we suppose that the remaining 2¼% was included in the drachma paid under the name of ἀπαρχαί, the amount did not correspond to the common προσδιαγραφόμενα.[93] The ἀπαρχαί themselves are obscure. In the Septuagint this term means the first

---

[90] After the fire of 69, a second fire destroyed the temple in 80. The funds of the *fiscus Iudaicus* were probably used for their original purpose till the beginning of Domitian's reign. According to Tcherikover, when the temple was finally restored the income was assigned to other necessities and the tax changed name and became Ἰουδαικὸν τέλεσμα. We may simply suppose that the name conformed to the way most of the people called the tax, without a change in its use.

[91] On the Ἰουδαικὸν τέλεσμα S. Wallace 1938, pp. 170–176; on the surtax, S. Wallace, pp. 324–326.

[92] 1 tetradrachma = 25 obols.

[93] According to Alessandra Gara, the tax was paid in all the Empire; the amount was of two denarii, corresponding to a didrachmon and to half-shekel. In Egypt, the only province where the denarius did not circulate, the tax was paid in the local currency. Since the times of Vespasian, the name of the tax summarized the total amount in Egypt: the sum of the Egyptian currency changed into Roman currency plus the premium of this exchange. A similar operation is attested in Palestine, where the Temple offering was of half-shekel plus a *kollubos*, a monetary supplement that was the salary of the money dealer. A. Gara 1976, p. 83, p. 180.

fruits that people offered to the Temple and consecrated to God.[94] It could correspond to the bikkurim, the first fruits that, according to the Mishnah,[95] the Israelites offered in procession:[96] those who lived near Jerusalem carried fresh fruit, the others dried fruit. This ceremony was suspended when the half-shekel was no longer paid.[97] Tcherikover has a different opinion.[98] The half-shekel was not the only monetary offering that the Jews sent to the Temple: the ἀπαρχαί could have been a lump sum gathering all the smaller offerings.[99] Consequently, the (Egyptian) drachma mentioned in the papyri and

---

[94] According to Delling (G. Delling 1965, pp. 1289–1290), ἀπαρχή has three meanings in the Septuagint: A) the offering and the consecration of the first fruits: it is of common use, particularly in the Torah (Deut. 18:4, 25:2–10; Num. 18:8–12, 5:9, 18:15) but it is also attested elsewhere (Neh. 10:37; Ez. 45:13–16). B) Any offering to the Temple (2 Chr. 31:5). In some passages it is distinguished from the tithe to the Levites (Neh. 12:44; 13:5; 2Chr. 31:10–12–14). C) Special actions that the pagans do for the Temple and for God (Ex. 25:2; 35:5; 36:6; e Esd. 8:25; Ez. 20:31).

Philo (De Spec. Leg. 156; 216) uses the term for the offerings the Jews of Diaspora sent to Jerusalem: the *didrachmon* was part of the ἀπαρχαί. None of these meanings may correspond to the value the term has in the Egyptian evidence, but they show that it was not a juridical term either when the Temple existed.

[95] Bikkurim, 3rd chapter, written probably before the destruction of the Temple, according to the style and the reference to Agrippa II. *EJ* s.v. *Bikkurim*, coll. 993–994.

[96] The Talmud links the bikkurim with the seven kinds of fruit mentioned in Deut. 8:8: "a land of wheat and barley, vine, figs, and pomegranates, a land of olives bearing oil and of honey." It was probably a later tradition: in origin the term could have meant any offering of first fruits. (*EJ* s.v. *Bikkurim*, coll. 993–94). E. Schürer 1973–1986, II.1, p. 237.

[97] Mishnah Shekalim 8:8. We do not know why the *didrachmon* was suspended. According to Flavius Josephus (*BJ* VI, 94: ἐπέπυστο γὰρ ἐπ᾽ ἐκείνης τῆς ἡμέρας, Πανέμου δ᾽ ἦν ἑπτακαιδεκάτη, τὸν ἐνδελεχισμὸν καλούμενον ἀνδρῶν ἀπορίᾳ διαλελοιπέναι τῷ θεῷ καὶ τὸν δῆμον ἐπὶ τούτῳ δεινῶς ἀθυμεῖν.) the daily sacrifice (*tamid*) was suspended twelve days after the first violent attack to the Temple, on 17 Panemos 70, corresponding in the Hebrew calendar to 17 Tammuz (June/July): there were not enough priests to perform the rite. Rabbinic sources (M. Ta'an. 4.6 and Pes. Rab. 26.6) report the information and confirm the dating, but justify the suspension by the lack of animals for the sacrifices. According to Grätz (H. Grätz 1905–1908, III.2, p. 537 n. 2), ἀνδρῶν ἀπορίᾳ could be corrected with ἀρνῶν ἀπορίᾳ: after a few lines, Josephus says that many priests and two high priests were still in the Temple (BJ VI, 114) and were slaughtered by the Romans (BJ VI, 271). Notwithstanding the famine, some animals and the food for their nourishment were kept in the Temple area. Archaeological findings confirm this information: according to Price, during the excavation in the upper city containers for food, which the Jews hid from the requisitions of the authorities during the siege, have been found. (J. Price 1992, section VII, chapter 6).

[98] CPJ II, p. 115.

[99] The half-shekel, together with donations of notables, was the most important income the Temple had. The sources mention other monetary offerings. Less wealthy

in the ostraka as ἀπαρχαί was not a peculiarity of the Egypt, due to the exchange of the local currency into the Roman one, but was a small amount that had to be paid everywhere in the Empire. This interpretation contrasts with the passages of Josephus and Cassius Dio, according to which the amount of the tax was of exactly two (Attic) drachmae. To overcome this difficulty, Wallace identifies the ἀπαρχαί with the *terumot*, offerings paid in kind and used to support the priests.[100] The amount of the *terumot* was never fixed and could come to 1/40 or 1/60 of the harvest. In his opinion, in Egypt these offerings were assigned to the temple of Leontopolis, and, turned into a monetary offering in an unknown moment, were maintained by the Romans as the drachma for the ἀπαρχαί. Although in origin the ἀπαρχαί were spread all over the Jewish world, they originated mainly in Egypt where they are actually attested. It is a smart theory, but it is not supported by any evidence.

Who were the people that had to pay the tax? According to Josephus and Cassius Dio, the tax was based on the half-shekel offering. The Egyptian evidence is much more precise. In Egypt the tax was paid by Jewish males and females probably aged between three and sixty-two years old, regardless of their rank and their status.[101] It was a heavy worsening of the Jewish status both from a social and economic point of view.[102] The Jews had to undergo a special ἐπίκρισις;[103] the procedure was different from that of the

---

Jews could give offerings to the Temple for personal necessities. A Jew (even a woman) could offer money to a *cohen* seen as "holy of God" (Lev. 27): this offering depended on the age of the person.

[100] S. Wallace 1938, p. 176.

[101] Some ὄστρακα of Edfu attest that the sons of Ἀντώνιος Ῥοῦφος, probably a Roman citizen, paid the Jewish tax: Νίγερ Ἀντωνίου Ῥούφου (CPJ II, 162, 164 and 178), Θεόδωρος Ἀντωνίου Ῥούφου (CPJ II, 170 and 173), Νίκων Ἀντωνίου Ῥούφου (CPJ II, 174) and Θεόδωτος Ἀντωνίου Ῥούφου (CPJ II, 176 and 178). These receipts were issued from 28th January 72 to 28th July 79. We also know of freedmen as Ἀκυντὰς Καικιλλίας ἀπελεύθερος Σάρρας in CPJ II, 171–179–180. Tcherikover supposes that the husband, the father or an ancestor of Sarah was a freedman of the Roman family of the Caecilii. On the slaves see below.

[102] The tax was added to all the other taxes paid in Egypt, as the receipts clearly show. For example, an ὄστρακον of 30th May 75 (CPJ II, 259) registers the "common" taxes Νίκων Ἀντωνίου Ῥούφου had to pay, in addition to the Jewish tax. According to Wallace (S. Wallace 1938, p. 175), the worsening of the economic condition due to the payment of the Jewish tax was at the base of the Alexandrian revolts in 72–73.

[103] S. Wallace 1938, p. 111.

λαογραφία, whose aim was to establish the age of the taxpayers, not their social conditions.

Notwithstanding the high quality of the documents, some details are still unclear. The slaves could not pay the tax because they had no income. Egyptian and Greek masters would have hardly paid a high annual tax for each Jewish slave: according to Tcherikover, all the slaves mentioned in the ὄστρακα belonged to Jewish masters.[104] A Jew had to pay the tax for his own slaves, regardless of their origin, as a member of his *familia*: the same problems arose with women and sons who were not economically independent. The receipts support this theory:[105]

Name of the slave	Name of the master	Date	Nr. ὄστρακον
Κοπρεύς	Ἀντιπάτρου καὶ ἀδελφοῦ	24th October 104	201
Κοπρεύς	Ἀντιπάτρου	9th December 106	207
Δεκᾶς	Ἀπανίου Βελάρου	21st August 106	206
Σπόρος	Ἀνινίου	20th December 107	212
Ζωσίμη	Υἱῶν Πεσουρίου διὰ Μελχίωνος Πεσουρίου[106]	1st September 108	218
Θερμαῦθος	Ἀνινίου	18th May 116	229

The names of the masters, when not explicitly Jewish, are attested among the Egyptian Jews, with the exception of Ἀπάνοις Βέλαρος, an hapax in the province.[107] On behalf of the slaves, the evidence

---

[104] CPJ II, p. 114.

[105] We can take into account only the receipts from Edfu; the papyrus of Arsinoe mentions only the name and the age of the taxpayers, not their status.

[106] The woman became a slave of the sons of Πεσοῦρις but was bought only by Μελχίων.

[107] Ἀντίπατρος is no more attested in Edfu. An Ἀντιπάτρου Ἰουδαίου is attested in a document of the mid-third century B.C. (CPJ I, 125); similar names appear in CPJ I, 28 of 150 B.C. (Ἰωάννης Ἀντιπάτρου), in CPJ I, 29 (Ἀντίπατρος Δωσιθέου) and in CPJ II, 407, which are vaguely dated to the first/second centuries C.E.. Ἀνίνιος could be a variation of Ἀνανίας, the Hebrew חנניה and is attested in Hellenistic period in a document of 259 B.C. (CPJ I, 1: . . . . .]ος Ἀνανίου), of 259/8 B.C. (CPJ I, 35: Πτολεμαίωι Ἀ[ν]αν[ίου]) and of 174 B.C. (CPJ I, 24: Ἀνανίας Ἰωνάθου Ἰουδαῖος). An Ἀνινᾶ is mentioned in a papyrus of the end of the fifth century (CPJ III, 504). Πεσοῦρις occurs about 50 times in Edfu, while his son Μελχίων 25 times: the genealogy of this family has been completely reconstructed (CPJ I, 118). All these names are not attested among the Jewish inscriptions in Egypt.

is less clear. Ζωσίμη is attested in a Jewish inscription from Cyrene,[108] while the other names do not appear in Jewish inscriptions or papyri.[109] Consequently, in the Trajan period, some Jewish families of Edfu owned non-Jewish slaves for whom they paid the Jewish tax.

The ὄστρακα do not mention the age of the tax-payers; according to a section of the papyrus of Arsinoe (CPI II, 421), it has been thought that the lowest limit was the age of three. It is a strange age, which was not inspired by the Temple tax, or by the *tributum capitis* that had to be paid both in Egypt and in Syria since the age of fourteen. According to Wallace, this rule depended on a particular "bureaucratic laziness". The register of the ἀμφοδάρχης is based on the ἐπίκρισις of the fourth year of Vespasian, to which the data collected in the ἐπίκρισις of the fifth year should be added: the two lists of Jews who had paid the tax between 29th August 71 and 29th August 73 are united in one. Ll. 163–166 register two children who were respectively three years old in the fourth year of Vespasian and one year old in the second year, according to what is said few lines above; then, (l. 173) they register the little Σεύθ[ης] who in the third year was one year old, while in the fifth was three years old. It is added (l. 174) that when this child was registered in the ἐπίκρισις of the fourth year he was two years old. The Imperial years follow the Egyptian calendar: in the second Egyptian year of Vespasian Jerusalem had not yet fallen. This is a fiscal peculiarity that will be debated later on. According to the information we have from Edfu, it is supposed that in Egypt the tax was paid for the first time in the fourth year of Vespasian, plus the outstanding taxes of the second and third years. According to Wallace, the accuracy the ἀμφοδάρχης shows in registering the children is not superfluous. The new tax was probably introduced immediately after the destruction of the Temple, and was paid by all Jews who were at least one year-old. In the fourth year of Vespasian, when the lists were completed, these children were three years old. This age became the lowest limit

---

[108] W. Horbury – D. Noy 1992 C72; the name in the masculine form occurs among the Jewish witnesses of an assignment (CPJ I, 22 of 201 B.C.).

[109] An Ἰσίδωρος Κοπρέως (CPJ III, 475) is mentioned among the night watchmen in the temple of Serapis in 295 B.C.; probably he was not a Jew. Θερμαῦθος is not mentioned anywhere else. Similar names are attested among the Jews: Θερμουθίων (CPJ III, 406, first/second centuries C.E.) and Θερμουθία (CPJ III, 508 of the 542 C.E.). Δεκᾶς and Σπόρος are not attested.

to collect the tax. The lists of the fifth year echo this novelty: the officer clarifies the position of these children, writing down the actual age and the Imperial year when they were one year old. But, if the Emperor had decided that the tax had to be paid from the first year of life, we could hardly suppose that a provincial bureaucracy had raised the limit to three year without an Imperial permission. Nonetheless, such a fiscal policy is not mentioned in the sources we have and contrasts with the financial crisis Vespasian had to fight against in the early Seventies. This papyrus is the only evidence we have on how old the people were when they began to pay the tax: we cannot say whether this rule lasted or not.

The maximum age is unknown too. Ll. 182–184 register a woman ἀπὸ ὑπερετῶν,[110] words that Tcherikover translated as "old persons": she was 59 years old in the fourth year of Vespasian, 61 in the fifth. Neither Tcherikover nor Wallace remarks this peculiarity[111] that can be hardly justified, unless we suppose that the ἐπίκρισις was not done each year in the same month.[112] In their opinion the maximum age was 62 years old, as for the λαογραφία. Instead, Smallwood sustains that (ἐτῶν) ξα was not the age of the woman, who in the fifth year was 60 years old, but the maximum limit for the collection, as occurred for the λαογραφία.[113] The "bureaucratic convenience" that Smallwood foresees in establishing the same limits for two taxes was

---

[110] 182b γυναῖκες τέλειαι | 182 Τρύφαι[να..]σπατος το(ῦ) Καλῆτος μῆ(τρος) Δωσαρίου | 183 ἀπὸ [ὑπερ](ετῶν) (ἐτῶν) ξα ἐπικ(εκριμένη) τῶι α(ὐτῷ) | 184 (τετάρτῳ) (ἔτει) (ἐτῶν) νθ Tcherikover (CPJ II, p. 208) translates: "Tryphaina, daughter of . . . spas, granddaughter of Kales, mother of Dosarion, of those who are over age, having been adjudged in the fourth year to be 59 years old, now 61 years old." Smallwood does not suggest a translation of the passage; on the basis of her idea, we may translate: "Adult women. Tryphaina, daughter of . . . spas, grand-daughter of Kales, mother of Dosarion, among the persons over the limit of 61 years, having been adjudged in the fourth year to be 59 years old . . ." The only reason why the ἀμφοδάρχης should have mentioned the limit was the age of the woman. This detail was probably a memorandum for the ἐπίκρισις of the following year.

[111] S. Wallace 1938, p. 170.

[112] To be 59 years old in the fourth Egyptian year of Vespasian (71–72), Tryphaina was possibly born in 12/13 C.E. Her birthday could have fallen after the ἐπίκρισις of 72 but before that of 73: this could explain the age the woman declares in the two ἐπικρίσεις. Let's suppose that Trypheina was born on 15th February 12 C.E.: if the ἐπίκρισις of 72 was organized on 30th January, the woman would have been 59 years old. If the following year the ἀμφοδάρχης had drawn up the lists on 4th March 73, the woman would have been 61 years old.

[113] E. Smallwood 1981, p. 373 nr. 60.

in fact useful only in Egypt, where the λαογραφία was paid: but we know that the Jewish tax was paid in all the Empire.

The last problem concerns the moment when Vespasian introduced this tax.[114] As we have already seen, Cassius Dio affirms that the tax was introduced immediately after the seizure of Jerusalem, possibly in the autumn of 70, during the second year of Vespasian; on the contrary, Flavius Josephus attests that the tax was created after the triumph, when Judaea had already been pacified, probably during the third year of Vespasian (71–72). The most ancient receipts of Edfu are dated to the fourth Egyptian year of Vespasian, between 29th August 71 and 29th August 72: the information given by Josephus is confirmed. It has to be remarked that Josephus attests the moment when Vespasian created the tax, not when the tax was actually collected: from that moment onwards months were spent compiling the lists. The ὄστρακα attest also that in the fourth year there was a retroactive collection for the second year.[115] The Egyptian calendar did not correspond to the Roman one: the second Egyptian year ran from 29th August 69 to 29th August 70, a period when Jerusalem had not yet fallen. This was not a mistake. In the papyrus of Arsinoe it is said that children that were three years old in the fourth and in the fifth year of Vespasian, were one year old in the second and in the third year of his government: in Arsinoe too, the second year of Vespasian was considered the beginning of the collection. All these data are not contradictory, although some aspects cannot be explained yet. According to Tcherikover, the Egyptian evidence definitely confirms the information given by Flavius Josephus.[116] The fourth Egyptian year, during which the first ἐπίκρισις

---

[114] For this purpose it could be useful to schematize the Roman and the Egyptian counting of the years of Vespasian:

Official years	Roman calendar	Egyptian calendar
First	1/7/69–1/7/70	1/7/69–29/8/69
Second	1/7/70–1/7/71	29/8/69–29/8/70
Third	1/7/71–1/7/72	29/8/70–29/8/71
Fourth	1/7/72–1/7/73	29/8/71–29/8/72
Fifth	1/7/73–1/7/74	29/8/72–29/8/73

[115] CPJ II, pp. 164–166: a payment for the third year was probably done, but is not attested.

[116] CPJ II, pp. 113–114.

took place, corresponded roughly to the third year of Vespasian: as Josephus says, the tax could have been collected since 71–72. In the meantime, Vespasian could have possibly decided the payment of the arrears of the second year, during which Jerusalem was seized. In Egypt, the second year preceded this event; nonetheless, the provincial government carried out the order and compelled the Jews to pay the arrears for both the second and the third Egyptian year of Vespasian. As a matter of fact, the Jews paid the tax from 70 onwards: Cassius Dio's statement is confirmed too.

Wallace's opinion is different.[117] He affirms that, after having celebrated the triumph (third year), Vespasian issued a decree in which he fixed how the tax had to be paid and ordered an extraordinary payment for the previous year by all the Jews that were more than one year old. This policy is clearly attested in the papyrus of Arsinoe, in which it is (unnecessarily) stated that two children were one year old in the second year of Vespasian. Josephus, the ὄστρακα of Edfu and the ἐπίκρισις in the fourth year mentioned in the papyrus of Arsinoe confirm the date when the tax was actually introduced. In 71–72, the tax was created, and lists were drawn up, where the names of all the Jews who were over one year old were registered; supplementary lists included the names of the tax-payers who were one year old in the second year of Vespasian. Because of the differences between the two calendars, this order supposedly raised doubts and problems in Egypt. The evidence of Edfu shows that in Egypt two years of arrears were collected instead of one: the bureaucracy took advantage of the different calendars and collected the payment for a period when Jerusalem had not yet fallen. As the papyrus of Arsinoe shows, the children who were one year old in the second Egyptian year of Vespasian, were three in the fourth, when the payment began. The minimum age for the payment became three years old, instead of one, as Vespasian had decided. The bond with the temple of Juppiter Capitolinus was of primary importance. According to Cassius Dio and Tacitus, the ceremonies for the restoration were celebrated in 70, immediately after the seizure of Jerusalem;[118] on the contrary,

---

[117] S. Wallace 1938, pp. 172–173.
[118] Cass. Dio., *Hist. Rom.* LXVI, 10,2: Τόν τε νεὼν τόν ἐν τῷ Καπιτωλίῳ εὐθὺς οἰκοδομεῖν ἤρξατο, αὐτός τε τοῦ χοῦ πρῶτος ἐκφορήσας καὶ δῆλον ὅτι καὶ τοῖς ἄλλοις τοῖς ἐπιφανεστάτοις τὸ αὐτὸ τοῦτο ποιῆσαι κελεύσας, ἵνα καὶ τῷ λοίπῳ πλήθει ἀπαραίτητον τὸ διακόνημα γένηται. Tac. Hist. IV, 53. Tacitus dates the rite to XI

Jerome maintains that the temple began to be rebuilt only in 73.[119] Consequenly, we may suppose that in 70 Vespasian decided to rebuild the temple and to finance the works with the Jewish tax; the building yard was opened when the income began to pour in. It was 72–73 C.E.

To summarize, not everything we know of the Jewish tax is clear and regarded the whole Empire. During the siege, the Jewish authorities suspended the ancient half-shekel offering. With the fall of Jerusalem, Vespasian created a tax of two denarii modeled on this offering, but changed it in some important details: the tax was due by all the Jews, male and female, over one year of age. After the triumph and the seizure of Masada, the Emperor ordered the collection of the tax to begin: the lists were drawn up in 71–72 but included pax-payers of the previous year. The name of the tax was in these years τιμὴ δηναρίων δύο Ἰουδαίων, and could be paid in local currency. It is questionable whether the age limits attested in Egypt were in force everywhere in the Empire; the smaller amounts (2 obols) are present only in Egypt and are not mentioned in the literary sources. The tax, a regular income for the Roman economy, was probably created to restore the temple of Juppiter Capitolinus, which was set on fire during the civil war in 69, and assumed a political and ideological value that, in many Jews' view, overlooked the heavy economic burden.

III

With the new tax a new section of the Imperial *fiscus* was born, the *fiscus Iudaicus*. Scanty evidence attests this tax. Cassius Dio and Josephus do not add any details on the administrative organization linked to its collection. The first historian who speaks of this side of the problem is Suetonius: he says that under Domitian *fiscus Iudaicus acerbissime actus est*.[120] To support his statement, he recalls that when he

kalendas Iulias of the 70, eleven days before the Kalendae of July, on 21st June, the summer solstice.

[119] S. Wallace 1938, p. 429 nr. 18.

[120] Suet., *Dom.*, 12: *Iudaicus fiscus acerbissime actus est; ad quem deferebantur qui vel inprofessi Iudaicam viverent vitam vel dissimulata origine imposita genti tributa non pependissent.*

was young he had witnessed the examination a *procurator* carried out on a ninety year-old man to investigate whether he was circumcised or not. Nerva put an end to this violence and celebrated the return to a fiscal equity with the emission of the well-known monetary series whose *titulus* reads: *fisci Iudaici calumnia sublata*.[121] The *fiscus* is attested in an inscription roughly dated to the Flavian period: the inscription was dedicated to T. Flavius Euschemon, Imperial freedman, *procurator ad capitularia Iudaeorum*.[122] After Domitian, the tax continued to be collected,[123] as is shown both by a papyrus of Karanis (CPI III 460) dated to the mid-second century on palaeographic basis,[124] and by a passage of Origen.[125] But no direct evidence of the collection remains today.

Vespasian ordered that new lists were drawn up. As the Egyptian evidence shows, these lists were based on a special ἐπίκρισις that had to establish the "Jewishness" of the taxpayers and, possibly, their age. Domitian intervened in the tax. As we have already said, the ὄστρακα of Edfu attest that in a moment between 89 and 93 C.E. the name was changed from τιμὴ δηναρίων δύο Ἰουδαίων in Ἰουδαίων τέλεσμα while the amount and the way it was paid remained unchanged.

According to Suetonius, Domitian hardened the methods of collection, allowing the use of violence and including new categories.

Interfuisse me adulescentulum memini cum a procuratore frequentissimoque consilio inspiceretur nonagenarius senex an circumsectus esset.

[121] H. Mattingly – E. Sydenham 1926, p. 227 nr. 58; p. 228, nr. 80. They are dated to 96–97.

[122] CIL VI, 8604 (ILS 1519): *T. Flavio Aug(usti) lib(erto) | Euschemoni | qui fuit ab epistulis | item procurator | ad capitularia | Iudaeorum | fecit | Flavia Aphrodisia | patrono et coniugi | bene merenti.* The finding place is unknown. Dessau (ILS 1519) quotes both de Rossi, who states that the inscription was found "extra portam Latinam", and CIL, who states that it comes from porta Pinciana.

[123] Wallace (S. Wallace 1938, p. 176 and 348) remarks that the ὄστρακα are attested until the reign of Trajan and supposes that Hadrian finally suppressed the tax. Later evidence contradicts this theory. The Jews could have left Edfu after the revolt in 115–117 (V. Tcherikover, CPJ II, p. 108): the few ὄστρακα dated between 151 and 165 (CPJ II, 375–403), which are not related to the Jewish tax, show the presence of only one Jewish family living in Edfu.

[124] CPJ II, 460 (col. I, l. 7): Ἰουδ(αϊκοῦ) τελέσμ(ατος) ϑ (διώβολον). The papyrus is dated in l. 1, but this indication is not enough: ϑ (ἔτους). "The 9th year mentioned in l.1 gives no certain date, but on palaeographic grounds the year in question may be either 145/6 or 167/8" (V. Tcherikover, vol. III, p. 17).

[125] Origenes, *Ad Africanum*, 14: καὶ νῦν γοῦν Ῥωμαίων βασιλευόντων, καὶ Ἰουδαίων τὸ δίδραχμον αὐτοῖς τελούντων.

Consequently, the *fiscus Iudaicus* was created before Domitian, who did not change the pre-existing organization. The only evidence for the years of Titus is the receipts of Edfu.[126] Most probably, Vespasian, in introducing the tax, established the way it had to be collected and organized a new fund.[127] The fiscus survived the Flavian dynasty. According to the numismatic evidence, Nerva did not suppress the fiscus but forbade the violent methods with which the tax was collected. This is also the last news we have of the fiscus: the tax is still attested in the third century, but any later evidence concerns its collection.

The *fiscus Iudaicus* was an independent branch of the Imperial fiscus, and had the sole function of collecting the Jewish tax.[128] According to T. Flavius Euschemon's inscription, at the head of this fiscus there was a *procurator ad capitularia Iudaeorum*. Dessau translates this office as "préposé aux listes d'impôt des Juifs"; more probably he was responsible for all the operations required in collecting the tax.[129] Altough a freedman, and not a person of equestrian rank filled the post, this office was not of secondary importance in the *a rationibus* department, as the carrier Euschemon shows. As Boulvert remarks, after this procuratorship he filled an office in the department *a epistulis* as subordinate of a *ducenarius* equester: the previous experience was probably enough.[130]

Suetonius speaks of a *procurator* who, with the help of a *consilium*, examines an old man accused of evading the tax. No more details

---

[126] CPJ II, 179–182.

[127] Contra Modrzejewski (J. Mélèze-Modrzejewski 1991, p. 174); he claims that Domitian created the fund, because the fiscus is mentioned from his reign on, and remarks that Euschemon's inscription cannot be clearly dated.

[128] S. Wallace 1938, p. 335; M. Rostovzeff in P.W. s.v *Fiscus*, coll. 2403–2405; V. Tcherikover, CPJ II, pp. 80–81. Stern (M. Stern 1974–1980, II, p. 129) supposes that the term *fiscus Iudaicus* indicated the income of the Jewish tax and not a branch of the fiscus.

[129] M. Stern 1974–1980, II, p. 128 (nr. 320); P. Brunt 1966, p. 77; G. Boulvert 1974, p. 140. Smallwood (E. Smallwood 1981, p. 375 nr. 69) suggests that he could have been an office-worker.

[130] G. Boulvert 1974, pp. 139–140. The speed with which offices were filled was a character of the *fiscus Alexandrinus*, of the *fiscus Iudaicus* and of the *fiscus Asiaticus*. Analogies in the three funds are studied by Rostovzeff (M. Rostovzeff, P.-W., s.v. *Fiscus*, coll. 2402–2405): A) Vespasian created these taxes (as a matter of fact Cicero already attests the payment of the Asian tax). B) the three funds were placed in Rome and not in the provinces because of the dispersion of the taxpayers; C) the procurator at the head of the fund was a freedman. Brunt implicitely agrees (P. Brunt 1966, p. 77).

are shown. He could possibly be identified with the *procurator ad capi-tularia Iudaeorum*, because the operation, however brutal, could be included in the control of the taxpayers' lists that figures among the duties of the office.[131] The examination takes place in a court where a suit between a fiscal officer and a citizen charged of evasion is discussed. How these kinds of suits were discussed is questionable, and depends on the value the ancient sources attach to the term *fiscus*.[132] As Pomponius says, as from Nerva the *actor* or the Imperial *procurator* in charge of the *fiscus* would have submitted the fiscal suits (including those concerning the *bona caduca* and the *bona damnatorum*)[133] to the judgment of a court chaired by a praetor.[134] An *advocatus fisci* would have defended the position of the fiscus:[135] the procurator was not present at the trial.

This picture does not fit in with Suetonius. In some periods and in the provinces fiscal suits were not discussed according to the pri-vate procedure but with a *cognitio extra ordinem*;[136] an officer of the fiscus (a procurator) took the *iurisdictio* on fiscal suits and could deliver a judgment. If the trial that Suetonius describes took place in Rome, this interpretation must be rejected. But this point is debated. Therefore, we should ignore this theory.

With regard to the procedures which the local authorities followed to collect the tax, we have again scanty evidence. The papyrus of Arsinoe (P. Lond. II, 260–261) attests that the list of the taxpayers was drawn by an ἀμφοδάρχης. He had to list the nominatives of the inhabitants of the area within his province and to make a note of the taxes they had to pay in the current year.[137] Apart from the τιμή (P. Lond. II, 261 II section coll. 11–13; CPJ II; 421), he had to draw the lists of allowance (P. Lond. II, 261 II section col. 4), and the lists of those who had to pay both the λαογραφία (P. Lond. II, 261, I sect. 1–31; II sect. coll. 1–3; Pap. Lond II, 260 coll. 1–5) and the trade tax (coll. 7–10). Apparently the direct collection of the Jewish tax was not one of his duties.

---

[131] M. Stern 1974–1980 II, p. 128 (nr. 320).
[132] See Brunt 1966.
[133] Certainly with Tiberius (Tac. *Ann.* II, 48) and Trajan (Pl. *Pan.*, 36).
[134] Pomponius, Dig. 1,2,2,32: *adiecit divus Nerva (praetorem) qui inter fiscum et privatos ius diceret.* The praetor applied the *ius commune.*
[135] P. Brunt 1966, pp. 80–81; pp. 84–85.
[136] Under Claudius (Tac. *Ann.* XII, 60) and in the Severian period (*Dig.* I,16,9; II,15,8,19; XXXIX 4,16.1).
[137] S. Wallace 1938, pp. 112–115.

In the ὄστρακα of Edfu a πράκτωρ Ἰουδαικοῦ τελέσματος, who signed a receipt on 14 November 80,[138] is mentioned: most probably he was the officer in charge of the collection. This is the only evidence we have of this office, of which we do not know important details, such as how much time he was in office how he was appointed.

The evidence does not allow us to reconstruct the collection and the remittance of the tax to Rome where the fund was possibly placed.[139] We can suppose that the person in charge of the fiscus Iudaicus was the *procurator ad capitularia Iudaeorum*, an office an Imperial freedman could hold. Rome uses the local bureaucracies to draw the lists of taxpayers:[140] the ἀμφοδάρχης is responsible not only for the ἐπίκρισις of the Jewish tax, but also for other taxes paid in Arsinoe in Flavian period. In Egypt an officer was entirely devoted to the Jewish tax: πράκτωρ Ἰουδαικοῦ τελέσματος. However, his duties are not so clear: we know that he had to collect the tax and to issue receipts, but we cannot say if he was in charge of the tranfer of the money to a collection centre.

The tax itself has obscure aspects. The receipts of Edfu show that it could be paid by instalments. But who decided the amount of the instalments and when they had to be paid? The central authorities or the local bureaucracy? Before sending the money to Rome, it was gathered in centres we do not know anything about. The Jewish communities are apparently extraneous to this mechanism, but for the Flavian period we can suppose that they collaborated with the Roman fiscal functionaries. The tax was modeled on the δίδραχμον paid to the Temple: the core of these lists was probably the lists of Jews who had sent the half a shekel to Jerusalem. The synagogues or notables of the communities could help the Romans give the names of the Jews that, because of their age or their sex, did not

---

[138] CPJ II, 181: . . .]ναῖος Καλλιστράτου πράκτωρ | [Ἰουδαϊκ]οῦ τελέσματος Τρυφᾶτι | [Νίκων]ος χαίρειν. ἀπέχω διὰ | [. . . . Ἀ]πολλωνίου τιμὴν |5| [δηναρίων] δύο Ἰουδαίων σοῦ τε καὶ | [. . . . .] ὑπὲρ β (ἔτους) Τίτου Καίσαρος | [τοῦ κυρίου (δραχμὰς)] ις (τετρώβολον) κα(ὶ) ὑ(πὲρ) ἀπαρχ(ῶν) (δραχμὰς) β. | (ἔτους) γ Ἀθὺρ ιη.

[139] Not because T. Flavius Euschemon's inscription was found in Rome, but for the nature of the tax that was paid by an *ethnos* spread in the whole Empire.

[140] One of the goals of this book is to show how the communities of the Jewish Diaspora were different. We could suppose that the State would relate to the leaders of the communities, whoever these were. As we have discussed in the first chapter, we do not know how the Roman community was structured and who "the first of the Jews" were.

have to pay the δίδραχμον. In the aftermath of the fall of Jerusalem the contacts with the Jewish communities in Diaspora were probably intense. The sources do not show a Jewish presence in the management of the *fiscus Iudaicus*; the few names of functionaries we have can not be related to a Jewish context.[141] However, we could suppose that the communities helped the Romans draw the lists in the following years as well. The newborn babies, as sons of taxpayers, were registered for the fiscus. As both the papyrus of Arsinoe and the ὄστρακα of Edfu show, the father paid the tax for his sons too: the fiscus registered automatically their existence. But the fiscus missed out the conversions that occurred after 70–72, when the first lists were made. The proselyte, as an active member of a Jewish community, certainly had to pay the tax, but he could not be checked as the newborn babies.[142] Unless we assume that the proselyte had to inform the fiscus of his new status, a procedure which the sources do not mention, we should believe that the authorities checked the Jewish communities for the presence of new members.

---

[141] CPJ II, 240: Ἰσχύλος Ἰωσήφου | Τρυφᾶτι Νίκονος. | ὁμολογῶ ἔχειν παρὰ | σοῦ περὶ τοῦ βα(λανευτικοῦ) γ (ἔτους) (δραχμὰς) ς |5| περὶ σοῦ καὶ περὶ Νίκονος | Ἀντονίου Ῥούφου καὶ περὶ | Θεοδότου ἀδελφοῦ. The receipt, issued in 70–71, shows the presence of Jews in collecting the taxes in Edfu: their activity was not explicitly related to the Jewish tax. The name of the πράκτωρ mentioned in CPJ II, 181, is lost, but his father has a Greek name, *Callistratos*. The ἀμφοδάρχης too had a Greek name, *Erakleides*. However, the names of the Jews living in Diaspora are seldom of Hebraic origin: most of them are Greek or, more rarely, Latin and local.

[142] As we will see soon, Oesterley (W. Oesterley 1932, p. 455) rejected this hypothesis and supposed that Domitian included the proselytes in the lists. The proselytes were full members of the community: there is no reason why Vespasian should have exonerated this group.

DOMITIAN

In the few years of his government, Titus did not intervene in the Jewish tax. According to the sources, Domitian intensified the collection and, at the same time, enlarged the number of taxpayers. Meaningful evidence of the Imperial intervention on the *fiscus Iudaicus* is shown in the ὄστρακα of Edfu: as we have already seen, in the 80s the State changed the name of the tax into Ἰουδαικὸν τέλεσμα. Why and when Domitian adopted this policy can hardly be said.

Before studying the little evidence we have on this problem, a remark has to be made: Domitian intervened in a tax which was collected everywhere in the Empire, not only among the Jews of Rome. For the following two centuries the sources report the Empire's attitude and policy towards the Jews, but they are silent on the life of the Roman community. It has been supposed that Domitian's policy, which was valid in the whole Empire, was pursued with exceptional violence in Rome.[1] The involvement of this community was supposedly attested in the passage by Suetonius that we have already studied. However, as Stern shows, the incident could have happened in Rome or in Hippo Regius in Numidia, a town that, according to an inscription found in loco, could be considered his true birthplace.[2] Even if the incident happened in Rome, no evidence shows

---

[1] H.J. Leon 1995², p. 33; E. Smallwood 1981, p. 376.

[2] CRAI, 1952, pp. 76–86: *C. Suetoni[o] · fil (tribus)] Tra[nquillo | f]lami[ni -c.10– | adlecto i]nt[er selectos a di]vo Tr[a | iano Parthico p]on[t(ifici) Volca[nal]i | [-c.16– a] studiis a byblio[thecis | ab e]pistulis | [imp. Caes. Trai]ani Hadrian[i Aug. | Hipponienses Re]gii d.d.p.p.* M. Stern 1974–1980, II, p. 131. The inscription opened a discussion on Suetonius' birth-place. According to some scholars (A. Cook 1956–7, pp. 18–22 and J. Gascou 1978, pp. 436–444), Suetonius was born in Rome and visited Hippo Regius later in his life, while Syme (R. Syme 1958, II, p. 780; id. 1980, p. 80) supposes that he was born in Pisaurum, but considered Hippo his motherland. Meiggs (R. Meiggs 1960, p. 584) rejects the hypothesis that he was from Ostia and claims that in Ostia he was only appointed pontifex Volcani (ll.3–4 are restored with *p]on[t.] Volca[n]i [in colonia Ostiens.]*). In Wallace-Hadrill's opinion (A. Wallace-Hadrill 1983, p. 5), his education could have taken place in a town different from his birth-place. The episode of the ninety-year-old man, but also the way he reports the rumors on the false Nero (*Nero*, 57,2) which spread in Rome, and the memory of the Roman schools of rhetorics (*Gramm.* 4,9) implied a permanence in Rome which went back to his youth.

the Imperial will to persecute the local community. The attention I pay to this event must be related to the involvement that the Roman Jews probably had in the events we are going to study.

I

The first piece of evidence is a passage from Suetonius' biography of Domitian, which attests an intensification in the collection of the tax and the presence of informers that denounced those "who without publicly acknowledging that faith yet lived as Jews, as well as those who concealed their origin and did not pay the tribute levied upon their people".[3] Most of the scholars share the opinion that Domitian enlarged the number of taxpayers, including categories once exempted or extraneous to this tax.[4] The collectors began to use violence systematically; secret accusations or blackmailing were accepted as positive proofs during the inquiries. This last point is clearly attested in the passage. Consequently, the scholars' attention has focused on the identification of these new taxpayers, sometimes with questionable outcomes. In my opinion, there is a different point at issue. The sudden violence Domitian introduces in the collection of the Jewish tax is not isolated: the whole chapter XII deals with fiscal abuses and (illegal) forfeitures established in a period of economic crisis due to extra expenses.[5] What makes the collection of

---

[3] Suet., *Dom.*, 12,2: *Praeter ceteros Iudaicus fiscus acerbissime actus est; ad quem deferebatur, qui vel [ut] inprofessi Iudaicam viverent vitam vel dissimulata origine imposita genti tributa non pependissent. Interfuisse me adulescentulum memini, cum a procuratore frequentissimoque consilio inspiceretur nonagenarius senex, an circumsectus esset.*

[4] Some scholars suppose that the proselytes were involved (W.O. Oesterley 1932, II, p. 455; H.J. Leon 1995², p. 33; P. Keresztes 1973, pp. 10–11). This thesis has been rejected in the previous chapter. Someone else thinks about the "Judaizers" (E. Smallwood 1956a, pp. 1–13 and ead. 1981, pp. 376–380; M. Stern 1974–1980, II, p. 130), the apostates or groups of *peregrini* (L.A. Thomson 1982, pp. 329–342). Bruce (I. Bruce 1964, pp. 3–45) affirms that B.J. VII, 218 was inaccurate and that Vespasian had imposed the tax only in the Oriental provinces, a tax that Domitian began to collect in Italy too. There are no valid reasons why we should consider the passage by Flavius Josephus untrustworthy.

[5] To put in order the budget ruined by the expenses for public buildings, games and the rise of the *stipendium*, Domitian at first tried to lower the military expenses, reducing the number of legions. With such an operation he was risking dismantling the *limina* dangerously. Consequently, he began to forfeit goods on the basis of the charge *de maiestate*, to take possession of important inheritances (with legitimate heirs still living), although the will did not mention legacies to the Emperor, and to collect the taxes more agressively. An analysis of this passage in P.M. Rogers 1984, pp. 75–76.

the Jewish tax "*acerbissima*" is the indiscriminate use of secret accusations: the episode of the ninety-year-old man—an abuse because people of that age were exempted[6]—shows a climate of suspicion due to constant checks. The risk of being sued as a consequence of secret accusations affected two groups in particular, whose description apparently fits in with this kind of procedure: those who have adopted a Jewish style of life and those who have not declared their Jewish origin. But what could have been the charge? Domitian persecuted only these categories or promoted a more complex fiscal policy that regarded all Jews, but that targeted these groups in particular. It seems that the sentence reports the Imperial intervention only in its first part (*fiscus Iudaicus acerbissime actus est*), which shows a bitter struggle against the evasion; the second part concerns the activity of the police informers against people whose bond with Judaism was doubtful. These words do not report the content of a state act, and are of secondary importance.

Suetonius attests that peculiar investigations were made on people who lived as Jews without having declared their faith and people who evaded the tax, not having declared their Jewish birth.

With regard to the first group, the tax can refer both to a pagan and a Jewish ambit.[7] In fact, the *inprofessi* could be identified with the "Judaizers", pagans who did not have to pay the Jewish tax.[8] As Williams remarks, these charges were an abuse because they compelled a non-Jew to pay the tax of an *ethnos* they did not belong to.[9] Keretzs notices an important detail: *qui. . . . Iudaicam viverent vitam* almost corresponds to τοὺς τὰ πάτρια αὐτῶν ἔθη περιστέλλοντας, the phraseology Cassius Dio uses in describing those who had to pay the δίδραχμον to Rome.[10] In the same way, in the passage we will soon analyse, Cassius Dio describes the conversion to Judaism and the adoption of Jewish customs, saying ἐς τὰ τῶν Ἰουδαίων ἤθη ἐξοκέλλοντες.[11] Again Cassius Dio says that Nerva, inaugurating a new policy

---

[6] Bruce (I. Bruce 1964, pp. 40–41) supposes that the overage limit was suspended, but Stern (M. Stern, 1974–1980, II, p. 131) considers the detail an evidence of Domitian' *acerbitas*.

[7] *Ad quem deferebatur, qui vel[ut] in professi Iudaicam viverent vitam.*

[8] E. Smallwood 1981, pp. 376–380.

[9] M. Williams 1990, p. 199; L. Thomson 1982, p. 341.

[10] Cass. Dio., *Hist. Rom.* LXVI, 7,2: Καὶ ἀπ᾽ ἐκείνου δίδραχμον ἐτάχθη τοὺς τὰ πάτρια αὐτῶν ἔθη περιστέλλοντας τῷ Καπιτωλίῳ Διὶ κατ᾽ ἔτος ἀποφέρειν. P. Keresztes 1973, pp. 10–11.

[11] Cass. Dio., *Hist. Rom.* LXVIII, 1,2: τοῖς δὲ δὴ ἄλλοις οὔτ᾽ ἀσεβείας οὔτ᾽ Ἰουδαικοῦ βίου καταιτιᾶσθαί τινας συνεχώρησε.

towards the Jews, forbade charges of Ἰουδαικὸς βίος, words that closely recall Suetonius. Besides, the Romans used this expression in legal terms to recognize a Jewish community. In the documents concerning the communities of Asia Minor the expression τοῖς πατρίοις ἔθεσι καὶ ἱεροῖς χρῆσθαι recurs frequently.[12] Suetonius probably paraphrased this official phraseology: these people were Jews belonging to the Roman community who did not declare their faith (inprofessi) to avoid the payment. The "Judaizers" are automatically excluded.[13] Without the fiscus' strict checks, this option could have been considered.[14] Some scholars affirmed that the proselytes could have been exempted from the payment because of their non-Jewish birth.[15] As we have already discussed, it is possible that the new members escaped the fiscus's checks illegally. Nonetheless, as members of the community, they were certainly supposed to be included in the lists of taxpayers.

At first sight, the second group[16] could be more easily defined and should include the Jews who hid their faith to avoid paying the tax.[17] Why? If we suppose that under Titus the tax was not aggresively collected, many Jews could have evaded the tax with the confidence that they would not undergo strict checks.[18] Besides, people of Jewish

---

[12] *Ant.* XIV, 213–216 epistle sent to the Jews of Parium in the Throas. *Ant.* XIV, 223, request to Dolabella of the Jews of Asia: . . . τὰ πάτρια τηρεῖν αὐτοῖς ἔθη, καὶ κατὰ ταῦτα ζῆν ἐπιτρέπειν. *Ant.* XIV, 227, answer of Dolabella to the Jews of Ephesus: . . . καὶ συγχωρῶ χρῆσθαι τοῖς πατρίοις ἐθισμοῖς, ἱερῶν ἕνεκα καὶ ἁγίοις συναγομένοις, καθὼς αὐτοῖς νόμιμον, καὶ τῶν πρὸς τὰς θυσίας ἀφαιρεμάτων. *Ant.* XIV, 242, epistle of G. Rabirius to Laodicea: . . . ἵνα τά τε σάββατα αὐτοῖς ἐξῇ ἄγειν καὶ τὰ λοιπὰ ἱερὰ ἐπιτελεῖν κατὰ τοὺς πατρίους νόμους. *Ant.* XIV, 246, epistle of G. Servilius Galba to Miletus: . . . μὴ κωλύεσθαι Ἰουδαίους τοῖς αὐτῶν ἔθεσι χρῆσθαι. *Ant.* XIV, 258, decree of Alicarnassus: . . . τά τε σάββατα ἄγειν καὶ τὰ ἱερὰ συντελεῖν κατὰ τοὺς Ἰουδαικοὺς νόμους. *Ant.* XIV, 260, decree of Sardis: . . . ἵνα κατὰ τὰ νομιζόμενα ἔθη συνάγωνται. *Ant.* XIV, 263–264, decree of Ephesus: ἐπεὶ ἐντυχόντων . . . ὅπως ἄγωσι τὰ σάββατα καὶ πάντα ποιῶσι κατὰ τὰ πάτρια αὐτῶν ἔθη . . . ὁ στρατηγὸς συνεχώρησεν . . . ἐπιτετράφθαι δ’ αὐτοῖς πάντα ποιεῖν κατὰ τοὺς ἰδίους αὐτῶν νόμους.

[13] Williams (M. Williams 1990, p. 199) remarks the idea of a fight against the evasion implied in the terms *inprofessi* and *dissimulata*.

[14] M. Stern 1974–1980, II, p. 130. Though he recognises the proselytes in this group, Leon (H.J. Leon 1995², p. 33) remarks that it was easy to evade the fiscus in a period of low control. Of this opinion L. Troiani 2000, p. 387.

[15] W.O. Oesterley 1932, II, p. 455; P. Keresztes 1973, pp. 4–5; H.J. Leon 1995², p. 33.

[16] *vel [qui] dissimulata origine imposita genti tributa non pependissent.*

[17] Probably a large group.

[18] M. Williams 1990, pp. 199–200 on the basis of Suet., *Titus*, 8,5, in which Titus punished the *delatores mandatoresque* and *vetuit inter cetera de eadem re pluribus legibus agi quaerive de cuiusquam defunctorum statu ultra certos annos*; V. Tcherikover (CPJ II, p. 115;

birth, but who converted to other faiths, could have decided not to pay the tax.[19] Many of them were possibly Jewish Christians whose fiscal status we do not know.[20]

However obscure Suetonius is, the secret accusations seem to concern Jews; it is hard to state if these accusations echoed an act of Domitian. We know that Nerva changed policy and with a measure of large visibility such as a monetary issue, proclaimed the suspension of the fiscal abuse of his predecessor.[21] *Calumnia* could be referred both to the way the tax was collected and to the decision to include exempted categories in the payment.

A detail could help us understand what the official position of the Emperor was. Suetonius uses the expression *imposita genti tributa*, which closely reminds us of a similar sentence by Flavius Josephus who says that "On all the Jews, wheresoever resident, he imposed a poll-tax of two drachms" (B.J. VI, 218). The tax should be paid by all Jews according to their birth and not to their faith. Nonetheless, the lists were probably drawn with the help of the communities and mirrored the ancient lists of the Israelites who had paid the half a shekel: non-observant Jews could avoid the tax. Cassius Dio describes the procedure that was probably used to collect the tax that was paid only by people of Jewish faith. During a harsh economic crisis, Domitian probably required payment from all people of Jewish birth, including the apostates. The groups Suetonius mentions included people that had eluded the payment without being pursued. Domitian

---

182) remarks that the tax could be paid at one or by two instalmnets, in the attempt to make the amount easier to pay. This practice is attested in two ὄστρακα of the time of Titus (CPJ II, 180 of 15 June 80 and CPJ II, 182 of 80–81) and in two of Domitian (CPJ II, 186 of 30 July 89 and CPJ II, 192 of 18 August 95), but it becomes a common procedure with Trajan. Eighteen ὄστρακα (CPJ II, 195, 196, 200, 202, 206, 209, 211, 213–217, 220, 222, 224, 225, 227, 228) were issued between 100 and 116 for the payment of 4 drachmae; an ὄστρακον of 108 (CPJ II, 218) attests a payment of 6 drachmae, an ὄστρακον of 109 (CPJ II, 190, dated also to 93 C.E.) of 2 drachmae, while an ὄστρακον of 105/106 (CPJ II, 203) and of 109 (CPJ II, 219) of 1 drachma together with the payment of 5 drachmae of another taxpayer. Two ὄστρακα attest the payment of 4 and 3 obols (CPJ II, 207 of 106 and CPJ II, 229 of 116).

[19] Thomson 1982, pp. 338–340.

[20] This hypothesis is widely accepted (among others M. Stern 1974–1980, II, p. 130; E. Smallwood 1981, p. 377; P. Rogers 1984, pp. 338–339; P. Keresztes 1973, p. 5). It is hard to claim that the purpose of Domitian was to fight Christianity (M. Sordi 1960, p. 21).

[21] H. Mattingly – E. Sydenham 1926, p. 227 (nr. 58), p. 228 (nr. 82); H. Mattingly 1966, pp. 15–19, nr. 88, p. 98, pp. 105–106.

broke with the policy his family had on this tax, but his action ultimately resumes the act of Vespasian. What probably caused the reaction of Nerva was the way the tax was collected. Both Vespasian
and Titus had forbidden secret accusations:[22] for this reason, Syme
can speak of a persecution against the Jews.[23] According to Goodman,
after Domitian the *fiscus Iudaicus* was reorganized.[24] It was probably
decided that the tax had to be paid only by observant Jews, who
could obtain freedom of cult in exchange. As Tertullian says, the
Jews obtained a *vectigalis libertas*, a freedom reached with the payment of a tax.[25]

Suetonius places the measures on the *fiscus Iudaicus* among fiscal
and economic reforms that Domitian promoted to relieve the economy.[26] This problem is the subject of chapter twelve: Domitian
intensifies the collection of the Jewish tax and of other taxes (*praeter
ceteros . . .*) and forfeits the *bona vivorum ac damnatorum* also on the base
of secret accusations. The general context is vague. Suetonius says
that after the revolt of L. Antonius Saturninus in 89 c.e. the Emperor
became "more cruel" and behaved in a way opposite to that of the
previous period.[27] It has been supposed that the reform belonged to
the 90s, which were characterized by an "*inopia rapax*", due, according to Rogers, to extra expenses which were not offset by adequate
incomes. This dating finds confirmation in a passage by Martial in

---

[22] According to Suetonius, Vespasian quickened the trial procedures and forbade
the trial *sine causa*: *Vesp.*, 10,1: *sorte elegit per quos rapta bello restituerentur quique iudicia
centumviralia, quibus peragendis vix suffectura litigatorum videbatur aetas, extra ordinem diiudi-
carent redigerentque ad brevissimum numerum. Vesp.* 15,1: *Non temere qui punitus insons repe-
ritur nisi absente eo et ignaro aut certe invito atque decepto.* For Titus see Suet., *Tit.*, 8,5.

[23] R. Syme 1930, p. 67 nr. 2.

[24] R. Syme 1930, p. 67 nr. 2.

[25] Tert. (*Apol.*, 18,9) speaking of the Greek Bible kept in the library of Alexandria
says: *Sed et Iudaei palam lectitant. Vectigalis libertas; vulgo aditur sabbatis omnibus.*

[26] Rogers (P. Rogers 1984, pp. 75–76) notices that the *stipendium* was slightly lowered in the last decade of his reign: rather than disappointing his soldiers, Domitian
chooses to disband some troops: Suet., *Dom.* 12,1: *Exhaustus operum ac munerum inpen-
sis stipendioque, quod adiecerat, temptavit quidem ad relevandos castrenses sumptus numerum mi-
litum diminuere.*

[27] Suet., *Dom.*, 10,5: *verum aliquanto post civilis belli victoriam saevior.* The biography
of Domitian is divided in two sections: in the first the Emperor focuses on works
of repairs (ch. V), on the fight against the Chatti and the Daci (ch. VI) and on a
fair management of the State (ch. VIII and IX) that induces him to refuse the
legacy in the presence of living relatives (behaviour opposite to that of the following years); chapter X and XI mark the sudden passage to the new policy. Suet.,
Dom., 10,1: *Sed neque in clementiae neque in abstinentiae terrore permansit, et tamen aliquanto
celerius ad saevitiam descivit quam ad cupiditatem.*

which the fall of Jerusalem and the harsh fiscal policy are mentioned.[28] The passage is dated to 92 on the basis of a reference to the impending return of Domitian from the campaign against the Sarmates.[29] Martial clearly knows of the existence of a Jewish tax, but he does not attest the intensification which occurred exactly in the period when he was writing the epigram.[30]

Some inner references in Suetonius's passage suggest a different dating. He says that the investigation on the ninety-years-old man occurred "*me adulescentulum*". We do not know when Suetonius was born, but in the biography of Nero he says that he was adulescens in 88.[31] Moreover, in the twelveth chapter he affirms that the new fiscal policy was ultimately a consequence of the raising of the *stipendium*.[32] According to Cassius Dio,[33] the raise was made after the war against the Chatti,[34] whose conclusion is dated to the autumn of 83 or to the winter of 82/83.[35] Moreover, the tax was originally introduced for the temple of Juppiter Capitolinus which was destroyed in the year of the four Emperors. The building was damaged by a fire in 80:[36] it has been supposed that the restoration, concluded with

---

[28] Mart., *Epigr.*, VII, 55, 7–8: . . . *sed quae de Solymis venit perustis | damnatam modo mentulam tributis.*

[29] Particularly in VII, 5 where the defeat of the Sarmates has already been announced and the return of the Emperor is awaited. Domitian reached Rome in January 93. The campaign started after the Sarmates Iazyges had invaded Pannonia and destroyed the legion stationed in the province. The war is briefly summarized in Suet., *Dom.*, 5, 1 and in Cass. Dio, *Hist. Rom.*, LXVII,5,2.

[30] As Smallwood supposes. E. Smallwood 1956a p. 12 nr. 23; ead. 1981, p. 377 nr. 78.

[31] Suet., *Nero*, 57,2: *Denique cum post vigenti annos adulescente me exstitissent condicionis incertae qui se Neronem esse iactaret, tam favorabile nomen eius apud Parthos fecit, ut vehementer adiutus et vix redditus sit.* His name was Terentius Maximus. Another false Nero appeared in 70 C.E. (Tac., *Hist.* II,8).

[32] Suet. *Dom.*, 12,1: *Exhaustus operum ac munerum inpenis stipendioque, quod adiecerat.* . . .

[33] Cass. Dio., *Hist. Rom.*, LXVII,3,5: καὶ μετὰ ταῦτα εἰς Γαλατίαν ἐξορμήσας, καὶ λεηλατήσας τινὰ τῶν πέραν Ῥήνου τῶν ἐνσπόνδων, ὠγκοῦτο ὥς τι μέγα κατωρθωκώς, καὶ τοῖς στρατιώταις ἐπηύξησε τὴν μισθοφοράν, τάχα διὰ τὴν νίκην· πέντε γὰρ καὶ ἑβδομήκοντα δραχμὰς ἑκάστου λαμβάνοντος ἑκατὸν ἐκέλευσε δίδοσθαι. Μεταμεληθεὶς δὲ τὴν μὲν πεσότητα οὐκ ἐμείωσε, τὸ δὲ πλῆθος τῶν στρατευομένων συνέστειλε. Καὶ ἑκατέρωθεν μεγάλα τὸ δημόσιον ἔβλαψε, μήθ᾽ ἱκανοὺς τοὺς ἀμυνόντας αὐτῷ καὶ τούτους μεγαλομίσθους ποιήσας.

[34] Suetonius mentions the war, but not the raise of the *stipendium*.

[35] B.W. Jones 1973, pp. 70–93.

[36] The fire is mentioned in Suet., *Tit.*, 8,3: *Urbis incendio nihil publice nisi periisse testatus* and in Jerome among the events of 80 (ed. Helm p. 189): *Romae plurimae aedes incendio concremantur.* In both texts the temple is not explicitly mentioned, although the fire seems of considerable dimensions. The repairs of the building in Suet. *Dom.* 5,1: *Plurima et amplissima opera incendio absumpta restituit, in quis et Capitolium, quod rursus arserat.*

a ceremony of inauguration at the end of the decade, had been expensive and required a more careful collection of the tax traditionally related to the temple.[37] Finally, the change in the name of the tax could suggest a change in the tax itself, a change that was made, according to the ὄστρακα of Edfu, between the eighth (88–89) and the twelfth (92–93) Egyptian year of Domitian.[38] All these elements suggest that the abuses occurred in the second half of the 80s.

To summarize, according to Suetonius, Domitian does not include new categories in the taxpayers but persecuted fiscal evasions with exceptional harshness and allowed the use of unconventional procedures of investigation, such as the secret accusations and the violent physical checks. The change in the fiscal policy traditionally pursued by the Flavians is seen as the answer to extra expenses that could not be covered because of lack of liquidity.[39]

II

According to Cassius Dio, the consul Flavius Clemens, nephew of Domitian, his wife Flavia Domitilla and M' Acilius Glabrio, who was consul in 91 together with Trajan,[40] were charged with atheism because they had drifted into Jewish ways.[41] Some, like Glabrio,[42]

---

[37] Jerome places the inauguration in 89 (ed. Helm, 191: multa opera Romae facta, in quis Capitolium, forum transitorium, Isium ac Serapium, stadium, correa piperataria, Vespasiani templum, Minerva Cahalcidica, Od[e]um, forum Traiani, termae traianae et titianae, senatus ludus matutinus, mica aurea, Meta sudans et Pantheum.).

[38] ὄστρακα dated between the eighth and the twelfth year of Domitian have not been found.

[39] Rogers (P. Rogers 1984, p. 75) notices that the forfeiture of lands and goods, both of senators and of equestrians, is carried out for need of liquidity.

[40] PIR I, 9–10 n. 67.

[41] Cass. Dio., Hist. Rom. LXVII, 14, 1–3: 1. Κἀν τῷ αὐτῷ ἔτει ἄλλους τε πολλοὺς καὶ τὸν Φλάουιον ⟨τὸν⟩ Κλήμεντα ὑπατεύοντα, καίπερ ἀνεψιὸν ὄντα καὶ γυναῖκα καὶ αὐτὴν συγγενῆ ἑαυτοῦ Φλαουίαν Δομιτίλλαν ἔχοντα, κατέσφαξεν ὁ Δομιτιανός. 2. ἐπηνέχθη δὲ ἀμφοῖν ἔγκλημα ἀθεότητος, ὑφ᾿ ἧς καὶ ἄλλοι ἐς τὰ τῶν Ἰουδαίων ἤθη ἐξοκέλλοντες πολλοὶ κατεδικάσθησαν, καὶ οἱ μὲν ἀπέθανον, οἱ δὲ τῶν γοῦν οὐσιῶν ἐστερήθησαν· ἡ δὲ Δομιτίλλα ὑπερωρίσθη μόνον ἐς Πανδατερίαν. 3. τὸν δὲ δὴ Γλαβρίωνα τὸν μετὰ τοῦ Τραιανοῦ ἄρξαντα, κατηγορηθέντα τά τε ἄλλα καὶ οἷα οἱ πολλοὶ καὶ ὅτι καὶ θηρίοις ἐμάχετο, ἀπέκτεινεν.

[42] There are two different versions of the death of Glabrio. According to Cassius Dio (LXVII, 14,3), he died in the arena, because during his consulship he excited envy in Domitian for having killed a lion during the Iuvenalia. Conversely, Suetonius states (Dom. 10,2): Complures senatores, in aliquot consulares, interemit: ex quibus Civicam Cerealem, in ipso Asiae proconsulatu, Salvidium Orfitum, Acilium Glabrionem in exilio, quasi molitores rerum novarum, ceteros lievissime quemque de causa.

were sentenced to death, the rest were deprived of their properties. Flavia Domitilla was banished to Pandataria. The fate of Clemens is unknown. The episode is precisely dated to 95, during the consulship of Clemens.

Although Judaism is explicitly mentioned, some scholars used this passage as evidence of a persecution against Christians; Flavius Clemens was even identified with Clemens, who was bishop of Rome at the end of the first century.

The misunderstanding is due to a passage from the Historia Ecclesiastica in which Eusebius states that in the fifteenth year of Domitian (95 c.e.), a violent anti-Christian persecution broke out and Flavia Domitia was one of the victims.[43] The two passages differ in important details: Flavius Clemens and M' Acilius Glabrio are not mentioned, and the woman—who was the niece and not the wife of Clemens—was banished to Ponza. In his Chronicle, Jerome claims of having read this information in Bruttius, an almost unknown author,[44] but he reports the same episode mentioned by Eusebius.[45] The first historian who mentions Clemens is Syncellus, a Byzantine historian of the ninth century, who quotes Jerome and, on the authority of Bruttius, adds that Clemens was condemned ὑπὲρ Χριστοῦ while Flavia Domitilla, his niece, was banished to Ponza.[46] The picture is complex. As Stern shows, it is unlikely that ancient Christian sources

---

[43] Eus., *Hist. Eccl.*, III, 18,4: ὡς καὶ τοὺς ἄποθεν τοῦ καθ᾽ ἡμᾶς λόγου συγγραφεῖς μὴ ἀποκνῆσαι ταῖς αὐτῶν ἱστορίαις τόν τε διωγμὸν καὶ τὰ ἐν αὐτῷ μαρτύρια παραδοῦναι, οἵ γε καὶ τὸν καιρὸν ἐπ᾽ ἀκριβὲς ἐπεσημήναντο, ἐν ἔτει πεντεκαιδεκάτῳ Δομετιανοῦ μετὰ πλείστων ἑτέρων καὶ Φλαυίαν Δομέτιλλαν ἱστορήσαντες, ἐξ ἀδελφῆς γεγονυῖαν Φλαυίου Κλήμεντος, ἑνὸς τῶν τηνικάδε ἐπὶ Ῥώμης ὑπάτων τῆς εἰς Χριστὸν μαρτυρίας ἕνεκεν εἰς νῆσον Ποντίαν κατὰ τιμωρίαν δεδόσθαι.

[44] He is quoted in Johannes Melalas, a later Christian chronographer: A. Schekn von Stauffenberg, *Die roemische Kaisergeschichte bei Malalas*, Stuttgart 1931, p. 237.

[45] Jer., ed. Helm p. 192: *Scribit Bruttius plurimos Christianorum sub Domitiano fecisse martyrium. Inter quos et Flaviam Domitillam, Flavii Clementis consulis ex sorore neptem, in insulam Pontiam relegatam.* Few lines before, he had mentioned the persecution against the Christians (ed. Helm, p. 192) dated to 94: *secundus post Neronem Domitianus Christianos persequitur, et sub eo apostulus Iohannes in Patmum insulam relegatus apocalypsin vidit. Quam [H]irenaeus interpretatur.*

[46] G. Sync., *Chronographia* (ed. L. Dindorf), vol. I, p. 650: Οὗτος μετὰ Νέρωνα δεύτερος Χριστιανοὺς ἐδίωξε, καὶ Ἰωάννην τὸν θεολόγον ἄπολιν ἐν Πάτμῳ τῇ νήσῳ περιώρισεν, ἔνθα τὴν ἀποκάλυψιν ἑώρακεν, ὡς ὁ ἅγιος Εἰρηναῖός φησι. Πολλοὶ δὲ Χριστιανῶν ἐμαρτύρησαν κατὰ Δομιτιανόν, ὡς ὁ Βρέττιος ἱστορεῖ, ἐν οἷς καὶ Φλαυία Δομετίλλα ἐξαδελφὴ Κλήμεντος Φλαυίου ὑπατικοῦ, ὡς Χριστιανὴ εἰς νῆσον Ποντίαν φυγαδεύεται· αὐτός τε Κλήμης ὑπὲρ Χριστοῦ ἀναιρεῖται. The two facts are literally translated from Jerome. He adds only the detail of the persecution against Clemens.

omitted the martyrdom of a consul;[47] Jerome, who quotes Bruttius as (apparently) Syncellius does, is aware only of the banishment of Flavia Domitilla. On the basis of a meaningful ex-silentio proof, we can conclude that Clemens was not at all charged as a Christian, a conversion that would have been certainly recorded in Christian sources. Keresztes supposes the existence of two Domitilla: a wife of Clemens who was condemned with her husband for her interest in Judaism and banished to Pandataria, and a niece of the consul, who became a Christian and was banished to Ponza.[48] The hypothesis that two members of the same family converted to concurring faiths could in part explain the silence of Eusebius and Jerome on the anti-Jewish policy of Domitian. Both works speak of Christianity in commendatory terms: it was probably useless to remind readers that the Jews too converted members of the Imperial family and underwent a persecution. In my opinion, it is unlikely that two women belonging to the same family and bearing the same name converted to two different faiths and were both eventually banished to an island. It seems to be a duplication of an episode that was interpreted from two opposite points of view.

Clemens and his family are charged with atheism (ἔγκλημα ἀθεότητος) "a charge on which many others who drifted into Jewish ways were condemned". According to Cassius Dio, Nerva ordered that "no one was permitted to accuse anybody *de maiestate* or to adopt the Jewish mode of life".[49] The two passages are linked. In texts by Graeco-Roman authors, atheism and impiousness are peculiarities of the Jewish faith:[50] nevertheless, these words do not have a political or

---

[47] M. Stern 1974–1980, II, p. 382. Contra M. Sordi 1960, pp. 11–13.

[48] P. Keresztes 1973, pp. 15–20.

[49] Cass. Dio., *Hist. Rom.*, LXVIII 1,2: καὶ ὁ Νέρουας τούς τε κρινομένους ἐπ' ἀσεβείᾳ ἀφῆκε καὶ τοὺς φευγόντας κατήγαγε, τούς τε δούλους καὶ τοὺς ἐξελευθέρους τοὺς τοῖς δεσπόταις σφῶν ἐπιβουλεύσαντας πάντας ἀπέκτεινε. Καὶ τοῖς μὲν τοιούτοις οὐδ' ἄλλο τι ἔγκλημα ἐπιφέρειν ἐπὶ τοὺς δεσπότας ἐφῆκε, τοῖς δὲ δὴ ἄλλοις οὔτ' ἀσεβείας οὔτ' Ἰουδαϊκοῦ βίου κατατιᾶσθαί τινας συνεχώρησε.

[50] In the Roman world the accusation of atheism against the Jews has some peculiarities: 1) The Jews do not recognise the gods: this accusation, moved for the first time by Apion (Fl. Jos. *C. Ap.* II, 65), marks the distance between the Jewish and the pagan words, because it is interpreted as a contempt for pagan cults (Pl. *NH*, 13,46: *Iudaea gens contumelia numinum insignis*). For this reason the Jews are impious (Florus, *Epit.* I, 40, 29: *inpia gens*): The Jews distinguish themselves from all non-Jewish people. This attitude has heavy consequences on their political life, which cannot be reconciled with the rhythm imposed by Judaism: for example, Persius (*St.* V.180–184) speaks ironically of a candidate who interrupts his political activities

juridical value, but are used to remark the dangerous distance the Jews show towards the traditional cults. The charge of atheism does not imply a capital sentence or the forfeiture of properties.[51] In the light of the measures Nerva decided at the beginning of his reign,[52] it has been supposed that the charge moved against Clemens and his family was not of ἀθεότητος but of ἀσέβεια, the legal term that Cassius uses for the Latin *maiestas*.[53] It is hard to say why a charge *de maiestate* could be applied to those who lived as Jews. Smallwood, and the scholars that agree with her, remarks that it was an abuse, an illicit charge: an action *de maiestate* could be moved against citizens who refused to celebrate the civic cults, while the Jews were probably exempted from these ceremonies.[54] But, as we have already

---

because of the sabbath. Julian the Apostate discusses the question and argues that the will of isolation and the "savage and barbaric" rites are the core of the problem: "while the Romans recognise the god of the Jews, they refuse to worship the other gods" (M. Stern 1974–80, II, n. 481, p. 483). The most complex theorization of anti-Jewish accusations is in the V book of Tacitus' *Historiae*. The *mos Iudaeorum* is not only *absurdus sordidusque* (5,11) but was thought by Moyses to be contrary to the rites of all the other human beings (4, 1: *Moyses quo sibi in posterum gentem firmaret, novos ritus contrariosque ceteris mortalibus indidit. Profana illic omnia quae apud nos sacra, rursum concessa apud illos quae nobis incesta.*). Their solidarity becomes hate against the non-Jews (5,2: *apud ipsos fides ostinata, misericordia in promptu, sed adversus omnis alios hostile odium*), while the circumcision (5,4) and the half-shekel offering (5,2) are tangible signs of separation. Their worst peculiarity is the contempt towards the public rites and the cult of the Emperor (5,9: *Igitur nulla simulacra urbibus suis* [. . .]; *non regibus haec adulatio, non Caesaribus honor*). The proselytes are more guilty than the Jews themselves because they freely choose a religion that teaches *contemnere deos, exuere patriam, parentes, liberos, fratres vilia habere* (5,5). On the attitude of the Graeco-Roman authors towards Judaism see M. Stern 1974–1980, P. Schäfer 1999, pp. 53–95, L. Troiani 2000, pp. 379–391.

[51] E. Smallwood 1981, p. 379; M. Williams 1990, p. 208.

[52] On this question the sentence is not so clear: the two charges are not mentioned in a relation of cause-effect, but are merely juxtaposed.

[53] So W. Nawijn, *Cassii Dionis Cocceiani Historiarum Romanarum index graecitatis*, Berlin: Weidmann 1931, p. 119. In particolar in LXVI, 9,1: Ὁ δὲ (Vespasian) ἐκείνους μὲν εἴα, ἐς δὲ τὴν Ῥώμην ἐπέστειλε, τήν τε ἀτιμίαν τῶν καταψηφισθέντων ἐπὶ ταῖς λεγομέναις ἀσεβείαις ὑπὸ Νέρωνος καὶ τῶν μετὰ ταῦτα ἀρξάντων, τῶν τε ζώντων καὶ τῶν τεθνεώτων ὁμοίως, ἀπαλείψων, καὶ τὰς γραφὰς τὰς ἐπὶ τοιούτοις ἐγκλήμασι καταλύων; LXVI, 19,1: τάς τε δίκας τὰς τῆς ἀσεβείας οὔτ' αὐτός ποτε (Titus) ἐδέξατο οὔτ' ἄλλοις ἐπέτρεψεν, λέγων ὅτι· ἐγὼ μὲν οὐδὲν οὔθ' ὑβρισθῆναι οὔτε προπηλακισθῆναι δύναμαι; LVII, 9,2: ἐπεὶ τό γε ὑβρίσθαι πρός τινος ἢ καὶ τὸ ἠσεβῆσθαι πρός τινος (ἀσέβειάν τε γὰρ ἤδη καὶ τὸ τοιοῦτον ὠνόμαζεν, καὶ δίκας ἐπ' αὐτῷ πολλὰς ἐσήγον) ἥκιστα προσεποιεῖτο, οὐδὲ ἔστιν ἥντινα τοιαύτην ἐφ' ἑαυτῷ γραφὴν προσεδέξατο, καίπερ τὸν Αὔγουστον καὶ ἐν τούτῳ σεμνύνων. An exception LXIV, 15,2a in which Xiphilinus, speaking of the death of Otho, uses this term at the place of ἀσέλγειαν (*impietas*): τὴν ἀσέβειαν καὶ πονηρίαν τοῦ βίου συνεσκίασε.

[54] P. Schäfer 1999, pp. 160–164.

seen, the passages of the 14th book of the Antiquities that attest these privileges are not a "magna charta" of Jewish rights, as Juster said, but they show the privileges that some communities of Asia Minor gained. Consequently, could the Jews be charged *de maiestate* if they refused to celebrate the civic cults?

According to Cassius Dio, not all Jews were charged with atheism/*maiestas*, but only those Jews who ἐς τὰ τῶν Ἰουδαίκων ἤθη ἐξοκέλλοντες. As in the passage of Suetonius, Cassius Dio resumes the official phraseology: "to follow the Jewish ways" was the criterion Vespasian established to define who had to pay the δίδραχμον. Consequently, the "persecution" concerned the pagans converted to Judaism, so to say the proselytes. The passage on Nerva is not enlightening: the brief expression Ἰουδαικοῦ βίου κατατιᾶσθαί τινας can be translated as "to accuse of adopting the Jewish mode of life"[55] or "to accuse of living a Jewish life".[56]

In regard to this question, the rabbinic tradition conveys elements of some interest. The Talmud carries the story of the nephew of the Titus, called Kolonymos or Kolonikos, who became a Jew and was arrested, even if he escaped the capital sentence.[57] A more complex tradition concerns a senator, whose Jewish name was Keti'ah bar Shalom, who became a Jew together with his wife; he openly opposed an order to exterminate Jewish people, which was supposedly issued by Domitian at the end of the first century. It was a crucial moment. A committee of four rabbis rushed to Rome so promptly that they had to celebrated the feast of Sukkoth on their journey.[58] When they

---

[55] E. Cary, Cambridge Mass.: Harvard University Press; London: W. Heinemann (Coll. Ed. Loeb) 1961–1969, vol. 8, ad. loc.; E. Smallwood (1981, p. 378), M. Stern (1974–1980, II, p. 385) and P. Schäfer (1999, p. 170 nr. 64) quote the translation of Cary.

[56] H. Leon 1995², p. 36.

[57] BT Gittim 56b; BT Avodah Zarah 11a.

[58] The patriarch Rabban Gamaliel II *nasi* of the sanhedrin of Jabneh (v. E.J. VII, col. 298), Joshua ben Hananiah (E.J. X, col. 280), the person in charge of the *bet din* of Peki'in, who opposed Gamaliel in the rabbinical disputations but supported his position in Jabneh, Eleazar ben Azariah, *nasi* of the sanhedrin of Jabneh after the removal of Gamaliel (E.J. VI, coll. 586–587) and Rav Akiva. The trip to Rome is mentioned in BT Sukkah 41b ומעשה ברבן נמלאל ורבי יהושע ורבי אלעזר בן עזריה ורבי עקיבא שהיו באין בספינה "And it once happened that when R. Gameliel, R. Joshua, R. Eleazar b. Azariah and R. Akiba were travelling on a ship . . ."; BT Erubin 41b: מעשה שבאו מפלנדרסין והפלינה בים ומעשה ברבן נמלאל ורבי אלעזר בן עזריה "It once happened that they were coming from Brindisi and while their ship was sailing on the sea, R. Gamaliel and R. Eleazar b. Azariah. . . ." Mishnà Shabbath 16:9: מעשה ברבן נמליאל והזקנים שהיו באין בספינה "Rabban Gamaliel and

reached Rome Keti'ah bar Shalom was their point of reference, but the man was arrested and sentenced to death or induced to commit suicide. Before dying, he asked to be circumcised.[59]

The news of a persecution against the Jews of Rome is vaguely reported in a Christian tradition as well. According to the apocryphal Acts of John, Domitian decided to persecute the Jews but, on suggestion of some convincing Jews, diverted his intervention onto the Christians.[60]

The episode of Kolonikos shows only that a member of the Imperial family had become a Jew. Although he was said to be a nephew of Titus, like Clemens, his identity is still unknown. We cannot be sure of his full conversion either: a confessional source could have had interest in showing the spreading of Judaism in the high society.[61] The episode of Keti'ah bar Shalom, narrated in more sources with a few variations, is more revealing. Both he and Clemens are senators (Clemens as a consul was actually a member of the senate), become Jews together with their wives and die for their faith in a moment of crisis in the relationship between Romans and Jews. These are suggestions more than actual evidence. According to Cassius Dio, the consul did not compromise himself to save the Jews who in any case were not in danger of being exterminated. In the Roman-Jewish inscriptions a proselyte has a Jewish name: consequently Keti'ah bar Shalom is likely to have been a proselyte too. But the tradition almost unanimously reports that he asked to be circumcised before dying: did he become a Jew at that very moment or was he already a Jew before then? Despite the Jewish name with which he is mentioned,[62] the senator could have been a Judaizer who decided to become a Jew at the end of his life.

How could a proselyte become a senator or a consul? If we extend this question to Cassius Dio's passage, we have to wonder whether ἐς τὰ τῶν Ἰουδαίκων ἤθη ἐξοκέλλοντες is truly technical phraseology:

---

the elders were once travelling in a ship . . ." Mishnà Maasar Shenì 5:9: מעשׂה ברבן נמליאל והזקנים שהיו באין בספינה "Once when R. Gamaliel and the elders were sailing on a ship . . .".

[59] BT Avodah Zarah 10b; Midrash Deut. Rabba II, 24.

[60] *Acta Apocrypha Sancti Johannis*, in M. Bonnet, *Acta Apostolorum Apocrypha* II (1), Leipzig 1898, pp. 151–153.

[61] As it happened, on the Christian side, to Domitilla.

[62] This detail is not meaningful: the senator could have received the Jewish name before dying. This was the name that interested rabbinical sources.

the consulship, an office bound to the traditional values of the *res publica*, could hardly be assigned to a Jew. The object of Domitian's measures could have been the Judaizers, the people partially converted to Judaism. Proselytism became illegal only with Antoninus Pius:[63] the government probably had some difficulties in finding charges that could restrain the spreading of Judaism in the Roman society. In a moment when the cult of the Emperor was at its peak, as during the reign of Domitian, the Jews could be accused of atheism and of negligence towards the cult of the Emperor, and charged *de maiestate*.

Probably the Emperor was not concerned with Judaism as such but with a religion that could deter large strata of the Roman population from the traditional religion and the Imperial cult. As Cassius Dio states, "many persons were condemned": we could argue that Judaism was increasingly present in Rome, and produced the hard reactions of the Emperor. Evidence of the spreading of Judaism within high society is the fact that two members of the Imperial family could be charged with atheism and be condemned. It is hard to say if this charge proved a true interest of Flavius Clemens in Judaism or, as it has been supposed, if it was instead a political accusation moved to eliminate people that Domitian considered dangerous.[64]

III

The sources attest two different interventions against Judaism. Probably in the last decade of his government, Domitian ordered a stricter collection of the Jewish tax by issuing an act whose nature is unknown: the non-observant Jews and the apostates were compelled to pay the tax as well as the Jews who live according to the Jewish mode of life. The act was actually legal and possibly echoed the original wording of Vespasian; what aroused the disdain of Suetonius and the political reaction of Nerva was the use of violence in the collection procedures and secret accusations used as proofs in the inquiries.

In 95 the consul in office, his wife (both members of the Imperial family) and an ex-consul were charged *de maiestate* together with others and were sentenced to death or banished. The basis of this charge

---

[63] Mod. *Digesta*, XLVIII, 8,11: *circumcidere Iudaeis filios suos tantum*. The proselytes who probably had to undergo circumcision could no longer be admitted in the communities.

[64] Domitian had probably chosen his two sons as his heirs.

was the interest they showed in Judaism. It was a violent repression that probably made an impression on the contemporaries: the rabbinical literature, with some inaccuracies, speaks of a hard time, in which the very existence of the Jewish people was menaced.

The two events are not correlated: the first act is part of the Imperial fiscal policy and concerns only the Jews, while the second intervention regards, non-Jews, people, persons near to the Emperor, and seems to be a consequence both of the spreading of Judaism in the high society, and of the bad relationships between Domitian and the senate or some members of his family in the last years of his reign.

What links the episodes is the violence used in carrying out these measures: the inquiries led to personal violation; the accusation of a Jewish mode of life sometimes led to death.

Did Domitian support an anti-Judaic policy? Although he did not take part in the Jewish war, he issued coins with the title *Iudaea capta*, as his father and especially his brother had done.[65] Treading in the footsteps of his predecessors, he built an honorary arch to Titus on the south-eastern side of the circus Maximus.[66] The monument was inaugurated in 81; an inscription exalted the seizure of Jerusalem as one of the most glorious victories of Roman history.[67] A second arch

---

[65] The series is attested between 70 and 85 with some variations both in iconography and in the legenda. In the issuing of Vespasian, together with the common *Iudaea Capta S.C.* (H. Mattingly – E. Sydenham 1926, II, p. 63 nr. 393; p. 68 nr. 424–427; p. 73 nr. 489–491; p. 84 nr. 595–596; p. 101 nr. 733; p. 104 nr. 762), is attested also *Iudaea devicta* (p. 32 nr. 148b; p. 49 nr. 289; p. 67 nr. 419), *Iudaea* (p. 16 nr. 15–16; p. 18 nr. 34; p. 20 nr. 45; p. 44 nr. 254; p. 46 nr. 266; pp. 48–49 nr.287–288 issued between 70 and 73) and *de Iudaeis* (p. 31 nr.143; p. 50 nr. 301). The recto bears the portrait of Vespasian. To remark the importance Titus had in the war, Vespasian issued five series with the portrait of the son on the recto and on the verso the legenda *Iudaea devicta* (p. 59 n. 373 of unknown dating, minted in Tyre), *Iudaea capta S.C.* (p. 86 n. 608 and p. 87 n. 620 minted in 72 at Rome; p. 107 n. 786 minted in 77/78 at Lugdunum). Titus, as Emperor, resumed the legenda *Iudaea capta s.c.* (p. 127 n. 93 NAD p. 131 n. 128) but shortened it in *Iud. Cap. S.C.* (p. 127 n. 91–92 and p. 133 n. 141). Apart from this last issue, the other series are of the year 80. Even if he had not taken part in the Jewish war, Domitian, as Emperor, issued the series *Iudaea Capta S.C.* (p. 189 n. 280 of 85 C.E.). On this problem see S. Cappelletti 2004.

[66] S. De Maria 1988, pp. 285–6 n. Cat. 73. The foundations show the existence of an arch at three barrel-vaults.

[67] CIL VI, 944: *Senatus populus(que) Romanus | imp(eratori) Tito Caesari divi Vespasiani f. Vespasian[o] Augusto | pontif(ici) max(imo), trib(unicia) pot(estate) X, imp(eratori) XVII, | [c]o(n)s(uli) VIII, p(atri) p(atriae), principi suo, | quod praeceptis patri[s] consiliisq(ue) et auspiciis gentem | Iudaeorum domuit et urbem Hierusolymam, omnibus ante | se ducibus regibus gentibus aut | frustra petitam aut omnino intemptatam, delevit.* Boffo (L. Boffo 1994, p. 313) speaks of a "theology of the victory" after the triumph on the Jews.

was erected on the slope of Palatine, where it can still be seen, with an honorary inscription[68] and bas-reliefs representing the triumph over Judaea and the apotheosis of Titus.[69] In Overman's opinion, this policy was typically Flavian.[70] Vespasian and, with more consciousness, Titus built a important programme of propaganda around this war, and transformed the annexation of an area that was already within the Roman sphere of influence into a victory of world-wide importance. Vespasian was in Judaea when he was acclaimed Emperor; the seizure of Jerusalem and the pacification of Judaea were the most important military events of Titus's life: through this war the Flavians could present themselves as bearers of peace and order to the whole Empire.

Conversely, the passages in question concern independent acts of Domitian. Schäfer calls the atmosphere described in Suetonius a "witch-hunt",[71] although we have no evidence of a fury against the Jewish faith, but only against the Jews who evaded the fiscus. It is a rather different point of view. In the same period illegal procedures were carried out also to take possession of rich legacies of senators or equestrians. The methods used to collect the tax remind us of a persecution, but the reason why this act is undertaken is not *odium* but a compelling need of liquidity. The second act was different. At the end of the first century, an interest in Judaism is likely to have spread among the Roman high society. In Cassius Dio's opinion, consuls and members of the Imperial family could be genuinely interested in this faith. Domitian himself chose this accusation to eliminate people whom he probably saw as political adversaries. Although he does not make Judaism a *religio illicita* (on this point even the rabbinical sources are silent), he links the Jewish mode of life with the

---

[68] CIL VI 945: *senatus | popolusque Romanus | divo Tito divi Vespasiani f. | Vespasiano Augusto*. The arch was built after the divinization of Titus in 81.

[69] S. De Maria 1988, pp. 27–289, nr. cat. 74. The most important elements of the iconography are two panels of the inner side of the barrel-vaul that represent Titus on the triumphal quadriga crowned by Victory and followed by the procession (northern side), and the Temple vassels carried during the triumph (southern side). It was not built on the via Sacra, but on a stretch of road bent towards the east, which was considered part of the via Triumphalis.

[70] J.A. Overman 2002, p. 215; Meshorer (Y. Meshorer 1962, p. 98) on this question remarks that the mint of Caesarea produced series with different iconographies and legends: for example, the type with the half-naked prisoner was eliminated, not to hurt the feelings of the losers. On the typologies attested in Judaea see I. Carradice 1982–3, pp. 14–20.

[71] P. Schäfer 1999, p. 163.

charge *de maiestate*. Such policy did not cause a large persecution against the Jews: apparently only high rank people were involved, while the rabbinic literature speaks of menaces and fears, not of a real extermination. Domitian probably had a double purpose: he meant to eliminate political adversaries and to prevent the spreading of what he considered a dangerous religion. This latter attempt shows an anti-Judaic attitude, a natural consequence of the core of Domitian's religious policy: the Imperial cult.

SECTION THREE

ARCHAEOLOGICAL AND EPIGRAPHIC EVIDENCE

THE CATACOMBS

The Jewish community of Rome left late archaeological evidence that dates back to the third and the fourth centuries. According to the inscriptions, there were eleven synagogues, some of which can be dated to the beginning of the Empire. No evidence of these buildings has been found, and the attempt to localize their position has turned out questionable and fallacious. The five Jewish catacombs found in the *suburbium* also open many questions. Apart from the areas of Villa Torlonia and Vigna Randanini, which can still be visited, the other catacombs were dug up in a rush and were subsequently destroyed through geological events or through negligence. For instance, the plan of the excavated area of Monteverde is inaccurate, while there is not even a map of the catacombs of Via Labicana and vigna Cimarra. The difficulties in dating the catacombs are reflected in the difficulties in dating the inscriptions discovered inside, which are almost the totality of the inscriptions of Rome.

The Catacomb of Monteverde[1]

Discovery

According to Binyamin of Tudela, who visited Rome around 1160, on a hill on the western bank of the Tiber there was a quarry used for burials.[2] Although it was quite a vague suggestion, in this passage scholars have seen the first reference to a catacomb not far from the river, along via Portuense.[3] The catacomb was actually discovered in 1602: Antonio Bosio explored the galleries for two hours on 14th December, and noticed the extreme instability of the bearing walls and the presence of collapsed areas. In the account that he published in "Roma sotterranea", he mentions painted and scretched menorot, three lamps with a stamped menorah and an inscription

---

[1] The catacomb is also known as catacomb of via Portuense.
[2] I could check only the Italian translation. Binyamin da Tudela, *Itinerario* (Sefer massa'ot) a cura di G. Busi: Rimini 1988, p. 20: "In un'altra caverna, in una collina sulla riva del Tevere, sono sepolti i 10 pii messi a morte dalle autorità."
[3] A. Berliner 1893 (It. ed. 1992), pp. 96–97.

where he could read συναγογ-: the catacomb was clearly Jewish.[4] He
noticed signs of violation and some damaged or crushed inscriptions.
The catacomb was apparently forgotten up to the middle of the
seventeenth century: in few years Cardinal Passionei (ca. 1740)[5] and
Gaetano Migliore (1748) visited the site.[6] Migliore observed the risk
of further collapses. In a few hours he could transcribe 42 inscriptions, the core of the corpus of Monteverde's inscriptions.[7] Approximately in the same years, Gaetano Marini copied 37 inscriptions
kept in the Museo Borgiano of Velletri and in the Benedectine nun-
nery of S. Paolo fuori le Mura, and claimed that this group came
from Monteverde. On an unknown date and by means of unknown
people, a group of inscriptions were transported out of the catacomb.
According to Ferrua, Marini often used secondary sources such as
the Cod. Vat. Lat. 9074, and ascribed the inscriptions to Monteverde
not on the basis of positive evidence, but because this was the only
Jewish catacomb known in Rome.[8] In the nineteenth century, the
remembrance of the catacomb seems to fade away. In 1840, about
a century after the first exploration, Marucchi and de Marchi could
hardly find the site,[9] while in 1864 de Rossi stated that it had completely collapsed.[10] In the autumn of 1904 the catacomb was re-dis-
covered. Some workers who were digging in the area accidentally
found graves: Müller recognised the forgotten catacomb of Monteverde.
He began to excavate between November 1904 and January 1905
and, on two further occasions, in March–April and in September–
October 1906. The undertaking went on with difficulties, the galleries were in danger of collapse, the diggers could remain inside
only few hours a day. In 1915 he published an essay and a map of
the catacomb (map 1).[11] As Vismara shows,[12] Müller explored quite

---

[4] A. Bosio 1632, pp. 141–143; an English translation in H. Leon 1995[2], pp. 48–49.

[5] As Leon states (H. Leon 1928, p. 303).

[6] The texts of the inscriptions and the account of the exploration in Cod. Lat.
943. This latter part, written in Latin, is transcribed in Frey, CIJ I, pp. 206–207.
H. Leon 1928, p. 302; H. Leon 1995[2], pp. 49–50.

[7] A. Ferrua 1936, p. 462.

[8] A. Ferrua 1936, p. 462.

[9] S. de Ricci 1905, pp. 245–247; S. de Ricci, s.v. *Palaeography*, in J.E. (1905),
coll. 471–5 ("Greek and Latin Inscriptions").

[10] M.S. de Rossi 1864, p. 50.

[11] N. Müller 1912. His work was enlarged and translated into Italian: *Il cimitero
degli antichi Ebrei sulla via Portuense*, Dissertazioni della Pontificia Accademia Romana
di Archeologia, 12 (1915), pp. 205–318.

[12] C. Vismara 1986, vol. II, p. 362.

a wide area (ca. 80 × 65 m), an area that seems different from the one described by Bosio "fatta alla rustica e rozzamente non havendo altro che due soli cubicoli e quelli ancora molto piccioli e ignobili, com'è tutto il cimiterio".[13] 151 inscriptions and stamps from the excavated area were gathered in a collection in Museo Laterano, and then transferred to Museo Vaticano. Bees published the inscriptions in 1919, after the death of Müller in 1912.[14] His work was based on Müller's notes without any attention to the place where the inscriptions were found. Probably, what Bees saw did not correspond to the material Müller found few years before. In a posthumous essay by Müller published in 1915,[15] he includes in the list of the inscriptions a Κλ(αύδια) 'Ρουφῖνα and a *Magius* which had been omitted both in the work of Bees and in the notes of Marucchi and Iosi who attended the excavation.[16] Apart from supposing a mistake by Müller, probably some inscriptions disappeared in the period between the discovery and Bees' essay.[17] New excavations were carried out in 1911. Kanzler excavated a new area in 1913. He published a brief note narrating what he had observed in the little time he could spend in the galleries, and added an inaccurate map drawn by Schneider Grazioli without orientation and scale (map 2).[18] In June 1914 he looked after the removal of the inscriptions in the Jewish room of the Museo Laterano.[19] The area collapsed before the publication of the essay. Paribeni excavated in 1919 and took out nine inscriptions that were carried to the Museo Nazionale Romano.[20] Already in June 1928,[21] Frey could visit only a limited area that finally collapsed on 14th October 1929.[22] In 1935 d'Angelis d'Ossat surveyed the geological sequence of the area and took the last known pictures of the galleries.[23] D'Ossat remarked that the collapses were

---

[13] A. Bosio 1632, pp. 142–3. H. Leon 1995[2] p. 49: "It is crudely and roughly constructed, containing only two private chambers (*cubicoli*) and even these are very small and mean, as is the entire cemetery."

[14] N. Müller – N.A. Bees 1919.

[15] N. Müller 1915, pp. 286–7.

[16] Ferrua published their notes in 1988. A. Ferrua 1988, pp. 5–33.

[17] As Noy suggests. JIWE I, p. 2.

[18] R. Kanzler 1915, pp. 152–157.

[19] According to G. Filippi 1991, pp. 74, 96.

[20] R. Paribeni 1919, pp. 143–155. We have a photograph of his excavation.

[21] J.B. Frey, Intr. to CIJ, p. LXI; he photographs the access and adds that the structure was already collapsed at the time of the publication of the CIJ (1935).

[22] G. de Angelis d'Ossat 1939, p. 26.

[23] G. de Angelis d'Ossat 1939, pp. 361–9.

caused by the lithoid tufa in which the galleries were excavated,[24] a problem Müller had already pointed out.[25] The collapse of the cata-comb was due to two simultaneous factors: the stratum of tufa is surmounted by a compact, impermeable stratum of sandy marl mixed with limestone, while the stratum of lithoid tufa that lies beneath the catacomb level was constantly removed to extract the tufa of Monteverde, which had been used as a building material since Roman times. Large latomiae with thin walls could not support a heavy stra-tum and finally collapsed. In 1935 d'Ossat denounced the risk of razing that the archaeological area was subject to: already in 1960 it was entirely occupied by a block of flats.[26]

The Structure

The catacomb lay on a slope of the hill of Monteverde, between via Vincenzo Monti and the Circonvallazione Gianicolense, about 400 m. west from Trastevere railway station. As we have seen, it was exca-vated in three phases and in three different areas: at present it is hard to establish what the relation between these sections was and to assess definitively whether they belonged to the same cemetery or not.

The area Bosio explored, of which no plan was made, seems to have been excavated with narrow galleries; the graves are poorly carved, the private chambers very small and mean, "so is the entire cemetery, since not even a fragment of marble or any painting can be seen", a peculiarity that this catacomb shared with other Jewish cemeteries in Rome.[27] The graves are excavated in the walls or in the floor and are enclosed by bricks, sometimes with stucco-covering, "on which the epitaphs were in nearly every instance inscribed in red letters". None of these inscriptions was ever transcribed. We do not know the average number of loculi that were carved in the walls, a datum that could have helped us calculate the height of the galleries.

The area Müller excavated is actually the best known.[28] He testifies that he found a vestibule with a vaulted ceiling built in bricks and about 2 m. high. According to Goodenough,[29] who resumes a the-

---

[24] G. de Angelis d'Ossat 1939, pp. 25–7.
[25] N. Müller 1915, p. 225.
[26] H. Leon 1995², p. 58.
[27] A. Bosio 1632, p. 142.
[28] Description in N. Müller 1915, pp. 219–229.
[29] E. Goodenough 1953–1968, II, p. 4.

ory by Müller,[30] the atrium was a חצר, the vestibule the Mishnah requires for the funerary services;[31] as happens in the Jewish catacomb of Vigna Randanini and in the Christian catacomb of Domitilla, this area at a certain moment was occupied by burials: its original function had changed. From this room, one moved into the proper catacomb through a stairway in bricks 3 m wide (stairway I) that led to the level of the galleries. Müller could recognize three areas running radially around the central landslide:

- a South-eastern area, near the stairway.[32] The galleries have a haphazard development; there is a great variety in the types of sepulture. The theory that the extraordinary number of private chambers could depend on the union of more hypogea is rejected by Müller who points out that there was no other entrance;[33] it could be explained with the adaptation of grotto or tufa quarries to sepulchral aims. A second section departs from the rear of the stairway, with wide galleries and a few burials. In the middle of the ninth gallery two graves are carved in the floor, across the wall, probably because the gallery was no longer used: in fact no burial is attested in the final part.
- A South-western area, at the left hand side of the entrance. The area was partially explored. The plan shows some attempts at regularity, and the galleries were intended to cross at right angles. In this area there were the only three cubicula that Müller could find, two of which are decorated with corner columns. The density of burials is lower than in the other section; most of the graves are excavated in the pavement.
- A North-eastern area, in front and at the right hand side of the entrance. Like the just mentioned section, the area was probably planned. The galleries have a regular development, with the exception of a group of a few galleries excavated in the north, whose belonging to this section is uncertain. This area too is characterized by graves excavated in the pavement. Consequently, the density

---

[30] N. Müller 1915, p. 222.
[31] Mishnah Baba Bathra VI, 8.
[32] As Vismara remarks (C. Vismara 1986, p. 362) the orientation of the map Müller drew is wrong: he inverted the East with the West. The topographic elements given in the present work consequently do not follow Müller's description.
[33] As occurred in Vigna Randanini.

of the burials is low and seems to have been planned: at the end
of the twenty first branch, the most eastern one, only two graves
were found.

The area Müller excavated lies entirely on the same level, a chamber apart: this room was opened at the North-East of the stairway,
and could be entered with few steps.[34] Müller noticed a loculus inside
the chamber but was not able to understand whether the room was
connected to a lower area for a landslide. De Angelis d'Ossat studied the geological section after the general collapse of the catacomb
and claimed that the galleries occupied a level included between −10/
−7 m of fine and homogenous tufa and a level at about −7/−6 m
made of lithoid tufa and coarse volcanic detritus, an inhomogeneous
and permeable stratum.[35]

According to Müller, on the surface of the catacomb there was a
cemetery that he considered of a later period than the catacomb,
but that he ultimately could not investigate.[36] In his brief note, he
speaks of inscriptions that fell down in the lower strata when he
cleared the galleries below. He compares this situation to that of the
Christian catacomb of S. Callisto where two cemeteries were attested,
one on the surface, and one underground. Vismara is convinced by
the validity of this interpretation and suggests that the inscriptions
(whose Jewishness is not clear) could have been brought to the surface at the moment of the great landslide that devastated the stratigraphy and the planimetry of the catacomb.[37]

Also, the area Kanzler excavated in 1913 is on the side of the
landslide, but is clearly independent from the areas Müller discovered: its only entrance was a stairway opening on via Portuense and
a (no better specified) "access" had already collapsed at the time of
the excavation. He produced a map that is not very useful for our
purposes because it was not made in scale and was not orientated.
On the basis of this untrustworthy evidence it is possible to deduce
that there were perpendicular galleries and four cubicula. The most
peculiar element is a chamber in a wall (the northern wall?) of gallery
Q where a burial was placed, as happened in Venosa as well.[38]

---

[34] N. Müller 1915, p. 226.
[35] G. de Angelis d'Ossat 1939, pp. 23–25.
[36] N. Müller 1915, p. 220.
[37] C. Vismara 1986, p. 363.
[38] As Vismara remarks (C. Vismara 1986, p. 365).

Dating

Various attempts have been made to assign dates to this catacomb. Frey based his study only on the survey of the 204 brick stamps on the masonry and on the tiles that closed the burials.[39] He deduced that the catacomb was likely to have been in use since the first century, that it underwent intensive use in the second/third century and was finally abandoned in the IV century. The last dated stamp was produced under Diocletian.[40] Leon, and, in more recent times, Williams agrees with this reconstruction.[41] In 1988 Ferrua criticized this dating and affirmed that most of the brick stamps have to be dated to the III/IV century.[42] On the basis of renewed studies on this matter, in the early '90s Rutgers surveyed the brick stamps again and affirmed that most of the evidence should be dated to Trajan and Hadrian, together with a significant group dated to the Severians:[43] he concluded that the third century was the terminus post quem for the excavation of the catacomb.[44] The brick stamps cannot be used as the only dating material because of their irregular production[45] and because the bricks[46] were often reused. This catacomb did not produce other dating evidence, such as paintings or large fragments of sarcophagi.[47] Noy tried to grasp some elements from the inscriptions.[48] On one

---

[39] J.B. Frey, Intr. to CIJ, I, p. LIV and list of the brick stamps on pp. 211–227.

[40] The most ancient brick stamps are the nr. 1 (CIL XV, 1355), 2 (CIL XV, 1388), 3 (CIL XV, 1535) that he dates to the end of the Republic or to the Early Empire. The latest are 13 stamps that he considers of Diocletian period: 192 (CIL XV, 1623), 193 (CIL XV, 1569), 194–195 (CIL XV, 1569a), 196 (CIL XV, 1575), 197–198 (CIL XV, 1605), 199 (CIL XV, 1606), 200 (CIL XV, 1613); 201–204 cannot be compared to brick stamps published on the CIL because too fragmentary.

[41] H. Leon 1995², p. 66. Leon supposed that the catacomb was used since the end of the first century B.C. when we have the first literary evidence of the presence of a Jewish community in Rome. M. Williams 1994, pp. 165–182.

[42] A. Ferrua 1988, p. 31.

[43] Of 144 brick stamps, 10 stamps belong to 98–113 C.E., 7 to 114–122 C.E., 7 of 123 C.E. and 2 to 124–140 C.E. 8 brick stamps dated to 198–211 C.E., 36 to 198–211 C.E. and 32 to 212–217. L. Rutgers 1998, pp. 51–52.

[44] A. Ferrua 1988, p. 31.

[45] M. Steinby 1978, p. 1495 and pp. 1514–1516.

[46] Ferrua noticed this phenomenon in Monteverde. It is a principle widely accepted in archaeology.

[47] The most important fragment bears the representation of a kid and of erotes; this is why it has been supposed that the fragment did not belong to the material of the catacomb, but was subsided from the impending cemetery. The funerary furnishings too may not belong to an external context. C. Vismara 198, p. 366. The fragments of sarcophagi are described in E. Goodenough 1953–1968, II, pp. 12–14.

[48] D. Noy, JIWE I, p. 4.

hand, the rarity of the nomen *Aurelius* suggests that the effects of the *Constitutio Antoniniana* were not significant;[49] on the other hand, the abbreviated form *Aur(elius)* in JIWE II, 40 is not attested before the third century. Even if most of the inscriptions are in Greek, there are few texts in Hebrew and Aramaic in a numeric relation that reminds us of the early stage of the catacombs of Venosa; moreover, the lettering is similar to that of the Hebrew inscriptions of Beth She'arim, a burial area mainly used in the III/IV century.[50] On the whole, the epigraphy suggests the III and the IV centuries as the period of utilization of Monteverde. Vismara quotes some notes that Müller wrote on the kinds of burial he could see in the cemetery.[51] Notwithstanding the presence of loculi carved in the walls of the galleries, most of the graves were excavated in the floor; he adds that the *arcosolia* are, oddly, attested once. The graves carved in the floor, a type found only in Monteverde, are concentrated in the area around the stairway, the first to be exploited. In some cases, sarcophagi in brickwork were built on these burials. Müller consequently deduced that this was probably the most ancient kind of grave, and that it was then abandoned for other typologies, such as the sarcophagi and the loculi, not the arcosolia which for their rarity were possibly introduced only in the latest period of life of the catacomb. We can accept the relation he traces between the graves excavated in the pavement and the sarcophagi, but not the reason he suggests for the absence of arcosolia. As in the case of the *koch*,

---

[49] *Aurelius* is attested in Monteverde only in JIWE II, 40: *Aur(elius) Oly|mpius fil|io beneme|renti Bo[e?]|to q[ui vix(it)]* || [- - -] and JIWE II, 184: Αὐρη[λ]ία Ζωτική. Outside this catacomb, *Aurelius* is attested only in Vigna Randanini: JIWE II, 206, 226, 241, 265, 279, 284, 325, 378.

[50] JIWE II, 33, Aramaic and Greek: [- -] אסודרה ברת | [- - ᾿Ισ]ιδώρα θυγά|[τηρ --] ἄρχ(οντος) ῾Εβρέων Ar.: Isidora daughter of. . . . Gr.: Isidora daugher of. . . . *archon* of the Hebrews; JIWE II, 58 in Aramaic: דבר כולבריה | אניה חתנה Annia (?) son-in-law (?) of Bar-Calabria (?); JIWE II, 53: שלום Peace; JIWE II, 92: שלום על שאל Peace upon . . .; JIWE II, 153 in Aramaic: לברכתה זהי May it be for a blessing (?); JIWE II, 183 Greek and Hebrew: ἔνθα κῖτε ᾿Αμμι|ὰς ᾿Ιουδέα ἀπὸ | Λαδικίας ἥτις | ἔζησεν ἔτη (menorah) | שׁ'פלם Gr.: Here lies Ammias, a Jewess from Laodicea, who lived 85 years. Peace; JIWE II, 186 Greek and Hebrew: ἐνθάδε κῖτεν ᾿Ιούδας | νίπιος· ἐν εἴρνε κύμυ|σες αὐτοῦ. | ישראל Here lies Judas, child. In peace his sleep. Israel; JIWE II, 193 Greek and Hebrew: ἐνθάδε {ε} κεῖθεν | Σαββάτις δὶς ἄρχων | ἔζησεν ἐτῶν λε᾿· | ἐν ἰρήνῃ κύμησις αὐτοῦ | שאלום על ישראל Here lies Sabbatius, twice archon. He lived 35 years. In peace his sleep. Peace upon Israel.

[51] C. Vismara 1986, pp. 364–5. N. Müller 1915, p. 223.

attested only in Vigna Randanini, we could say that this kind of burial was in use in social or cultural groups, and probably did not depend on a different dating.

The catacomb of Vigna Randanini[52]

Discovery

The catacomb was discovered and explored by Ignazio Randanini, the landowner of the area. Already in 1862 Guarducci made the first excavation on behalf of the Pontificia Commissione d'Arte Sacra, and gave a brief account of the results the following year.[53] At that time there was a map of the structures on the ground level, but not of the catacomb itself; in this work he also published some inscriptions of which he neglected to add details regarding the stones and the places where they had been found. In 1862 and 1863 Visconti copied few more inscriptions that de Rossi transcribed and that came together in the work of Frey.[54] In the same decade, in an unknown year, many inscriptions that laid on the floor of the galleries were moved to more visible points and fixed to the walls. This was not an isolated episode: the policy of moving the inscriptions from their original places lasted for decades. We know that in 1884 Marucchi visited the catacomb and transcribed the inscriptions he could see, annotating the places where they were kept.[55] Frey, in the visits he paid while compiling the CIJ, had to remark that many inscriptions were not in the same places Marucchi had pointed out.[56] Leon stresses that the number of inscriptions kept in the catacomb decreases with time, although this movement was mostly due to a new collocation in museums.[57] Guarducci counts 195 inscriptions carved in stones and an unspecified number of graffiti that were published for the

---

[52] The catacomb is also known as the catacomb of via Appia.

[53] R. Garrucci 1862.

[54] J.B. Frey, CIJ, I, 53. The inscriptions Visconti copied were gathered in a manuscript of J.B. de Rossi, Cod. XLI, nr. 16270–16273, known to Frey. Visconti published also an essay on the catacomb: C.L. Visconti 1861, pp. 16–22.

[55] O. Marucchi 1903, II, p. 224; at pp. 208–224 he re-published his "Breve guida del cimitero giudaico di Vigna Randanini", Roma 1884.

[56] J.B. Frey 1933, pp. 27–50. In the appendix he published the map which is still used (though revised) both by Vismara and Noy (map 3).

[57] H.J. Leon 1995², pp. 70–71.

first time in the CIJ; in 1922, when Leon visited the catacomb, he could count only 122 texts. Frey, who entered the catacomb repeatedly in the '30s, could find only 119 inscriptions, a number that diminished when Leon visited the area in 1951, possibly as a consequence of the damage the catacomb underwent in 1943/44 when it was used as an air-raid shelter.

In 1951 Goodenough too visited Vigna Randanini and was able to photograph the paintings and details that were subsequently ruined by heavy seepages from the impending ground.[58] The Pontificia Commissione d'Arte Sacra restored the area in 1970, under the direction of Mazzoleni.[59] In 1986 Vismara published a new map of the catacomb, elaborating the map Frey had published in the CIJ (map 4).[60] In 1986 the catacomb was put under the management of the Soprintendenza Archeologica.[61] Because of important static problems in some areas (in particular in the galleries A and B) it is necessary to obtain a permit to enter the catacomb, although all the galleries are actually free from debris. The last visit paid to the catacomb mentioned in the bibliography is that of Noy on July 1994, before his re-edition of the Jewish inscriptions of Rome and the publication of a new map, which was a re-elaboration of the map of Frey too (map 5).[62]

Structure

The central body of the catacomb has a compact plan: it develops on the slope of the hill, almost always at the same level. No entrance steps were required nor steps to go from one area to another. The main entrance is on via Appia Pignatelli, a short distance from the Christian catacomb of Pretestatus, and is structured as a rectangular atrium with its long axis running south-west and north-east, which originally had a roof. The original building was later modified.[63] The earliest phase was in opus reticulatum mixtum;[64] in the north and in

---

[58] E. Goodenough 1953–1968, II, p. 15.
[59] D. Mazzoleni 1975, p. 295.
[60] C. Vismara 1986, p. 372.
[61] M. Vitale 1976, pp. 176–186.
[62] D. Noy, JIWE, II, p. 174; the map in the appendix.
[63] C. Vismara 1986, pp. 371–373.
[64] C. Vismara 1986, p. 372. It is an *opus reticulatum* alternated with three lines of bricks. Leon (H. Leon 1995², pp. 56–7) speaks only of *opus reticulatum*; Frey does the same. He took a photograph of the masonry (Intr. to CIJ, p. LV).

the south walls there were two wide niches. The second phase was
built in opus vittatum, and large sections of these can still been seen
today. In this phase a transverse from east to west was built, the
perimetrical walls were lengthened and were occupied by monu-
mental archosolia in brickwork (no more than three impending burials), while the pavement was covered with a black and white mosaic
with a geometric decoration.[65] The relation between the two structures is not clear. According to Guarducci, the building was always
Jewish and was used as a synagogue; the vestibule was near a spring
that could have been used for the purification rites; it was built in
the suburbs, as the other synagogues, and was divided into two rooms
to separate men and women. The mosaic pavement added elegance
and dignity to the whole structure.[66] This opinion can hardly be
accepted: apart from the fact that the localization of the Roman
synagogues is questionable and actually unknown, the proximity to
a burial area could violate the purity rules.[67] No positive reference
to burial activities can be foreseen in the first stage of this building:
probably in this period the construction was only a hall—in the open
air in the opinion of Noy[68]—that non-Jewish groups used for funerary purposes.[69] In a second stage, when the Jews took possession of
the area, it was restored and used as the atrium of the newly excavated catacomb. It is questionable whether the arcosolia were contemporary or subsequent to this phase, as it occurred in the lower
catacomb of Villa Torlonia. In any case, the atrium was probably
used for the funerary service. Possibly in connection with the vestibule
and its use, but on a lower level, a square room with a well in the
middle, from which departed a pipe that led to the atrium, was
opened. This is the room that suggested to Guarducci the hypothesis

---

[65] Frey could take a photograph of the mosaic when it was free from vegetation
Intr. to CIJ, p. LIX.

[66] R. Garrucci 1862, p. 6.

[67] This is a common opinion among scholars. In particular, Goodenough
(E. Goodenough 1953–1968, II, pp. 15–16) reminds us that the cemeteries could be
dug only at a long distance from the houses and were signalled by an inscription
that warned of the risks of impurity. The synagogue rites were forbidden, above
all, the opening of the Torah scrolls. Leclerq supposed that the room was used for
funerary banquets, as occurred for the cells used during the ἀγάπη in the vestibule
of the Christian catacomb of Domitilla (H. Leclerq 1907, I, p. 500).

[68] D. Noy, JIWE, II, p. 175.

[69] If the presence of arcosolii in the apses is correct. The news is attested in
Barbini but not in Vismara.

that the atrium was a synagogue. What was its original use can
hardly be said; most probably it was the heritage of an abandoned
pagan structure. At the north-east and the south-west of the entrance
there were two areas, which had already collapsed at the time of
Frey's visit.[70] The catacomb is structured around a central gallery
that runs along the imaginary axis of the vestibule. Six cubicula open
on this gallery, of which the third—counting from the entrance—
was painted with red lines that underline the architecture and with
Jewish symbols.[71] From its terminus, lit by the only light well of the
catacomb, two more galleries depart: one—with a south-west orientation—has both cubicola and arcosolia, the other—with a north-
west orientation—had already collapsed when Frey visited the catacomb
and is likely to have had no burials. The corridor crosses a perpendicular gallery that, following an odd course, reaches a new area.
This gallery, although on the same level of the preceding one, has
some interesting peculiarities: the cunicula are smaller, the galleries
cross perpendicularly at modular distances as if they drew a grille;
the height of the galleries diminishes dramatically and does not exceed
two metres. This latter detail may depend on the massive presence
of kochim, the graves cut perpendicularly to the walls under the
floor level, with superimposed burials—rigidly separated—found in
Rome probably only in this catacomb,[72] but well attested in Palestine:[73]
to excavate at the base of the walls and to make the galleries too
high would have dangerously altered the structure.[74] On the northern wall of the main gallery there is a cubiculum whose paintings
had already been destroyed at the time of Frey's visit.[75]

---

[70] As the dotted line on the map shows.

[71] Cubiculus 3 (according to Noy) or painted room IV (according to Frey and
Vismara). Description in E. Goodenough 1953–1968, II, p. 21 and photographs,
III, fot. 759–761.

[72] Vismara said to have seen these burials also at the ending of gallery D5 of
the lower catacomb of Villa Torlonia (C. Vismara 1986, p. 371).

[73] The koch is the most common burial in Palestine from 200 B.C. up to the
end of the Second Temple period. After the fall of Jerusalem, its use decreases.
E. Goodenough 1953–1968, I, p. 66; L. Rutgers 1995, pp. 61–62. Williams too
(M. Williams 1994, p. 177) connects the use of caves and kochim with the influence
of methods of burials attested in Palestine in the first century; in her opinion, the
innovative element was the large dimensions of the catacombs, considering that the
only Palestinian cemetery comparable to these catacombs is that of Beth She'arim,
which, however, developed in the second half of the second century. Clearly she
still dates Monteverde to the first century.

[74] C. Vismara 1986, p. 371.

[75] Cubiculus 12 or painted room III. Description of the few traces that could

The extreme offshoot of this area is closely connected to an area that originally was not included in the catacomb. A second entrance was opened on via Appia, a three-lamp stairway that descends to the level of the catacomb, to about −9 m. At the base of this entrance there is a vaulted atrium, like the one found in the lower catacomb of Villa Torlonia, which, according to Vismara, should be interpreted as the vestibule prescribed in the Mishnah.[76] Mazzoleni has a different opinion and, as in the case of the atrium on via Appia Pignatelli, supposes that it was a pre-existent structure that the Jews inherited and utilized.[77] This area is connected with two galleries one of which is the already mentioned connection with the main body of the catacomb. Most of the burials found in these galleries are *kochim*. Through a hiatus that can be easily recognised in the masonry, the second gallery reaches a new area, mostly collapsed, with narrow galleries. The interpretative problem concerns two cubicula that were opened at a lower level compared to the floor of the gallery, and which are decorated with paintings with pagan subjects, such as a naked athlete crowned by a winged Victory and Fortuna with the cornucopia.[78] Rutgers remarks the presence of signs on the walls, caused by the original excavations and carved in two different directions.[79] The traces show that the fossores who excavated the area around the cubicula came from the east, while those who dug the gallery connecting the area with the Jewish catacomb came from the west. He recognized around the two cubicula many unexcavated galleries, that could possibly hide a separate entrance to the hypogeum.[80] The relation between this area and the Jewish catacomb is actually unknown and for decades it has been the object of a lively debate for the presence of paintings that openly contradict the idea that Jewish art did

---

still be seen in E. Goodenough 1953–1968, II, pp. 20–21 and photographs, III, fot. 757–758.

[76] C. Vismara 1986, p. 375.

[77] D. Mazzoleni 1976, pp. 82–98.

[78] Cubicula 13 and 14 or painted room I and II.

[79] L. Rutgers 1995, pp. 54–55.

[80] In 1930, Frey (J.B. Frey 1933, pp. 27–50; map at p. 386) suggested the existence of a staircase that led from one of these galleries to the surface, which was placed on the western side of the two cubicula, and drew it on the map. Rutgers (L. Rutgers 1998, p. 62) could not find any trace of it, and has doubt about the validity of Frey's statement. All the other scholars who drew maps of the catacomb, although they based them on that of Frey, considered this corner unexplored and traced a dotted line.

not have any icons and the prohibition to represent images in places of worship.[81] Most probably, this section was originally an independent hypogeum whose entrance (or entrances) went lost; at that time, it was probably used by pagans. Then, this area was included in the Jewish burial area and a connecting gallery was excavated. As Rutgers remarks, the use of family cemeteries or hypogea of pagan origin is well attested among the Christians and can be recognised in the so called Villa Piccola of the catacomb of S. Sebastiano and in the "Flavian hypogeum" of the catacomb of Domitilla; only in this latter case were Christian symbols added to the original iconographic programme.[82] Consequently, I cannot accept the idea Vismara suggested that the cubicula were included in the Jewish catacomb to avoid altering the statics of the galleries and were actually an extraneous body within the cemetery. Apart from the fact that the diggers could have in any case separated the cubicula from the galleries by erecting a wall, Rutgers points out the presence of two kochim in the cubiculum 14, which Noy saw too:[83] the room was clearly used by Jews. I will discuss the implications of this question later on in the conclusions.

Dating

Various attempts have been made to assign dates to this catacomb, as to all the Jewish catacombs of Rome. Most probably Vigna

---

[81] Ex. 20:4 (לא־תעשה לך פסל וכל־תמונה אשר בשמים ממעל ואשר בארץ מתחת ואשר במים מתחת לארץ "You shall not make yourself an image, or any likeness of what is in the heaven above, or on the earth below, or in the water under the earth") Rabbinic Judaism frequently studied this question. In TB 'Abodah Zorah 42b the painting itself was forbidden. If a Jew found a pre-existent painting, he was allowed to keep it, but not to sell it. Consequently, a number of scholars, especially among the first who commented the cubicula, argued that the rooms were used by pagans. There are some interesting differences: Guarducci (R. Garrucci 1862, p. 156) thought that the rooms were never used by Jews, while Frey (Intr. to CIJ, p. CXXIV), on the basis of the above mentioned passage in the Talmud, claimed that the rooms could have been used as a Jewish burial area. Recently, Vismara (C. Vismara 1986, p. 377) rejected the possibility of a Jewish use. Conversely, Goodenough (E. Goodenough 1953–1968, II, pp. 30–32), at first, and Leon (H. Leon 1995², p. 60), radicalized the Talmud's idea, and, considering that only at a few points did the burials ruin the frescoes, claimed that the decoration of the rooms was made by the Jews. Rutgers (L. Rutgers 1995, p. 54 e L. Rutgers 1998, pp. 61–62) pointed out that no evidence shows that the rooms were distinguished or divided from the Jewish catacomb. No detail in the paintings can be compared to a Jewish symbology; most probably, the cubicula had a pagan origin. There are clear traces of a Jewish reuse of the rooms for funerary purposes.

[82] L. Rutgers 1995, p. 55.

[83] L. Rutgers 1995, p. 55; D. Noy, JIWE, II, p. 177.

Randanini was used from the end of the II to the IV century. Beginning from the eastern structures, the atrium has some dating elements. On the basis of the shape of the decorative details, Vismara dates the mosaic that paves the atrium to a period not preceding the Severians, as Leon and Rutgers have already supposed.[84] The opus reticulatum mixtum of the original structure should be dated to the second century too,[85] while the opus vittatum mixtum, the masonry used in the second phase, probably belongs to the III/IV century.[86] Rutgers found a brick-stamp walled in the opus reticulatum, which dated back to the first quarter of the second century, and which he used as terminus post quem.[87] The mosaic is likely to have been created during the enlargement of the room, as it shows its correspondence with the walls, which can still be seen in the photographs taken by Frey.[88] The fragments of sarcophagi found in this area belong to the end of the third century.[89]

The paintings of the cubicula 13 and 14 (known as painted rooms I and II), by comparison with Christian paintings drawn in similar catacombs, could be dated, according to Rutgers, to the beginning of the third century,[90] while those of cubiculum 12 (painted room III), which at present are heavily damaged, should date back to the first half of the IV century.[91] The cubiculum 3 (painted room IV) that inside has also a painted arcosolium is the only one with a Jewish iconography, a peculiarity that, however, does not allow any comparisons

---

[84] H.J. Leon 1995[2], p. 56; L. Rutgers 1998, p. 56; C. Vismara 1986, p. 373.

[85] C. Vismara 1986, pp. 372–373 and Rutgers (L. Rutgers 1998, p. 56). Though Leon (H. Leon 1995[2], p. 56) considered the masonry an opus reticulatum, he dated it to the second century anyway.

[86] D. Noy, JIWE, II, p. 178; L. Rutgers 1998, p. 56. If there is a correspondence between the brickworks in opus vittatum and the mosaic, further study would be needed to explain the chronological gap between the two interventions.

[87] L. Rutgers 1998, p. 56; The brick-stamp was walled up in one of the niches of the southern wall and bears the inscription: IIICOSSVLP.

[88] J.B. Frey, Introduction to CIJ, p. LIX. Thick vegetation covers the mosaic.

[89] Described in E. Goodenough 1953–1968, II, pp. 25–30 and L. Rutgers 1998, pp. 67–68.

[90] L. Rutgers 1998, p. 60. The closest comparisons were made with the cubicula X/Y of the catacomb of S. Callisto, dated to the early third century, and with the contemporary hypogeum of the Flavians in the catacomb of Domitilla. Goodenough (E. Goodenough 1953–1968, II, p. 31) dated the frescoes to the late second or early third centuries.

[91] The floral decoration has been compared to the cubiculum B of the catacomb of via Latina, dated to the fourth century, while the use of panels of false marble dates to the beginning of the fourth century. L. Rutgers 1998, p. 63.

with the contemporary Christian art;[92] in the arcosolium there was a fragment of a sarcophagus dated to the end of the third century, an element that can hardly be used to date the whole cubiculum.

The development of the galleries is unclear, but the chronological relation between the areas, particularly in the western sections, is not clear either. Before the Jewish use, the area was occupied by non funerary structures built at the end of the second century, as some clear traces in the building of via Appia Pignatelli indicate. As from the Severian period, certainly in the third century, the area was run by the Jewish community that restored and modified the buildings on the surface and begun the excavation of the galleries along a north-east and south-west axis that led naturally towards via Appia. Apart from the pipe connecting the square room to the atrium, which may belong to a pre-Jewish phase, the whole area does not indicate a previous use of the underground. If the dating of the cubiculum 3 is correct, it could be argued that the catacomb developed in the III/IV century. In the western outskirts, the kinds of burials change radically: the loculi and the arcosolia, hitherto the most common typologies, are replaced by the kochim. Whether this should be explained by a different chronology is questionable. A hypogeum beginning from via Appia was opened. A gallery belonging to this structure crosses a peripheral gallery of the Jewish catacomb, and it was connected to this one through a narrow stairway. In this regard, I would like to point out that a secondary gallery running from a southern area of the main catacomb accurately avoids, with sudden corners, crossing the above mentioned gallery belonging to the hypogeum of via Appia. Summarizing these pieces of information, we could argue that the hypogeum was created as an independent burial area; during enlargement works, a gallery orientated towards via Appia Pignatelli opened a gallery of the main catacomb, a fact that suggested to the diggers the possibility of connecting the cemeteries with a narrow service stairways "di servizio", as Fasola said. When the structure of the hypogeum became well known, a second widening of the main catacomb was decided, and a gallery that, as the map points out, avoids crossing any of the main galleries of the hypogeum was opened. Apart from these considerations, other chronological limits could hardly be established: at this stage we have no

---

[92] So L. Rutgers 1998, p. 64.

dating details. We cannot establish if the excavation of these two areas began simultaneously either, because the masonry of the entrances and of the galleries does not support any chronological theory.

The north-east gallery of this second catacomb includes an hypogeum, probably of pagan origin, and opens a new area with a large presence of cubicula and with narrow galleries, an area that has not been explored because it had already collapsed at the time of the first excavations. The entrance stairway to this area has not been found, but, as we have already remarked, the area has totally collapsed. Unlike the fortuitous crossing with the gallery dug from via Appia Pignatelli, this gallery makes a 90 degree corner and stretches to the area with the painted rooms. Most probably, the diggers of the Jewish catacomb, who had taken over the management of the pagan hypogeum later, tried to reach and incorporate this new area that they decided to use as a burial place without religious bias. The site known today as the catacomb of Vigna Randanini originally was probably made of three distinct areas. Considering that the paintings of cubicola 13 and 14 date back to 220/250 C.E., the incorporation of the hypogeum was possibly decided after the end of the third century.

The digging and the use of the catacomb is roughly dated between the III and the IV century. Traces of a later use could be seen in an inscription dated precisely to 501/2 C.E., whose Jewishness, in Frey's views, is questionable.[93]

The Catacomb of Vigna Cimarra[94]

The catacomb was discovered during works in the estate of count Cimarra in 1864, an area between via Ardeatina and via Appia Antica, not far from the Christian catacomb of S. Sebastiano. The following year, the Pontificia Commisione d'Arte sacra entrusted De Rossi with the exploration of the galleries. In 1867 he wrote a brief

---

[93] JIWE II, 401: [- - p]ositus | Maias die | [- - Flavio Avi?]eno iunior|[e consule - -] luna prim[a]. The formula positus/depositus is common among Christians, but rare among Jews. The presence of the date is not a problem: also JIWE II, 210, from Vigna Randanini, is a dated inscription. At the beginning of the fifth century Latin was widely used in the Jewish inscriptions of Venosa. If the inscription is Jewish and comes from this catacomb, the catacomb had been (partially?) used for decades after its supposed desertion. Frey, CIJ I, pp. 580–1, nr. 81.

[94] Known also as the catacomb of Vigna Limiti.

note in which he remarked the importance of the epigraphic material, but left out a description of the structures and of the burials.[95]
According to Müller, apart from an arcosolium, all the burials were
loculi.[96] De Rossi's paper includes a map of the archaeological area,
but not a map of the galleries, on which nothing is known. Although
we assume that the area on the surface corresponded to the original
extent of the catacomb, we should speak of an hypogeum more than
of a catacomb.[97] The summary excavations made in the galleries
suggest that we should not exclude the existence of other areas which
have now collapsed. Berliner published the inscriptions only in 1893.[98]
They are four texts, only one of which can actually be seen and is
kept in the Pontificio Istituto di Archeologia Cristiana; the other three,
which were left in situ, were lost. At the end of the nineteenth century the precarious conditions of the catacomb worsened because of
heavy seepages; in the '30s, Frey could see only "vestiges informes".[99]
De Angelis d'Ossat could not enter the galleries and was forced to
draw the geologic sequence doing surveys in the neighbourhood.[100]
In the post-war period the area was cut up into building lots.

According to Rutgers, the inscription, carved on a fragmentary
sarcophagus with a decoration consisting of strigiles, should be dated
to the third century.[101] According to Noy, the formulae of the few
inscriptions that were copied are like those used in the corpus of
Vigna Randanini.[102] Consequently, it has been supposed that the two
catacombs were in use in the same period, an assumption that can
hardly be accepted, considering the few data we have on the site.

The Catacomb of via Labicana[103]

At the time of the discovery, the catacomb was crossed by via
Labicana and was divided into two estates, about two kilometres

---

[95] G.B. de Rossi 1867, p. 13 and p. 16.
[96] N. Müller 1915, p. 238.
[97] J.B. Frey, Intr. to CIJ, I, p. CXCIV.
[98] A. Berliner 1893 (It. ed. 1992), p. 46. Berliner published a copy of the inscriptions kept in the lapidarium of de Rossi residence, given by de Rossi himself.
[99] J.B. Frey, Intr. to CIJ, I, p. LX.
[100] G. de Angelis d'Ossat 1939, p. 253. He picks up two superficial strata of
earthy tufa and an in-depth stratum of red pozzolane.
[101] As base. L. Rutgers 1998, pp. 67–68.
[102] D. Noy, JIWE II, p. 332.
[103] Known also as the catacomb of via Casilina.

from Porta Maggiore. This area was heavily exploited for burial purposes: a few metres away there is the entrance of the wide Christian cemetery of Marcellino e Pietro, while on the surface Frey notices fragments of inscriptions and of sarcophagi that were probably pagan.[104] The catacomb was discovered by Marucchi who could enter through a quarry. Marucchi visited the galleries briefly on January 1884, but could remain inside only three days because of the continuous risk of collapses. In the same year he published an account with the only map ever drawn of the catacomb, which was a map in scale and orientated, although rather summary.[105] In the '30s, Frey tried to go in but had to give up.[106] He explored some isolated galleries, with completely bare loculi, and the pozzolana quarries that supported the catacomb, but could not find any trace of the cemetery. In 1943, De Angelis d'Ossat had to study the nearby hypogea to isolate the geological sequence.[107] As Leon supposes, the structure was probably destroyed with the enlargement of via Casilina.[108]

Marucchi had noted the presence of galleries which had partially collapsed: most probably, the area he could describe was only a part of the whole site. We do not know where the entrance the diggers used was. According to Marucchi's map and drawings, on average the galleries were more than a metre wide, had vaulted ceilings and often created perpendicular crossings. The most common burials were loculi closed by bricks or large tiles. He saw at least three cubicula, but only one of these could still be visited when the first explorations took place. Marucchi mentions sarcophagi made in brickwork—a type found also in the main vestibule of Vigna Randanini—and two arcosolia, a kind of burial well attested in Jewish contexts.

Schürer dates the catacomb to the Antonines, with no further explanations, probably because of the tendency of the scholarship of the past century to date the greatest development of the Jewish catacombs to the second century.[109] As Noy remarks, no peculiarity could be singled out in the few inscriptions found in this catacomb or in the phraseology or in the stone.[110] We have to conclude that no dating element coming from this catacomb has survived today.

---

[104] J.B. Frey, Intr. to CIJ, p. LX and p. 46.
[105] O. Marucchi 1884, pp. 497–532. See map 6 and 7.
[106] J.B. Frey, Intr. to CIJ, p. XLVI.
[107] G. de Angelis d'Ossat 1939, p. 128.
[108] H.J. Leon 1995², p. 52.
[109] E. Schürer 1973–1986, III.1, p. 80.
[110] D. Noy, JIWE II, p. 338.

Catacombs of Villa Torlonia[111]

Discovery[112]

In November 1919, a burial area was found in the gardens of Villa Torlonia, during works at the foundations of a new stable, near the intersection between via Spallanzani and via Nomentana. The following year Marucchi published a brief note on this discovery,[113] while Paribeni published the first inscriptions and drew a sketchy map of the galleries with the help of Gismondi.[114] The exceptional dimensions of the catacomb were clear from the first excavations; it was known that the area had two different entrances, although nobody supposed that it belonged to two independent cemeteries. Frey, who entered the galleries three times in 1928, transcribed 55 inscriptions coming from the lower catacomb, an inscription found in the upper catacomb and 4 inscriptions of unknown provenance.[115] Beyer and Litzmann published the first monograph in 1939; they described the net of galleries in detail, published again the inscriptions of which he reported the precise finding points, and included a map that turned out to be a milestone in the studies on this site till the Seventies.[116] The structure of the site is becoming clear: the area was originally occupied by two distinct catacombs whose galleries developed on different levels and crossed only incidentally.[117] Beyer, who worked on the topographical questions, affirmed that the upper catacomb preceded the lower one. When in the '40s, the Villa became the private residence of Mussolini, some important changes took places: the air shafts and the entrance to the upper catacomb were closed for fear of attacks.[118] The only entrance to the whole archaeological area was the stairway to the lower catacomb. The closure of the ventilating shafts had an impact on the static balance of the galleries, as we will see later. Emergency repairs were carried out in

---

[111] Known also as the catacombs of via Nomentana.

[112] I am indebted to dott.ssa Barbara, inspector of the Distretto nomentano della Soprintendenza Archeologica di Roma, for all the pieces of information she could give me on the structures and on the repairs of the catacombs.

[113] O. Marucchi 1920, pp. 55–7.

[114] R. Paribeni 1920, pp. 143–55.

[115] J.B. Frey, Intr. to CIJ, p. LX.

[116] H.W. Beyer – H. Lietzamann 1930.

[117] The geologic stratigraphy has never been studied. De Angelis d'Ossat could not study the catacombs, which were inaccessible in the '30s.

[118] M.R. Barbera – M. Magnani Cianetti 2002, p. 63.

1946.[119] Between November 1973 and June 1974 the Commissione Pontificia d'Arte Sacra entrusted Umberto Fasola with the overall repairs of the catacombs. In 1976 a long paper appeared in the Rivista di Archeologia Cristiana, and a new map was drawn, which is used today (map 8).[120] The galleries were completely freed from debris, the vaults and the walls were reinforced, both stairways, the one that was used as entrance to the lower catacomb, and the one that connects the two catacombs, were restored with the insertion of bricks that could easily be distinguished from the original masonry. The stratigraphy of the catacombs was precisely drawn; the engineer Santa Maria highlighted the existence of twelve strata.[121] The lower catacomb developed at a depth between −11.40 and −9.45 m, while the upper catacomb between −9.15 and −6.90 m. After this excavation not only the development of the galleries and the relations among the different areas became clear, but it was also understood that the lower catacomb was dug before the upper cemetery. Fasola could copy twenty-five new inscriptions from the lower catacomb, as many texts from the upper catacomb and an inscription of unknown provenance, which were all not included in the *CIJ*. Fifty-nine brick-stamps, which Frey had partially mentioned, were listed and used to suggest the dating of the area.[122] Some of Fasola's interventions during the restoring works are now considered questionable. Without registering the finding place or the criteria adopted in the choice, he gathered part of the clay pottery, mainly ollae and lamps, all in very good conditions, and placed them in the arcosolium A6, free from burials, and closed by a grating.[123] With similar aims he walled part of the inscriptions he found broken on the ground along the main gallery of the catacombs, as in an exhibition. The finding place again was not recorded. At the end of the works, for no apparent reason, he asked to secure the gardens, closing the only entrance to the catacombs, the stairway E; the ditch that probably existed since the '30 and was necessary to reach the original level of the entrance was filled with earth. In 1984 the management of the catacombs was given to the Soprintendenza Archeologica that immediately freed

---

[119] Leon 1995², p. 63.

[120] U.M. Fasola 1976, pp. 7–62.

[121] U.M. Fasola 1976, pp. 32–33. For new stratigraphic survey see M.R. Barbera – M. Magnani Cianetti 2002, pp. 56–59.

[122] J.B. Frey (*CIJ*, I, 10–11) mentions 13 brick-stamps, 3 of first century and 10 of second century.

[123] Mentioned and photographed in U.M. Fasola 1976, pp. 60–61.

the entrance. In 1994 Noy, for security reasons, was refused a permit and could not enter the galleries and verify Frey's reading of the inscriptions.[124] In June–July 1997 Prof. Leonard Rutgers, coordinator of a research group from the University of Utrecht, counted and studied the loculi (he could count 3828 loculi)[125] and collected skeletal fragments that were going to be submitted to chemical tests to reach a positive dating of the period when the catacombs were in use. Most of the burials have intact depositions, although they were partially violated and were no longer sealed. The terrible quality of the air that allows only quick visits prevented him from more in-depth studies on the bones.[126]

As no other areas are likely to exist, the main interest of the Soprintendenza is the reinforcement of the walls: at present, many peripheral galleries are in risk of collapse and the whole site needs urgent reclamation works. In regard to the first problem, Fasola had already reinforced the unsafe areas with supports in brickworks, but some galleries are still in danger of collapse.[127] Beside the differences between the geological strata, most of the responsibilities had to be ascribed to the roots that, penetrating from the soil for 8–10 m, emerged in the vaults and in the walls of the galleries. A map of the most damaged area was drawn.[128] Clearly, the upper catacomb that is nearer to the surface has been heavily compromised. The problem is not an easy one. The surface corresponding to the site belongs to the park of Villa Torlonia, an area of high naturalistic interest: in the impossibility of uprooting age-old plants, the roots were contained and building on the area was forbidden. The irrigation of the gardens and an inadequate hydraulic net for the rain water caused seepages, abundant in the area near via Spallanzani and by the entrance E, which can also be recognized at a glance for the presence of limestone concretions in the tufa.[129] Completely different problems concern the air quality. Chemical tests[130] indicated high percentages

---

[124] D. Noy, JIWE II, p. 341.

[125] A map of the loculi is projected by the Sovrintendenza.

[126] M. Barbera – M. Magnani Cianetti 2002, p. 63.

[127] See map 9.

[128] By prof.ssa Giulia Caneva. M. Barbera – M. Magnani Cianetti 2002, p. 59. See map 10.

[129] See map 11.

[130] By the ASL and the Laboratorio di Chimica dei fluidi profondi dell'Università la Sapienza of Rome. See map 12. M. Barbera – M. Magnani Cianetti 2002, p. 62.

of radon, a radioactive gas that develops naturally in the rocks (an average figure of 17.2 Bq/L with hits of 30.7 Bq/L in the less ventilated cubicula versus the limit of 0.148 Bq/L fixed by the Environmental Protection Agency)[131] and of carbon dioxide (3.000 ppm on average with hits of 9100 ppm versus the limit of 5.000 ppm accepted not to cause respiratory problems). While the latter is probably produced by the activity of the roots and by the presence of volcanic rocks, the radon is probably transmitted in the catacombs through rifts in the stata of tufa and pozzolane into which the galleries were dug. The short ventilation caused by the closure of the air shafts worsened an already precarious situation. In 2001, the Ministero dei Beni Culturali invested in the estate, repairs could begin and works on the ventilation of the galleries were carried out. The collapses and the depth of the structures did not allow the use of georadar to localize the air shafts, which were eventually found with the help of electromagnetic equipment.[132] It was decided to open only the air shaft in front of the arcosolium A6, but the new air circulation cannot reach all the corners, and causes dangerous air pockets of carbon dioxide, whose formation is favoured by sudden lowering of the ceilings. In the future all the air shafts will be opened to re-create the original environment. Another consequence of the new ventilation was the urgent repairs of the paintings that were already kept under strict control;[133] during my visit to the catacombs in September 2003, the works were about to begin.

Structure

A stairway with traces of opus latericium leads to the lower catacomb,[134] into an irregular landing partly occupied by depositions. It has been supposed that this room was originally used as the atrium described in the Mishnah to fullfil the funerary duties, as it occurred—according to a current of opinion—also in the vestibule opened on the side of via Appia in the catacomb of Vigna Randanini.[135] As for

---

[131] See map 13.
[132] M. Barbera – M. Magnani Cianetti 2002, p. 56.
[133] Microbiologic tests of the air and of the painted walls were made by dott.ssa Lidia Barcellona, while mineralogic tests on the painted film by dott.ssa Marisa Laurenzi Tabasso (M. Barbera – M. Magnani Cianetti 2002, pp. 60–61).
[134] U.M. Fasola 1976, p. 62.
[135] C. Vismara 1986, p. 368.

its location, most probably the burials belonged to a late period, when the cemetery itself was no longer in use. With few more steps one descends to the proper catacomb and enters the gallery E1, at level –9 m. At the base of the short stairways there are two completely different areas. The first (E) was dug in the south with an irregular net of galleries, as can be seen in the ending of E5 that crosses E3, causing the collapse of the wall "d" of a loculum. The ceiling is modulated with small arches jutting out and carved in the tufa; the distance from each other roughly corresponds to the average length of a loculum. An air shaft, still closed, was placed at the intersection between E4 and E5. In a second period, when the gallery E1 was deepened, new galleries were excavated in the south and in the north. The main one of these is the long corridor E6 whose termination reaches a gallery coming from area D; according to the haphazard running of D14, we could argue that the diggers tried to reach the gallery E6, which at that time had already been opened, as the depositions destroyed after the crossing clearly show.[136] The ending of E6 joins the cuniculum "f". The burials, scantly attested in the area around the intersection between E6 and D12, disappears in F: the cuniculum is probably not a connection to a new, unknown, region. At the end of F there is another air shaft that, as in the previous case, has been localized but not yet opened. The area has both arcosolia and loculi placed in the spaces between two arches.

Area D was dug northwards from the stairways, at a lower level. Nine steps connect the region with the base of the stairway. The first galleries have orthogonal intersections and outline a regular net. The vaults are decorated with arches and crosses drawn with white lime at a modular distance. Similar strips of white lime can be seen on the walls. The correspondence between these strips and the placement of the loculi suggests that the former were guidelines for the carving of the burials: the few cases where the strips were ignored depended on peculiarities in the geological nature of the ground.[137] In a second stage, the region was widened and new galleries were dug; the original scheme was respected. Gallery D2 belongs to this phase. This corridor gets over the entrance stairway without crossing it (the gallery, in fact, is at a deeper level) and joins the termi-

---

[136] U.M. Fasola 1976, p. 48.
[137] U.M. Fasola 1976, pp. 53–55.

nation of E6 destroying a deposition: with no doubts, gallery E6 had already been opened when the ending of D2 was dug. The region D has burials excavated in the floor, loculi, arcosolia and the only cubiculum found in the lower catacomb, at the beginning of D12, with corner columns carved in the tufa.[138] Vismara mentions the presence of kochim at the end of D5.[139]

Coming back to the main gallery of the catacomb, corridor E1 runs eastwards. Its ceiling, after the intersection with E6, was abruptly lowered, a fact that at the moment causes a heavy worsening of the air quality for the stagnation of carbon dioxide; while in the first part of the gallery up to seven burials could be put one on top of the other, in the ending section no more than five loculi could be superimposed. No arcosolium or cubiculum has been found.

The intersection between E1 and C1 marks the connection with the upper gallery. As said above, the area was freed from debris during the first excavation, but underwent radical repairs during the campaign of 1976. The reading of the area is difficult because of the presence of more interacting elements: gallery E1, two cubicula opening on this one, gallery C1 and a stairway of about twenty steps that leads to level –8.25 m.[140] Fasola noted that the end of gallery E1 was filled with the debris of C1 and from this detail deduced that the lower catacomb was dug in before the upper cemetery, contrary to Beyer's authoritative opinion.[141] The ending of E1, in fact, had already been opened at the time of the excavation of C1.

The stairway was rebuilt in 1976, to facilitate the passage to the upper catacomb.

Region C opens at the left of the stairway. The map of this area has few peculiarities. Gallery C4, a peripheral corridor, with its haphazard routes, goes over gallery E10, but cannot join the lower catacomb for the difference of level the two cemeteries have. Gallery C1 exploits a hydraulic pipe whose traces can be still seen at the end of the gallery. Region C was occupied by both arcosolia and

---

[138] Fasola's map omits the arcosolia of the lower catacomb.

[139] C. Vismara 1986, p. 370. Contra L. Rutgers 1998, p. 86. I cannot verify this detail because the area was considered dangerous for the presence of gas.

[140] U.M. Fasola 1976, p. 33; the difference between the levels is about 1,40 m.

[141] U.M. Fasola 1976, pp. 9–12. C1 ruined a loculus placed at a higher level than E1. When the staircase and C1 were opened, that loculus was transformed into two arcosolia. Only the bottom in tufa was preserved; all the others walls were built in brickwork.

loculi. The main body of the upper gallery develops towards South-East, around a stairway that today is closed and covered with earth, but that can still be recognised in the few traces of opus listatum with which the ending part was built.[142] The region A, possibly the most ancient area of the catacomb because of its proximity to the entrance, was dug to the North-East of gallery A2. The plan for this section was orthogonal and regular. As for the lower catacomb, the upper cemetery was organized along an axis, gallery A2, from which corridors and regions depart. After the intersection with E1, A2 is crossed by the same hydraulic pipe exploited for C1. In this very point, the pipe is broken by the ceiling of B4 that runs at a lower level: this interesting crossing has been cleared with the excavation of Fasola. Along A2 there are three arcosolia and two cubicula, wholly painted with frescos that represent Jewish symbols or Jewish subjects. Goodenough, Leon and, more recently, Rutgers, studied these paintings, also for the importance they have in dating the catacombs.[143] We refer to these works for a full description. The ending of A1, after the intersection with the staircase A, still has some relevant burials, six arcosolia and a cubiculum that show traces of paintings. Though it was a blind gallery, it belongs to the most ancient area of the catacomb, an area that was long used for depositions. Perpendicularly from gallery A1, which starts at the foot of the staircase, three more galleries were opened. As occurs with E1, A1 runs in straight line, but the floor lowers after the cross with A3; according to Fasola, it may be argued that the ending part of the gallery belonged to a later period. In this regard, the gallery A9 broke into a loculus that belongs to the ending of A1: most probably, the gallery was opened after the prolongation of A1. Unlike the main corridor, galleries A6 and A7 are enriched by five arcosolia and a cubicula with no traces of paintings but with corner columns carved in the tufa, as in the cubiculus "a" of the lower catacomb. At the crossing of the two galleries the only air shaft of the upper catacomb was opened; the Soprintendenza decided to open only this well, and, in recent works of repairs, reinforced the structure with a tube that obstructs the entrance to A7.

---

[142] U.M. Fasola 1976, p. 41.
[143] E. Goodenough 1953–1968, II, pp. 36–41; photographs vol. III, plates 806–817; H.J. Leon 1995[2], pp. 206–209; L. Rutgers 1998, pp. 64–66.

The region B was dug at a lower level behind the staircase. It can be reached through a few steps carved in the tufa. This area consists of an intersection of two galleries: the first (B1) runs westwards, while the second (B2), is oriented towards the north and exploits the same pipe used for B3 and C1. The low number of depositions found in the ending of B2 indicate a loss of interest in this area and may explain why the central section of the pipe was never used for funerary purposes. In any case, attempts were made to join the region C starting from region B: as seen above, gallery B4 broke into gallery C1 at a point near the staircase; the difference in the level of the two areas (about 1 m) prevented the connection. However, the lowering in the level of B1, the correction in the gallery E7, whose ending, according to a recent survey, turns abruptly southwards, could depend on an aborted attempt to surmount the differences in the levels and to eventually connect the two galleries.

Dating

Most scholars have dated the catacombs to the III/IV century. After Fasola's excavation, the stages of development of the galleries can be more clearly read. Contrary to the former studies, the lower catacomb turned out to be the most ancient: the original core of the whole site consequently was the stairway of the lower catacomb and the galleries E2, E3 and E1 (before the crossing with E6). The lengthening of E1, the remaining galleries of region E and the first parts of D1, D2, D3, D4, D5 belong all to a later stage.[144] The opening of the upper gallery should be dated back later: it includes the staircase A, the gallery A1 up to the crossing with A3, the gallery A2 without the cubicula that were opened at a lower level and the whole region C, excavated, as seen above, after the prolongation of E1. Gallery A1 was subsequently deepened and prolonged, and the galleries A4–A6 (with the cuniculus "e") and the four cuniculi of A2 were opened. Because the gallery A9 breaks into a loculus of A1, Fasola supposed that this gallery and A8, from which it starts, were dug in the aftermath. Recent repairs confirmed his theory.

However, as we look for evidence supporting an absolute chronology of the catacombs, we meet an overwhelming lack of information. Following a hint by Beyer-Lietmann, Frey dates the catacombs

---

[144] All the galleries up to the intersection with D5.

on the basis of elements depending on the brick-stamps put on the tiles that closed the burials or on other building materials found during the excavations.[145] In the introduction to the CIJ published in 1936, he supposes that the catacombs developed between the first and the third century, but saw their maximum use in the second century. Leon shared his position.[146] Fasola too used this method, but felt the risks that this could imply.[147] In describing the galleries he distinguished between walled brick stamps and brick-stamps not found *in situ*; these latter could not be assigned to a precise context or, supposedly, to the catacombs themselves, as pagan burials were found at the surface and in the neighbourhoods. Crossing the data obtained from the brick-stamps and the developing stages of the galleries, he could deduce some positive post quem terms. Considering that in gallery A1 two brick-stamps of Severian age[148] and a number of brick-stamps lying at the ground dating back to the same period were found, he argued that the origin of the upper catacomb should be fixed to the beginning of the third century. According to the relations between the galleries he had pointed out after the excavations, he supposed that the original body of the lower catacomb up to the crossing with C1 had possibly been dug some time before, while the deepened area of region A and the opening of cubicula apparently belonged to the middle of the third century. Without further information, the finding of a brick-stamp probably of Diocletian age walled in A7 led to dating the intersection A6–7 and the ending of A1 (all on the same level) to the early fourth century. No brick-stamps were found in the widening of area D, where most of the inscriptions were found. Fasola could only argue that this region was opened in an early period: the prolongation of D2 breaks into a loculus of E11, as seen above. This method has been subjected to substantial criticism. On the one hand, he does not take into consideration the irregular trend of production, according to which periods of massive production could be followed by the almost total disappearance of brick-stamps; on the other hand, he almost ignores the phenomenon of reuse of stamped building material. In his essay we can see an interesting example. The area B has a lower number of

---

[145] J.B. Frey, *Introduction to CIJ*, p. LV.
[146] H.J. Leon 1995[2], pp. 65–66.
[147] This position is summarized in U.M. Fasola 1976, pp. 61–62.
[148] Probably he was thinking to CIL XV, 180 and CIL XV, 195.

loculi than the average registered in the whole catacomb, an element that could support the dating to a later period, when the loculi were partially replaced by other kinds of burials.[149] Conversely, in this area a brick-stamp of the first century (CIL XV, 122) walled in the closure of a loculus has been found, as well as two brick-stamps lying at the ground and belonging the first to the Hadrian period (CIL XV, 115), the other to 123 c.e. (CIL XV 486a). The two pieces of evidence clash. One more brick-stamp of the first century was found in the filling of the staircase A, but it was not used for dating purposes because it could come from other contexts. Moreover, although we think that the brick-stamps originally walled up on the galleries did not belong to materials of reuse—a questionable assumption—the brick-stamps could be of bricks used in a later period. For instance, it is not sure that the intersection A6–7 was opened in the Diocletian period because a brick-stamp (probably) of those years was walled up on a gallery. A re-examination of the evidence reveals some discrepancies in the dating Fasola suggested.[150] Most of the brick-stamps dated back to the government of Commodus and Caracalla. A core of evidence belongs to an earlier period, mostly the years of Antoninus Pius and Marcus Aurelius (with scarce evidence of Hadrian). The only brick-stamp belonging to the Late Antiquity is that of Diocletian, mentioned above. Apparently, no positive element can be deduced from the material found in the galleries. Evidence of second century is always mixed with brick-stamps of the third century; a comparison with the stages of development of the galleries is in any case necessary. We can only legitimately argue that the moment of maximum exploitation of the catacombs was the third century, probably after Caracalla, and is likely to have continued in the fourth century. The limits of such a survey are clear.

According to Rutgers, the entrance to the lower catacomb, built in opus latericium, and the entrance to the upper catacomb, in opus listatum, could date back to the end of the second century.[151] Because we know that the peripheral galleries of the lower catacomb were

---

[149] A completely different dating could be supported by the fact that B4 breaks into the pipe used for C1, but at a lower level and when the gallery had been already opened.

[150] S. Cappelletti 2002, pp. 261–278.

[151] L. Rutgers 1998, p. 55. Fasola (U.M. Fasola 1976, p. 62 nr. 42) suggested this dating. In Leon's opinion (H. Leon 1995², p. 65), the staircase E belonged to the third century.

dug before the upper catacomb, but we cannot definitely date the staircase E, we cannot exclude the possibility that the excavation of the two catacombs began in the same period. The dating of the frescoes is debated. Fasola compares these paintings with frescoes found in Christian contexts and suggests the mid-third century as a possible dating.[152] On the same basis, Rutgers supports a later dating, the fourth century.[153] In particular, the paintings in the cubiculus Aa belonged to 320–350 C.E.,[154] while those in the two arcosolia in A2 (eastern and western wall) dated back to 350–370 C.E.[155] The paintings in cubicula b-c-d are too ruined to be studied and dated. According to Rutgers interpretation, the catacombs were probably used during the whole of the fourth century.[156]

To conclude, the catacombs developed as two independent cemeteries with different entrances, different kinds of burials, a different and incomparable plan of galleries and on different levels, but were dug, apparently, roughly in the same period.[157] According to the little evidence we have, we are inclined to suggest the late second century or the early third as the moment when both catacombs were opened. The lower catacomb reached its maximum development (as for the region E) before the upper catacomb was widened, as the intersection E1–C1 clearly shows. Although the catacombs were actually connected, they were still considered two different cemeteries: the staircase built for this purpose, both because of its dimensions and for its steepness, is to be considered a "scala di servizio", a back

---

[152] U.M. Fasola 1976, p. 61 and P. Pergola 1997, p. 140. Vismara (C. Vismara 1986, pp. 369–370) described the paintings but did not suggest any dating, while Leon (H. Leon 1995², p. 66), who still considered the lower catacomb later than the upper one, dated the frescoes to the second century, and affirms that they were contemporary to the opening of the cubiculum.

[153] L. Rutgers 1998, pp. 64–66.

[154] The paintings on the ceiling and on the arcosolium of the cubiculum could be compared with frescoes of the catacomb of Pietro and Marcellino, while the imitation marble *strigiles* sarcophagus on the front of the arcosolium is supposedly contemporary to the spreading of this kind of sarcophagi, in the first half of the third century.

[155] The paintings have been compared to the catacomb of Marcellino e Pietro (J. Deckers (ed.) 1987, pp. 66–67, p. 381, p. 384).

[156] L. Rutgers 1995, p. 54.

[157] In the lower catacomb, the burials are usually closed with tufa covered with marble, while slabs of terracotta prevail in the upper ones. In the lower catacomb most of the burials are loculi carved in the walls, and, seldom, in the floor. There are traces of kochim (Vismara 1986, p. 370). The number of arcosoli (2) and of cubiculi (1) is surprisingly low. In the upper catacomb there are 5 cubiculi and about thirty arcosoli. No koch has been found.

stairway, to quote Fasola. Possibly the enlargement of the upper catacomb (as the opening of the peripheral galleries of the area C and
A and the opening of area B) dated back to the third century or to
the early fourth. We do not know for sure if the building structure of
the painted rooms, at a lower level than A2,[158] belonged to the same
period as the frescoes which are dated—with a wide margin of variation—to a period between the third and the late fourth century.

Conclusions

The Jewish catacombs have significant elements in common with the
Christian cemeteries. The condition of four of the six Jewish catacombs found in Rome does not allow a general study on this topic.
However, the data that has been surveyed supports the idea that
few positive differences distinguish the catacombs of the Christian
from those of the Jewish communities. Like the Christians—or the
"pagans",—the Jews in a first moment excavated underground hypogea
of limited dimensions. Subsequently, they connected these small burial areas and created a wider catacomb, as can be seen clearly in
Vigna Randanini. They too exploited the morphology of the area, such
as the presence of caves, reused abandoned quarries or shaped the
galleries on pre-existent hydraulic pipes. The plan of the galleries
can also be easily compared: corridors with a haphazard route co-
exist with well-organized areas. Jewish burial areas are not clearly distinguished from the Christian or pagan ones either. Christian catacombs
or pagan hypogea are in close contact with Jewish burial areas: the
Christian catacomb of S. Agnese is near the catacombs of Villa
Torlonia, along via Nomentana, while Frey remarks that on the surface of the Jewish catacomb of via Labicana he could see fragments
of pagan sarcophagi and of pagan funerary inscriptions. The best
example of fusion between a Jewish and a non-Jewish context is
undoubtedly the double cubiculus of Vigna Randanini. The existence
of an independent hypogeum originally distinguished from the Jewish
catacomb had already been supposed in the first studies. Who were
the owners that commissioned the paintings on mythological subjects
is a point that has been harshly debated. The discovery of a koch
inside one of the cubiculi of Vigna Randanini showed that the Jewish

---

[158] A peculiarity that Fasola explains with a later dating.

reuse of the rooms could no longer be denied. Picking up a consideration by Rutgers,[159] we do not know whether these paintings were made by Jews, but it is clear that the Jews could bury their dead in rooms with pagan decoration. Whether this position was considered heterodox at that time is hard to establish. The Judaism of this period was not gathered around a unitary interpretation of the Law. What was considered forbidden in Babylon was possibly accepted in Rome. Apparently, the Jews of this community did not wish to be divided or clearly distinguished from the Christians and the pagans.

Not all the features of the Jewish catacombs are similar to the pagan and the Christian cemeteries, with regard to the kind of burials. The Jewish depositions contain only one body; in case of wide graves such as the arcosolia, the bodies are separated by small brick walls or with strata of tiles. Though the arcosolia and the loculi are well-attested in the Christian cemeteries too, the kochim are typically Jewish. The difference in the burials has provoked many questions. Their belonging to different periods can not be suggested as a possible explanation, because loculi, arcosolia, painted rooms and sarcophagi do not occupy an exclusive area, but are all placed at close contact with each other. As can clearly be seen in the gallery A2 of the upper catacomb of Villa Torlonia, loculi are carved in the walls, while two painted arcosolia and two cubicula opened on the sides. The area of Vigna Randanini, where most of the kochim were found, has important evidence of loculi and a cubiculus. Most probably, as Williams supposed, the differences in the burials depend on economic reasons: those who could be buried in (family) cubiculi or in decorated sarcophagi were likely to have been of a higher rank than those who had access to a loculus.[160] However, this answer is not enough. The presence of a typically Jewish deposition such as the koch could indicate that in life the dead had kept close religious bonds with his motherland and with traditional rites. Unfortunately, as Rutgers remarks, these burials were never studied in depth.[161] In this regard, he affirms that the kochim were used also in Rome—as in Palestine—for burying the bones, but no positive evidence of this custom was ever found in this community.[162]

---

[159] L. Rutgers 1995, p. 54.
[160] M. Williams 1994, pp. 179–180.
[161] L. Rutgers 1995, pp. 61–62.
[162] L. Rutgers 1995, pp. 63–64. There are few traces. Rutgers takes into con-

Many details are still unknown. We do not know whether there were structures of worship or small buildings on the surface in correspondence to the catacombs. As seen above, the vestibule of Vigna Randanini has given rise to many interpretations, but no definitive answer because of the lack of recent archaeological data concerning the surface around the entrance to the catacomb. We do not know by which right the Jews could use the soil (and the subsoil) for funerary purposes. However, on this point the excavations have been of some help. The hypogeum of via Appia, included in the catacomb of Vigna Randanini at a second stage, developed northwards and incorporated a pagan hypogeum: a new plot was possibly added to the original area the community could use. The area D of the lower catacomb of Villa Torlonia is a net of galleries whose northern side is traced by the ends of three blind galleries: the walls do not show any decrease in the number of burials. Similarly, gallery A2 was suddenly interrupted around the same point of gallery F. Probably the widening of an area corresponded to the acquisition of a new plot, whose limits the diggers could not cross. We could deduce that both the soil and the subsoil were managed by the community. However, it cannot be established who actually managed these plots or if the *fossores* were all Jews.

---

sideration an inscription (JIWE II, 180) coming from Monteverde decorated with a little rose whose drawing recalls the decoration represented in the ossuaries of Jerusalem. However, the text is fragmentary and the original dimensions of the stone are unknown. In some small inscriptions the names of more dead people are mentioned. Rutgers himself, however, admits that in the Jewish catacombs of Rome there was no relation between the dimension of the burials and that of the inscriptions, which, often placed between two graves, could refer to more than one burial.

THE INSCRIPTIONS

Most of the Jewish inscriptions of Rome were found during the excavations in the catacombs, walled up in the *loculi* and in the galleries or crashed on the ground. A smaller group was found by chance during road works in other areas of the town. Although these inscriptions are similar to those discovered in the catacombs, we cannot say if they belonged to a Jewish context. Neither group can be dated for certain. The inscriptions found outside the catacombs are dated on the basis of a comparison with the funerary inscriptions. However, these inscriptions are often scratched or roughly carved and usually do not bear any dating elements. They are considered contemporary to the catacombs and are dated to the third/fourth century.[1] As we have already seen, the catacombs themselves can hardly be dated. Moreover, the way the inscriptions were found and, subsequently, kept, raises many questions. Since the first accounts by Müller and De Bees on the catacomb of Monteverde, the data concerning the inscriptions were desultory: we know that an inscription comes from a catacomb, but we do not know the gallery it was placed in. This is an important question and involves also the fictile and vitreous finds. If we agree on the fact that a catacomb developed in many decades, a dating based solely on the context cannot be considered definitive. Unfortunately, even Fasola, who excavated the area of Villa Torlonia in recent times, is quite inaccurate in recording these data.[2] The problem is even more complex. The excavators of Vigna Randanini moved some inscriptions from their (unknown) finding places to put them in more visible points along the main gallery that crosses the catacomb: Frey remarks that many inscriptions were moved from the place registered by Marucchi in 1884.[3] Probably something similar happened also in Villa Torlonia. Fasola in his essay

---

[1] H.J. Leon, dates the catacombs to the first/third century and the inscriptions to the second/third century (1995[2], pp. 87, 89, 91–2); H. Solin (1983, p. 656, 684, 694, nr. 235, 701, 718 nr. 287), D. Noy and L. Rutgers (1998, p. 57) date the inscriptions to the third/fourth century, whil A. Ferrua (1936, pp. 309–311) to the fourth/fifth century.

[2] S. Cappelletti 2002.

[3] J.B. Frey 1933, pp. 27–50.

says that he repeatedly found crashed inscriptions: all these finds were walled up in the galleries. We do not know whether the finding point corresponded to the place where the inscriptions are kept at present; most of the inscriptions are actually walled along the main galleries. Moreover, in the accounts of the excavators of the nineteenth century the overall number of inscriptions registered diminished instead of increasing. According to the reports on Vigna Randanini the number of inscriptions kept in the catacombs, 195 in 1862, becomes 122 in 1922 and 119 in the '30s; this trend depends only in part on assignments to museums or removals organised by the Pontificia Commissione d'Arte Sacra.[4] The two main catacombs were accessible for decades and probably underwent despoliations.

Notwithstanding these problems, the information these inscriptions gives us is enormous. The number of finds can be compared to the corpus of Beth She'arim in Eretz-Israel and of Venosa. This evidence gives us information on the organization of the community: the titles discussed in the first section of the present work are mentioned only in this source.

The inscriptions are a privileged source to understand the degree of Romanization of the Jewish community. The attempt to "make the inscriptions speak" is quite common among scholars and has been re-proposed with the publication of the new corpus. According to stricter criteria and to the data about the discovery, Noy could establish when a text has to be considered certainly Jewish.[5] Consequently, some inscriptions coming from contexts other than the cat-

---

[4] H.L. Leon 1995[2], pp. 70–71.

[5] In J.B. Frey's opinion (Intr. to CIJ, p. XII), an inscription cannot be considered surely Jewish only on the basis of the place of finding: other criteria, such as a Jewish name, Jewish phraseology, symbols, and Jewish ideology, are required. In the appendix he gathers inscriptions that he considers pagan (CIJ 4*–47*) or Christian (CIJ 80*–87*). He regards inscriptions of unknown provenance (CIJ 500–514) and inscriptions on glasses found outside the catacombs (CIJ 512–526) as Jewish. The collection of Porto is regarded as evidence of an autonomous community (CIJ 535–551). A few years later V. Tcherikover applies similar criteria in organising the CPJ (CPJ I, pp. XVII–XX). A papyrus is certainly Jewish if it presents terms such as Ἰουδαῖος, συναγωγή or sabbath, or a Jewish name and if it was found in a Jewish context. However, as P. van der Horst (1991, pp. 16–17) has pointed out, the presence of only one criterion does not prevent us from making mistakes in establishing whether an inscription (or a papyrus) is Jewish or not. For example, a term as συναγωγή, which is considered typically Jewish, has been found also in non-Jewish contexts. In 1960 H.J. Leon in the appendix to "The Jews of Ancient Rome", re-published the inscriptions, using Frey's system of numbering (criteria at p. 263).

acombs, have been expunged and put in an appendix, while the group of Porto, studied by Leon,[6] has been divided into inscriptions of unknown provenance and inscriptions coming from a definite catacomb.[7] Consequently, the data concerning the languages used in the inscriptions diverge from the conclusions suggested both by Leon and by Rutgers in his first work on the community, published before Noy's corpus.[8]

Monteverde: 155 inscriptions in Greek, 39 in Latin, 4 in Hebrew,[9] 2 in Aramaic,[10] 2 bilingual Latin/Greek, 2 bilingual Greek/Aramaic.[11] *Vigna Randanini*: 126 inscriptions in Greek, 63 in Latin, 7 bilingual Greek/Latin.

He adds inscriptions that Frey had not considered Jewish, while expunging others (for instance CIJ 24*, 30*–35* from Monteverde). The inscriptions of Porto are considered of unknown provenance or are gathered with the evidence of a catacomb, wherever possible. The inscriptions on the golden glasses (CIJ 515–522) are expunged: although these objects were in use among the Jews and often have a Jewish symbology, the inscriptions are not clearly Jewish and can be brought back to a Christian context too (H. Leon, p. 341). In 1975 B. Lifshitz re-published the first volume of the CIJ with a new introduction. He does not change Frey's organization but adds new inscriptions. The group of Villa Torlonia, which Fasola would publish the following year, is clearly not included. In the edition Noy published in 1995 (intr. I, pp. IX–XI) an inscription is considered Jewish if it is written in Hebrew or Aramaic, if it has Jewish symbols (in particular the menorah, the ethrog and the shofar that seldom occur among the Christian inscriptions), if it has a Jewish phraseology or typically Jewish epithets, if presents a Jewish name and if it cannot be brought back to a pagan or Christian context. In comparison with the other editions, more attention is paid to the provenance of the inscription. The collection of Museo Borgiano at Velletri and of S. Paolo fuori le Mura are studied again, the notes of Marini are reconsidered: the inscriptions are included in the groups of Monteverde, Vigna Randanini or in the inscriptions of unknown provenance, as most of the inscriptions from Porto. The inscriptions with DM are supposed to have re-used pagan inscriptions, are considered "possibly Jewish" and are gathered in APP. 2. Frey had expunged this group as certainly pagan. APP. 3 includes an inscription that was erroneously considered Roman (CIJ 514–JIWE II, 613). APP. 4 gathers non-Jewish texts, among which there are two inscriptions of Porto (CIJ 542, 551b) and one of Monteverde (CIJ 470–JIWE II, 627) and the group of Vigna Pignatelli that is no longer considered a Jewish catacomb (CIJ 79,89–JIWE II, 628).

[6] H.J. Leon 1952, and H.J. Leon 1995[2], p. 73.

[7] CIJ 535–551.

[8] H.J. Leon 1995[2], pp 75–78; L. Rutgers 1995, pp. 176–191.

[9] JIWE II, 53 [ם]שלון; JIWE II, 92: שלום על שאל (sic); JIWE II, 161: illegible letters; JIWE II, 253.18: א.

[10] JIWE II, 58: דבר כולבריה | אניה חתנה the text can hardly be reconstructed. Noy, pp. 51–52. He translates: Annia (?) son il law (?) of Bar Calabria (?). JIWE II, 153: תחי | לברכתה "May it be for a blessing (?)".

[11] JIWE II, 33: the Greek and the Aramaic texts are similar: אסודרה ברה | [-- Ἰσ]ιδώρα θυγά|[τηρ – –] ἄρχ(οντος) Ἑβρέων.

Villa Torlonia: 112 inscriptions in Greek, 5 in Latin, 1 in Hebrew.[12]
Vigna Cimarra: 5 inscriptions in Greek.
Via Labicana: 3 inscriptions in Greek.
Inscriptions found in other places: 46 in Greek, 3 in Latin, 4 bilingual Greek/Hebrew,[13] 2 bilingual Greek/Latin, 1 bilingual Latin/ Hebrew,[14] 1 trilingual Greek/Latin/Hebrew.[15]
Inscriptions of unknown provenance: 32 in Greek 2 in Latin, 1 bilingual Greek/Hebrew,[16] 2 bilingual Greek/Latin.[17]

Interesting data comes also from the glasses[18] and other evidence found in the excavations:[19]
Greek: 4 inscriptions.
Latin: 6 inscriptions.
Bilinual Latin/Greek: 2 inscriptions.
Bilinual Greek/Hebrew: 1 inscription.[20]

Greek is used in about 75% of the inscriptions, while Latin occurs only in 20% of the texts.[21] Semitic languages are rare. At first sight, the data are homogeneous. However, even if most of the inscriptions found in Monteverde are in Greek, 9 texts are written in Hebrew and Aramaic, an outstanding number in comparison with the information we have on the other catacombs. Conversely, in Vigna Randanini no Semitic text has been found, but eleven of the

---

[12] JIWE II, 529: שלום על ישראל H. Leon (1995², p. 63) claims that he saw the inscription inside the catacomb. The text went lost.

[13] JIWE II, 535 found in via Appia: in Hebrew only שלום; JIWE II; 545–546 both found in Trastevere: the Hebrew letters are illegible; JIWE II, 560: kept in S. Paolo fuori le Mura: in Hebrew שלום.

[14] JIWE II, 550 found in in via Portuense: in Hebrew only בשלום.

[15] JIWE II, 539 found in Trastevere (V C.E. ?).

[16] JIWE II, 560: in Hebrew l.7 . . . שלום. JIWE II, 551: the inscription is in Greek; one word is in Latin with an Hebrew letter: Barῶeoda.

[17] JIWE II, 564 and 577: in both inscriptions Greek is transliterated.

[18] On the gold-glasses, found in Christian and Hebrew contexts. Rutgers 1998, pp. 68–69 and 1995 pp. 81–85; J. Engemann 1968–69, pp. 7–25.

[19] JIWE II, 568 on a glass medallion; JIWE II, 599–600 on two seals.

[20] JIWE II, 596: in Hebrew l. 5: שלום.

[21] Leon (H. Leon 1927) studied the Greek the Jews of Rome spoke. In the monograph on the community he summarizes his conclusions and adds a short list of examples (H. Leon 1995², pp. 75–92). He affirms that "the Jews of ancient Rome essentially spoke the same Greek that was prevalent in the lower class", an interpretation recently shared by P. van der Horst (1991, pp. 23–32) who gathered even more evidence, by L. Rutgers (1995, pp. 184–186) and by D. Noy (1997).

sixty-three Latin inscriptions are written with Greek characters, while in three Greek/Latin inscriptions the Greek part is written with Latin characters. In these last two groups Greek is used only in the final formula. The picture of Villa Torlonia is more simple: most of the evidence is in Greek, the Hebrew is used once, and in the bilingual one Greek is again reduced to the final formula. The catacombs of via Labicana and Vigna Cimarra have hardly been studied and cannot be considered in this analysis. How should we interpret these data? In the past a catacomb was thought to have been used by specific groups, which were distinguished according to wealth or, more probably, to religious and cultural identity. Considering that most of the Semitic inscriptions come from Monteverde, it has been suggested that this catacomb was used by traditional Jews.[22] Conversely, the absence of Semitic inscriptions, the massive find of Latin inscriptions and the discovery of two cubicula with figurative paintings on the ceilings supported the assumption that the area of Vigna Randanini was used by Rominized Jews.[23] In regard to Villa Torlonia, the proportion between Latin and Greek inscriptions suggests that the catacombs were used by Ellenophone Jews, possibly coming from a Graeco-Jewish environment.[24] Although the presence of different levels of Romanization and of different religious sensibilities is prudently suggested, this picture of the Roman community is, in my opinion, inconsistent. Above all, the interpretation of the evidence is incorrect on some details. The three Hebrew inscriptions discovered in Monteverde contain only the short formula *shalom*; the Aramaic inscriptions, unusually long, will be discussed later on. During the excavations no typically Jewish grave has been found: Bosio's statement attesting kochim is no longer valid. Most of the inscriptions found in Villa Torlonia were written in Greek. But, actually, this is not a typical aspect of this burial area: from Hellenistic times, the Greek became the language used both in everyday life and in holy rites in large communities such as Cyrene and Alexandria. With regard to Vigna Randanini, the Greek inscriptions are prevalent, though inscriptions in Latin are well attested too. In the bilingual texts, the Greek is used only for salutation formulae. As said above,

---

[22] H. Leon 1995², p. 77.
[23] H. Leon 1995², p. 77.
[24] H. Leon 1995², p. 77.

no inscription in Hebrew has been found. How should we interpret the inscriptions in Latin language but written in Greek characters? Recently it has been suggested that the Latin inscriptions were later than the Greek ones.[25] At Venosa, the Greek inscriptions are attested in the most ancient phase of the site, while Latin is used from the late fifth century c.e. on.[26] The Latin inscriptions were not contemporary to the Greek evidence, but belonged to a later period, and were the result of an age-long process of integration with the Roman culture. The Latin texts written in Greek characters could attest an intermediate phase, when Greek was still in use and Latin had not yet prevailed. As we will see, a similar interpretation has been suggested for the lack of evidence in Hebrew or Aramaic.

As Noy remarks, unlike the other groups of foreigners living in Rome, for centuries the Jews maintained the language that they possibly used on their arrival, the language in which the Bible was written, the language used during holy rites.[27] Consequently, we should suppose that the Roman community was largely bilingual, that most of the Jews spoke Greek as their first language, but that there were smaller groups who spoke predominantly Latin.

Most probably, Greek was the language in use during the rites, as the bilingual inscriptions of Vigna Randanini show.[28] In these texts, Greek occurs only in the holy formulae, to the point that they are transliterated—not translated[29]—in Latin characters. Moreover, the Jewish titles are all in Greek, are seldom Latinized but never

---

[25] L. Rutgers 1995, pp. 178–184.

[26] At Venosa, the Latin inscriptions are later than the Greek ones; many Greek texts seem to have been written by people who thought in Latin, with the use of Latin cases and of Latin expressions transliterated into Greek. Opposite data has been gathered in Rome. Probably, in the first centuries of their permanance in Italy the Jews spoke Greek. Later on, Latin became the language of daily life, and eventually supplanted Greek as the ritual language (D. Noy 1994, p. 175).

[27] D. Noy 2000, p. 264 and Noy 1997, pp. 301–308; according to P. van der Horst (1991, p. 34), the use of Latin indicated a better education and a higher social rank. It is certainly possible, but the small number of inscriptions found (in comparison to the importance of the community) does not allow any definitive conclusion on this matter.

[28] JIWE II, 217, 265, 298, 322, 352, 359, 379: it was the usual formula ἐν εἰρήνῃ ἡ κοίμησις αὐτοῦ with small linguistic variations.

[29] JIWE II, 157 from Monteverde: irene; JIWE II, 204 from Vigna Randanini: en irene quimesis su; JIWE II, 217 from Vigna Randanini: iren cybis aut; JIWE II, 352 from Vigna Randanini: en hirene e cymesis autoes; JIWE II, 379 from Vigna Randanini: en irene ae cymesis su; JIWE II, 577: en irenae ay cymisis autis.

reduced to Hebrew. As Rajak stresses, data coming from inade-
quately explored areas could be controversial and should be studied
with caution.[30] Even if we agree with the idea of two phases of linguistic development or with the theory of the contemporary presence of Latin and Greek speaking groups, the inscriptions do not
show any religious peculiarity of the people buried in this catacomb.
Conversely, the archaeological discoveries show two areas with kochim,
tombs usually connected to traditional Judaism, in close proximity
to the painting cubicula. The idea that this catacomb was used by
Romanized Jews is inconsistent: actually, it is difficult to say whether
or not there was a prevailing identity among the people buried in
this catacomb.

In this context the absence of inscriptions in Semitic languages is
apparently surprising. However, this is not a striking peculiarity. The
epigraphic evidence in Hebrew found in Rome is limited to the usual
formulae *shalom* and *shalom al Israel*, whose spelling is in two cases
incorrect.[31] Much more interesting are the two inscriptions in Aramaic
found in Monteverde. These inscriptions were thought to belong to
a later period, when the Hebrew returned to be the everyday language. However, the lettering is similar to that attested in the inscriptions of the third/fourth century in Beth She'arim. Consequently, it
has been supposed that the people mentioned in the inscriptions had
close links with Eretz-Israel. In any case, it is worth noting that in
the third century the Hebrew language has not yet seen the flourishing
attested in the fifth/seventh century in the inscriptions of Venosa. The
lack of evidence of Semitic inscriptions in Rome is not so meaningful.

The importance of the Greek language in the ritual can be deduced
from the way the Bible is quoted in the inscriptions. A gold glass
bears the inscription "οἶκος ἰρή | [νη]ς. λά | βε εὐλογία".[32] If εὐλογία is

---

[30] T. Rajak 1994, p. 232.

[31] JIWE II, 183 l.5 from Monteverde: שׁ׳עלπ‎ם and JIWE II, 193, l.5 from
Monteverde: שׁאלום על ישׂראל. Conversely, in P. van der Horst's opinion (1991, p.
23), the presence of these Hebrew formulae shows that Hebrew was still considered the holy language, although it was no longer used during the rites.

[32] JIWE II, 588. This is a well-known gold glass, with the representation of the
Temple and of a menorah in its upper section. It was found by De Rossi in the
Christian catacomb of SS. Pietro e Marcellino in 1882. It is not clear why a Jewish
glass was kept in an expressly Christian cemetery. Around a picture of temple and
menorah is an inscription reading: οἶκος ἰρή[νη]ς. λάβε εὐλογία. Around outside:
[- - μετὰ τῶν] σῶ[ν] πάντων.

corrected with εὐλογίαν, the sentence, λαβὲ εὐλογίαν is a quotation from 2Kings 5:15, as it appears in the Septuagint.[33] A less evident quotation can be found in JIWE II, 584. The inscription, which belongs to the Porto's collection, is of unknown provenance. It certainly belonged to the Roman context, as there the synagogue of the Calcaresians, well-attested in the Capital, is mentioned. On ll. 7–8 it is said: εἶδεν ἐκ τῶν τέκνων | αὐτῆς ἔγγονα. In Noy's opinion, the sentence could echo Psalm 127,6, according to the Septuagint: καὶ ἴδοις υἱοὺς τῶν υἱῶν σου. Actually, it is more a suggestion than a true quotation.

The presence of other biblical references is still less assured. In JIWE II, 25, a long, poetic inscription, on ll. 2–3 there is an invocation: νῦν δέσ|ποτα ἐν εἰρήνῃ κόμησιν αὐτοῦ. Although this expression is evidently shaped on the formula ἐν εἰρήνῃ ἡ κοίμησις αὐτοῦ, the invocation is very similar to that in Luke 2,29–30: νῦν ἀπολύεις τὸν δοῦλόν σου, δέσποτα, κατὰ τὸ ῥῆμά σου ἐν εἰρήνῃ. This passage, full of Old Testament references,[34] reflects Genesis 15,15, again according to the Septuagint: σὺ δὲ ἀπελεύσῃ πρὸς τοὺς πατέρας σου μετ' εἰρήνης, ταφεὶς ἐν γήρει καλῷ.[35] Moreover, in JIWE II, 327 it is said: ἡ δόξα | Σωφρονί|ου, Λουκίλ|λα εὐλογη|μένη, an unusual expression.[36] According to Ferrua, there is a parallel with I Corinthians 11:7 (ἡ γυνὴ δὲ δόξα ἀνδρός ἐστιν), a passage that recalls the creation of man in Genesis 1:27.[37]

---

[33] 2 Kings 5,15: καὶ νῦν λαβὲ τὴν εὐλογίαν παρὰ τοῦ δούλου σου.

[34] A. Plummer 1956, p. 68: ἀπολύεις is used for the death of Abraham (Gn. 15:2), of Aaron (Num. 20:29), of Tobit (Tb. 3:6) and of a martyr (2Macc. 7:9). Δεσπότης is rare in the NT (Acts 4:24; Rev. 6:10), but is attested in the Septuagint (Pv. 29:28, Is. 1:24, Jonah 4:3). Flavius Josephus uses this term to translate the name of God (J.B. Fisher 1948–1949).

[35] Gn 15:15 ואתה תבוא אל־אבתיך בשלום תקבר בשיבה טובה "As for you, you shall join your forefathers in peace; you shall be buried at a happy old age".

[36] Attested only in JIWE II, 103 and in IGCVO 1033, a Christian inscription.

[37] Gn. 1:27: ויברא אלהים את ־ האדם בצלמו בצלם אלהים ברא אתו זכר ונקבה ברא אתם "And God created man it his image; in the divine image created he him, male and female created he them". In the Septuagint the passage is translated: καὶ ἐποίησεν ὁ θεὸς τὸν ἄνθρωπον, κατ' εἰκόνα θεοῦ ἐποίησεν αὐτόν, ἄρσεν καὶ θῆλυ ἐποίησεν αὐτούς. Among the fragments of Aquila, this passage is translated: καὶ ἔκτισεν ὁ θεὸς σὺν τὸν ἄνθρωπον ἐν εἰκόνι αὐτοῦ, ἐν εἰκόνι θεοῦ ἔκτισεν αὐτούς. Paul could have modified the passage because he was more interested in the relationship between man and woman than between woman and God. A. Robertson – A. Plummer 1955, p. 251; A. Ferrua 1936, p. 300.

Three inscriptions almost quote Proverbs 10:7: "the memory of the just man with praise".[38] In ll. 2–3 of JIWE II, 307, an inscription of Vigna Randanini, can be read: "μνήμη δικαίο[υ] σ[ὺ]ν | ἐνκωμίῳ. The quotation is based on the Septuagint (μνήμη δικαίων μετ᾽ ἐγκωμίων), quite faithfully cited.[39] The same passage is quoted in JIWE II, 112, coming from Monteverde. On ll. 6–7 it is said: μνία δικαίου εἰς | εὐλογίαν. This time, the Aquila version is used, which had spread in the Diaspora since the second century (μνήμη δικαίων εἰς εὐλογίαν).[40] In a third inscription discovered in Vigna Randanini (JIWE II, 276) the versions of the Septuagint and of Aquila are cast together: μνήμη | δικαίου ἰς εὐλογίαν | οὗ ἀληθῆ τὰ ἐνκώ|μια.[41] JIWE II, 153 may be considered too. This inscription, found in Monteverde in 1913, was written in Aramaic: לברכתה | תהי, "May it be for a blessing (?)". Unfortunately, this inscription is fragmentary and the large lacuna does not allow us to understand whether it was a true quotation of Prov. 10:7 or not. This passage was cited in a funerary context not only in Rome: actually this was the most cited Biblical passage in the Jewish inscriptions found in Italy. Unlike those of Rome, all these inscriptions date to a later period (sixth-eighth century) and are written only in Hebrew.[42]

From these few inscriptions it is hard to deduce which version of the Greek Bible was in use in the community, and when and if the Septuagint was replaced by the Aquila version in the ritual of the Roman Jewry.

Deissmann supposed that, at a certain moment, the community used a Latin version preceding the *Vulgata*.[43] The inscription of *Regina*,

---

[38] Prov. 10:7: [זכר] צדקת לברכה.

[39] In the Septuagint ἐγκώμιον is used to translate ברכה as in Ex. 2:23 (E. Hatch – H. Redpath 1975, vol. I, p. 367).

[40] The version of Aquila uses the term εὐλογία as a translation of ברכה also in Dt. 11:27, Iob. 29:13, Is. 44:3 and Ez. 34:26 (N. Turner 1966, p. 100 and p. 268).

[41] P. van der Horst 1991.

[42] JIWE I, 118 from Taranto (third/fourth century); JIWE I, 120 (seventh/eighth century) from Taranto JIWE I, 122 and 131 (seventh/eighth century) from Taranto; JIWE I, 137 (fifth/seventh century) from Oria; JIWE I, 183 (fifth/sixth century) in which the passage is mentioned at the feminine, [זכר] צדקת | לברכהם. Only one Latin inscription quotes this passage: JIWE I, 120 (fourth/fifth century) quoted above: *memoria iustorum ad benedictionem*.

[43] A. Deissmann 1927, pp. 447–450.

the only Jewish inscription in hexameters found in Italy, was entirely built on Biblical passages, many of which are apparently inspired by a translation of the Bible in Latin.[44] In his opinion, this inscription attested the diffusion of a Latin Bible in the Diaspora, before the Vulgata and the version of Aquila were written. This theory is inconsistent.[45] As part of the Roman corpus, this inscription dates to the third/fourth century.[46] In this period, the community probably used Greek both in daily life and in the rites: on this question the inscriptions in Latin seem quite clear. The passages that Deismann considered Biblical quotations are more likely echoes of the Bible, words that because of their meaningfulness often recur in the Vulgata.[47]

The content

A source of primary importance for the knowledge of the community and the mentality of the Roman Jews, the inscriptions found in Rome are only funerary documents. As said above, this is not a striking peculiarity: in Italy the honorary inscriptions made by Jews are rare.[48] Probably inscriptions of this kind were placed in the exte-

---

[44] JIWE II, 103: *Hic Regina sita est tali contecta sepulcro | quod coniunx statuit respondens eius amori. | Haec post bis denos secum transsgresserat annum | et quartum mensem restantibus octo diebus; | rursum victura reditura ad lumina rursum. | | Nam sperare potest ideo quod surgat in aevom | promissum, quae vera fides, dignis piisque | quae meruit sedem venerandi ruris habere. | Hoc tibi praestiterit pietas, hoc vita pudica, | hoc et amor generis hoc observantia legis, | | coniugii meritum cuius tibi gloria curae. | Horum factotum tibi sunt speranda futura, | de quibus et coniunx maestus solacia quaerit.*

[45] Of this same opinion T. Rajak 1994, p. 232 and D. Noy in editing the inscription.

[46] T. Reinach (1920 p. 118) supposed the inscription was of the first century because of the archaic accusative *aevom*.

[47] For instance: l.1 *contecta sepulchro* could remind Qoh. 38:16 *contege corpus*, while l. 3 *transsegerat annum* Gn. 41:56 *transactis annis*; l.6 *nam sperare potest* could recall the eschatological promise in 2Macc. 12:44: *nisi enim eos resurrecturos speraret*, while l.8 *quae meruit* could be seen as a quotation of Esth. 16:18: *deo reddente ei quod meruit*.

[48] JIWE I, 18: *[synagoga (?)] Iudeorum | [in col(onia) Ost(iensi) commor]antium qui compara | [verunt ex conlat(?)]ione locum C(aio) Iulio Iusto | [gerusiarche ad m]unimentum struendum | [donavit, rogantib(?)]us Livio Dionysio patre et | | [. . . . .]no gerusiarche et Antonio | [. . . . dia] biu anno ipsorum, consent(iente) ge[r | us(ia). C(aius) Iulius Iu]stus gerusiarches fecit sib[i] | [et coniugi] suae lib(ertis) lib(ertabusque) posterisque eorum. | [in fro]nte p(edes) XVIII, in agro p(edes) XVII.* The inscription was found at Castel Porziano and could be dated to the second century. The community of Ostia dedicated it to a gerusiarches and probably placed it on his grave. JIWE I, 15: Ostia (around 253–260 C.E.): *M(arco) Aurel[io .] f(ilio) Ter(entina) Py[ladi] | A[. .]SCI[. . .] Scythop[oli] | p[an]tomim[o*

rior of the synagogues, as is shown in Elche and in Aegina, but no evidence has been found yet.

Most of the inscriptions are painted in red or, sometimes, in white or scratched on the loculus closure, according to a use well-attested in Beth She'arim and Venosa. These texts, which were composed with little attention to the lettering and the layout, are usually short, and contain the name of the dead and often a Jewish symbol. A sample of this category of evidence could be JIWE II, 506, which can still be seen in the gallery A1 of the superior catacomb of Villa Torlonia: *Blerinos*. The name is not attested anywhere else, and Fasola takes it for *Verinus*.[49] The inscription is scratched on the plaster of the wall beside the loculus of a child. A little menorah is scratched above.

A smaller number of inscriptions is carved on plaques of travertin or of marble. At times, the high quality of the materials is accompanied by a greater accuracy in the making of the text. The inscription of Regina (JIWE II, 103) is carved on a white marble plaque, 84 x 43 cm, and shows and excellent layout: the final letter of each line, except the last, is aligned vertically. Even more interesting for this porpuse is the only trilingual inscription found in Rome (JIWE II, 539) in 1842 during building works between Ripa Grande and the Tiber. It is dated to the fifth century. The inscription was carved on a thick marble plaque (24.5 × 46.5 × 6.0 cm); the Greek and Latin texts are exactly equivalent to each other, the letters (with serifs) have medium hight of about 2.6 cm and two menorot of the same measures (7.5 × 6.0 the first; 7.7 × 6.0 the second) are carved aside the Hebrew text.

---

sui] *tempor*[*is*] | *primo in c*[. . . . . .]*to et probato* | *a*[*b imp*(*eratoribus*) *Valeriano*] | [*e*]*t Gal*[*lien*]*o* [- -] | *ex provincia* [*Iuda*]*e*[*a* . . . . . . *post*] | *mortem patr*[*is s*]*ui Iud*[*ae; item de*]*cu* | *rioni civitat*[*iu*]*m Ascalo*[*nitan*]*orum et* | *Damascen*[*or*]*um. Huic s*[*ecu*]*ndus* | *ordo Augus*[*ta*]*lium non solum* | *propter memo*[*ri*]*am patr*[*i*]*s eius, sed* | *et propter plenam* [*ipsius pe*]*ritiam postul*[*antibus*] | *omnibus pariter civibus* [- -] [—]. JIWE I, 13: *pro salute Aug*(*usti*). | Οἰκοδόμησεν κὲ αἰπο[ί] | ησεν ἐκ τῶν αὐτοῦ δο | μάτων καὶ τὴν κειβωτὸν || ἀνέθηκεν νόμῳ ἁγίῳ | Μίνδις Φαῦστος με | [τὰ τῶν ἰ]διῶ[ν]. The inscription, which is fragmentary, was found in the building material reused to floor the vestibulum of the synagogue of Ostia. Probably, Mindios Faustos built and paid for the architectural element that bore the inscription. When the floor was remade, in the last phase of the building the inscription was reused. JIWE I, 17: Porto (IV d.C.): [– – –] σὺν [. . . . . . κ]αὶ Θεοδώ | [ρου (?) κα]ὶ Ἑλλὴλ φρον | τιστῶν. The inscription can not be referred to a synagogue.

[49] U. Fasola 1976, p. 21.

In regard to the formal aspects, some interesting differences distinguish the inscriptions in Latin from those in Greek.[50] In the Greek inscriptions a closer attention to the formulae has been noted. Sixty-three of the 633 inscriptions in Greek open with the formula ἐνθάδε κεῖται, with both lexical and morphological variants.[51] The most attested closing formula (35 finds) is ἐν εἰρήνῃ ἡ κοίησις αὐτοῦ and was probably so common that it was transliterated (not-translated) in some Latin inscriptions of Vigna Randanini.[52] In this case too, some variants have been registered.[53] The two formulae are often united in the same inscription. The concluding expression is the most modified. Eleven inscriptions wish the deceased to rest "with the justs", μετὰ τῶν δικαίων[54] or μετὰ τῶν ὁσίων;[55] according to a bilingual inscription (Greek/Hebrew) found in Otranto and dated to the third/

---

[50] H. Leon 1995², L. Rutgers 1995, D. Noy 1999. With Noy's edition, some data change, but not significantly.

[51] Ἔνθα (7 times) and ὧδε (13 times) can be found in place of ἐνθάδε. The verb is attested also in the first person: JIWE II, 25; JIWE II, 342: κεῖμε; JIWE II, 360: κῖμαι; JIWE II, 488: κεῖμε. All morphological variants reflects the spelling phenomena attested in the Jewish corpus (H. Leon 1995², pp. 79–86 and L. Rutgers 1995, pp. 184–186). The diphthong αι can become an ε: κεῖται is written κεῖτε 98 times. The diphthong ει is often written as an ι: κεῖται becomes κῖται (10 evidences) or κῖτε (50 evidences). Often the aspirate consonant is missplaced or eliminated: ἐντάδε (9 evidences), κῖθε (JIWE II, 128), χῖτε (JIWE II, 543). Often the variants depend on wrong assimilations to the aspirate letter that follows or precedes the syllable (JIWE II, 402: ἐνθάδε χεῖθε ἐθῶν) or on a methatesis (JIWE II, 52: εἰτάδε χεῖθε). A ν is sometimes added at the third person singular (4 instances).

[52] This formula is also used in the later inscriptions (fourth/seventh century) found in Southern Italy (JIWE I, 50, 118, 46, 101, 53, 48.16). In JIWE I, 75 the formula is transliterated in Hebrew characters: קימיסי אן ירינא. Similar formula are attested also in the Latin inscriptions: JIWE I, 33 cuius anima in reque (sic); sit pax in requie eius (JIWE I, 120, 122, 127, 128, 129a, 130), sit pax super dormitorium eorum (JIWE I, 121). A similar version in Hebrew is well-attested: שלום על משכב (JIWE I, 107, 89, 85, 70, 87, 111, 75, 132).

[53] According to the phenomena mentioned above, αἰν can be found in place of ἐν (3 evidences), or ἰρήνη for εἰρήνη (41 evidences). One of the best attested variants concerns the diphthong οι of κοίμησις, written with an υ: κύμησις (26 evidences). Again in κοιμήσις, the η can be written as ι (27 evidences). Leon (1927, pp. 214–216) explains this phenomenon as an assimilation of the vowel of the inner syllable, placed between an υ and a ι. Probably the vowel was written in the way it was pronounced. Consequently, this phenomenon differs from the substitution of η with ι as in the term νήπιος (JIWE II, 186 νίπιους). This last variant is seldom attested in Rome, but is used in the later inscriptions of Venosa.

[54] JIWE II, 235, 270, 329, 342, 406, 533. In JIWE II, 343 the formula is partly translated, partly transliterated into Latin: dormitio tua inter dicaeis.

[55] JIWE II, 50, 463, 465, 481.

fourth century, the expression is probably a translation of עַם הַצַּדִּיקִים.[56] In elaborate texts, a formula that is attested also in Christian context is used: θάρσει, οὐδεὶς ἀθάνατος.[57] Simon remarks that in this case the deceased was often a child or a young person.[58] According to the lexicon, there is a strong homogeneity in the use of adjectives and epithets describing qualities of the deceased. Beside terms such as γλυκύτατος,[59] ἡδύς (JIWE II, 282) and ὅσιος[60] (which are separate from the formula mentioned above), many epithets include the prefix φιλο-. This prefix can stress the love the deceased had towards his family, as in the cases of φίλανδρος,[61] φιλάδελφος,[62] φιλογονέους (JIWE II, 414), φιλοπάτωρ[63] and φιλότεκνος (JIWE II, 127,171). This a characteristic that the Jewish inscriptions share with the non-Jewish epigraphy. The peculiarity is the use of this prefix to remark the love for the community (φιλοσυνάγωγος,[64] φιλόλαος,[65] φιλοπένης[66]) or for the Law (φιλόνομος,[67] φιλέντολος).[68] The latter is similar to expressions such as εὐδιδακτή,[69] ἀμίαντος (JIWE II, 270), δικαία.[70] Belonging to the community and faith in the Law were priorities in the life of the Roman Jews.

---

[56] JIWE I, 134: ἔνθα κατ|άκητε Γλύ|κα, θυγάτερ | Σαβίνου καὶ | [. .]αης τῶν ‖ προαναπαυ|σάμαινων. ‖צדיקים | עם | מִשְׁכַּב L. Rutgers 1995, p. 194; C. Colafemmina 1975, pp. 131–137. As Rutgers shows, the similarity between the two formulae is strenghtened by the fact that ὅσιος translates חסיד in the Septuagint.

[57] JIWE II, 31, 99, 172, 187, 326, 557, 586.

[58] JIWE II, 172 of Gaudentia, 19 years old, JIWE II, 557 of Nicodemos, 30 years old, JIWE II, 187 of Samuel, 5 months, JIWE II, 99 of Euphrasius, 3 years and 10 months. [58] M. Simon 1936, pp. 188–206.

[59] JIWE II, 25, 29, 244, 257, 259, 340, 345, 353, 354, 358, 556. The adjective γλυκύς is also attested (JIWE II, 25, 108).

[60] JIWE II, 127, 171, 173, 209, 212, 227, 236, 257, 347, 373, 376, 552, 556, 564. This adjective is commonly used in a Jewish context, but is never attested in Christian and Roman inscriptions.

[61] JIWE II, 251, 362, 376.

[62] JIWE II, 127, 171, 344, 528.

[63] JIWE II, 254, 344, 559.

[64] JIWE II, 171.

[65] JIWE II, 240, 576.

[66] JIWE II, 240.

[67] JIWE II, 212, 502.

[68] JIWE II, 240, 281, 576. In JIWE II, 564 the term is transliterated in Latin: filentolia.

[69] JIWE II, 390. the woman is called μαθητής: probably, she studied the Law. This could be an evidence of the active role women played in the synagogue after the fall of Jerusalem (P. van der Horst 1991, p. 108).

The inscriptions in Latin do not show recurrent formula. The expression *hic pausat/hic requiescit*, a translation of ἐνθάδε κεῖται, or similar variants are scarcely attested in Rome, while it is used in later inscriptions found in Southern Italy and at Venosa.[71] Similar expressions are attested only in two inscriptions.[72] The final formulae are equally rare: *quiecet in pace* (sic) and *in pace* are attested only in one inscription.[73] The Latin epitaphs are more similar to the Christian and Pagan ones with the remarkable exception of JIWE II, 233: *bona Iudea*. The most common epitets are the generic *benemerens*[74] and *dulcissimus*,[75] a translation of the well-attested γλυκύτατος.

One of the main peculiarities of the Jewish inscriptions is the use of synagogue titles, prestigious enough to be mentioned in a funerary inscription. Conversely, the job and the place the deceased had in the Roman society is seldom recorded. The few references come solely from the catacomb of Vigna Randanini. We know of a doctor,[76] a painter,[77] a trader[78] and a botularus,[79] this latter a hapax that could have something to do with the butchering or the sale of meat. No

---

[70] JIWE II, 171, 127. JIWE II, 564 transliterates the formula in Latin: *dicea*.

[71] Hic requiescit: 33 instances; hic iacet: 2 instances; hic pausat: 3 instances; hic positus est: 2 instances; hic receptus in pace: 1 instance; heic obdormivit in pace (sic): 1 instance. This is not the place to study the phonetical and morphological variants of these formulae.

[72] JIWE II, 550 (hic requiescit); JIWE II, 103 (hic sita est).

[73] JIWE II, 196 and JIWE II, 7.

[74] 37 instances.

[75] JIWE II, 179, 214, 224, 249, 291, 381, 491, 553. In JIWE II, 332 the adjective is transliterated into Greek: δουλκισειμε.

[76] JIWE II, 341, ll. 1–4: Αὐλο[ς] | Βήδιο[ς] | Κολλή[γα] | ἀρχίατρ[ος]. The inscription, with a good lettering, is carved on a sarcophagus: the deceased probably belonged to a wealthy family.

[77] JIWE II, 277: ἐνθάδε | κῖτε Εὐδό|ξιος ζωγ|ράφος· ἐν | εἰρήνη ἡ κύ⟨μ⟩ησις⟩. The subjects Eudoxios painted in some detail were probably symbolic or natural elements, although frescoes with human subjects painted in Jewish contexts have been found.

[78] JIWE II, 360 ll. 6–7: Πούπλις Κατίλις Ἑρμι|ᾶς ἔνπορο⟨ς⟩ ἐνθάδε κῖμαι.

[79] JIWE II, 343: *Alexander | butularus de ma | cello q(ui) vixit annis | XXX, anima bona, om | nium amicus | dormitio tua inter | dicaeis*. The *t* of botularus is badly carved. Seneca (*Ep.* LVI, 2) uses *botularius*, while in CIL VI 30743 from *Hadrumentum* a *bublarus* is attested. The Forma Urbis mentions a [vicus bu]blarus (CIL VI, 29844.46) and, according to Suetonius (*Aug.* 5), Augustus was born on the Palatine *ad capita bubula*. Whatever Alexander's job was, he probably worked with beef. The identification of the macellum is uncertain. It could have been the macellum Liviae restored at the end of the fourth century or the macellum magnum built by Nero on the Celium and still in use in the third/fourth century. See also M. Williams 2002.

civil or military office is mentioned. The scarce amount of evidence does not allow us to trace an exhaustive economic picture of the community, but is, in some ways, meaningful: according to the inscriptions, the primary interest of Roman Jews was not to integrate with Roman society, but to preserve their own cultural and religious identity.[80]

---

[80] Many words have been spent in the past to show that the Jewish community of Rome was poor. Apart from the scanty pieces of information that can be grasped from the inscriptions, great importance has been attached to the literary sources. In the Acts (Acts 18:3) it is said that Aquila worked as a tent maker in Corinth but we do not know whether this was his job when he lived in Rome too. Poets such as Martial (*Ep.* 12,57,12–13) and Juvenal (*Sat.* 3,12–16; 3,290–296; 6, 542–547) speak of Jewish beggars, fortune-tellers and sellers of broken glasses, but they also mention poets who were close to the Imperial court (Mart., *Ep.*, 7,82 and 11,92). This picture cannot correspond to a community as large as that of Rome. Philo's statement (*Leg. ad Gaium*, 155) that the core of the community was composed of freedmen, who were once war prisoners, cannot be considered evidence of a low economic level. Notwithstanding the jobs the Jews probably had (an involvement in the workshops that produce lamps, sarcophagi and glasses with a Jewish symbology is highly probable, as suggested by L. Rutgers 1995, pp. 92–99), the community grows in the first four centuries of the Empire and is not significantly touched by the expulsions. It is difficult to estimate the part that prosperity and economic growth played in this period. H. Leon 1995², pp. 233–238; S. Applebaum 1974, pp. 720–722. On the passages mentioned above see M. Stern 1974–1980, II passim.

CONCLUSIONS

The pieces of evidence we have on the Jewish community of Rome are often late and fragmentary. The picture emerging from the survey of the sources is not completely satisfactory even on aspects that the Roman community shares with other centres of the Jewish Diaspora within the Imperial borderlines. I do not intend to revisit problems that have already been discussed, but to focus on three questions that could be developed in future works.

1. According to the literary tradition, the Jews frequented Rome already in 139 B.C., possibly temporarily. This could be deduced from the order of *redere domos suas* that the praetor peregrinus Hispalus/Hippalus enacted, according to the late evidence of the epitome of Valerius Maximus compiled by Iulius Paris (in codex Vat. Lat. 4929). In the following years their presence is attested during the trial against L. Valerius Flaccus (66 B.C.) and at the arrival of Jewish delegations in the aftermath of Herod's death (14 B.C.). Cicero's passage actually does not describe a permanent community, but the large presence of Jews who were in Rome for business and to take part in the trial. Philo (*Leg. ad Gaium*, 155) attests abruptly that in the period of Caligula there was a permanent and organized community, that this community was placed in the XIV regio Transtiberim, that had built some προσευχαί, houses of prayer where the Jews met to celebrate the shabbath and to share the communal meals, and that it was composed of Ῥωμαῖοι freedmen who once were war prisoners. Of which war? How did the community form and develop? If we accept Paris' account, we could deduce that Jewish merchants frequented Rome since the middle of the second century B.C., as happened some decades later at Puteoli. Then, new groups joined them, people who came from Judaea as prisoners captured during the campaigns in the East. Guignebert suggested that the first arrivals of prisoners could be dated back to the Syriac war, which was fought few years after Syria had occupied Palestine, but this hypothesis cannot be validated in any way. Possibly, a substantial group of prisoners reached Rome with the fall of Jerusalem in 63 B.C. and with Pompey's return to Italy in the following year. Many scholars share

this view, and it is admittedly a likely hypothesis, but it cannot be definitively proved, as the sources describing the triumph—including the long account by Plutarch—do not mention the presence of Jews, unlike the accounts of the triumph of Vespasian and Titus in 71 C.E. Within half a century, the community seems to be well-rooted and integrated, and is probably composed of freedmen who had found their place in the social fabric of Rome. We can suppose that until the end of the war of Bar Kochba in 135 C.E., the community grew up both because of a natural demographic increase and because of the periodic arrivals of war prisoners. However, the sources completely ignore this problem and it is actually mentioned only by Philo.

2. Philo does not describe the organization of the community; the inscriptions mention offices and titles, but do not explain their meaning and degree of importance. Our survey has shown that the picture we have of the stucture of the Roman community is scant and shifty. Apart from the problem concerning the legal equalization of the synagogues with the *collegia sacra*—a point that in my opinion should be shelved—the organization of the community is not clear. Some activities—such as passing judgements and arbitrages, managing lots used as cemeteries or collecting the half-shekel offering and the Jewish tax—required coordination between the groups, an assembly with representative and decisional powers, but such an assembly is not clearly attested. According to Acts 28.17, when Paul reached Rome in the spring of 56, "the first ones among the Jews" could take decisions on religious matters and kept links with the motherland. But this account is vague. Undoubtedly, the inscriptions show the presence of a γερουσία, but it is uncertain what the duties of this assembly were.

It is a peculiar problem. The trend of most of the Jewish communities in the Diaspora was to create a pyramidal structure, regardless of the dimensions and the importance that these centres had. The presence of ἄρχοντες and of a γερουσιάρχης suggested the presence of a γερουσία at Antioch,[1] while at Berenice inscriptions attest

---

[1] According to Schwabe (Schwabe 1954 p. 252). Applebaum (Applebaum 1974, p. 485) resumed this hypothesis. Flavius Josephus mentions the ἄρχωντες during the turmoil that occurred in 69 A.D. (*BJ*, VII, 47). John Chrysostomus, who wrote in the fourth century, reports their presence (*Adv. Iud.* VI, 5). The γερουσιάρχης is

the presence of a πολίτευμα that coordinated the public life of the community.[2] The structure of the Jewish community of Alexandria was even more complex. Here too the Jews had a πολίτευμα that was probably created in the period between the reign of Ptolemy VI and of Ptolemy VIII in the middle of the third century B.C., according to recent studies that have reassessed the disputed evidence of Strabo (in Flav. Jos., *A.J.* XIV, 117 = FGrHist. 91 F7). According to Philo (*In Flaccum* 74, 76) at the death of the γενάρχης in 10/11 C.E., his duties were undertaken by a γερουσία. As we have already discussed, this passage is inconsistent with what Flavius Josephus says of that event and of its institutional consequences (*A.J.* XIX, 283). Whatever the value of this evidence is, the community was strictly centralised. In the aftermath of the conflicts between Cleopatra II and Ptolemy VIII in 145 B.C., a πολίτευμα was created in Leontopolis, while a plentiful papyrological documentation (P.Pol.Jud.) shows the presence of a πολίτευμα at Heracleopolis in the period between 144/3 and 133/2 B.C., during the kingdom of Ptolemy VIII Euergetes II. The πολίτευμα, which passed judgements both in Heracleopolis and in the χώρα, was constituted by ἄρχοντες and chaired by a πολιτάρχης, primus inter pares as to his colleagues.

Conversely, what the sources on the Jewish community show is not an administrative centralization, but the existence of different groups. In Rome, the term συναγωγή seems to apply to the congregation, while προσευχή is found for synagogue, house of prayer, both in literary and epigraphic evidence, as happens in Egyptian Judaism.[3]

---

attested in a funerary inscription found at Beth Shea'rim (IJO III, *Syr74*, cat. 12, hall B, entrance from room III to Room IV, date 200–352 C.E.): ἀψὶς | Αἰδεσίου | γερου⟨σ⟩ιάρχου | Ἀντιοχέως. On this topic see Kraeling 1932 and Kasher 1982. In the opinion of Noy and Bloedhorn (notes to IJO III, *Syr74*, pp. 118–119), the inscription does not definively prove the presence of a supra-synagogal γερουσία. A γερουσιάρχης is mentioned in one of the nineteen mosaic inscriptions found in the synagogue of Apamea: IJO III, *Syr53* (CIJ 803) Date 7 Jan. 392 A.D.: ἐπὶ τῶν τιμιοτάτων ἀρχισυνα|γώγων Εὐσεβίου καὶ Νεμίου καὶ Φινέου | καὶ Θεοδώρου γερουσιάρχου καὶ τῶν | τιμιοτάτων πρεσβυτέρων Εἰσακίου | καὶ Σαούλου κ⟨α⟩ὶ λοιπῶν, Ἱλάσιος ἀρχισυνά|γωγος Ἀντιοχέων ἐποίησεν τὴν ἰσόδον τοῦ | ψηφίου πό(δας) ρν'· ἔτους γψ', Εὐδυνέου ζ'· εὐλογία πᾶσι.

[2] See S. Applebaum 1979, pp. 160–161; G. Luederitz 1989.

[3] Philo, *Leg. ad Gaium*, 23; Juvenal *Sat.* III, 296.

JIWE II, 602 (App. 1: Non-Jewish inscriptions concerning Jews): *Dis M(anibus). | P(ublio) Corfidio | Signino | pomario | de agger || a proseucha, | Q(uintus) Sallustius | Hermes | amico benemerenti | et numerum | 10 | ollarum decem.* The inscription comes from a pagan burial area in via Gabina and is dated to the first/second century C.E.

This situation is attested also elsewhere, in Berenice,[4] Aegina,[5] Kyme or Phocaia,[6] Akmonia[7] and, in Italy, Brixia.[8] In declarations of *manumissio* found at Penticapeum[9] and Phanagoria[10] on the Black Sea, the προσευχή is distinguished from the συναγωγή τῶν Ἰουδαίων: while the first term means the synagogue, the building, the second one is referred to the community that was responsible for acts of freedom. Likewise, at Stobi in Macedonia the expression τῷ ἁγίῳ τόπῳ means the synagogue, while συναγωγή is the community that gathers in the building to pray.[11]

Consequently, if συναγωγή can be correctly interpreted as "community" and not as "synagogue", we could argue that the Roman community was composed by partially independent groups that kept their identities but did not create conflicts that actually are not attested in the sources. In Rome the community stuck to a model that apparently was different from the patterns attested in other populous centres of the Diaspora. The presence of an assembly was required to coordinate some activities that the community developed, but nothing definitive can be said of this assembly.

---

[4] SEG XVII (1960) nr. 823 (CZJC nr. 72) dated to 55 C.E. The term stands both for the prayer's house (l. 5) and the community (ll. 3–4: ἐφάνη τῇ συναγωγῇ τῶν ἐν Βερνεικίδι Ἰουδαίων).

[5] IJO I, *Ach59* (CIJ I 723): ll. 2–3 [ἐκ τῆς πρ]ο[σ]όδου τῆς | συναγ(ωγῆς).

[6] IJO II, 36 (CIJ II 738): the building is called τὸν οἶκον (l. 2), while ἡ συναγωγή . . . τῶν Ἰουδαίων (ll. 6–7) is clearly referred to the community. On the doubts concerning the finding place see the introduction to the inscription: IJO II, p. 163.

[7] IJO II, 168 (CIJ II 766). This inscription is controversial. The synagogue is called both ο[ἶ]κον (l. 1) and συναγωγή (l. 13). But this latter term is used also with the meaning of community (l. 11).

[8] JIWE I, 5 (CIJ I, 639): *Coeliae Paternae | matri synagogae | Brixianorum*.

[9] IJO I, BS5 (CIJ I 683): act of *manumissio* of Ἡρακλᾶν dated to Jan./Febr. 81 C.E. ll. 13–15: χωρὶς ἰς τ[ὴ]ν προσευ|χὴν θωπείας τε καὶ προσκαρτε|ρήσεως. Ll. 18–19: συνεπ[ιτ]ροπεούσης δὲ καὶ τῆς | συναγωγῆς τῶν Ἰουδαίων. Similar evidence in IJO I, BS 6 (CIJ I 684) ll. 20–23; IJO I, BS7 (CIJ 2nd ed., 683 a) ll. 7–10, both dated to late 1st–early 2nd century A.D. IJO I, BS9 (CIJ 2nd ed., 683 b), date: 1st–2nd century A.D., fragmentary stone: [τῆς συναγω]γῆς τῶν | [Ἰουδα]ίων.

[10] IJO I, BS18 (SEG XLIII 1993, nr. 510) ll. 13–19 dated to Mar./Apr. 52 A.D. IJO I, BS17 (CIJ I, 691) dated to May/June 17 A.D., fragmentary stone, l. 9 τῆς προσευχῆς].

[11] IJO I, *Mac*.1 (CIJ nr. 694) date: second half of 2nd–first half of the 3rd century A.D.: ll. 1–10 (passim): [Κλ.] Τιβέριος Πολύ|χαρμος ὁ καὶ Αχύρι|ος ὁ πατὴρ τῆς ἐν | Στόβοις συναγωγῆς | ὅς πολιτευσάμε|νος πᾶσαν πολιτεί|αν κατὰ τὸν Ἰουδαι|σμὸν, εὐχῆς ἕνεκεν | τοὺς μὲν οἴκους τῷ | ἁγίῳ τόπῳ . . .

3. The period that follows the fall of Jerusalem is not documented. The first epigraphic and archaelogical evidence date to the III/IV century. In those years the community was largely grecophone, although a minority spoke Latin as their main language. The Semitic languages (Aramaic and Hebrew) are hardly attested and are used only in a few common formulae. The large set of bilingual inscriptions (in Latin/Greek languages) points to a confused situation, with groups or families speaking Latin, but with the majority of the community speaking Greek. The presence of inscriptions in that part of the text which was transliterated into Greek or Latin reflects this moment of change and still requires more scholarly attention.

The bilingualism of the Roman community can hardly be considered exceptional. In Venosa, adjacent inscriptions were written both in Latin and in Greek or, in a later period, in Hebrew.[12] While in the early V century Greek is predominant, Latin becomes more popular over time, though Greek is still in use even when, at the beginning of the sixth century, Latin is the main language in the daily life. A similar phenomenon seems to be attested in Northern Italy,[13] although the number of inscriptions is low. Although the inscriptions found in this area can hardly be dated, they roughly belong the same period as the Roman ones (or to a few decades later): nine are written in Latin, while two are in Greek. Hebrew is used only for the formula *shalom* carved on a Latin inscription of Mediolanum (JIWE I,2) probably belonging to the V century, and scratched on an amphora dated to the fifth/sixth centuries found in Ravenna (JIWE I, 10).

In Rome, Greek is not only the language of the daily life, but also of the ritual: Hebrew is relegated to a few formulae, but the Bible is quoted (sometimes approximately) according to the Septuagint. Apparently, at some point the Bible of Aquila is used too, while there is no evidence of diffusion of the Latin versions that preceded the Vulgata. What was happening in the Roman community was not exceptional: the linguistic mixture of the community corresponded to characteristics well attested in other areas of the Diaspora during the III/IV century. But the cultural reality is definitely more complex. As we have seen, Acts 28.17 shows the preservation of close

---

[12] Still in the early fifth century, Hebrew is used in common formulae such as *shalom*, or *shalom al Israel*, in the turn of the century, this language is increasingly used, mainly in bilingual inscriptions.

[13] S. Cappelletti 2003.

religious links between the community and the motherland. In the period that followed the destruction of the Temple, rabbis from Jamnia reached Rome and taught in the local yeshivah: as happens in the whole Diaspora, the wars of 70 and 135 do not weaken the bonds between Palestine and the Diasporan communities. But the archaeological data are in some respects controversial. Loculi and painted rooms stand beside typically Jewish sepultures as the kochim, while paintings with non-Jewish subjects were drawn alongside Jewish symbols. Was there a religious unity among the Roman Jews? Did a more autonomous Judaism develop in Rome? The evidence seems to attest a cultural unity in the use of Greek as the ritual (and daily life) language and in the reading of the Greek Bible. In this environment the sepulchres show the survival of different religious lines: on the one hand, integration with a non-Jewish culture; on the other hand, the preservation of typically Jewish customs, such as the kochim burials. In my opinion, the presence of different trends within the community is quite clear and could have partially depended on the lack of a strong central authority. In any case, this was not a peculiarity of the Roman Jewry. A well-known episode in Acts could suggest that a kind of pluralism characterized Judaism at the end of the Second Temple period. When Paul reached Ephesus, he began to preach in the synagogue but, driven out, moved to the school of a Tyrannos, an independent rabbi who taught in what was likely to be a *bet midrash* (Acts 19.9).

MAPS

1. Catacomb of Monteverde—area discovered in 1904–1906 (Noy, JIWE II)

2. Catacomb of Monteverde—area discovered in 1913 (Noy, JIWE II)

3. Catacomb of Vigna Randanini (Frey 1975[2])

4. Catacomb of Vigna Randanini (Vismara 1986)

5. Catacomb of Vigna Randanini (Noy, JIWE II)

6. Catacomb of via Labicana (Vismara 1986)

7. Catacomb of via Labicana (Noy, JIWE II)

8. Catacombs of Villa Torlonia (Fasola 1976)

9. Actual collapse of ceilings, or danger thereof (from Barbera—Magnani Cianetti 2002)

10. Galleries affected by root penetration (from Barbera—Magnani Cianetti 2002)

11. Penetration of water in the catacombs (from Barbera—Magnani Cianetti 2002)

12. Points used for chemical tests (from Barbera—Magnani Cianetti 2002)

13. Percentages of radon (from Barbera—Magnani Cianetti 2002)

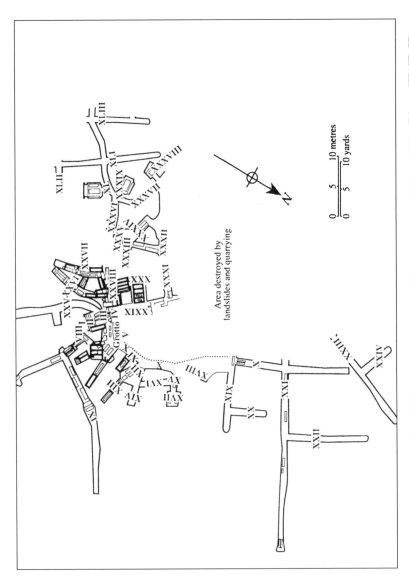

Map 1. Catacomb of Monteverde—area discovered in 1904–1906 (Noy, JIWE II)

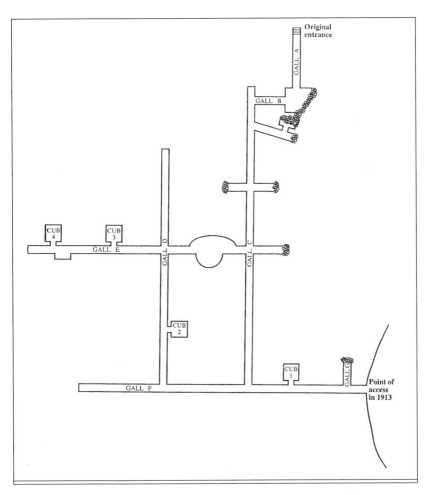

Map 2. Catacomb of Monteverde—area discovered in 1913
(Noy, JIWE II)

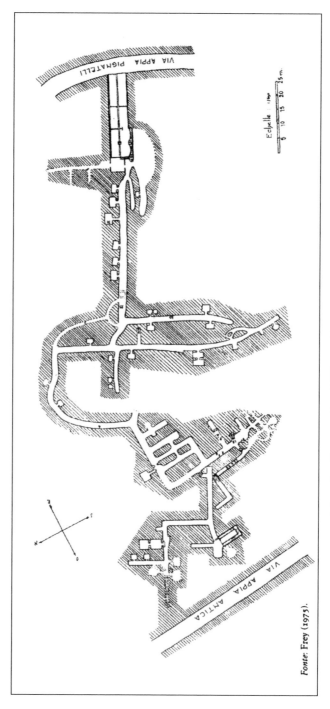

Map 3. Catacomb of Vigna Randanini (Frey 1975[2])

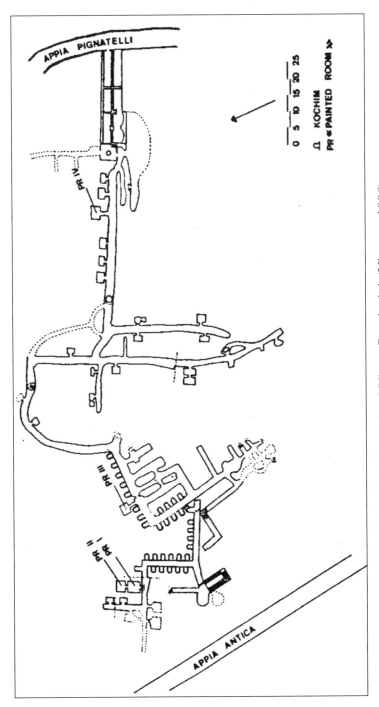

Map 4. Catacomb of Vigna Randanini (Vismara 1986)

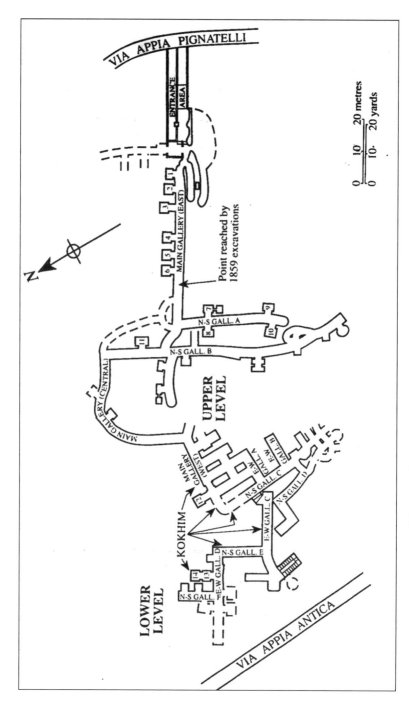

Map 5. Catacomb of Vigna Randanini (Noy, JIWE II)

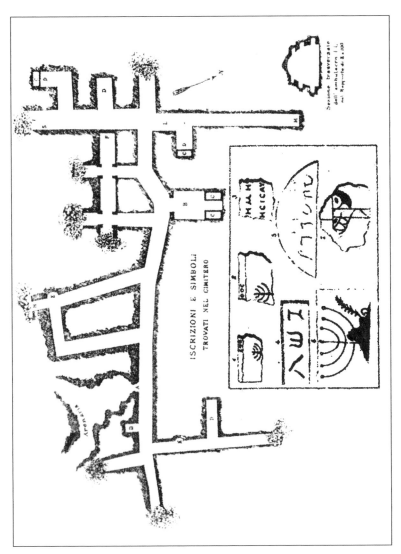

Map 6. Catacomb of via Labicana (Vismara 1986)

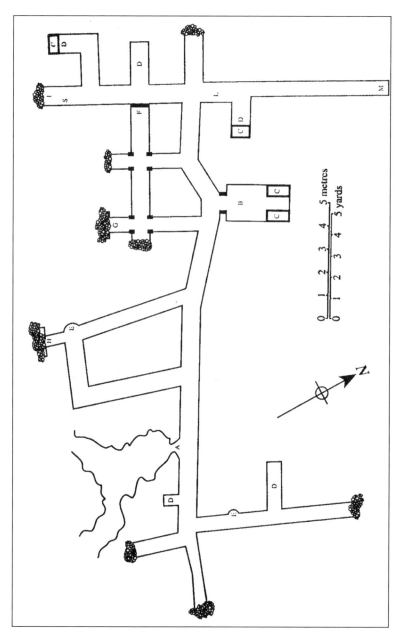

Map 7. Catacomb of via Labicana (Noy, JIWE II)

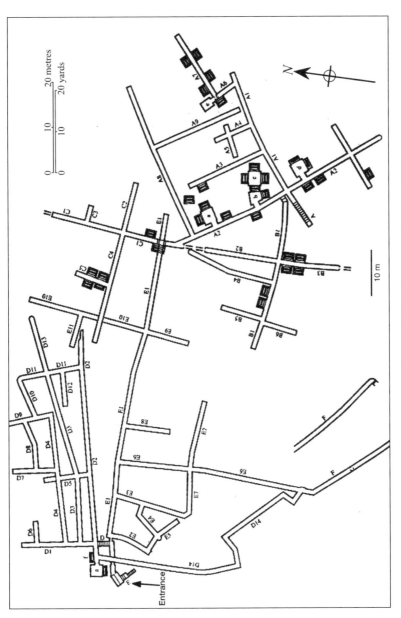

Map 8. Catacombs of Villa Torlonia (Fasola 1976)

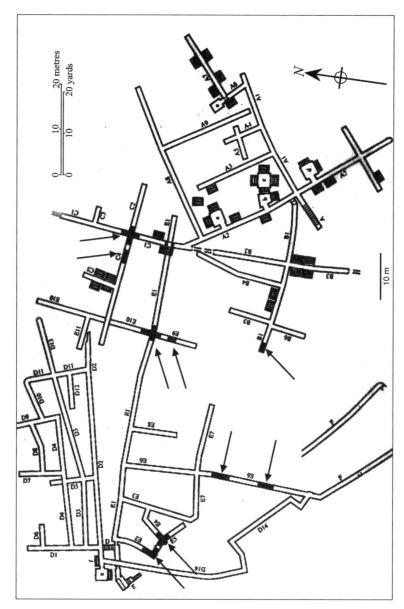

Map 9. Actual collapse of ceilings, or danger thereof (from Barbera—Magnani Cianetti 2002)

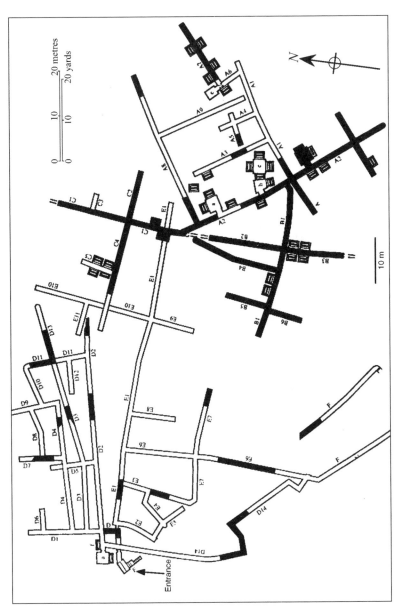

Map 10. Galleries affected by root penetration (from Barbera—Magnani Cianetti 2002)

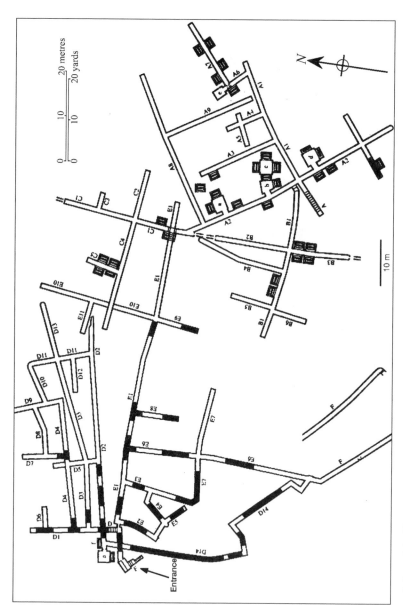

Map 11. Penetration of water in the catacombs (from Barbera—Magnani Cianetti 2002)

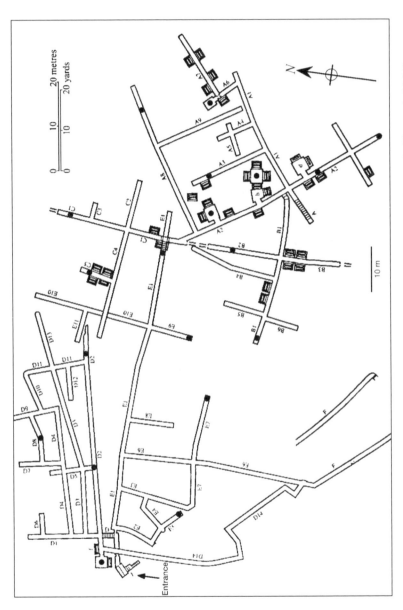

Map 12. Points used for chemical tests (from Barbera—Magnani Cianetti 2002)

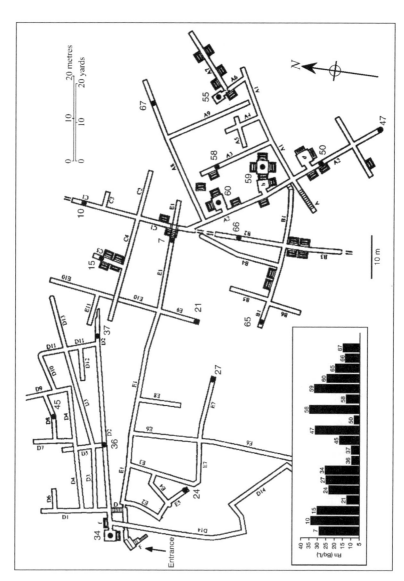

Map 13. Percentages of radon (from Barbera—Magnani Cianetti 2002)

BIBLIOGRAPHY

Primary Sources

Greek and Roman Literary Sources

Appianus, *La storia romana. Libri 13–17, le guerre civili*, E. Gabba and D. Magnino (eds.), Torino: Unione tipografico-editrice torinese 2201

Flavius Arrianus, *Tactica*, ed. A.G. Roos e G. Wirth, in *Flavii Arriani quae supersunt omnia*, vol. 2, Leipzig: Bibliotheca Scriptorum Graecorum et Romanorum Teubneriana 1968

Q. Asconius Pedianus, *Argumentum in M. Tullii Ciceronis orationem Pisonianam*, C. Mueller (ed.), in *M. Tullii Ciceronis scripta quae manserunt omnia*, vol. III pars II, Leipzig: Bibliotheca Scriptorum Graecorum et Romanorum Teubneriana 1904

M. Tullius Cicero, *In L. Pisonem*, C. Müller (ed.), in *M. Tullii Ciceronis scripta quae manserunt omnia*, vol. III pars II, Leipzig: Bibliotheca Scriptorum Graecorum et Romanorum Teubneriana 1904

M. Tullius Cicero, *Pro L. Valerio Flacco*, C. Müller (ed.), in *M. Tullii Ciceronis scripta quae manserunt omnia*, vol. II pars II, Leipzig: Bibliotheca Scriptorum Graecorum et Romanorum Teubneriana 1904

M. Tullius Cicero, *In Vatinium testem interrogatio*, C. Müller (ed.), in *M. Tullii Ciceronis scripta quae manserunt omnia*, vol. III pars II, Leipzig: Bibliotheca Scriptorum Graecorum et Romanorum Teubneriana 1904

M. Tullius Cicero, *Epistolarum ad Q. fratrem libri I–III*, C. Müller (ed.), in *M. Tullii Ciceronis scripta quae manserunt omnia*, vol. I pars III, Leipzig: Bibliotheca Scriptorum Graecorum et Romanorum Teubneriana 1904

Cassius Dio, *Cassii Dionis Cocceiani historiarum Romanarum quae supersunt*, ed. U.P. Boissevain, 3 vols., Berlin: Weidmann, 1:1895; 2:1898; 3:1901

M. Valerius Martialis, *Epigrammaton libri XIV*, ed. W. Gilbert Leipzig: Bibliotheca Scriptorum Graecorum et Romanorum Teubneriana 1907[2]

A. Persi et D. Iuni Iuvenalis Saturae, ed. W.C. Clausen, Oxford: Clarendon Press 1959

C. Plinius Secundus, *Naturalis Historia*, L. Ian and C. Mayhoff (eds.), in 6 vols., Leipzig: Bibliotheca Scriptorum Graecorum et Romanorum Teubneriana 1892–1904[2]

C. Plinius Caecilius Secundus, *Panegyricus Traiano imperatori dictus*, ed. R.C. Kukula Leipzig: Bibliotheca Scriptorum Graecorum et Romanorum Teubneriana 1908

Plutarchus, *Numa*, ed. B. Perrin, in Plutarch's Lives, vol. 1, Cambridge Mass.: Harvard University Press 1914 (2nd ed. 1968)

Plutarchus, *Pompeius*, ed. B. Perrin, in Plutarch's Lives, vol. 5, Cambridge Mass.: Harvard University Press 1917 (2nd ed. 1968)

Scholia in Iuvenalem vetustiora, ed. P. Wessner, Leipzig: Bibliotheca Scriptorum Graecorum et Romanorum Teubneriana 1931

L. Annaeus Seneca, *Ad Lucilium epistularum moralium libri XX*, O. Heuse (ed.), vol. III, Leipzig: Bibliotheca Scriptorum Graecorum et Romanorum Teubneriana 1898

Strabo, *Strabonis geographica*, ed. A. Meineke, 3 vols., Leipzig: Bibliotheca Scriptorum Graecorum et Romanorum Teubneriana 1877 (ristampato Graz: Akademische Druck- und Verlagsansalt, 1969)

C. Suetonius Tranquillus, *De vita Caesarum libri VIII*, M. Ihm (ed.), Leipzig: Bibliotheca Scriptorum Graecorum et Romanorum Teubneriana 1907

Q. Aurelius Symmachus, *Q. Aurelii Symmachi V. C. consulis oridinarii epistulae editae post eius obitum a Q. Fabio Memmio Symmacho V. C. filio* (libri I–IX), ed. O. Seeck, in Monumenta Germaniae Historica, Auctores Antiquissimi, vol. VI.1, Berlin: Weidmann 1883

P. Cornelius Tacitus, *Annalium ab excessu divi Augusti libri*, ed. C.D. Fisher, Oxford: Clarendon Press 1906

P. Cornelius Tacitus, *Historiarum libri V*, ed. C.D. Fisher, Oxford: Clarendon Press 1911

Valerius Maximus, *Factorum et dictorum memorabilium libri IX*, ed. C. Kempf, Leipzig: Bibliotheca Scriptorum Graecorum et Romanorum Teubneriana 1888[2]

Jewish and Christian Literary Sources

Novum Testamentum Graece, K. Aland, J. Karavidopoulos, C.M. Martini, B. Metzger (eds.), Stuttgart: Deutsche Bibelgesellschaft 1898 (27th ed. revised 1993)

Septuaginta, ed. A. Rahlfs, Stuttgart: Württembergische Bibelanstalt 1935 (repr. 1971)

Hebrew-English edition of the Babylonian Talmud, ed. rabbi dr. I. Epstein, London: The Soncino Press 1983–1990

Le Talmud de Jérusalem, M. Schwab (ed.), Paris: G.-P. Maisonneuve, 1960

The Tosefta: translated from the Hebrew, J. Neusner (ed.), New York: Ktav Publishing House Inc. 1979

Acta Apocripha Sancti Johannis, in *Acta Apostolorum Apocripha* II (1), A. Lipsius – M. Bonnet (eds.), Hildesheim-New York: G. Olms 1972 (2nd. repr. of the Leipzig 1891–1903 ed. with pref. and bibl.)

Aurelius Augustinus, *De Civitate Dei*, ed. B. Dombart e A. Kalb, Leipzig: Bibliotheca Scriptorum Graecorum et Romanorum Teubneriana 1929 (4th ed.)

Eusebius, *Historia ecclesiastica*, ed. G. Bardy, Eusèbe de Césarée. Histoire ecclésiastique, 3 vols, Paris: Cerf 1:1952; 2:1955; 3:1967

Die Chronik des Hieronymus (ed. R. Helm), Leipzig: J. Hinrischssche Buchhandlung 1913

Flavius Iosephus, *Antiquitates Iudaicae*, ed. B. Niese, Flavi Iosephi opera, vols. 1–4, Berlin: Weidmann, 1:1887, 2:1885, 3:1892, 4:1890 (repr. 1955)

Flavius Iosephus, *Iosephi vita*, ed. B. Niese, Flavi Iosephi opera, vol. 4, Berlin: Weidmann, 1890 (repr. 1955)

Flavius Iosephus, *Contra Apionem*, ed. B. Niese, Flavi Iosephi opera, vol. 5, Berlin: Weidmann, 1889 (repr. 1955)

Flavius Iosephus, *De bello Iudaico* libri VII, ed. B. Niese, Flavi Iosephi opera, vol. 6, Berlin: Weidmann, 1895 (repr. 1955)

Isidorus Episcopus Hispalensis, *Originum seu etymologiarum libri XX*, ed. W. Lindsay, Oxford: Clarendon Press 1911

Orosius, *Historiarum adversus Paganos libri VII*, ed. C. Zangemeister, Leipzig: Bibliotheca Scriptorum Graecorum et Romanorum Teubneriana 1889

Philo, *De plantatione*, ed. Wendland, Philonis Alexandrini operae quae supersunt, vol. 2, Berlin: Reimer 1896 (repr. De Gruyter, 1962)

Philo, *De ebrietate*, ed. Wendland, Philonis Alexandrini operae quae supersunt, vol. 2, Berlin: Reimer 1896 (repr. De Gruyter, 1962)

Philo, *De migratione Abrahami*, ed. Wendland, Philonis Alexandrini operae quae supersunt, vol. 2, Berlin: Reimer 1896 (repr. De Gruyter, 1962)

Philo, *De fuga et inventione*, ed. Wendland, Philonis Alexandrini operae quae supersunt, vol. 3, Berlin: Reimer 1898 (repr. De Gruyter, 1962)

Philo, *De somnis* (lib. I–II), ed. Wendland, Philonis Alexandrini operae quae supersunt, vol. 3, Berlin: Reimer 1898 (repr. De Gruyter, 1962)

Philo, *De vita Mosis* (lib. I–II), ed. L. Cohn, Philonis Alexandrini operae quae supersunt, vol. 4, Berlin: Reimer 1902 (repr. De Gruyter, 1962)

Philo, *De mutatione nominum*, ed. Wendland, Philonis Alexandrini operae quae supersunt, vol. 3, Berlin: Reimer 1898 (repr. De Gruyter, 1962)

Philo, *De Abrahamo*, ed. L. Cohn, Philonis Alexandrini operae quae supersunt, vol. 4, Berlin: Reimer 1902 (repr. De Gruyter, 1962)

Philo, *De specialibus legibus* (lib. I–IV), ed. L. Cohn, Philonis Alexandrini operae quae supersunt, vol. 5, Berlin: Reimer 1906 (repr. De Gruyter 1962)

Philo, *De posteritate Caini*, ed. Wendland, Philonis Alexandrini operae quae supersunt, vol. 3, Berlin: Reimer 1898 (repr. De Gruyter 1962)

Philo, *Legatio ad Caium*, ed. L. Cohn and S. Reiter, Philonis Alexandrini operae quae supersunt, vol. 6, Berlin: Reimer 1915 (repr. De Gruyter 1962)

Philo, *In Flaccum*, ed. L. Cohn and S. Reiter, Philonis Alexandrini operae quae supersunt, vol. 6, Berlin: Reimer 1915 (repr. De Gruyter 1962)

Georgius Syncellus, *Chronographia* (ed. L. Dindorf), in *Corpus Scriptorum Historiae Byzantinae*, ed. B. Niebuhr, Bonn: ed. Weber 1829

Q. Septimius Florens Tertullianus, *Apologeticum*, ed. J.P. Waltzing, Paris: Les Belles Lettres 1929

Juridic Sources

Codex Iustinianus, ed. P. Krüger, *Corpus Iuris Civilis*, vol. II, Dublin-Zuerich: Weidmann 1970 (15th ed.)

Digesta Iustiniani Imperatoris, ed. T. Mommsen, *Corpus Iuris Civilis*, vol. I (Digesta), Dublin-Zuerich: Weidmann 1973 (22nd ed.)

Institutiones, ed. P. Krüger, *Corpus Iuris Civilis*, vol. I, Dublin-Zuerich: Weidmann 1973 (22nd ed.)

Codex Theodosianus, ed. T. Mommsen, *Theodosiani libri XVI cum constitutionibus Sirmondianis et leges novellae ad Theodosianum pertinentes*, in 3 vols., Berlin: Weidmann 1905

Inscriptions, Papyri

Corpus Inscriptionum Iudaicarum, ed. J.B. Frey, 2 vols., Roma: Istituto Pontificio di Archeologia Cristiana 1936–1952, 1st vol. revised by B. Lifshitz New York: Ktav 1975 (with Prolegomenon)

Jewish Inscriptions of Greco-Roman Egypt, ed. W. Horbury – D. Noy, Cambridge: University Press 1992

Jewish Inscription Western Europe: The City of Rome, ed. D. Noy, Cambridge: University Press 1995

Jewish Inscription Western Europe: Italy (excluding the City of Rome), Spain and Gaul, ed. D. Noy, Cambridge: Cambridge University Press 1993

Inscriptiones Judaicae Orientis, Vol. I (Eastern Europe), ed. by David Noy, Alexander Panayotov, Hanswulf Bloedhorn, Tübingen: Mohr Siebeck 2004

Inscriptiones Judaicae Orientis, vol. II (Kleinasien), ed. by Walter Ameling, Tübingen: Mohr Siebeck 2004

Inscriptiones Judaicae Orientis, Vol. III (Syria und Cyprus), ed. by David Noy and Hanswulf Bloedhorn, Tübingen: Mohr Siebeck 2004

Luederitz G., *Corpus jüdischer Zeugnisse aus der Cyrenaika. Mit einem Anhang von J.M. Reynolds*, Wiesbaden 1983

Inscriptiones Christianae Vrbis Romae Septimo Saeculo Antiquiores, coepit Joannes Baptista De Rossi, complevit edidítque Angelus Silvagni: nova series, vol. 1.: *Inscriptiones incertae originis*, ed. A. Silvani, Roma: Officina libraria doct. Befani 1922; vol. 2: *Coemeteria in viis Cornelia, Aurelia, Portuensi et Ostiensi*, ed. A. Silvani, Roma: Pont. Institutum archaeologiae christianae 1935.; vol. 3: *Coemeteria in via Ardeatina*: cum duabus appendicibus, ed. A. Silvagni et A. Ferrua, Roma: Pont. Institutum archaeologiae christianae, 1956; vol. 4: *Coemeteria inter vias Appiam et Ardeatinam*, ed. A. Ferrua, Roma: Pont. Institutum archaeologiae christianae 1964; vol. 5: *Coemeteria reliqua viae Appiae*, ed. A. Ferrua, Roma: Pont. Institutum archaeologiae christianae 1971; vol. 6: *Coemeteria in viis Latina, Labicana et Praenestina*, ed. A. Ferrua, Roma: Pont. Institutum archaeologiae christianae 1975; vol. 7: *Coemeteria viae Tiburtinae*, ed. A. Ferrua, Roma: Pont. Institutum archaeologiae christianae, 1980; vol. 8: *Coemeteria viarum Nomentanae et Salariae*, ed. A. Ferrua, Roma: Pont. Institutum archaeologiae christianae 1983; vol. 9: *Viae Salariae coemeteria reliquia*, ed. A. Ferrua e D. Mazzoleni, Roma: Pont. Institutum archaeologiae christianae 1985; vol.10: *Coemeteria viae Salariae veteris et viae Flaminiae*, ed. D.Mazzoleni et C. Carletti, Roma: Pont. Institutum archaeologiae christianae 1992

Corpus Inscriptionum Latinarum, vol. VI: *Inscriptiones urbis Romae*: 1 (Bormann, Henzen, 1879); 2 (Bormann, Henzen, Huelsen, 1882); 3 (idd., 1886); 4.1 (Huelsen, 1894); 4.2 addimenta (id., 1902); 4.3 (Bang, 1933); 5 (Bormann, Henzen, Huelsen, 1885: falsae); 6.1 (Bang, 1926: index nominum); 6.2 (Vidman 1980, index cognominum); 7.1 (Jory, Moore, 1974: indices vocabulorum nominibus propriis inclusis); 7.2–6 (Jory, Moore, 1975: id.), 7.7 (Jory, 1989: id.)

Inscriptiones Latinae selectae, ed. H. Dessau, Berlin: Weidmann vol. I: 1892; vol. II:1906; vol. III, pars I (indices): 1914; pars II (addenda et corrigenda et indices): 1916
Corpus Papyrorum Iudaicarum, ed. V. Tcherikover – A. Fuks, 3. vols., Cambridge Mass.: Harvard University Press 1957–1964

Cowey J. – Maresch K., *Urkunden des Politeuma der Juden von Herakleopolis (144/3–133/2 v. Chr.) (P. Poli. Iud.). Papyri aus den Sammlungen von Heidelberg, Köln, München und Wien*, Wiesbaden 2001 (Abhandlungen der Nordrhein-Westfälischen Akademie der Wissenschaften, *Papyrologica Coloniensia* XXIX)

Modern Authors

Abel, E.L. 1968. *Were the Jews Banished from Rome in A.D. 19?*, Revue des Études Juives 127, pp. 42–49.

Achtemeier, P. 1996. *1 Peter. A Commentary on First Peter*, in Hermeneia. A critical and historical commentary on the Bible, Minneapolis.

Alessandri, S. 1968. *La presunta cacciata dei Giudei da Roma nel 139 a. Cr.*, Studi Classici e Orientali 17, pp. 187–198.

Alföldy, G. 1987. *Storia sociale dell'antica Roma*, Bologna.

Alon, G. 1980. *The Jews in their Land in the Talmudic Age (70–640 C.E.)*, Jerusalem.

Aly, W. 1957. *Strabon von Amaseia*, Bonn.

Aperghis, G. 2004. *The Seleucid Royal Economy*, Cambridge University Press.

Appelbaum, S. 1974. *The Social and Economic Status of the Jews Diaspora*, in M. Stern and S. Safrai (eds.), *The Jewish People in the First Century II*, Assen, pp. 701–727.

——— 1979. *Jews and Greeks in Ancient Cyrene*, Leiden.

Armstrong, K. 1996. *Jerusalem*, Jerusalem.

Avi-Yonah, M. 1968. *The Second and the Third Walls of Jerusalem*, Jewish Exploration Journal 18, pp. 98–115.

Barag, D. 1978. *The Palestinian "Judaea Capta" Coins of Vespasian and Titus and the Era on the Coins of Agrippa II Minted under the Flavians*, Numismatic Chronicle 137, pp. 14–23.

Barbera, M.R. – M. Magnani Cianetti, 2002. *Lo stato attuale delle catacombe Torlonia*, in *I beni culturali ebraici in Italia* (ed. M. Perani), Ravenna, pp. 55–70

Barclay, J.M. 1996. *Jews in the Mediterranean Diaspora, from Alexander the Great to Trajan (323 B.C.E.–117 C.E.)*, Edinburgh.

Bar Kochva, B. 1989. *Judas Maccabeus*, Cambridge.

Baron, S. 1952. *A Social and Religious History of the Jews*, New York.

Barrett, C.K. 1994–1998. *A Critical and Exegetical Commentary on the Acts of the Apostles*, Edinburgh.

Bartlett, J. 2002. *Jews in the Hellenistic and Roman Cities*, London.

Bell, H.I. 1924. *Jews and Christians in Egypt*, London.

Beloch, J. 1886. *Die Bevölkerung der Griechisch-Römischen Welt*, Leipzig.

Benko, S. 1980. *Pagan Criticism of Christianity During the First Two Centuries*, Aufstieg und Niedergang der römischen Welt II, 23.2, pp. 1055–1118.

Berliner, A. 1992. *Storia degli Ebrei di Roma dall'antichità allo smantellamento del Ghetto*, (A. Audisio It. ed.), Milano, (original ed.: *Geschichte der Juden in Rom von der ältesten Zeit zum Gegenwart (2050 Jahre)*, Frankfurt a. M. 1893).

Beyer, H.W. – H. Lietzmann, 1930. *Die Jüdische Katakombe der Villa Torlonia in Rom*, Studien zur spätantiken Kunstgeschichte 4, Jüdische Denkmäler, vol. I, Berlin-Leipzig.

Bianco, E. 1968. *Indirizzi programmatici e propagandistici nella monetazione di Vespasiano*, Rivista Italiana di Numismatica e scienze affini 70 vol. 16 sr. 5, pp. 143–224.

Bickerman, E. 1926. *Das Edikt des Kaisers Caracalla in P. Giss. 40*, Diss. Berlin.

——— 1937. *Der Gott der Makkabäer*, Berlin.

——— 1958. *The Altars of Gentiles. A Note on the Jewish "ius sacrum"*, Revue internationale des droits de l'antiquité 5, pp. 11–38; reprinted in E. Bickerman, *Studies in Jewish and Christian History*, vol. 3, Leiden 1986, pp. 137–164.

——— 1991. *Gli Ebrei in età greca*, Bologna (original edition: *The Jews in the Greek Age*, Harvard 1988, (It. tr. L. Troiani).

Billanovich, G. 1956. *Dall'antica Ravenna alle biblioteche umanistiche*, Aevum 30, pp. 319–353.

Bloch, H. 1947–1948. *The Roman Brick-Stamps not published in volume XV 1 of the "Corpus Inscriptionum Latinarum"*, Harvard Studies in Classical Philology 56–57 and 58–59, pp. 1–128.

——— 1947. *I bolli laterizi e la storia dell'edilizia romana*, Roma.

——— 1948. *Indices to the Roman Brick-Stamps Published in Volumes XV 1 of the "Corpus Inscriptionum Latinarum" and in LVI–LVII of the HSCP*, Harvard Studies in Classical Philology 58–59.

——— 1953. *I bolli laterzi e la storia edilizia di Ostia*, Scavi di Ostia vol. I, Roma.

Boffo, L. 1994. *Iscrizioni latine e greche per lo studio della Bibbia*, Brescia.

Borg, M. 1972–3. *A New Context for Romans XIII*, New Testament Studies 19, pp. 205–218.

Bosio, A. 1632. *Roma sotterranea*, Roma: G. Severani, (2nd ed. 1650).

Bottermann, H. 1996. *Das Judenedikt des Kaisers Claudius*, Hermes Einzelschriften 71, Stuttgart.

——— 2003. *Die Maßnahmen gegen die Stadtrömischen Juden im Jahre 19 n. Chr.*, Historia 52.4, pp. 410–455.

Boulvert, G. 1974. *Domestique et fonctionnaire sous le Haut-Émpire romain. La condition de l'affranchis et de l'esclave du Prince*, Paris.

Brooten, B. 1982. *Women Leaders in Ancient Synagogues* (Brown Judaic Studies 36), Chico.

Broshi, M. 1978 *Estimating the Population of Ancient Jerusalem*, Biblical Archaeology Review 4, pp. 10–15.

Broughton, T. 1951. *The Magistrates of the Roman Republic*, New York.

Brown, R. 2001. *Introduzione al Nuovo Testamento*, (It. ed. Gastone Boscolo), Brescia (original edition *An Introduction to the New Testament*, New York 1997).

Bruce, I. 1964. *Nerva and the Fiscus Judaicus*, Palestine Exploration Journal 94, pp. 34–35.

Brunt, P. 1966. *The "Fiscus" and its Development*, The Journal of Roman Studies 56, pp. 75–91.

Buttrey, T. 1972. *Vespasian as Moneyer*, Numismatic Chronicle 132, pp. 91–109.

Cadbury, H.J. 1955. *The Book of Acts in History*, London.

Cappelletti, S. 2002. *Sulla cronologia delle catacombe giudaico-romane di Villa Torlonia*, Acme: Annali della facoltà di lettere e filosofia dell'Università degli Studi di Milano 55.1 (January–April 2002), pp. 261–278.

——— 2003. *La presa di Gerusalemme: influsso demografico sulla comunità giudaica di Roma*, Materia Giudaica 8.2, pp. 269–277.

—————— 2004. *Note sulla presenza ebraica in Italia Settentrionale*, in V. de Angelis (ed.), *Sviluppi recenti nell'antichistica*, Quaderni di Acme 68, pp. 23–48.

—————— 2004. S. Cappelletti, *La campagna giudaica nella monetazione di Vespasiano*, Rivista Italiana di Numismatica e scienze affini 105, pp. 6, 9–92.

Carcopino, J. 1931. *Ancore le réscript impérial sur les violations de sépulture*, Revue Historique 166, pp. 77–92.

Carradice, I. 1982–83. *Coinage in Judaea in the Flavian Period, A.D. 70–96*, Israel Numismatic Journal 6–7, pp. 14–20.

Chambolu, A. 1885. *Flaviana. Untersuchen zur Geschichte der flavischen Keiserzeit*, Philologus: Zeitschrift für antike Literatur und ihre Rezeption 44, pp. 106–131 e pp. 502–517.

Charlesworth, M.P. 1939. *Documents Illustrating the Reigns of Claudius and Nero*, Cambridge.

Chilton, B. 1989. *The epitaph of Himerus from the Jewish catacomb of the Via Appia*, Jewish Quarterly Review 79.2–3, pp. 93–100.

Chilver, G. 1985. *A Historical Commentary on Tacitus' Histories IV and V*, Oxford.

Colafemmina, C. 1975. *Di un'iscrizione greco-ebraica di Otranto*, Vetera Christianorum 12, pp. 131–137.

Collins, J. 2000. *Between Athens and Jerusalem: Jewish Identity in the Hellenistic Diaspora*, Gran Rapids MI.

Collon, S. 1940. *Remarques sur les quartiers juifs de la Rome antique*, Mélanges d'Archéologie et d'Histoire de l'École Française de Rome 57, pp. 72–94.

Cook, J.A. 1956–7. *Suetonius ab Epistulis*, Proceedings of the Cambridge Philological Society 4, pp. 18–22.

Cotton, H. 1989. *The Date of the Fall of Masada: the Evidence of the Masada Papyri*, Zeitschrift für Papyrologie und Epigraphik 78, pp. 157–162.

—————— 1999. *Some Aspects of the Roman Administration of Judaea/Syria-Palaestina*, in W. Eck (ed.), *Lokale Autonomie und römische Ordnungsmacht in den kaiserzeitlichen Provinzen von 1. bis 3. Jahrhundert*, München.

Cranfield, C. 1986–87. *A Critical and Exegetical Commentary on the Epistle to the Romans*, Edinburgh.

Cumont, F. 1906. *Les Mystères de Sabazius et le Judaisme*, Comptes rendus de l'Académie des Inscriptions et Belles-Lettres, pp. 63–79.

—————— 1930. *Un réscript impérial sur la violation de sépulture*, Revue Historique 163, pp. 241–266.

De Angelis d'Ossat, G. 1935. *La catacomba ebraica di Monte Verde in Roma*, Roma 13, pp. 361–9.

—————— 1939. *La geologia delle catacombe romane*, in Roma Sotterranea Cristiana 3, Città del Vaticano.

Deissmann, A. 1927. *Light from Ancient East*, London.

De Maria, S. 1988. *Gli archi onorari di Roma e dell'Italia romana*, Roma.

de Ricci, S. 1905a. *Catacombe juive de la vie Portuensis*, Comptes rendue de l'Académie des Inscriptions et des Belles Lettres, pp. 245–247.

—————— 1905b. s.v. *Palaeography*, in Jewish Encyclopedia, vol. 8, coll. 471–5.

De Robertis, F. 1938. *Il diritto associativo romano. Dai collegi della Repubblica alle corporazioni del Basso Impero*, Bari.

de Rossi, M.S. 1864. *Analisi geologica ed architettonica delle catacombe romane*, in G.B. de Rossi, *Roma sotterranea cristiana*, vol. 1, Roma.

—————— 1867. *Scoperta di un cimitero giudaico sull'Appia*, Bollettino di Archeologia Cristiana 5, p. 16.

De Sanctis, G. 1929–1931. *Il rescritto imperiale di Nazaret*, Rendiconti della classe di scienze morali, storiche e filologiche dell'Accademia dei Lincei 7, pp. 13–17.

Deckers, J. 1987. *Die Katakombe "Santi Marcellino e Pietro". Repertorium der Melereien*, Città del Vaticano.

Delia, D. 1991. *Alexandrian Citizenship during the Roman Principate*, Atlanta.

Delling, G. 1965. s.v. ἄρχω, in *Grande Lessico del Nuovo Testamento*, F. Montanini,

G. Scarpat and O. Soffritti (eds.), Brescia, vol. I, coll. 1289–1290 (original ed. by G. Kittel and G. Friedrich, Stuttgart 1938).

De Visscher, F. 1963. *Le droit des tombeaux romains*, Milano.

Eck, W. 1969–70a. *Die Eroberung von Masada und eine neue Inschrift des L. Flavius Silva Nonius Bassus*, Zeitschrift für die Neutestamentliche Wissenschaft und die Kunde der älteren Kirche 60–61, pp. 282–289.

———— 1969–70b. Année Epigraphique, nr. 183.

———— 1999. (ed.), *Lokale Autonomie und römische Ordnungsmacht in den kaiserzeitlichen Provinzen von 1. bis 3. Jahrhundert*, München.

Edmondson E., Mason S., Rives J. (eds.), *Flavian Josephus and Flavian Rome*, Oxford 2005 (non vidi).

Engemann, J. 1968–69. *Bemerkungen zur römischen Gläsern mit Goldfoliendekor*, Jahrbuch für Antike und Christentum 11–12, pp. 7–25.

Fabre, G. 1981. *Libertus, Recherches sur les rapports patron-affranchi à la fin de la république romaine*, Rome: Collection de l'école française de Rome vol. 50.

Fasola, U.M. 1976. *Le due catacombe ebraiche di Villa Torlonia*, Rivista di Archeologia Cristiana 52, pp. 7–62.

Feldman, L. 1984. *Josephus and Modern Scholarship* (1937–1980), Berlin-New York 1984.

———— 1989. *Proselytes and "Sympathizers" in the Light of the New Inscriptions from Aphrodisias*, Revue des Études Juives 148, pp. 265–305.

———— 1993. *Jew and Gentile in the Ancient World: Attitudes and Interactions from Alexander to Justinian*, Princeton.

———— 1995. *[On] Leonard Victor Rutgers, "The Jews in Late Ancient Rome; Evidence of Cultural Interactions in the Roman Diaspora"*, Jewish Quarterly Review 86,3–4 (1996) 439–443.

Feldman, L. – M. Reinhold, 1996. *Jewish Life and Thought among Greeks and Romans*, Edinburgh.

Ferrua, A. 1936. *Sulla tomba dei Cristiani e quella degli Ebrei*, Civiltà Cattolica 87.3, pp. 298–311.

———— 1988. *Via Portuense*, Archivio della Società Romana di Storia Patria 111, pp. 5–33.

Fezzi, L. 2001. *La legislazione tribunizia di Publio Clodio Pulcro (58 a.C.). La ricerca del consenso a Roma*, Scritti Classici ed Orientali 47.1, pp. 274–278.

Filippi, G. 1991. *Nuovi dati sui laterizi bollati della catacomba ebraica di Monteverde*, Monumenti Musei e Gallerie Pontificie. Bollettino 11, pp. 69–103.

Firpo, G. 2002. *La distruzione di Gerusalemme e del Secondo Tempio nel 70 d.c.*, Rivista Storica Italiana 114.3 (dic. 2002), pp. 774–802.

Fisher, J.B. 1958–59. *The Term δεσπότης in Josephus*, Jewish Quarterly Review 49, pp. 132–138.

Foraboschi, D. 2000. *Aspetti dell'opposizione giudaica. La differenza specifica delle rivolte giudaiche*, in M. Sordi (ed.), *L'opposizione politica*, Contributi dell'Istituto di Storia Antica 26, Milano, pp. 31–60.

Frascati, S. 1989. *Un'iscrizione giudaica dalle catacombe di villa Torlonia; nota su CIJ, I 69*, Rivista di Archeologia Cristiana 65,1–2, pp. 135–142.

Fraser, P.M. 1972 *Ptolemaic Alexandria*, Oxford.

Frey, J.B. 1930. *Les communautés juives à Rome*, Recherches de Science Religieuse 20 (1930), pp. 267–297.

———— 1931. *La catacombe juive de la vie Nomentane*, Rivista di Archeologia Cristiana 8, pp. 359–363.

———— 1933. *Nouvelles inscriptions inédites de la catacombe juive de la via Appia*, Rivista di Archeologia Cristiana 10, pp. 27–50.

Fuchs, L. 1924. *Die Ägyptens in ptolemäischer und römischer Zeit*, Berlin.

Fuks, G. 1985. *"Where Have All the Freedman Gone?" On an Anomaly in the Jewish Grave-Inscriptions from Rome*, Journal of Jewish Studies 36, pp. 25–32.

Galimberti, A. 2001. *I Giulio-Claudii in Flavio Giuseppe (AJ XVIII–XX)*, Alessandria.

Gara, A. 1976. *Prosdiagraphomena e circolazione monetaria: aspetti dell'organizzazione fiscale in rapporto alla politica monetaria dell'Egitto romano*, Milano.

Garner, G. 1986. *How Many People? Archaeology and Population Numbers*, Buried History 22, pp. 98–125.

Garrucci, R. 1862. *Il cimitero degli antichi Ebrei scoperto recentemente in Vigna Randanini*, Roma.

Gascou, J. 1978. *Nouvelles données chronologiques sur la carrière de Suétone*, Latomus 37, pp. 436–444.

Ghilardi, M. 2003. *La sinagoga di Ostia Antica e gli ebrei di Roma: riflessioni in margine ad un libro*, Mediterraneo Antico 6.1, pp. 311–324.

Gibson, E.P. 1978. *The "Christians for Christians" [χριστιανοὶ χριστιανοῖς]. Inscriptions of Phrygia*, Harvard Theological Studies 32.

Giordano, C. – I. Kahn, 2001. *Testimonianze ebraiche a Pompei, Ercolano, Stabia e nelle città della Campania Felix*, Roma.

Goldenberg, R. 1979. *The Jewish Shabbath in the Roman World up to the Time of Constantine the Great*, Aufstieg und Niedergang der römischen Welt II, 19.1, pp. 414–447.

Goldstein, J. 1989. *The Hasmonean Revolt and the Hasmonean Dynasty*, in *The Cambridge History of Judaism* (ed. W. Davies and L. Finkelstein), vol. 2, Cambridge University Press, pp. 292–349.

Goodenough, E. 1953–1968. *Jewish Symbols in Greco-Roman Period*, New York.

Goodman, M. 1987. *The Ruling Class of Judaea: the Origins of the Jewish Revolt against Rome, A.D. 66–70*, Cambridge.

——— 1989. *Nerva, the Fiscus Judaicus and Jewish Identity*, Journal of Roman Studies 79, pp. 41–42.

——— 1992. *Jewish Proselytizing in the First Century*, in J. Lieu – J. North – T. Rajak (eds.), *The Jews among Pagans and Christians in the Roman Empire*, London-New York, pp. 53–78.

——— 1994. *Mission and Conversion. Proselytizing in the Religious History of the Roman Empire*, Oxford.

Goodyear, F.R. 1981. *The Annales of Tacitus*, Cambridge University Press.

Gotbrod, W. 1968. s.v. Ἰσραήλ, Ἰουδαῖος, in *Grande Lessico del Nuovo Testamento*, F. Montanini, G. Scarpat and O. Soffritti (eds.), Brescia 1968, vol. 4 coll. 1167–1172 (original ed. by G. Kittel and G. Friedrich, Stuttgart 1938).

Grätz, H. 1905–1908. *Geschichte der Juden*, Leipzig.

Grayzel, S. 1947. *History of the Jews*, Philadelphia.

Gruen, E. 1984. *The Hellenistic World and the Coming of Rome*, Barkley.

——— 2002. *Diaspora: Jews amindst Greeks and Romans*, Harvard.

Guarducci, M. 1941–42. *L'iscrizione di Nazareth sulla violazione dei sepolcri*, Rendiconti della Pontificia Accademia di Archeologia 18, pp. 85–98.

Guignebert, C. 1950. *Le monde juif vers le temps de Jesus*, Paris.

Hadas-Lebel, M. 1994. *Flavius Josephus, Historian of Rome*, in F. Parente – J. Sievers (ed.), *Josephus and the History of the Graeco-Roman Period, Essays in Memory of Morton Smith*, Leiden 1994, pp. 99–106.

Hatch, E. – H. Redpath, 1975. *A Concordance to the Septuagint and Other Greek Versions of the Old Testament Including the Apocriphal Books*, Graz (I ed. Oxford 1897).

Havas, L. 1983. *Rome and the aurum sacrum*, Oikumene 4, pp. 233–248.

Heyob, S. 1975. *The Cult of Isis among Women in the Graeco-Roman World*, Études preliminaries aux Religions Orientales dans l'Empire romain 5, Leiden.

Hoelscher, G. 1930. s.v. *Masada*, Pauly-Wissowa, Real-Encyclopedie der classischen Altertumswissenschaft, vol. 14.2, coll. 2056.

Honigman, S. 2002. *Jewish "Politeumata" in Hellenistic Egypt. About P. Pol. Iud. (P. Colon. XXIX)*, Scripta Classica Israelica 21, pp. 251–266.

——— 2003. *Politeumata and Ethnicity in Ptolemaic and Roman Egypt*, Ancient Society 33, pp. 61–102.

Horsley, G.H. 1982. *New Documents Illustrating Early Christianity*, Mac Quarte.

Jacques, X. 1972. *Index des mots apparentés dans la Septante*, Rome.

Jeremias, J. 1979. *Jerusalem in the Time of Jesus* (3rd ed. transl. by H. & C.H. Cave), London 1969.

Jones, B.W. 1973 *The Dating of Domitian's War against the Chatti*, Historia 22, pp. 70–93.

———— 1984. *The Emperor Titus*, London & New York.

———— 1989. *Titus in Judaea*, *A.D. 67*, Latomus 48.1 (1989), pp. 127–134.

Johnson, E. 1984. *The Present State of Sabazius Research*, Aufstieg und Niedergang der römischen Welt II, 17.3, pp. 1538–1613.

Johnson, L. 2001. *The First and Second Letters to Timothy. A New Translation with Introduction and Commentary*, The Anchor Bible (volume 35A), New York-Toronto-London-Sydney-Auckland.

Juster, J. 1914. *Les Juifs dans l'empire romain. Leur condiction juridique, economique, sociale*, Paris.

Kajanto, I. 1963. *Onomastic Studies in the Early Christian Inscriptions of Rome and Carthage*, Helsinki.

Kant, L.H. 1987. *Jewish Inscriptions in Greek and Latin*, Aufstieg und Niedergang der römischen Welt II, 20.2, pp. 671–713.

Kanzler, R. 1915. *Scoperta di una nuova regione del cimitero giudaico della via Portuense*, Nuovo Bollettino di Archeologia Cristiana 21, pp. 152–157.

Keresztes, P. 1973. *The Jews, the Christians and Emperor Domitian*, Vigiliae Christianae 27, pp. 1–28.

Kasher, A. 1982. *The Rights of the Jews of Antioch on the Orontes*, Proceedings of the American Academy for the Jewish Research 49, pp. 69–85.

Köhler, L. – W. Baumgartner, 1967–1996. *Hebräisches und Aramäisches Lexicon zum Alten Testament*, Leiden.

Konikoff, A. 1986. *Sarcophagi from the Jewish Catacombs of Ancient Rome. A Catalogue Raisonné*, Wiesbaden.

Köstermann, E. 1967. *Ein folgenschwerer Irrtum des Tacitus (Ann. 15,44,2 ff.)?*, Historia 16, pp. 456–469.

Kraeling, C. 1932. *The Jewish Community at Antioch*, Journal of Biblical Literature 51, pp. 130–160.

Krauss, S. 1922. *Synagogale Altertümer*, Berlin-Wien.

Lacerenza, G. 1999. *L'iscrizione di "Claudia Aster Hierosolymitana"*, Biblica et Semitica, pp. 303–313.

La Piana, G. 1927. *The Foreign Groups in Rome*, Harvard Theological Review 20, pp. 117–144.

de Lange, N. 1996. *The Rivaval of the Hebrew Language in the Third Century*, Jewish Studies Quarterly 3, pp. 342–358.

Lane, E.N. 1979. *Sabazius and the Jews in Valerius Maximus: a Re-examination*, Journal of Roman Studies 69, pp. 35–38.

Lelercq, H. 1907. *Manuel d'archéologie chrétienne depuis les origines jusqu'au VIII siècle*, Paris.

Leon, H.J. 1927. *The Language of the Greek Inscriptions from the Jewish Catacombs of Rome*, Transactions and Proceedings of the American Philological Association 58, pp. 210–233.

———— 1928. *The Jewish Catacombs and Inscriptions of Rome; an Account of their Discovery and Subsequent History*, Hebrew Union College Annual 5, pp. 299–314.

———— 1952. *The Jewish Community of Ancient Porto*, Harvard Theological Review 45, pp. 165–175.

———— 1995². *The Jews of Ancient Rome*, updated ed. (1st ed. Philadelphia 1960), Peabody 1995.

Leonhard, R. 1925. s.v. *Lex Aelia Sentia*, Pauly-Wissowa, Real-Encyclopädie der classischen Altertumswissenschaft, Stuttgart, vol. 12.2, coll. 2321–2322.

Linder, A. 1987. *The Jews in Roman Imperial Legislation*, Detroit-Jerusalem.

Levine, L. 1989. *Synagogue Leadership: the Case of the Archisynagogue*, in M. Goodman, *Jews in a Graeco-Roman World*, Oxford 1998.

———— 2001. *The Hellenistic-Roman Diaspora C.E. 70–C.E. 235: the Archaeological Evidence*, in *The Cambridge History of Judaism* W. Horbury – W. Davies – J. Sturdy (eds.) vol. 3, Cambridge, vol. 3, pp. 991–1024.

Lo Cascio, E. 2000. *La popolazione*, in E. Lo Cascio (ed.), *Roma Imperiale*, Roma.

Luederitz, G. 1989. *What is the Politeuma?*, in J. Van Henten – P.W. van der Horst (eds.), *Studies in Early Jewish Epigraphy*, Leiden, pp. 183–225.

Luzzatto, G.I. 1942. *Epigrafia giuridica greca e romana*, Milano.

Madden, F. 1967. *History of the Jewish Coinage*, San Diego.

Manzella, S. 1989. *L. Maecius Archon, centurio alti ordinis. Nota critica su CIL VI, 39084–CIJ I, 470*, Zeitschrift für Papyrologie und Epigraphik 77, pp. 103–112.

Marshall, B.A. 1985. *A Historical Commentary of Asconius*, Columbia.

Marucchi, O. 1884a. *Breve guida del cimitero giudaico di Vigna Randanini*, Roma 1884; reprinted in O. Marucchi, *Éléments d'archéologie chrétienne*, Paris 1903, vol. 2, pp. 208–224.

———— 1884b. *Di un nuovo cimitero giudaico scoperto sulla via Labicana*, Dissertazioni della Pontificia Accademia Romana di Archeologia 2, pp. 497–532.

———— 1920. *Scoperta di un nuovo cimitero giudaico sulla via Nomentana*, Nuovo Bollettino di Archeologia Cristiana 26, pp. 55–57.

Mason, H. 1974. *Greek Terms for Roman Institutions, a Lexicon and an Analysis*, Toronto.

Mattingly, H. 1966. *Coins of the Roman Empire in the British Museum*, London 1966, vol. 3.

Mattingly, H. – E. Sydenham, 1926. *The Roman Imperial Coinage*, London, vol. 2.

Mazzoleni, D. 1975. *Le catacombe ebraiche di Roma*, Studi Romani 23, pp. 289–302.

———— 1976. *Les sépultures souterraines des Juifs d'Italie*, Dialoghi di Archeologia 19, pp. 82–98.

Meiggs, R. 1960. *Roman Ostia*, Oxford.

Mélèze-Modrzejewski, J. 1990. *Entre la cité et le fisc: le statut grec dans l'Egypte romaine*, Symposion 1982. Actas de la Sociedad de Historia del Derecho Griego y Helenistico (Santander, 1–4 septiembre 1982), éd. F. Fernandez Nieto Valencia 1985, reprint. in J. Mélèze-Modrzejewskj, *Droit impérial et traditions locales dan l'Egypte romaine*, pp. 241–280.

———— 1991. *Les Juifs d'Egypte de Ramsès II à Hadrien*, Paris.

———— 1999. *Espérances et illusions du Judaisme alexandrin*, in Aa. Vv., *Alexandrie: un mégalopole cosmopolite*. Actes, Cahiers de la Villa « Kérylios » (Beaulieu-sur-mer) n° 9, Paris, pp. 129–144.

———— 2003a. *La Diaspora juive d'Egypte*, in M.T. Le Dinahet (ed.), *L'Orient Méditerranéen. De la mort d'Alexandre au 1ᵉʳ siècle avant notre ère. Anatolie, Chypre, Egypte, Syrie*, pp. 330–353.

———— 2003b. *«Filios suos tantum»: Roman Law and Jewish Identity*, in M. Mor – A. Oppenheimer – J. Pastor – D. Schwartz (eds.), *Jews and Gentiles in the Holy Land in the Days of the Second Temple, the Mishnah and the Talmud*, Jerusalem 2003, pp. 108–136.

Merrill, E. 1919. *The Expulsion of the Jews from Rome under Tiberius*, Classical Philology 14 (1919), pp. 365–372.

Meshorer, Y. 1962. *Notes on the Judaea Capta Coins*, Israel Numismatic Bulletin 3–4, p. 98.

———— 1967. *Jewish Coins of the Second Temple Period*, New York.

Momigliano, A. 1930. *Prime linee di storia della tradizione maccabaica*, Roma.

———— 1931. *I nomi delle prime sinagoghe romane e la condizione giuridica della comunità in Roma sotto Augusto*, in Rassegna mensile d'Israel 6,7 (2nd series), pp. 283–292; reprinted in Terzo contributo alla storia degli studi classici e del mondo antico, Roma 1966, pp. 523–533.

———— 1934. *Claudius the Emperor and his Achievement*, Oxford.

———— 1967. *Ricerche sull'organizzazione della Giudea sotto il dominio romano (63 a.C.–70 d.C.)*, Amsterdam.

Mommsen, T. 1843. *De collegiis et sodaliciis Romanorum*, Kiel.
Müller, N. 1912. *Die Jüdische Katakombe am Monteverde zu Rom*, Leipzig.
——— 1915. *Cimitero degli Ebrei posto sulla via Portuense*, Dissertazioni della Pontificia Accademia Romana d'Archeologia, Serie II, 12, pp. 205–318.
Müller, N. - N.A. 1919. Bees, *Die Inschriften der Jüdischen Katakombe am Monteverde*, Leipzig.
Mussies, G. 1974. *Greek in Palestine and Diaspora*, in Z. Safrai - M. Stern (eds.), *The Jewish People in the First Century*, Assen, pp. 1040–1064.
Musurillo, H. 1979. *The Acts of Pagan Martyrs*, New York.
Nawijn, W. 1931. *Cassii Dionis Cocceiani Historiarum Romanorum Index Graecitatis*, Berlin.
Niese, B. 1893. *Zur Chronologie des Josephus*, Hermes 28, pp. 194–229.
——— 1900. *Kritik der beiden Makkabaerbücher*, Hermes 35, pp. 268–307.
Norden, E. 1966. *Josephus und Tacitus über Jesus Christus und eine messianische prophetie*, Kleine Schriften zum klassische Altertum, Berlin.
Noy, D. 1994. *The Jewish Community of Leontopolis and Venosa*, in J. van Henten and P. van der Horst (eds.), *Studies in Early Jewish Epigraphy*, Leiden, pp. 163–182.
——— 1997. *Writing in Tongues: the Use of Greek, Latin and Hebrew in Jewish Inscriptions from Roman Italy*, Journal of Jewish Studies 48, pp. 300–311.
——— 1999. *Jewish Inscriptions from Western Europe: Language and Community*, in XI Congresso di Epigrafia Greca e Latina (Roma 18–24 settembre 1997), Roma, pp. 163–182.
——— 2000. *Foreigners at Rome, Citizens and Strangers*, London.
Oesterley, W. 1932. *A History of Israel*, Oxford.
Olsson, B. - D. Mitternacht - O. Brandt (eds.), 2001. *The Synagogue of Ancient Ostia and the Jews of Rome. Interdisciplinary Studies*, Acta Instituti Roman Regni Sueciae, serie IV, 17, Stockolm.
Otranto, G. 1982. *Note sul sacerdozio femminile nell'antichità in margine a una testimonianza di Gelasio I*, Vetera Christianorum 19 (1982), pp. 341–360.
Overman, J.A. 2002. *The First Revolt and Flavian Politics*, in A. Berlin - J.A. Overman (eds.) *The First Jewish Revolt: Archaeology, History and Ideology*, London and New York, pp. 213–219.
Parente, F. 1968. *Escatologia e politica nel tardo Giudaismo e nel Cristianesimo primitivo*, Rivista Storica Italiana 80.2 (June 1968), pp. 234–296.
Paribeni, R. 1919. *Via Portuense. Iscrizioni del cimitero giudaico di Monteverde*, Atti dell'Accademia Nazionale dei Lincei. Notizie degli Scavi di Antichità 16, pp. 143–155.
——— 1920. *Catacomba giudaica sulla via Nomentana*, Atti dell'Accademia Nazionale dei Lincei. Notizie degli Scavi di Antichità 17, pp. 143–155.
Pergola, P. 1997. *Le catacombe romane*, Roma.
Pflaum, R. 1950. *Les procurateurs équestres dans le Haut-Empire romain*, Paris.
Plummer, A. 1956. *A Critical and Exegetical Commentary on the Gospel According to St. Luke*, Edinburgh 1922 (5th ed. 1956).
Price, J. 1992. *Jerusalem Under Siege: the Collapse of the Jewish State (66–70 C.E.)*, Leiden.
Pucci Ben Zeev, M. 1996. *Ant. 14.186–267: A Problem of Authenticity*, in R. Katzhoff, Y. Petroff and D. Schaps (eds.), *Classical Studies in Honor of David Sohlberg*, Bar Ilan, pp. 15–31.
——— 1998. *Jewish Rights in the Roman World: the Greek and Roman Documents quoted by Flavius Josephus*, Tübingen 1998.
——— 2001. *Were They Seditious? The Jews of Rome in the Sixties BCE*, Studi e ricerche sulla storia, la cultura e la letteratura degli Ebrei d'Italia 13–15 (2001), pp. 9–24.
Rabello, A. 1980. *The Legal Condition of the Jews in the Roman Empire*, Aufstieg und Niedergang der römischen Welt II, 13, pp. 662–762.
——— 1996. *Jewish Law in Talmudic Period*, in N. Hecht - B. Jackson - S. Passamaneck - D. Piattelli - A. Rabello (eds.), *An Introduction to the History and the Sources of Jewish Law*, Oxford, pp. 141–168.
——— 2000. *The Jews in the Roman Empire: Legal Problems, from Herod to Justinian*, Aldershot-Burlington USA-Singapore-Sydney.

Rabin, C. 1974. *Hebrew and Aramaic in the First Century* in Z. Safrai – M. Stern (eds.), *The Jewish People in the First Century* Assen, pp. 1007–1039.

Radin, M. 1915. *The Jews among Greeks and Romans*, Philadelphia.

Rajak, T. 1984. *Was There a Roman Charter of the Jews?*, Journal of Roman Studies 84, pp. 107–123.

———— 1992. *The Jewish Community and its Boundaries*, in J. Lieu – J. North – T. Rajak (eds.), *The Jews among Pagans and Christians*, London and New York, pp. 9–28.

———— 1994. *Inscription and Context: Reading the Jewish Catacombs of Rome*, in J. van Henten e P. van der Horst (eds.), *Studies in Early Jewish Epigraphy*, Leiden, pp. 226–241.

Rajak, T. – D. Noy, 1993. *Archisynagogoi: Office, Title and Social Status in the Graeco-Jewish Synagogue*, Journal of Roman Studies 83, 75–93.

Reicke, B. 1965. *Neutestamentliche Zeitgeschichte. Die Biblische Welt*, Berlin (Engl. transl. Philadelphia 1968).

Reinach, T. 1893. *Quid Iudaeo cum Verre?*, Revue des Études Juives 26, pp. 36–46.

———— 1920. *Le cimetière juif de Monteverde*, Revue des Études Juives 71, pp. 113–126.

———— 1921. *Une nouvelle nécropole judéo-romaine*, Revue des Études Juives 72, pp. 24–28.

———— 1924. *L'Emperateur Claude et les Juifs d'apres un nouveau document*, Revue des Études Juives 89, pp. 113–144.

Reynolds, J. – R. Tannenbaum, 1987. *Jews and Godfearers at Aphrodisias*, Proceedings of the Cambridge Philological Society 12–13 Suppl.

Ricci, C. 1995. *L'affranchi impérial T. Flavius Euschemon et le "fiscus judaicus"*, Revue des Études Juives 154,1–2, 89–95.

Rinaldi, E.G. 1991. *Procurator Felix*, Rivista Biblica 29, pp. 45–61.

Robertson, A. – A. Plummer, 1967. *A Critical and Exegetical Commentary on the First Epistle of St. Paul to the Corinthians*, Edinburgh.

Rogers, R.S. 1932. *Fulvia Paulina C. Sentii Saturnini*, American Journal of Philology 53, pp. 254–255.

Rogers, P. 1984. *Domitian and the Finances of State*, Historia 33.1, pp. 60–78.

Rostovzeff, M. 1909. s.v. *Fiscus*, Pauly-Wissowa, Real-Encyclopedie der classischen Altertumswissenschaft, vol. VI.2, coll. 2385–2405.

Roth, J. 1995. *The Length of the Siege of Masada*, Scripta Classica Israelica 14, pp. 87–110.

Royden, H.L. 1988. *The Magistrates of the Roman Professional Collegia in Italy from the First to the Third Century A.D.*, Pisa.

Rutgers, L. 1992. *Archaeological Evidence for Interaction of Jews and non-Jews in Late Antiquity*, American Journal of Archaeology 96, pp. 101–118.

———— 1994. *Roman Policy Towards the Jews: Expulsions from the City of Rome During the First Century C.E.*, Classical Antiquity 13.1.

———— 1995. *The Jews in Late Ancient Rome*, Leiden.

———— 1998. *The Hidden Heritage of Diaspora Judaism*, Leiden.

Safrai, Z. 1994. *The Communal Functions of the Synagogues in the Land of Israel in the Rabbinic Period*, in D. Urban – P. Flesher (eds.), *Ancient Synagogues*, Leiden, pp. 181–204.

Safrai, Z. – M. Stern (eds.), 1974. *The Jewish People in the First Century: Historical Geography, Political, Social, Cultural and Religious Life and Institutions*, Assen.

Sanders, E.P. 1992. *Judaism: Practice and Believe, 63 B.C.E. to 66 C.E.*, London & Philadelphia.

Schäfer, P. 1999. *L'antisemitismo nel mondo antico*, Roma. (orig. ed. Harvard 1997).

Schekn Von Stauffenberg, A. 1931. *Die römische Kaisergeschichte bei Melalas*, Stuttgart.

Scherillo, G. – A. Dell'Oro, 1987. *Manuale di diritto romano*, Bologna.

Sherwin, A.N. – White, 1963. *Roman Society and Roman Law in the New Testament*, Oxford.

Schram, T. 1974. *The Use of* ΙΟΥΔΑΙΟΣ *in the Forth Gospel*, PhD Th. Utrecht.

Schultz, F. 1995. *I principi del diritto romano*, Firenze (1st ed. Munchen 1934; tr. V. Arangio-Ruiz).

Schürer, E. 1973–1986. *The History of Jewish People in the Age of Jesus Christ (175 a.C.–135 A.D.)*, eds. G. Vermes, F. Millar, M. Black, M Goodman, Edinburgh 1973–1987.

Schwartz, J. 1983. *La communauté d'Edfou (Haute-Egypte) jusqu'a la fin du règne de Trajan*, in R. Kunzmann – J. Schlosser (eds.), *La communauté d'Edfou, Etudes sur le Judaisme hellenistique* (acts du Congrés, Strasbourg 1983), Paris 1984, pp. 61–70.

Schwier, H. 1989. *Tempel und Tempelzerstörung. Untersuchungen zu den theologischen und ideologischen Faktoren im ersten jüdischen-römischen Krieg (66–74 n.Chr.)*, Göttingen.

Simon, M. 1936. θάρσει οὐδεὶς ἀθάνατος. *Étude de vocabulaire religieux*, Revue de l'histoire des religions 113, pp. 188–206.

——— 1964. *Verus Israel: étude sur les relations entre Chrétiens et Juifs dans l'empire romain (135–425)*, Paris.

——— 1976. *Jupiter-Jahvé*, Numen 23, pp. 52–56.

——— 1981. *Remarques sur les origines de la chrétienté romaine*, in Religion et culture dans la cité italienne Actes du Colloque (Strasbourg 8–10 Novembre 1979), Strasbourg.

Slingerland, H.D. 1997. *Claudian Polycimaking and the Imperial Repression of Judaism at Rome*, South Florida Studies in the History of Judaism, Atlanta.

Smallwood, E. 1956a. *Domitian's Attitude toward the Jews and Judaism*, Classical Philology 51, pp. 1–13.

——— 1956b. *Some notes on the Jews under Tiberius*, Latomus 15, pp. 314–329.

——— 1981. *The Jews Under Roman Rule: From Pompey to Diocletian. A Study in Political Relations*, Leiden.

Solin, H. 1983. *Juden und Syrer in westlichen Teil der römischen Welt. Eine ethnisch-demographische Studie mit besonderer Berücksichtigung der sprachlichen Zustände*, Aufstieg und Niedergang der römischen Welt II, 29.2, pp. 587–789.

Sordi, M. 1952. *Il valore del trattato fra i Romani e i Giudei nel 161 a.C.*, Acme: Annali della facoltà di lettere e filosofia dell'Università degli Studi di Milano 5, pp. 509–519.

——— 1957. *I primi rapporti fra lo stato romano e il cristianesimo e l'origine delle persecuzioni*, Rendiconti della classe di scienze morali, storiche e filologiche del l'Accademia dei Lincei 8.12, pp. 58–69.

——— 1960a. *Sui primi rapporti delle autorità con il Cristianesimo. (A proposito della cronologia degli "Atti")*, Studi Romani 8, pp. 383–409.

——— 1960b. *La persecuzione di Domiziano*, Rivista di Storia della Chiesa in Italia 14, pp. 1–26.

——— 1965. *Il cristianesimo e Roma*, Bologna.

——— 1972. M. Sordi, *L'elogio dei Romani nel I libro dei Maccabei*, Contributi dell'istituto di Storia antica 27 Milano, pp. 95–104.

——— 1995. *L'espulsione degli Ebrei da Roma nel 49 d.C.*, in M. Sordi (ed.), *Coercizione e mobilità umana nel mondo antico*, Contributi dell'Istituto di Storia Antica 21, Milano, pp. 259–277.

Steinby, E.M. 1974. *La cronologia delle figlinae doliari urbane dalla fine dell'età repubblicana fino all'inizio del III secolo*, Bullettino della Commissione Archeologica Comunale di Roma 84.

Steinby, M. 1978. *Ziegelstempel von Rom und Umgebung*, Pauly-Wissowa, Real-Encyclopedie der classischen Altertumwissenschaft, Supplementband XV, coll. 1489–1531.

Stern, M. 1974. *The Jewish Diaspora*, in Z. Safrai – M. Stern (eds.), *The Jewish People in the First Century* Assen, pp. 117–183.

——— 1974–1980. *Greek and Latin Authors on Jews and Judaism*, Jerusalem.

Stroux, J. 1988. *Die Constitutio Antoniniana*, Philologus: Zeitschrift für antike Literatur und ihre Rezeption 88, pp. 25–48.

Syme, R. 1930. *The Imperial Finances under Domitian, Nerva and Trajan*, Journal of Roman Studies 20 (1930), pp. 55–70.

——— 1958. *Tacitus*, Oxford 1958.

———— 1980. *Guard Prefects of Trajan and Hadrian*, Journal Roman Studies 70, pp. 64–80.

Taübler, E. 1913. *Imperium Romanum*, Berlin.

Tcherikover, V. 1959. *Hellenistic Civilization and the Jews*, Philadelphia.

Thompson, L.A. 1982. *Domitian and the Jewish Tax*, Historia 31, pp. 329–342.

Trebilco, P. 1991. *Jewish Communities in Asia Minor*, Cambridge University Press.

Treggiari, S. 1969. *Roman Freedmen during the Late Republic*, Oxford: Clarendon Press 1969.

Troiani, L. 1977. *Commento storico al "Contro Apione" di Giuseppe*, Pisa.

———— 1992. *Il mondo giudaico e le origini del Cristianesimo*, Contributi dell'istituto di storia antica 18, Milano, pp. 195–210.

———— 1994. *The ΠΟΛΙΤΕΙΑ of Israel in the Greco-Roman Age*, in F. Parente – J. Sievers (eds.), *Josephus and the History of the Graeco-Roman Period*, Essays in Memory of Morton Smith, Leiden, pp. 11–22.

———— 1995. *La dispersione giudaica*, in M. Sordi, *Coercizione e mobilità nel mondo antico*, Contributi dell'istituto di storia antica 2,21, Milano, pp. 235–244.

———— 2000. *Il giudaismo negli autori greci e latini dei primi secoli d.C.*, in Proceedings of the Congress "Storia locale e storiografia universale" (Bologna 16–18 dicembre 1999), Como, pp. 379–391.

———— 2002. *L. Giunio Gallione e le comunità ebraiche*, Materia Giudaica 7.1, pp. 47–54.

Truemper, M. 2004. *The Oldest Original Synagogue Building in the Diaspora: The Delos Synagogue Reconsidered*, Hesperia 73.4 (October–December 2004), pp. 513–599.

Turner, N. 1966. *An Index to Aquila*, Leiden.

Urman, D. – P. Flesher, 1994, *Ancient Synagogues. Historical Analysis and Archaeological Discovery*, Leiden.

Van der Horst, P. 1991. *Ancient Jewish Epitaphs*, Kampen.

Visconti, C.L. 1861. *Scavi di Vigna Randanini*, Bullettino dell'Istituto di Corrispondenza Archeologica, pp. 16–22.

Vismara, C. 1986. *I cimiteri ebraici di Roma*, in A. Giardina (ed.), *Società romana ed Impero tardo-antico*, Bari, vol. 2, pp. 351–389.

———— 1987. *Orientali a Roma: nota sull'origine geografica degli Ebrei nelle testimonianze di età imperiale*, Dialoghi di Archeologia 5, pp. 119–121.

———— 1986–88. *Ancora sugli Ebrei di Roma*, Archeologia Classica 38–40, pp. 150–160.

Vogelstein, H.–P. Rieger, 1896. *Geschichte der Juden in Rom, 139 c. Chr.–1420*, Berlin.

Wallace, S. 1938. *Taxation in Egypt. From Augustus to Diocletian*, Princeton.

Wallace-Hadrill, A. 1983. *Suetonius*, London 1983.

Walser, G. 2001. *The Greek of the Ancient Synagogue: an Investigation on the Greek of the Septuagint*, Stockholm.

Walter, L. 1966. *A Critical and Exegetical Commentary on the Pastoral Epistles: I & II Timothy and Titus*, Edinburgh.

Walzing, J.P. 1895–1900. *Étude historique sur les corporations professionnelles chez les Romains*, Louvian.

Wardy, B. 1979. *Jewish Religion in Pagan Literature during the Late Republic and Early Empire*, Aufstieg und Niedergang der römischen Welt II, 19.1, pp. 621–631.

Wilken, U. 1909. *Zum alexandrinischen Antisemitismus*, Abhandlungen der Königlichen Sächsischen Geschichte Wissenschaft 27, pp. 783–839.

Will, E. – C. Orrieux, 1992. *"Proselitisme juif?" Histoire d'une erreur*, Paris.

Williams, M. 1989. *The Expulsion of the Jews from Rome in A.D. 19*, Latomus 48, pp. 765–784.

———— 1990. *Domitian, the Jews and the "Judaizers"—a Simple Matter of Cupiditas and Maiestas?*, Historia 39.2, pp. 196–211.

———— 1994a. *The Organization of Jewish Burials in Ancient Rome in the Light of Evidence from Palestine and Diaspora*, Zeitschrift für Papyrologie und Epigraphik 101, pp. 165–182.

——— 1994b. *The Structure of Roman Jewry re-considered. Were the Synagogues of Ancient Rome entirely Homogeneous?*, Zeitschrift für Papyrologie und Epigraphik 104, pp. 129–141.

——— 1997. *The Meaning and Function of* Ἰουδαῖος *in Graeco-Roman Inscriptions*, Zeitschrift für Papyrologie und Epigraphik 116, pp. 249–262.

——— 1998. *The Structure of the Jewish Community in Rome*, in M. Goodman (ed.), *Jews in Graeco-Roman Period*, Oxford, pp. 64–71.

———2000. *Exarchon; an unsuspected Jewish liturgical title from ancient Rome*, Journal of Jewish Studies 51.1, 77–87.

——— 2001. *The Jews among the Greeks and Romans. A Diasporan Sourcebook*, London.

——— 2002. *Alexander, bubularus de macello: Humble Sausage-seller or Europe's First Identifiable Purveyor of Kosher Beef?*, Latomus 61.1, pp. 122–133.

Wiseman, J. 1979. *Corinth and Rome, 228 B.C.–A.D. 267*, Aufstieg und Niedergang der römischen Welt II, 11.7.1, pp. 853–945.

INDEX OF ANCIENT SOURCES

I. *Jewish Inscriptions*

II. *Greek and Latin Inscriptions*

III. *Jewish Authors*

IV. *Graeco-Roman Authors*

V. Christian Authors

VII. *New Testament*

VIII. *Rabbinic Literature*

IX. *Papyri*

X. *Juridical Sources*

INDEX OF NAMES AND PLACES

INDEX OF SUBJECTS

Samaritans 81
Sanhedrin, συνέδριον 19, 21, 22, 23, 24
Sepolture 147, 190, 191
  arcosolium 150, 153, 154, 157, 158, 160, 161, 163, 165, 166, 167, 168, 172, 174
  atrium 147, 152, 153–158, 165
  cubiculum 145, 157, 148, 154, 155, 156, 167, 158, 159, 161, 165, 167, 168, 169, 170, 172, 173, 174, 181, 183
  fossores 155, 175
  hypogeum 147, 155, 156, 158, 159, 160, 161, 173, 175
  koch 150, 154, 155, 156, 158, 167, 181, 183
  loculus 146, 148, 150, 158, 160, 161, 164, 166, 167, 168, 169, 170, 171, 177, 187
  sarcophagus 149, 150, 157, 158, 160, 161, 173, 174
Servus 41, 50, 53, 60, 61, 62, 64
Sicarii 103
Stipendium 124, 128, 129
Synagogue 3, 5, 7, 8, 9, 10, 11, 12, 14, 16, 19, 21, 22, 24, 27, 28, 45, 46, 58, 72, 77, 82, 83, 88, 121, 143, 153, 154, 184, 187, 189, 190, 194, 195, 196, 198
  bet din 19, 22, 23, 107, 134
  bet-ha-midrash 8, 42

bet-ha-sefer 8
yeshivah 8, 23
προσευχή/proseucha 25, 42, 193, 195, 196
συναγωγή 9, 11, 24, 69, 71, 126, 144, 178, 195–196
Roman synagogues: Agrippesians 3, 16
  Augustesion 3, 16
  Calcaresians 3, 16, 184
  Campesians 3, 59
  of Elea 3
  Hebrews 3, 16, 150
  Secenians 3
  Siburesians 3
  Tripolitans 3
  Vernaclesians 3, 16
  Volumnesians 3, 16, 59
Superstitio 18, 49, 57, 58, 67
Symbolum Nicaeanum 54
Syncretism 36
Syria 38, 40, 41, 47, 48, 52, 54, 59, 63, 76, 80, 85, 92, 93, 97, 98, 102, 113, 193

Temple of Jerusalem 9, 23, 24, 50, 55, 53, 58, 67
Temple of Juppiter Capitolinus 104, 106, 109, 116, 117, 129
Testimonium Flavianum 54

Zealots 76